The Struggle for Iran

The Struggle for Iran

Oil, Autocracy, and the Cold War, 1951–1954

· ·

DAVID S. PAINTER AND GREGORY BREW

The University of North Carolina Press Chapel Hill

This book was published with the assistance of the Luther H. Hodges Jr. and Luther H. Hodges Sr. Fund of the University of North Carolina Press.

Set in Charis by Westchester Publishing Services
Manufactured in the United States of America

Library of Congress Cataloging-in-Publication Data
Names: Painter, David S., author. | Brew, Gregory, author.
Title: The struggle for Iran : oil, autocracy, and the Cold War, 1951–1954 /
    David S. Painter and Gregory Brew.
Description: Chapel Hill : The University of North Carolina Press, [2022] |
    Includes bibliographical references and index.
Identifiers: LCCN 2022025004 | ISBN 9781469671659 (cloth ; alk. paper) |
    ISBN 9781469671666 (pbk. ; alk. paper) | ISBN 9781469671673 (ebook)
Subjects: LCSH: Anglo-Iranian Oil Dispute, 1951–1954. | Petroleum industry
    and trade—Political aspects—Iran—History—20th century. | Petroleum
    industry and trade—Political aspects—United States—History—20th
    century. | Iran—History—Coup d'état, 1953. | Iran—Politics and
    government—1941–1979. | Iran—Foreign relations—United States. |
    United States—Foreign relations—Iran.
Classification: LCC DS318.6 .P35 2022 | DDC 955.05/3—dc23/eng/20220601
LC record available at https://lccn.loc.gov/2022025004

Cover illustration: Abadan refinery, 1949, with the Bawarda housing estate in the background. BP Archive ARC115890/001, © BP plc.

For my son Charles and in memory of my brother,
Joseph Graham Painter Jr. (1947–2022)

For Megan and Margot

Contents

Illustrations and Tables

Illustrations

Tables

Acknowledgments

I have been working on this book off and on since the late 1980s, and the number of people and institutions to whom I am indebted is daunting. I am happy to thank them now, and I apologize in advance to anyone whose assistance I have inadvertently neglected to acknowledge.

To begin, I want to thank my coauthor Gregory Brew. Without him, I am not sure this book would have made it to print. Greg brought not only wisdom and expertise, but also order, to an incomplete manuscript I began drafting many years ago but set aside in 2003, awaiting what I erroneously believed to be the imminent declassification of crucial documents.

Over the years, many friends and fellow scholars have provided invaluable insights, inspiration, and support; they include, but are not limited to, William Burr, Nathan J. Citino, Melvyn P. Leffler, Robert J. McMahon, John McNeill, James E. Miller, Geoffrey Roberts, John Tutino, and Anand Toprani.

Melvin Conant and Ian Skeet taught me about the oil industry and helped me arrange interviews with George Middleton and Peter Ramsbotham. Some of my early research on this topic was conducted for Robert J. Donovan for the second volume of his history of the Truman presidency. My Georgetown colleague John Voll organized a conference at Georgetown University in October 2003 that brought together scholars and participants, including James F. Goode, Malcolm Byrne, Nasser Jahanbani, Kennett Love, Thomas Stauffer, James C. Van Hook, and John Waller. I also benefited greatly from many informal conversations with Dr. Jahanbani. I am deeply indebted to Malcolm Byrne and the National Security Archive for making so much invaluable material available and for his insights and assistance.

I owe a tremendous debt to Georgetown University. I will always be grateful to Dean Peter F. Krogh of the School of Foreign Service for bringing me to Georgetown and to my colleagues in the Department of History whose scholarship inspired and informed me and whose friendship supported me for more than thirty years. I also want to thank my many students, undergraduates as well as graduates, whose enthusiasm for learning spurred me to think more deeply on how to make complex historical issues and the findings of specialists available to wider audiences. The Graduate School of

Arts and Sciences and the School of Foreign Service provided grants that helped fund some of the research for this study. The Truman and Eisenhower Libraries also assisted my research with travel grants.

Debbie Gershenowitz is my third editor at the University of North Carolina Press. I signed a contract with Lewis Bateman in the early 1990s, and Charles Grench waited patiently for years for me to finish. I am grateful to all three for their support and patience.

—David S. Painter

· · · · · ·

It is not often that a historian gets the opportunity to write not one, but two books on a fascinating and timely subject. In my case, both books happened to coalesce and emerge at the same time. I must thank my coauthor David S. Painter, first for asking me to assist him with this book, and second for introducing this subject to me many years ago, when I was a wide-eyed MA student at Georgetown University.

Particular thanks are owed to the Georgetown History Department, including Chad Frazier, Alex Finn MacArtney, Ben Feldman, Abby Holekamp, Nick Danforth, Eric Gettig, Oliver Horn, Graham Pitts, Tom Foley, Paul K. Adler, Aviel Roshwald, and Joseph Sassoon. In the realm of Iranian history, the history of oil, and the Cold War, I would like to thank Christopher Dietrich, Mark J. Gasiorowski, Roham Alvandi, Mattin Biglari, Dina R. Khoury, Touraj Atabaki, Kaveh Ehsani, Anand Toprani, Victor Macfarland, Brandon Wolfe-Hunnicutt, Karine Walther, Malcolm Byrne, Kian Byrne, James F. Goode, Siavush Randjbar-Daemi, Eskandar Boroujerdi, Ervand Abrahamian, Arash Azizi, and Rasmus Elling.

Work on this book was supported by postdoctoral appointments at Southern Methodist University and Yale University. My thanks to Jeffrey Engel, Ronna Spitz, Laiyee Leong, Sabri Ates, Thomas Knock, Hervey Priddy, Odd Arne Westad, Mike Brenes, and Ted Wittenstein.

—Gregory Brew

· · · · · ·

We hope our debt to the many fine scholars who have written about this topic is evident in the notes. At the risk of seeming to slight those we do not mention by name, we want to acknowledge the work of Fakhreddin Azimi, J. H. Bamberg, James A. Bill, Richard W. Cottam, Christopher R. W. Dietrich, Mostafa Elm, Steven G. Galpern, Mary Ann Heiss, Homa Katouzian, Habib

Ladjevardi, Wm. Roger Louis, Steve Marsh, Theodore H. Moran, Edith T. Penrose, George W. Stocking, Daniel Yergin, and Vladislav M. Zubok.

We also want to thank archivists at the National Archives and Records Administration, the United Kingdom National Archive, the Harry S. Truman Library, the Dwight D. Eisenhower Library, and the American Heritage Center at the University of Wyoming. A very special thanks to Peter Housego and Joanne Burman at the BP Archive for their timely assistance. The staff at the Lauinger Library at Georgetown University provided invaluable assistance over the years, and the Bodleian Library at the University of Oxford kindly sent us copies of transcripts of interviews conducted for the Granada television series *End of Empire*. Finally, an immense thanks to Debbie Gershenowitz and the team at UNC Press for helping to make this book a reality after decades of work.

Abbreviations in the Text

AIOC	Anglo-Iranian Oil Company (pre-1933 APOC, or Anglo-Persian Oil Company)
ARAMCO	Arabian American Oil Company
bpd	Barrels per day
CFP	*Compagnie française des pétroles*
CIA	Central Intelligence Agency
DPA	Defense Production Act
ICJ	International Court of Justice, The Hague
IPC	Iraq Petroleum Company
JCS	Joint Chiefs of Staff, United States of America
Jersey Standard	Standard Oil Company (New Jersey)
NIOC	National Iranian Oil Company
NSC	National Security Council
OSS	Office of Strategic Services
PAD	Petroleum Administration for Defense
PPS	Policy Planning Staff
Shell	Royal Dutch/Shell
SOCAL	Standard Oil Company of California
Socony	Standard Oil Company of New York
Texaco	The Texas Company

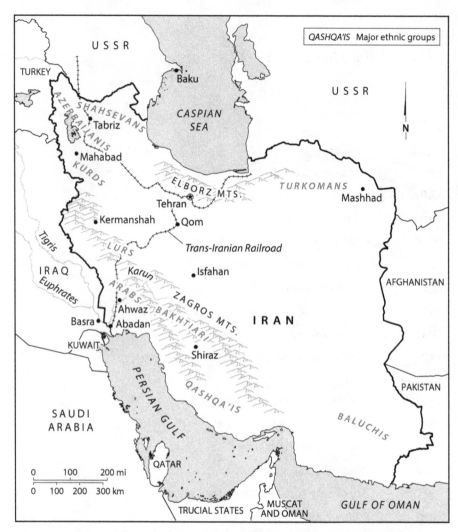

Iran, 1951. Adapted from Bamberg, *History of the British Petroleum Company*, vol. 2, iii; Keddie, *Roots of Revolution*, frontispiece; Cottam, *Nationalism in Iran*, frontispiece.

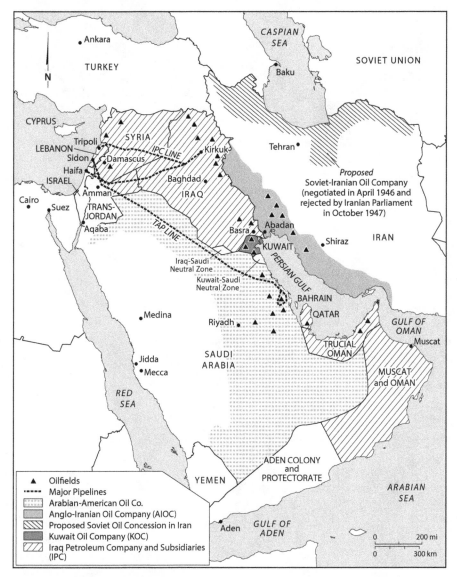

Major Middle East Oil Concessions, 1951. Adapted from Yergin, *The Prize*, 423; Painter, *Oil and the American Century*, 170, based on a map in Louis, *The British Empire in the Middle East*, 690.

The Struggle for Iran

The Struggle for Iran

· ·

The struggle of the Global South for political, economic, and cultural independence was a defining feature of the post–World War II world, rivaling if
not surpassing the Cold War in importance.[1] Though often treated separately from the Cold War, the fight against foreign domination of the Global
South was an integral part of a larger geopolitical struggle that included
balance of power concerns, an arms race, and economic and ideological conflicts.[2] Control of what was then called the Third World, in particular its
raw materials and strategic locations, had a significant impact on the global
balance of power, as well as efforts to rebuild and reform the global economy following the Great Depression and World War II.[3] Efforts by nations
and movements in the Global South to end external dominance deeply affected the United States and its allies, producing conflicts that often allied
national liberation movements with the Soviet Union or China and ran
counter to Western capitalist control of the global economy.[4] The postwar
period witnessed the rapid transformation of the global energy economy,
as oil became the industrialized world's most important energy source.[5]
The importance of oil to modern warfare and its growing importance in the
world economy, coupled with the uneven distribution of world oil reserves
and the domination of Anglo-American companies, ensured that the control of oil supplies and markets would be an important source of conflict in
international relations.[6] Finally, the struggle against foreign domination was
intertwined with challenges to political structures in Third World societies,
as imperial powers including the United States often exerted influence or
exercised control through local elites.

The origins, course, and outcome of the Iranian oil crisis of 1951–54 provide important insights into the processes that shaped the postwar world. In
the spring of 1951, Iran's parliament, the Majlis, passed legislation nationalizing the country's British-owned oil industry. Newly elected Prime Minister Mohammed Mosaddeq, an immensely popular nationalist committed
to governing according to Iran's constitution, hoped that nationalization
would free Iran from the intrigues of foreign powers and allow the nation
to liberalize its political system by reducing the power and prerogatives of

the shah, the country's monarch, and those of the ruling aristocratic elite. The Iranian action triggered an international crisis that both reflected and shaped the dynamics of international relations in the early Cold War. Fearing the loss of their most valuable overseas asset, the British rejected the nationalization and, together with the major Western oil companies and the tacit support of the U.S. government, enforced a boycott of Iranian oil to drive Mosaddeq from power.

Concerned that tension between Iran and Britain could lead to conflict and turmoil in the middle of the Korean War, the United States attempted to mediate a solution that would recognize the principle of nationalization but preserve Western corporate control over Iranian oil. Over time, American policymakers grew worried that pressure from the boycott and growing political instability within Iran caused by opposition to Mosaddeq's efforts to enact social, political, and economic reforms would lead to economic and political collapse and eventually communist control. In early spring 1953, the Eisenhower administration concluded that Mosaddeq would never agree to an oil settlement that preserved Western control over Iranian oil. The United States also believed that his reform efforts were undermining the power of the monarchy, which U.S. policymakers viewed as the chief guarantor of Western interests in Iran. These conclusions convinced U.S. officials to support a coup d'état to remove Mosaddeq.

On 19 August 1953, a coup d'état carried out by the Iranian military and local elites and organized, financed, and directed by the United States and Great Britain overthrew Mosaddeq and replaced him with a new government led by Fazlollah Zahedi and Mohammed Reza Pahlavi, the shah of Iran. The following year, Iran signed a deal with a consortium of major oil companies that returned the nationalized oil industry to foreign control. To ensure passage of the agreement and the survival of the new government, the United States provided Iran with financial and military assistance and supported the shah's efforts to establish a royal autocracy. The Anglo-American intervention not only reversed nationalization but also ended Iran's efforts to establish a secular, nationalist, and constitutional government. In the wake of the coup, Iran became an authoritarian state supported and shaped by revenues from oil and gas exports.

Sources and Limits

Understanding the Iranian oil crisis has been hampered for years by an unusual combination of too many and too few primary sources. The volume of documents in the United Kingdom National Archives on the Iranian oil crisis and related matters is gargantuan, but the British government has refused to declassify documents pertaining to the activities of its intelligence service. Similarly, the National Archives of the United States contains a wealth of documents on the crisis housed within several collections, and there are key documents in the Truman and Eisenhower presidential libraries. Large numbers of documents, especially those related to intelligence matters, remain classified or are otherwise unavailable, however. The records of the Anglo-Iranian Oil Company (AIOC, later renamed British Petroleum or BP), housed at the BP Archive at the University of Warwick, are available to researchers. Although archives in Iran are open to researchers, they can be difficult to access. Sources available outside of Iran include interviews with relevant figures and memoirs, both of which can be inaccurate and misleading. Soviet records on the crisis have only recently become available.[7]

In 1989, the U.S. State Department's Office of the Historian published a volume on the Iranian crisis in its venerable *Foreign Relations of the United States* series.[8] Though a valuable source of information for scholars studying the crisis, the volume was misleading because the State Department selectively censored its contents to downplay the U.S. role in Iranian politics and to avoid any mention of U.S. participation in the removal of Mosaddeq. The outcry over the omissions inspired Congress to pass new legislation mandating declassification of most government records regarding foreign policy within thirty years and specifying standards and processes to accomplish this goal.[9] In addition, the State Department promised to release a "retrospective" volume that would fill the gaps in the 1989 publication. Delays, both procedural and political, prevented publication of the volume until the summer of 2017. Prior to this release, the main sources from which historians could draw substantive evidence on U.S. covert actions were a secret Central Intelligence Agency internal history written in 1954 and leaked to the *New York Times* in 2000; unofficial accounts from interviews and memoirs; and whatever could be gleaned from the first *Foreign Relations* volume, the National Archives in College Park, Maryland, and various archival collections.[10]

The release of the retrospective *Foreign Relations* volume in 2017 provided an opportunity to gain a fuller understanding of the oil crisis and coup. The volume includes almost 1,000 pages of previously classified material related to U.S. policy in Iran from 1951 to 1954, including records on CIA operations surrounding the oil crisis, the 1953 coup d'état, and the coup's aftermath.[11] The new volume focused on intelligence matters and directed scholars to the 1989 volume for coverage of oil matters.[12] Although very valuable, it is still an incomplete account.[13] According to CIA Deputy Director Frank Wisner, the operation to remove Mosaddeq produced an "exceptionally heavy volume of traffic."[14] Unfortunately, many of the CIA's records were apparently destroyed in the early 1960s during an "office purge" when the agency's Near East division moved into new headquarters.[15] Nevertheless, the newly declassified documents from the *Foreign Relations* volume, as well as other material obtained by the National Security Archive based at George Washington University in Washington, D.C., have greatly expanded the available source base.[16]

This study reexamines the crisis in the light of new evidence and places it in the broader historical context of the global Cold War, the fight for control of the natural resources of the Global South, and the struggle over the political future of Iran. It draws on new material, four decades of research in U.S. and British archives, interviews with former American and British officials, oral history interviews conducted by other scholars, and a broad range of scholarly studies on the crisis, the global oil industry, the Cold War, U.S. and British foreign policy, and Iranian history.[17] The internal CIA history of the coup by Donald Wilber is very informative on the background of the coup and a useful corrective to high-ranking CIA official Kermit Roosevelt's 1979 book, *Countercoup*, which is so full of errors, distortions, and misrepresentations that it has been called "essentially a work of fiction."[18] There are many valuable books and articles on the Iranian oil crisis and coup of August 1953, though most were written before crucial documents became available. Although access to Iranian archives was not possible, this study addresses this gap by drawing on Persian-language sources available in the United States, including memoirs and interviews held by the Foundation for Iranian Studies (FIS) and Harvard Iranian Oral History Project (HIOHP) collections.

Approach and Argument

The Iranian crisis involved a host of actors, including the U.S., British, and Iranian governments, non-state actors such as major oil companies, international institutions such as the World Bank, and political actors inside Iran. Understanding the crisis requires a multilingual and multi-archival approach, representative of the international turn in diplomatic history, and careful attention to political economy as well as diplomatic and military issues.[19] While it is necessary to recognize the importance of the Cold War to the origins, course, and outcome of the Iranian crisis, it is critical to view the superpower struggle within the broader context of changes in the postwar political economy. Rather than focusing on any single factor, this study examines the interaction of a wide range of issues relating to geopolitics, political economy (both international and domestic), political developments in the Global South, and the rising importance of oil to the global political and economic order.[20]

Locating the Iranian oil crisis in the context of the early Cold War, especially the growing militarization of the conflict after 1949 and the outbreak of war on the Korean peninsula in 1950, remains crucial.[21] This period was one of heightened tensions, as the United States became more concerned about the possible threat of communism in the Global South and expanded its involvement in regional affairs, including in the Middle East, hitherto a British sphere of influence. The crisis should also be analyzed in the context of movements against European colonialism and domination, including the political struggle in Iran against foreign influence and authoritarian rule; efforts by the United States, Great Britain, and the major international oil companies to maintain control of the oil resources of the Global South; and the decline of Great Britain as an imperial power in the postwar Middle East.[22]

The Cold War involved not only Soviet-American military and political competition but also competition for control of resources and strategic locations in the Global South. This competition extended into the sphere of local politics, with the United States and its allies "backing elites" who were willing to concede control over resources in exchange for external support. Following World War II, a privately controlled but government-supported petroleum order emerged. By 1951, seven major international oil companies, later named the "Seven Sisters" by Italian oilman Enrico Mattei, maintained a dominant position in the world's primary oil-producing regions outside the United States and the Soviet Union. They managed the production, refining, and distribution of oil on a global scale, ensuring the flow of oil to markets in Western Europe and Japan.[23] Although the United States remained the world's leading major oil producer by a large margin, it still sought to control access to Middle East and Latin American oil to facilitate the rapid reconstruction of war-torn Western Europe and Japan while denying those resources to the Soviet Union.[24] Mosaddeq's nationalization constituted a threat to the stability of the postwar petroleum order. Were he to succeed, other oil-producing states such as Saudi Arabia, Kuwait, Iraq, or

Venezuela might follow Iran's example and wrest control of oil from Western corporations.

While the United States was concerned about communism—a concern that is immediately evident in the documentary record—policy toward Iran was also heavily affected by the desire to control Iranian oil. Throughout the crisis, the United States focused on preventing the "loss" of Iran to communism either through Soviet military intervention or internal subversion. U.S. officials feared that if the Soviets gained control of Iran, they would threaten the security of the Persian Gulf and important U.S. economic and security interests in the region. Soviet control of Iran would not only provide the United States' chief adversary with Iran's oil resources at a time when the Soviet oil industry had still not recovered fully from the damage of World War II; it would also place Soviet forces on the Persian Gulf, where they could threaten Western control of the rest of the region's oil. Loss of Iranian oil would retard European and Japanese recovery and impose severe financial hardships on Great Britain, which was deeply dependent on foreign exchange earnings from the sale of Middle East oil priced in sterling. Loss of Middle East oil would make the Western rearmament program impossible and would disrupt Europe's economy, which was in the process of moving toward a greater dependence on petroleum.[25] Finally, the United States worried that Iran would "collapse" into internal instability and eventually communist rule if it did not receive high levels of revenue from oil exports that could fund programs of economic development and reform. From this perspective, the flow of Iranian oil, both to meet Western needs and to ensure a sound financial basis for Iran's government, was a key factor in maintaining Iran's pro-Western strategic alignment. Oil and communism were closely linked in the U.S. official mind.[26]

U.S. policymakers believed that Iran was a key objective of Soviet expansion and tended to exaggerate the threat of a pro-Soviet government coming to power. Many officials including President Harry S. Truman initially viewed the Korean War as a diversion to mask Soviet aggression elsewhere, including an invasion of Iran.[27] Although the Soviets had precipitated a crisis in Iran in 1945–46 by refusing to withdraw their forces until Iran granted them an oil concession, Soviet foreign policy in 1951 was focused on Eastern Europe, Germany, the arms race, China, and the war in Korea.[28] In addition to the external threat of Soviet invasion, the United States was concerned about the possibility of the Tudeh, Iran's domestic communist party, seizing power. The Tudeh had around 20,000 members. It was the only organized political party in Iran and was able to stage large demonstrations in Tehran and other major cities. While aligned with the Soviet Union and opposed to British and American influence inside Iran, the Tudeh did not support Mosaddeq's National Front coalition, and the two only grew closer in 1953, by which point the United States had already set in motion plans to unseat Mosaddeq through covert action.[29] At no point during the crisis did U.S. intelligence officials believe the Tudeh was capable of seizing power, though that did not stop senior policymakers from worrying that an internal crisis might occur and allow for a communist takeover.[30]

British policy during the crisis was closely linked to economic interests. AIOC's operations in Iran, especially the massive refinery at Abadan, were crucial to Britain's balance of payments and aspirations to maintain sterling as a reserve currency, which were key components in British hopes of remaining a great power. Overseas investments played an important role in propping up the British economy and buttressing postwar economic recovery.[31] Oil nationalization threatened these interests. Sir Peter Ramsbotham, who worked on oil matters at the Foreign Office in this period, pointed out in a 1991 interview that British officials feared the loss of Iranian oil revenues would be a greater blow to the empire than Indian independence. "Abadan," he observed, was "the real end of empire."[32] The British were keenly aware that decisive action in Iran would not be possible without American cooperation and were concerned about the possibility of unilateral U.S. actions that went against British interests. Throughout the crisis, both the Labour government of Clement Attlee and the Conservative government of Winston Churchill worked hard to retain U.S. support.[33]

Although the U.S. and British governments were both determined to defeat nationalization, their views on how to respond to the crisis differed, as did their tactics for resolving it. Nevertheless, geopolitical concerns made the United States reluctant to pursue policies Britain opposed. Close cooperation with Britain was a cornerstone of U.S. foreign policy, especially in the Middle East, an area considered to be a British political and military responsibility. With its own resources stretched thin, the United States had to depend on British support throughout the world, which affected calculations regarding the Anglo-Iranian oil dispute. As President Truman noted in a letter to ex-Ambassador to Iran Henry F. Grady: "We had Israel, Egypt, near east defense, Sudan, South Africa, Tunisia, the NATO treaties all on fire. Britain and the Commonwealth nations were and are absolutely essential if these things are successful. Then on top of it all we have Korea and Indochina. Iran was only one incident."[34] Similarly, President Eisenhower noted in a National Security Council meeting in March 1953 that while the

United States should do what it thought necessary to prevent the loss of Iran, "we certainly don't want a break with the British."[35] Though the crisis strained the Anglo-American relationship, on the key issue of control of Iran's oil, the United States sided with Britain over Iran.

It is impossible to understand the crisis without a firm understanding of internal dynamics in Iran. Oil was an issue of immense political and economic importance, and historians of modern Iran have long regarded the nationalization period as a pivotal chapter in Iran's progression through the twentieth century. A secular nationalist prime minister who came to power supported by a popular mandate, Mohammed Mosaddeq wanted to return to the provisions of the 1906 constitution that vested power in the legislature and relegated the shah to the role of a constitutional monarch who reigned, rather than ruled. The rise of the National Front, Mosaddeq's political coalition, represented a shift away from authoritarianism, empowering Iran's parliament and its rising middle class rather than the traditional centers of power such as the shah, the military, the landowning aristocracy, and wealthy merchants. Nationalization of the British-owned oil industry not only symbolized Iran's escape from foreign influence; it was also a movement to restore constitutional government, born out of the brief liberal renaissance Iran experienced during the 1940s. In the summer of 1953, his popular mandate strained by the years-long oil crisis, Mosaddeq adopted undemocratic methods to retain power in the face of efforts by his domestic opponents and foreign powers to overthrow him. His constitutional experiment came to an end through the Anglo-American intervention of August 1953 and the rise of an authoritarian regime led by the shah and backed by the United States.[36]

U.S. and British officials feared that democracy in Iran would imperil Western strategic and economic interests and preferred an authoritarian monarchy based on military power to representative government. Cultural prejudices mattered as well. Many U.S. and British officials looked upon Iran, as they did other non-European countries and peoples, with an attitude of superiority, affected by notions of Iranian incompetence, irrationality, and vulnerability.[37] Mosaddeq appeared to many U.S. and British officials to be an absurd figure, and they often described him in feminine terms emphasizing his apparent emotionalism.[38] Noted U.S. diplomat George F. Kennan shared these views and argued in a 23 January 1952 letter to Secretary of State Acheson and State Department Counselor Charles E. Bohlen that Iranian nationalism was immature and fanatical. Like Soviet communism, it was "by nature hostile" to the United States and "incapable of contributing anything positive to the type of world we must back."

Facilities and positions like Abadan and Suez were "strategic assets not [for] ourselves alone but [for] the entire Western world," and the United States should not hesitate to use military force to retain control of them.[39] Similarly, a widely distributed report from John Stutesman, counselor at the embassy in Tehran until March 1952, focused on Mosaddeq's alleged demagoguery and the "immaturity" of the Iranian people, characterized by "peculiar national vanity and political irresponsibility." Stutesman drew connections between the National Front and other "fervent, though usually ill-defined, nationalist sentiments in Asia."[40] British attitudes were even more contemptuous and self-serving.

Iran was not an aberration, but rather was typical of U.S. and Western policy toward Third World nationalism during the Cold War.[41] Fearing that nationalist governments might fall to communist influence, the United States tended to back right-wing, authoritarian governments that were both anti-communist and generally favorable to private capital and foreign investment.[42] The decision to support the shah in Iran mirrored similar trends in Iraq, Saudi Arabia, and Venezuela, where the United States and Britain supported pro-Western authoritarian governments to protect the positions of private corporations.[43] When nationalist governments came to power, especially in countries with strong communist parties, the United States used covert action to remove them if economic pressure did not work and when alternative sources of leadership, including the military, were available.[44] Thus, the failure of Mosaddeq and his nationalization movement was the result of actions undertaken both *within* the domestic Iranian political scene and by foreign actors. The August 1953 coup was the culmination of a campaign to restrain liberal Iranian nationalism—the moment when Mosaddeq's enemies, both foreign and domestic, joined forces to thwart him and his movement, returning Iran to authoritarian government and Iran's oil to the hands of private Western oil companies.

The Iranian crisis shaped the postwar world and continues to hang like a shadow over Iran's relationship with the West, and the United States in particular, contributing to the air of suspicion, hostility, and confrontation that has endured for decades. A thorough understanding of the crisis can assist both the United States and Iran in moving past bitter legacies while shedding additional light on the ways in which the Cold War, the struggle for the natural resources of the Global South, the fight against foreign influence and authoritarian government, and the evolution of the global energy economy intersected in the mid-twentieth century and created the conditions that continue to shape the contemporary world.

1 A Crisis in the Making, 1901–1951

In the first half of the twentieth century, Iran formed part of a global oil economy dominated by private Western corporations. It was also a focus of great power competition, and Great Britain and Russia often intervened to secure economic concessions and power over Iran's political system. Within Iran, nationalists waged battles against foreign interference and the domination of the country's politics by an authoritarian monarchy and elite factionalism. The United States entered the struggle during World War II, developing a view of Iran as a strategically important country threatened by internal instability and communist pressure. In the early Cold War, the struggle for oil and the battle over Iran's political future erupted into crisis when nationalist leader Mohammed Mosaddeq led a successful campaign to nationalize Iran's British-owned oil industry. At the heart of the crisis was the question of who would control Iranian oil—whether its riches would pass primarily to the Iranian people or to foreign actors and Iranian elites intent on using them for their own ends.

Oil and Iran

In 1901, British-born Australian mining magnate William Knox D'Arcy reached an agreement with the Iranian government for a concession granting D'Arcy exclusive rights to search for and exploit any oil found within a 500,000 square mile area that included all of Iran except the five northern provinces bordering Russia. The concession would last sixty years. In return, Iran's government and its ruler, the Qajar shah, would receive payments equal to 16 percent of "net profits," plus a signing bonus of £20,000. The shah signed the agreement under fiscal duress, and D'Arcy's agents reportedly paid large bribes to various government officials to secure favorable terms. In 1905, D'Arcy's company became a subsidiary of the British-owned Burmah Oil Company. The company discovered oil at Masjed-e Suleiman in the southwestern province of Khuzestan in 1908, and early the next year the Anglo-Persian Oil Company (APOC) was formed to exploit the new find.[1]

The terms of the D'Arcy Concession, which were largely replicated in subsequent concessions throughout the Middle East, allowed APOC a measure of autonomy from the Iranian government. The company determined production levels and could drill wherever it wished within the concession area. It was under no obligation to relinquish unexplored territory to the Iranian government. The company could build pipelines and facilities where it wanted and was exempt from all taxation. While APOC was obligated to pay the Iranian government 16 percent of "net profits," it calculated these profits in secret. The company employed European engineers and Indian administrative staff, retaining Iranians only as low-skilled laborers. Mostafa Fateh, a former AIOC employee, noted that the Iranian people were mostly "unaware" that the oil industry even existed, "except for a few involved in the work."[2]

At the time of the D'Arcy Concession, the petroleum industry had grown into a sprawling global enterprise encompassing fields in the United States, Russia, Galicia, Romania, the Netherlands East Indies, Burma, and elsewhere. Demand for industrial lubricants and kerosene drove the industry's expansion, but by the early twentieth century oil had become an important source of energy and fuel as the development of the internal combustion engine and the emergence of the automotive industry created a new source of demand.[3] Oil had also taken on strategic significance. In June 1913, First Lord of the Admiralty Winston Churchill decided that the Royal Navy should switch the battle fleet from coal to oil as its predominant fuel. Motivated by technological considerations—oil-fired ships were faster, required less fuel and smaller crews, and eliminated dependence on overseas coaling stations—Churchill's decision presented the British government with a strategic dilemma. While rich in coal, Britain had almost no oil deposits, nor were sufficient reserves located elsewhere in the empire. Unwilling to depend completely on foreign oil companies, the British government decided to purchase a controlling stake in APOC in 1914. With the acquisition, APOC turned from a struggling firm to a quasi-official arm of British imperial policy. According to Churchill, the government stake in the company gave the British government "the power to regulate developments according to naval and national interest . . . over the whole of these enormous regions."[4] Control of oil was thus closely connected to British imperial policy.

Britain was deeply involved in the Middle East in the early twentieth century. The region had historically commanded British attention for its strategic location athwart the lines of communication linking the British Isles to India and East Asia. Iran, or "Persia" as it was still known, was never a formal British colony, but the British regarded it as strategically valuable. Iran was a buffer state lying between British India and Russia, and the two empires waged a "Great Game" for influence in Iran and Central Asia throughout the nineteenth century. Both powers routinely interfered in Iran's internal politics. Qajar statesmen sought to play the great powers off one another, a historic form of Iranian diplomacy that would later be known as "positive equilibrium." This allowed Iran to retain its independence, though efforts at domestic modernization and reform were repeatedly stymied by resistance from internal actors and pressure from foreign powers.[5]

While its interests in Iran were diverse, Britain came to value its position in southwestern Iran over all other considerations after oil was found there in 1908. Support from the British government, plus access to a steady supply of Iranian oil, facilitated APOC's rise from a small and struggling firm to one of the largest oil companies in the world. Iranian oil production expanded from 249,000 tons in 1913 to 1.7 million tons, or 34,700 barrels per day (bpd) in 1921.[6] As the company prospered, the returns for the British government also increased. In 1923, Churchill boasted that the government's stake had appreciated by £16 million, earned £6.5 million in dividends, and saved Britain £3 million on fuel costs.[7]

APOC's expansion coincided with a period of internal Iranian political instability. Though an absolute monarch who ruled as the "Shadow of God on Earth," the Qajar shah governed through alliances and informal arrangements with major elite factions.[8] National identity formed partly as a response to the country's apparent subjugation to foreign interests. In 1890, when the government granted a British firm a concession that included a monopoly over the production, sale, and export of tobacco, Grand Ayatollah Sayyed Mirza Shirazi of Qom, Iran's most prominent religious figure, issued a *fatwa*, or religious edict, against tobacco use in protest. Millions of Iranians abstained from tobacco, and the shah was forced to rescind the concession.[9] By the early twentieth century, Iranian nationalists in the intelligentsia and activists in the clergy had mobilized to demand political reform, which the Qajar shah conceded in 1906 in the form of a constitution that limited the power of the monarchy and created a parliamentary body, the Majlis. The fight against foreign control was thus closely linked to the struggle against autocratic government.[10]

Foreign intrigues undermined Iran's Constitutional Revolution. In 1907, Russia intervened in Iran in support of the shah, sabotaging the efforts of Iran's reformers. The same year, Britain and Russia agreed to a general rapprochement, splitting Iran into formal spheres of influence, with the British dominating the south and Russia the north. During World War I Iran, though technically neutral, suffered repeated military interventions by British, Russian, and Ottoman Turkish forces. Following the Russian Revolution of 1917, Iran signed a treaty with the communist regime in 1921 that settled previous debts while giving the Soviet Union the right to intervene in Iran with military force should another power threaten Iran's independence. The British, meanwhile, provided arms and support to an enterprising Iranian military officer, Reza Khan, and encouraged him to seize power in Tehran. In February 1921, Reza Khan deposed the feeble Qajar shah and established a new government with himself as dictator.[11]

Reza Shah and APOC

Energetic, imposing, and ruthless, Reza Khan used military power to bring the country under his control. For many of Iran's disgruntled intelligentsia, the rise of an assertive nationalistic dictator in the mold of Mustafa Kemal Atatürk of Turkey was a welcome change from the struggling constitutional government. The new dictator enforced a modernizing regime that had wide and lasting effects on Iranian society. These included the nation's first public school system, industrialization and transportation projects, a new legal code, the imposition of Western dress and the forced unveiling of women, a modern military, and a redesigned national capital. In 1925, the Majlis voted to dissolve the Qajar dynasty and named Reza Khan the new shah, Reza Pahlavi I. The measure passed with only the deputy from Khorasan, a constitutionalist named Mohammed Mosaddeq, offering an objection.[12] After his coronation, Reza Shah began a series of negotiations with APOC to gain a larger share of the company's profits and control over its operations, but the discussions resulted in stalemate.[13]

Although the British favored a strong government in Tehran that could impose order on the country, the rise of Reza Shah came at a time of new challenges for APOC. The company enjoyed booming profits, as it expanded Iranian oil production from 2,959,000 tons to 5,358,000 tons (109,361 bpd) between 1921 and 1928.[14] Output from the Middle East joined a wave of new oil from fields in the United States and Venezuela. Most of this output was controlled by a small group of private companies. Apart from APOC, there was Royal Dutch/Shell, which was Anglo-Dutch in ownership; and five American firms: Gulf Oil, the Texas Oil Company (Texaco), the Standard Oil Company of California (SOCAL), the Standard Oil Company of New York (Socony, later Socony-Mobil), and the Standard Oil Company of New Jersey

(Jersey Standard).[15] Amid the global Depression of the early 1930s, APOC's profits collapsed as the world was flooded with cheap crude oil. Lower profits meant reduced revenues for Iran: from £1.28 million in 1930, APOC's payment to Iran fell to £306,872 in 1931. A furious Reza Shah canceled the D'Arcy Concession on 28 November 1932.[16]

Pressured by the British and in need of cash to stabilize his regime, Reza Shah ignored advice from his ministers and agreed to the terms APOC chairman Sir John Cadman proposed during negotiations in April 1933. Iran received combined payments worth £4 million, guaranteed revenues of £750,000 per year, a 25 percent share of the company's annual dividend, and a reduction in the concession area to 100,000 square miles. While Cadman engineered the agreement to appear favorable to Iran, it was tailored to meet the company's long-term needs. The new agreement closed several loopholes in the D'Arcy Concession and extended the concession until 1993. A special added article prohibited unilateral cancellation, an important legal point the company would use to argue against the nationalization in 1951.[17]

Relations between the renamed Anglo-Iranian Oil Company (AIOC) and Reza Shah remained cordial for the remainder of the decade, though the monarch continued to press the company for more revenues.[18] At the same time, AIOC began developing oil fields elsewhere. In 1928, along with Shell, the French firm CFP (Compagnie française des pétroles), and five U.S. companies including Jersey Standard and Socony, AIOC had formed a company, renamed the Iraq Petroleum Company (IPC) the following year, to manage a concession in Iraq. In 1934 AIOC won a concession in Kuwait, which it split with Gulf Oil. AIOC sought unsuccessfully to gain a concession in Saudi Arabia in 1933, but was outbid by SOCAL, which brought in the Texas Company as its partner in 1936. As in Iran, the new concessions granted the companies sweeping rights to manage the oil fields as they saw fit, with little oversight or interference from local governments.[19]

The companies' control did not go entirely unchallenged. In March 1938, Mexican President Lázaro Cárdenas nationalized the country's oil industry, seizing the assets of Jersey Standard, Shell, and other foreign firms. Although nationalization did not damage the companies' overall commercial position, they boycotted Mexican oil exports and demanded heavy compensation for their lost property. The U.S. government eventually mediated a settlement involving U.S. companies in 1941.[20] The Mexican nationalization (or expropriation, as the companies termed it) established the precedent that governments could nationalize foreign-owned oil industries, provided compensation for lost assets was paid. This was very important during the Iranian crisis, where the legality of nationalization and the nature (and amount) of compensation were both key issues.

Occupation, Oil, and U.S. Policy in Iran

Upon the outbreak of World War II in 1939, Reza Shah resumed Iran's traditional neutrality. Having imprisoned, exiled, or executed most of his former advisors, he now ruled as an autocrat and enjoyed little popularity within his country.[21] Following the German invasion of the Soviet Union in June 1941, the British and the Soviets looked to Iran as a potential supply route linking the Persian Gulf to the Soviet Union and issued Reza Shah an ultimatum: expel all his German advisors or face invasion. The shah delayed responding, and Anglo-Soviet forces invaded, crushing the Pahlavi military within days. The Soviets occupied the five northern provinces, while the British concentrated their efforts on securing the Khuzestan oil fields and AIOC's refinery at Abadan. Reza Shah was forced to abdicate and sent into exile in South Africa, where he died in July 1944. Though they briefly considered placing the heir to the Qajar dynasty back on the Peacock Throne, the British opted for the shah's eldest son, twenty-one-year-old Mohammed Reza Pahlavi, as a suitable replacement.[22]

With troops from the Indian Army guarding Abadan, AIOC increased production. Iran became the main source of oil for countries east of Suez, following the Japanese seizure of the Netherlands East Indies in early 1942. Output rose from 181,690 bpd in 1940 to 357,605 bpd in 1945. Company profits also increased, from £2,843,000 in 1940 to £5,792,000 in 1945.[23] The occupiers inflated the currency to pay for their occupation and sequestered Iranian food supplies, leading to bread shortages in major cities.[24] Deprivation, famine, disease, and disorder struck most of the country. Karim Sanjabi, then a lawyer in Tehran, recalled how people refrained from riding the bus for fear of contracting disease from other passengers.[25]

In the absence of a powerful central authority, politics became diffuse and fluid, with different groups forming to represent the interests of distinct sections of Iranian society. These groups would play a role in the nationalization crisis and the politics of the Mosaddeq era. At the core was Iran's political elite, the landowning aristocracy. Together with major tribes—the Qashqa'i and Bakhtiyari being the largest—the aristocracy (sometimes known as the "Thousand Families") controlled politics in the provinces and held most of the seats in the Majlis. Below the elite was Iran's traditional middle class, consisting of bazaar merchants, shopkeepers, traders, and guildsmen, and the Shi'a clergy, who also owned land and engaged in commerce. The gradual spread of Western-style education and transnational intellectual exchange produced an intelligentsia that, along with military officers, civil servants, lawyers, bureaucrats, engineers, and other professionals, formed Iran's "modern" middle class. A small industrial working class resided in the major cities (particularly Tehran and the northern city of Tabriz) and in the southern oil fields. The majority of Iranians belonged to the rural working class and lived in the country's 45,000 villages. Most were illiterate and not active politically.[26]

In the wake of the occupation and Reza Shah's abdication, a variety of political forces attempted to fill the vacuum left by the absent dictator. The elite, clergy, bazaar merchants, and other notables vied for control of the Majlis, drawing on support from either the Soviets or the British.[27] New groups expressing alternative social and political ideas emerged from the modern middle class. Foremost among them were the Iran Party (originally known as the Engineers Association), a socialist-technocratic group comprising individuals drawn from the professional classes, and the Tudeh Party, a leftist organization founded by political prisoners released from Reza Shah's prisons in 1941. The Tudeh leadership accepted Moscow's support in 1943, becoming outwardly Marxist and pro-Soviet.[28]

Officials in the shah's government, including the young monarch himself, hoped for a third power to balance against the Anglo-Soviet occupiers. The shah was also anxious to recover the power lost after his father's abdication and reached out to the United States for assistance. Concerned that disorder within Iran could imperil the security of the supply line to the Soviet Union, the United States sent 30,000 troops to assist with the management of the supply route and several advisory missions to help strengthen the Iranian state, reform its finances, and train its armed forces. While American oilmen, diplomats, and missionaries had been visiting Iran since the nineteenth century, the war marked the beginning of substantive American engagement with the Iranian state and the Iranian people.[29]

Though U.S. policy in Iran focused on the security of the supply line, policymakers worried an unstable situation in Iran would threaten the large and valuable oil concessions held by American companies elsewhere in the region. While many of these fields had not yet entered commercial production, a survey of the Middle East's oil fields by geologist Everette Lee De-Golyer in 1943 concluded the region would become the new "center of gravity" in the global oil industry after the war.[30] The United States, which accounted for more than 60 percent of global production, supplied much of the oil for the allied war effort. Concerned about the drain on U.S. oil reserves due to the war, the U.S. government hoped to secure permanent and favorable access to Middle East oil, both to meet domestic demand and to ensure that American oil companies were well positioned to exploit major fields after the war. As Secretary of State Cordell Hull pointed out to President Roosevelt in August 1943: "it is to our interest that no great power be established on the Persian Gulf opposite the important American petroleum developments in Saudi Arabia."[31] Given that the British were already firmly entrenched in Iran, Iraq, and Kuwait, Hull's statement clearly referred to the Soviet Union.

Anxious to attract a permanent American interest in Iran, the Iranian government actively encouraged U.S. oil companies to seek concessions inside the country. Along with Royal Dutch/Shell, an Anglo-Dutch firm, two U.S. companies prepared concession bids in 1944. In September 1944, just as the U.S. and British companies were preparing to submit their bids to the Majlis for consideration, the Soviet Union sent an oil mission to Iran, claiming the right to a concession covering Iran's five northern provinces.[32] The Soviet intervention alarmed Iran's leaders, who feared a Soviet oil concession in the north might produce a permanent partition of the country. Iranian Prime Minister Mohammed Sa'id, with U.S. encouragement, ordered a halt in concession discussions.[33] In December, Majlis deputy Mohammed Mosaddeq—the same deputy who had opposed Reza Shah's ascension nineteen years before—proposed a bill banning all oil concession negotiations until foreign troops had left Iranian soil. Iran, Mosaddeq argued, should not offer any new oil concessions. Instead, the nation should pursue a policy of "negative equilibrium," remaining neutral while pursuing self-sufficiency. The speech struck a chord with Iran's budding nationalist movement, but it drew little attention from the United States, which now refocused its policy in Iran to combat the apparent increase in Soviet influence.[34]

The Cold War and Iran: The Azerbaijan Crisis

The Soviet intervention to secure an oil concession in 1944 was in response to the growing American presence in Iran, which Moscow viewed with alarm. After its bid for a concession in 1944 ended in failure, the Soviet Union took steps to solidify its influence in Iran's northern provinces. In December 1945, Soviet-backed separatist movements in Azerbaijan formed autonomous republics representing the Kurdish and Azeri minorities. Iranian troops sent to put down the separatists were blocked from entering the area by Soviet forces. In March 1946, with British and American forces withdrawn from Iran, Stalin warned the shah's government that the withdrawal of Soviet forces would be conditional on the offer of an oil concession covering the five northern provinces.[35]

Soviet interests were focused on securing Iranian oil. American intelligence estimated that the Soviet Union would face a deficit of at least 5 million bpd once the war ended. Soviet pursuit of a concession in northern Iran was motivated by "pragmatic economic interest."[36] The British also acknowledged this and seemed open to a permanent settlement whereby Iran remained divided, à la 1907.[37] For senior U.S. policymakers, the Soviet move in Azerbaijan added to mounting fears of Soviet aggression and territorial ambition and helped to consolidate the view of Iran as a country uniquely threatened by Soviet influence. The move seemed to confirm the analysis of George Kennan's "Long Telegram" from February 1946, which characterized the Soviet Union as an expansionist power inherently hostile to the global capitalist system.[38] In Iran, the stakes included control over the oil resources of the Middle East, since a communist government in Tehran could potentially threaten U.S. oil concessions elsewhere in the region.[39]

To manage the Soviet challenge, the shah appointed Ahmed Qavam, a veteran mainstay of Iranian politics known to be on good terms with Moscow, as prime minister. In negotiations with Joseph Stalin and Soviet Foreign Minister Vyacheslav Molotov in Moscow, Qavam insisted that withdrawal of Soviet troops from Iran was a prerequisite for settlement of other issues. In April, Iran and the Soviet Union agreed to establish a joint Soviet-Iranian oil company, with 51 percent Soviet ownership and exclusive rights to develop oil in Iran's northern provinces. Qavam promised to submit the agreement to the Majlis. Focused on other problems and concerned about lack of support in the United Nations, the Soviets withdrew their troops.[40]

With Soviet forces gone, Qavam moved to consolidate his power domestically. An ambitious, astute, and powerful aristocrat, Qavam took advantage of the country's unsettled political state and the weakness of the young shah to increase the power of his own faction. He announced a program of economic development and sought to control the Soviet-backed Tudeh Party by bringing three of its leaders into his government. The Tudeh had demonstrated new political strength by organizing a massive strike among AIOC's workers in Abadan in May 1946.[41] Though he appeared to be moving Iran closer to Moscow, Qavam was practicing positive equilibrium, playing foreign powers against each other. Several months after the strike in Abadan, Qavam expelled the Tudeh ministers from his cabinet and cracked down on the party at the local level. At the same time, he continued discussions with the British and American ambassadors.[42]

Qavam's efforts were only partially successful. U.S. Ambassador George V. Allen believed that supporting the young shah, with whom he was on close terms, was the best way to maintain Western influence in the country. In October 1946, Allen backed the shah against Qavam when the latter attempted to take full control of the government. The shah emerged victorious, thanks in part to Allen's support—a behind-the-scenes intervention by a U.S. official that set the template for future events.[43] In October 1947, the Majlis rejected the Soviet oil concession, ending the crisis and squashing Stalin's hope to retain influence in Iran. The Soviets ramped up support for the Tudeh and expanded propaganda beamed across the border, but otherwise took no action.[44]

The Postwar Petroleum Order, Iranian Politics, and Anglo-American Dynamics

Though it had escaped permanent Anglo-Soviet partition and now enjoyed support from the United States, Iran's government was weak and divided. The Majlis dominated politics. Most deputies were landlords, merchants, tribal leaders, or major religious figures elected through rigged voting. Different factions vied with one another, sharing power with Mohammed Reza Pahlavi, who, with U.S. support, forced Qavam out in December 1947 and began playing a larger role in Iranian politics.[45]

Born in October 1919, Mohammed Reza was the eldest son of Reza Shah and assumed the throne at the age of twenty-one in August 1941 following his father's abdication. Frequently seen as living in his father's shadow, he spent much of his youth abroad, attending boarding school in Switzerland. Inexperienced and lacking his father's ruthlessness, the second Pahlavi carefully husbanded his power, building his influence within the military (which he led as commander-in-chief) and cultivating U.S. support, particularly after the Azerbaijan crisis, when Washington viewed Iran as a country threatened by Soviet aggression.[46] While devoted to protecting Iran from foreign threats, the shah was personally interested in protecting his own position. After surviving an assassination attempt in February 1949, the shah capitalized on the subsequent surge in support for the monarchy to push through an amendment to the constitution, which gave him the power

President Harry S. Truman (left) with Mohammed Reza Pahlavi, the shah of Iran (center), and the shah's advisor and Minister of Court Hossein 'Ala (right). Truman Library, Accession No. 73-3146.

to dismiss the Majlis and call for new elections by royal decree.[47] As the amendments were made during a period of martial law and muscled through the assembly by the shah's supporters without a popular referendum, many Iranian nationalists considered them unlawful and refused to recognize their validity.

The United States regarded Iran as an important strategic asset. According to a report by the Joint Chiefs of Staff in October 1946, it was vital that "Soviet influence" be kept as far from the oil fields of the Persian Gulf as possible.[48] The downfall of Reza Shah had left Iran with a "weak constitutional regime," for which the Iranians were unprepared "by tradition or experience." A conservative strongman, wrote Ambassador Allen in December 1947, would be preferable "to the chaotic and corrupt condition we now have."[49] The United States supported the shah, largely due to the monarch's avowed anti-communism and his willingness to accept American assistance.[50] Despite Iran's strategic importance, President Harry S. Truman did not include Iran when he announced major aid packages for Greece and Turkey in March 1947. Iran did not face a communist-led insurgency like Greece or direct pressure from the Soviet Union like Turkey, and many U.S. officials believed that the shah's demands for aid and military hardware were excessive.[51]

Rather than direct assistance, the United States supported the shah's development plans, hoping that these would deliver stability and maintain the country's pro-Western strategic alignment. With U.S. support, Iran set out on a new economic development program, the Seven Year Plan, and applied for loans from the World Bank to cover the plan's $650 million price tag.[52] The Truman administration maintained the wartime military advisory mission and offered credits to Iran's government with which it could purchase military equipment.[53] The United States also increased its covert presence in Iran to counteract the spread of Soviet influence. In early 1947, John Waller of the Office of Strategic Services, a precursor to the Central Intelligence Agency, established an office in Tehran that focused on monitoring pro-Soviet groups including the Tudeh Party. OSS efforts included efforts to develop a "stay-behind" mission that would mobilize pro-Western elements inside Iran if the country fell to Soviet forces.[54]

By and large, however, the United States left Western policy in Iran in the hands of the British. After the September 1947 Pentagon talks, the United States and Britain agreed that the Middle East would remain an area of British preeminence.[55] British policies after 1946 focused on maintaining Iran's pro-Western strategic alignment, strengthening the shah's government, and protecting the AIOC oil concession.[56] AIOC contributed substantial taxes to the Treasury; 19 percent of its Iranian production served the British market, while 19.3 percent was sold to the Admiralty for a discounted price. Iranian oil was sold in sterling, buttressing Britain's weakening balance of payments and supporting sterling as an international reserve currency.[57] Any disruption of the Iranian oil industry could have "disastrous consequences" for the state of British finances.[58]

The growing importance of oil to Great Britain reflected the broader increase in oil's significance to the global economy. Working together, the U.S. and British governments and the major international oil companies erected what historians call the "postwar petroleum order," a system for delivering oil and refined products to Western markets.[59] American production, which had increased from 3.8 million to 4.7 million bpd during the war, began to decline relative to consumption, and in 1948 the United States

Middle East and World crude oil production, 1900–1950 (barrels per day)

	Iran	Iraq	Kuwait	Saudi Arabia	Total Middle East*	United States	Total World
1900	—	—	—	—	—	174,289	408,586
1905	—	—	—	—	—	369,091	589,285
1910	—	—	—	—	—	574,119	897,980
1915	9,899	—	—	—	9,899	770,146	1,183,652
1920	33,507	—	—	—	33,507	1,213,504	1,887,353
1925	95,595	—	—	—	95,595	2,092,447	2,928,584
1930	125,556	2,501	—	—	128,058	2,460,304	3,863,115
1935	156,912	75,090	—	—	235,468	2,730,400	4,532,864
1940	181,690	66,370	—	13,904	281,345	3,707,436	5,889,921
1945	357,605	96,197	—	58,386	532,214	4,694,945	7,108,753
1946	402,244	97,712	16,249	164,230	702,380	4,750,518	7,521,723
1947	424,652	98,175	44,452	246,170	839,232	5,087,636	8,278,729
1948	521,600	71,548	127,397	391,378	1,141,863	5,534,753	9,405,025
1949	560,855	84,814	246,575	476,734	1,401,389	5,046,411	9,325,584
1950	664,315	136,236	344,444	546,704	1,755,786	5,407,052	10,418,073

*Also includes Bahrain, Qatar, and Turkey.
Source: DeGolyer and MacNaughton, *Twentieth Century Petroleum Statistics*; Ferrier, *History of the British Petroleum Company*, vol. 1.

became a net importer of oil.[60] Apart from Venezuela, the cheapest and most abundant available reserves were in the Middle East. Much of this oil went to Western European reconstruction, with the U.S. government facilitating purchases of Middle East oil produced by U.S. companies through the Marshall Plan.[61] The major international companies cooperated to ensure that Middle East oil production increased in a manageable way, without producing another glut or price collapse.[62]

AIOC was a key element in this new system. In 1950, AIOC accounted for 50 percent of total regional output, with 915,000 bpd out of 1.8 million bpd.[63] This made the company's position among the most lucrative and important British assets left in the world. The United States considered continued corporate control over Middle Eastern oil a strategic and economic priority. Britain was its most important Cold War ally, and the United States depended on Britain to maintain strategic supremacy in the Middle East and parts of South and East Asia. In short, both the United States and Great Britain had a vested interest in maintaining AIOC's position in Iran.

The Oil Issue in Iran

Though not a formal colony of the British Empire, the oil fields of Khuzestan in southern Iran and the refinery town of Abadan bore the unmistakable signs of colonialism. British staff lived comfortably, with access to amenities including swimming pools, squash and tennis courts, and a cinema.[64] Conditions for Iranian workers were often very poor. In 1950, 80 percent of the company's non-skilled workers remained without company housing, according to a report from the International Labour Office.[65] Although company executives touted their achievements in bringing industrialization and modernization to Iran, many contemporary observers felt the company men were living in a bygone age. According to U.S. Ambassador John C. Wiley, "they have continued to celebrate Queen Victoria's Diamond Jubilee and time in its flight has passed them by."[66] The company ensured its position through a system of patronage, bribing Majlis deputies and newspaper editors and distributing propaganda advertising the benefits of its operations for the Iranian people.

Resentment of AIOC was closely connected to the development of Iranian nationalism in the late nineteenth and early twentieth centuries.[67] Educated Iranians questioned the legality of the company's concession in the 1930s, arguing that it violated Iranian sovereignty. As a sovereign landlord that owned the oil in the ground, the Iranian state should benefit from its production and sale, yet instead it struggled "with the blackest misery and hunger," according to one article in 1931.[68] Anger toward the company also reflected widespread animosity toward the British, who had interfered repeatedly in Iran's politics since the nineteenth century. These criticisms carried forward into the war years when Iran's press—liberated after years of suppression by Reza Shah—took stridently anti-British positions.[69]

Galvanized by the oil concession scramble of 1944 and the Azerbaijan crisis of 1946–47, Iran's small group of middle-class nationalists articulated new arguments based around the reduction, or possible elimination, of AIOC's dominance of Iranian oil. This movement grew alongside (but was separate from) similar anti-British rhetoric emanating from the Tudeh Party. In January 1949, a Majlis deputy accused Reza Shah's former finance minister of colluding with the British in 1933, prompting the aged minister to publicly disavow the agreement.[70] Nationalists in the assembly led by orator and journalist Hossein Makki denounced the 1933 agreement as illegitimate, arguing it had stemmed from Reza Shah's secret collusion with the

Abadan, the world's largest refinery, in 1949. The Bawarda housing estate, with its rows of large houses for the British staff, contrasts to the cramped slums nearer the refinery. BP Archive 115890 © BP plc.

British.[71] In time, the "oil issue" became the single most important concern in the country's political discourse, until it grew into a force for popular mobilization without precedent in Iran's modern history.[72]

Cash-strapped and anxious to secure funding for his development program and military mobilization scheme, the shah urged his negotiators to secure more favorable terms from AIOC. In addition to the company's alleged abuse of its workers, the government was especially interested in the gap between what it received for its oil and what AIOC and the British government received. According to published statistics, AIOC's net profits from 1933 through 1948 totaled £115,246,000; British government taxes on

AIOC profits, British taxes from Iranian oil, and payments to Iran, 1932–1950

	Oil Production (Thousand barrels)	AIOC Net Profits (Thousand £)	British Taxes (Thousand £)	Payments to Iran (Thousand £)
1932	49,471	2,380	190	1,525
1933	54,392	2,654	460	1,812
1934	57,851	3,183	770	2,190
1935	57,283	3,519	400	2,221
1936	62,718	6,123	1,170	2,580
1937	77,804	7,455	2,610	3,525
1938	78,372	6,109	1,690	3,307
1939	78,151	2,986	3,320	4,271
1940	66,317	2,842	4,160	4,000
1941	50,777	3,222	3,280	4,000
1942	72,256	7,790	6,600	4,000
1943	74,612	5,639	12,070	4,000
1944	102,045	5,677	15,720	4,464
1945	130,526	5,792	15,630	5,624
1946	146,819	9,625	15,590	7,132
1947	154,998	18,565	16,820	7,104
1948	190,384	24,065	18,030	9,172
1949	204,712	18,390	16,930	13,489
1950	242,457	33,103	36,190	16,032

Source: Galpern, *Money, Oil, and Empire*, 88; Bamberg, *History of the British Petroleum Company*, vol. 2, 325; Elm, *Oil, Power, and Principle*, 38; DeGolyer and MacNaughton, *Twentieth Century Petroleum Statistics: Historical Data*.

AIOC for the same period were £118,320,000, largely due to steep increases in taxes during World War II; and AIOC payments to Iran for the period were £69,402,000.[73] Finance Minister Abbasqoli Golsha'ian pushed for a deal that would split profits from oil "fifty-fifty," an idea modeled after an agreement between oil companies and the government of Venezuela in 1948.[74]

The British government encouraged the company to offer more generous terms while preserving the basic aspects of the 1933 concession agreement. AIOC felt its track record in Iran was sound and saw little reason to satisfy Iranian demands. Fifty-fifty would have been more costly for the company and exposed it to higher British taxes as well as increased payments to Iran because, unlike the U.S. tax code, British tax laws did not allow companies to take a credit for taxes paid to foreign governments. AIOC's leadership, particularly Chairman Sir William Fraser, regarded the Iranians with condescension and disdain, dismissing Golsha'ian as "nothing but a trader" who could be bought off just as Reza Shah had been in 1933. Fraser's negotiator Neville Gass offered Golsha'ian a deal whereby Iran's annual royalty would increase from 4s/ton to 6s/ton, retroactive to 1948, plus an increased contribution from the company's general reserve and annual dividend. Total payments covering 1948 and 1949 would increase from £22,662,000 to £41,558,000.[75] Other than more money, the deal offered Iran little else as AIOC ignored most of Iran's other demands. The terms of the 1933 concession, which was set to expire in 1993, remained the same. Facing a mounting budget deficit, the shah forced Golsha'ian to accept AIOC's terms on 17 July 1949. Known as the Supplemental Agreement, the terms would require Majlis ratification before becoming law.

Although the shah and his allies hoped a new oil agreement would provide financial support for the Seven Year Plan, public opposition to AIOC had grown into a groundswell of nationalist anger, and the opposition was better organized than the British or royalists had supposed. When the Supplemental Agreement came before the Majlis in late July, a small group of deputies led by Makki blocked the deal from proceeding to a vote. Those who dared speak out against the agreement, said Makki, did so "at the point of the bayonet. . . . On this sacred religious night, I pray God to set all those who have betrayed this country on the flames of oil."[76] Other deputies, fearful of appearing overly friendly to British interests, declined to challenge Makki. The assembly adjourned on 28 July without ratifying the agreement.[77]

The British embassy blamed the failure on internal divisions within the Iranian government and the "irresponsible self-seekers" inside the Majlis.[78] Both AIOC and the Foreign Office believed that the shah would force the agreement through the Majlis once elections for a new assembly were complete. The failure to ratify the Supplemental Agreement proved to be a crucial turning point, however. Nationalist animus toward AIOC and the British government developed into an organized political movement, one that challenged the status quo in a way the Pahlavi government and its foreign allies proved incapable of managing. Hossein 'Ala, the shah's minister of court and a reliably pro-Western fixture in Iranian politics, warned the U.S. State Department in early 1950 that unless AIOC quickly agreed to better terms, Iran's government might be forced to nationalize its assets.[79] Though initially discounted by AIOC, the movement to nationalize Iran's oil industry was quickly developing into a powerful political force. At its head was Mohammed Mosaddeq, Iran's most renowned and respected political figure.

The management of the Anglo-Iranian Oil Company (AIOC), 1947.
William J. Fraser (front row, second from right) was a stubborn negotiator
who regarded Iran's claims to national ownership of the oil industry as
ludicrous. BP Archive 180518 © BP plc.

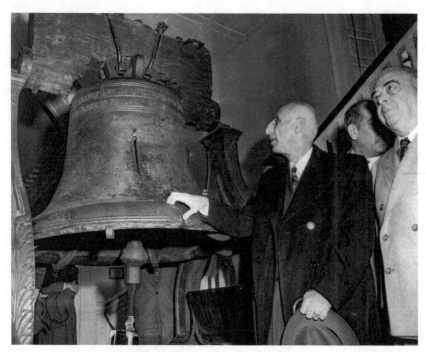

Mohammed Mosaddeq touches the Liberty Bell in Philadelphia, Pennsylvania, during a visit to the United States in October 1951. Truman Library, Accession No. 66-8004.

Mosaddeq and the National Front

Mohammed Mosaddeq was born on 16 June 1882. Raised among the aristocracy, Mosaddeq was descended from the Qajar dynasty that ruled Iran from 1796 to 1921.[80] Like many young Iranians of his class, Mosaddeq traveled to Europe for his education. He became the first Iranian to earn a Ph.D. in law from a European university, receiving his degree from the University of Neuchâtel in Switzerland in 1913. Mosaddeq first held public office at the age of fourteen, serving as the treasurer for the province of Khorasan. During the 1920s he held a series of government positions, including finance minister, foreign minister, governor of Azerbaijan, and minister of justice. Renowned for his probity, honesty, and diligence, Mosaddeq was the only Majlis deputy to categorically reject Reza Khan's ascension as Reza Shah Pahlavi I in 1925.[81]

Periodically suffering from a stomach ailment that would bring on fits of dizziness and indigestion, Mosaddeq went into retirement in the 1930s, as Reza Shah cracked down on the domestic opposition. He was briefly imprisoned by Reza Shah in 1940, returning to Tehran in 1942 after the shah's abdication. Mosaddeq won a seat in the Majlis in 1944 through a free and fair election in Tehran. Then in his sixties, Mosaddeq commanded the respect and admiration of the assembly through his oratory, incorruptibility, and defense of the constitution. His philosophy of negative equilibrium, once adapted to the context of the Cold War, presaged the concept of neutralism which would gain prominence during decolonization through the Bandung Conference of 1955 and the Non-Aligned Movement.[82] Other political figures in Iran found him "honest, trustworthy, and patriotic."[83] Although most foreign observers saw his rhetorical style as histrionic and theatrical, it made him very effective in the Majlis and in public fora, where he could keep crowds of thousands spellbound. While the British viewed him as a dangerous radical, early American assessments of Mosaddeq noted his reputation as an incorruptible politician.[84]

Mosaddeq's status as the country's most famous nationalist made him the natural leader of the anti-AIOC, anti-British, and pro-constitutional democracy movement that coalesced in 1949. That November, as the shah's allies attempted to rig the Majlis elections, Mosaddeq led his followers to the shah's palace, where they took *bast*, a protest sit-in reminiscent of tactics from the Constitutional Revolution. Once the protest concluded, Mosaddeq and his followers adjourned to the house of Hossein Fatemi, Mosaddeq's deputy, and formed the *Jebhe-ye Melli*, or "National Front." The shah relented and allowed new elections to be held, and Mosaddeq and ten of his supporters won seats. In a divided assembly where British influence was rife—as many as one-third of the deputies were indirectly controlled by Great Britain—Mosaddeq and his allies in the National Front formed a powerful and influential bloc advocating for national interests.[85]

The National Front was not a political party, but rather a loose grouping of factions united around the ideas of nationalization, opposition to British influence, and constitutional government over the dominance of the shah. Among the most important members were Mozaffar Baqa'i, a labor leader and organizer who founded the Toilers' Party in 1951 and published the paper *Shahed*; Hossein Fatemi, editor of *Bakhtar-e Emruz*, a popular paper that became the Front's major organ; a group of parliamentarians that included Hossein Makki, Allahyar Saleh, Ali Shayegan, Mahdi Azar, and Abdolhossin Haerizadeh; and the Iran Party, a group of Western-educated technocrats from which Mosaddeq would recruit administrators and bureaucrats. Mass politics were key to the Front's power, as huge crowds came out to see Mosaddeq and others deliver speeches denouncing the British. Baqa'i proved adept at this work, but the Front's clerical allies, who commanded wide audiences through Friday prayer services, had a much greater impact. Foremost among them was the Ayatollah Abolqassem Kashani, a cleric with a broad popular following.[86]

According to Mosaddeq's memoirs, Fatemi suggested the group demand nationalization of AIOC.[87] With a single action, Iran could take control of its most valuable economic asset, expel the British from the southern provinces, and chart a course toward national independence. Karim Sanjabi of the Iran Party argued that nationalization was internationally recognized; Britain had nationalized many industries, including the coal industry, after World War II, and would have to acknowledge Iran's nationalization so long as Iran paid compensation for AIOC's assets.[88] In 1950, the Front began disseminating the idea through major newspapers, including *Shahed* and *Bakhtar-e Emruz*. The coalition behind nationalization was broad and included members of Iran's traditional middle class in the bazaar and clergy as well as the intelligentsia. Organizing in the street was matched by the Front's Majlis representation, which soon dominated the assembly and made the shah's efforts to bring the Supplemental Agreement back for a vote virtually impossible.[89]

Staving Off the Crisis: The Razmara Government

The failure to ratify the Supplemental Agreement and the rise of the National Front brought the oil issue to the forefront of national politics. With the government facing a growing budget deficit, AIOC and the British government applied pressure on the shah to resubmit the Supplemental Agreement to the Majlis.[90] In May 1950, Prime Minister 'Ali Mansur struck a deal with Mosaddeq. Rather than force the Supplemental Agreement through the Majlis, Mansur formed an oil committee to examine the issue, with Mosaddeq as chair and five of its eighteen members National Front deputies. Intended as a stalling tactic, this had the effect of giving Mosaddeq a powerful position from which to attack the agreement and the British, raising his profile and ensuring the oil issue would dominate Majlis deliberations.[91]

While the British waited for Iran to act on the Supplemental Agreement, a combination of factors compelled the United States to increase its engagement in Iran. By March 1950 there were growing fears that economic problems, the government's ineptitude, and the public furor over the oil issue were causing instability that benefited Iran's communists and their allies in the Soviet Union. According to the U.S. embassy, the Tudeh Party was expanding its influence inside Iran.[92] Ambassador John C. Wiley warned that "economic deterioration and political helplessness" made Iran "ripe fruit for Communist exploitation."[93] Assistant Secretary of State for Near Eastern, South Asian, and African Affairs George C. McGhee spelled out the crisis in bleak terms in an April 1950 memorandum to Secretary of State Dean Acheson. The shah, once thought of as a possible reformer, "has neither the character nor the ability to offer his people guidance." Iranians were now "excellent targets for the clandestine but well-organized and well-financed Communist Party, whose influence appears to be expanding at an alarming rate."[94] Concern with Iran's internal stability and the expanding communist presence reflected broadening worries regarding the Cold War in the wake of the Soviet atomic test of August 1949, establishment of a communist government in China in October 1949, and the slowing of economic recovery in Western Europe. In the spring of 1950, the head of Truman's Policy Planning Staff, Paul Nitze, drafted NSC 68 (National Security Council Paper 68), which called for massive rearmament of the United States as a deterrent against growing Soviet influence.[95]

U.S. officials feared the oil issue and failing economy would lead to a general collapse and a communist takeover. According to Acheson, Iran's first problem was "government weakness." The shah could not offer the necessary leadership, and his refusal to back a powerful prime minister left his government rudderless.[96] U.S. officials in Tehran may have suggested to the shah that Army Chief of Staff 'Ali Razmara would make a suitable prime minister, though the degree to which the U.S. used direct pressure is unclear.[97] The only other possible choice for prime minister was Mosaddeq, whose prestige and popularity were on the rise.[98] Despite his own misgivings, the shah named Razmara the new prime minister on 25 June. The need to bolster Iran gained additional urgency following the North Korean attack on South Korea the same day.[99]

Razmara had previously served as minister of the interior as well as chief of staff of the army. He was anti-communist, ambitious, assertive, and pro-American. The shah distrusted Razmara, suspecting that he would use the office of prime minister to undermine the authority of the monarchy. However, the shah felt he had no choice but to back Razmara to retain American goodwill and support.[100] The U.S. preference for Razmara foreshadowed policy positions that would dominate the oil crisis, including the tendency to back figures associated with the military and an emphasis on stabilizing Iran through oil revenues—apart from his military background, Razmara appealed to U.S. officials because he seemed capable of pushing the Supplemental Agreement through the Majlis and restarting Iran's economic development plan.

Razmara had a broad agenda. Leaning on advice from the American development expert and former oilman Max Weston Thornburg, whom he took on as a personal economic advisor, Razmara announced a plan to decentralize the government's development program, refocusing efforts to the provinces. This would ensure Majlis deputies from the rural areas, where the National Front had little influence, would start to see immediate economic benefits and thus be more inclined to support Razmara's government. They would also be more inclined to support the Supplemental Agreement when Razmara brought it before the Majlis.[101] To accomplish these goals, Razmara needed money. He therefore reached out to the British and suggested AIOC begin paying higher royalties as mandated by the Supplemental Agreement—in other words, act as though the deal had been ratified and was in effect.[102]

Razmara's plan received the endorsement of the new U.S. ambassador in Iran, Henry F. Grady, a well-regarded economist who had spearheaded the postwar economic relief effort in Greece and later served as ambassador there and then in India. Grady, who arrived in July, promised Razmara a $25 million Export-Import Bank loan, which Iran could service using royalties from AIOC. After several meetings with Razmara, Grady suggested AIOC forward the funds available to Iran through the Supplemental Agreement, now approximately £50 million, as a gesture of good will. He agreed with Razmara that AIOC would have to offer additional concessions to make the agreement palatable to the new Majlis.[103] Grady was careful not to position himself as a mediator in the dispute and told Razmara that the Supplemental Agreement was fair and reasonable. Given the degree of anti-British feeling permeating the country, however, attempting to push through the agreement in its current form seemed suicidal. The British would have to sweeten the deal.[104]

AIOC Chairman Fraser refused to offer Iran more money. He insisted that Razmara ratify the Supplemental Agreement unaltered, suggesting the prime minister take some "bold action" and push the deal through the Majlis.[105] While the Foreign Office believed that AIOC should adopt a more flexible position, the Treasury refused to countenance a moderate strategy, citing Britain's unsteady balance of payments and the need to maintain access to Iranian oil on favorable terms.[106] "The company are convinced," wrote Foreign Office official Geoffrey Furlonge, "that more money is actually

[Razmara's] object," and that with more pressure he would crumble as Reza Shah had in 1933.[107] Foreign Office officials noted the "insatiable appetites of Near East states in matters of this kind," arguing to their American counterparts that Razmara's desire for funds was tantamount to blackmail.[108]

Frustrated by British intransigence, Razmara threatened to cancel the company's concession, as Reza Shah had in 1932. The United States took such threats seriously. Acheson argued that cancellation would have "almost total Iranian support," and he urged the British government to put more pressure on AIOC, "[the] last remaining obstacle."[109] The British dragged their feet throughout the summer, maintaining that pressure and time would force Razmara to concede and pass the Supplemental Agreement in its current form.[110] The divisions that appeared between the United States and Great Britain in the summer of 1950 foreshadowed the problems that would plague the allies during the oil crisis.

Concerned that rising regional nationalism would eventually threaten Middle East oil concessions, the U.S. government pressed all the companies operating in the Middle East to improve the terms of their concessions. The large U.S. concession in Saudi Arabia, where Aramco (owned by Jersey Standard, SOCAL, Socony, and Texaco) was under pressure from the Saudi government to improve its terms.[111] In September, U.S. officials met with AIOC executives and tried to impress upon them the importance of reaching a compromise with Razmara. "We have no doubt in our minds," wrote Richard Funkhouser, petroleum advisor, to McGhee in September, "that Persian Gulf oil operations have been and continue to [be] exceptionally profitable. . . . It is sophistry to suggest oil companies can't pay and do much more."[112] McGhee warned AIOC officials that Saudi Arabia was on the verge of making a new agreement with Aramco, one that might render the Supplemental Agreement obsolete. "Time is running out," and there was no chance of Razmara putting forward the Supplemental Agreement without meaningful improvements. The British would only consider a small loan of £2–3 million.[113] They also sabotaged Grady's plans for an Import-Export Bank loan, refusing to allow Iran to convert sterling to service the loan payments as a way to pressure Razmara to agree to the Supplemental Agreement. All of this proved immensely vexing to Grady. Iran's people lived "in animal-like poverty," and their government required foreign assistance. The United States must draw on all its resources, argued Grady, to rescue Iran from falling under Soviet domination "as a result of its sins of mismanagement."[114]

American frustrations stemmed in part from Razmara's unsuccessful efforts to assert himself over Iran's fractious political actors. From his seat at the head of the Majlis oil committee, Mosaddeq regularly denounced AIOC and the Supplemental Agreement.[115] The shah, forced to accept Razmara through U.S. pressure, intrigued against the prime minister behind the scenes. Razmara's plans to decentralize the development program stalled for lack of funds as the economic depression in Iran grew deeper. With little support inside Iran and the financial situation growing more desperate, Razmara buckled under AIOC pressure. In October, he abandoned his demands for cash payments, appointed a reliably pro-British figure as minister of finance, and promised to submit the Supplemental Agreement to the Majlis at the proper time. Razmara told the British embassy that a "face-saving" measure would be needed to mollify Mosaddeq's nationalists. Yet again, the British refused and pushed Razmara to submit the agreement in its existing form.[116]

American officials viewed the British approach to the situation in Iran with trepidation.[117] As McGhee saw it, AIOC was alone "in stubbornly refusing to face up to things as they are." The "wealthy tenant" was trying to outlast the "impoverished landlord."[118] Grady complained that months of pressure tactics from London had convinced him that the British were "bent on sabotaging our efforts to strengthen Iran in order to preserve [their] dubious supremacy and control." Further association with the British in Iran could become a "serious liability."[119] American misgivings were not enough to deter the British from demanding the Supplemental Agreement be ratified in its existing form. With no alternative, Razmara prepared to push the hated agreement through the Majlis, his efforts to fashion a new deal undone by British resistance.

Prelude to Nationalization

Attending a meeting of Mosaddeq's oil committee on 4 November, Razmara suggested the Supplemental Agreement would serve Iran's interests and argued that the country was not yet ready to run its own oil industry. His arguments carried little weight, however, and even the conservative deputies on the committee rejected his claims.[120] On 25 November, the committee released a statement declaring that the Supplemental Agreement did not protect Iran's interests and should be rejected. According to Grady, even the committee's pro-British members refused to support the agreement, "fearing that they would be branded as traitors if they did so."[121]

Facing mounting opposition from the National Front, conservatives in the Majlis, and the shah, Razmara sent his economic advisor Max Thornburg to London to meet directly with the British. Thornburg's goal, as he later related to a U.S. Treasury official, was to bring the two sides together around a settlement, "[and] head off any thought of Iran taking over the AIOC operations."[122] Thornburg failed to win over AIOC, however, and he left the meeting "disconsolate," complaining to an executive from Royal Dutch/ Shell of the "obdurate attitude" on display inside AIOC's headquarters at Britannic House: "in present world circumstances their standpoint was most deplorable."[123]

Thornburg's mission coincided with stunning news from Saudi Arabia. On 20 December, the Saudi government and Aramco announced a deal that split profits between them according to the fifty-fifty principle. Aramco agreed to pay half its profits to the Saudi government with the expectation that the payments could be deducted from its domestic tax liability in the United States. The "golden gimmick," as it was later known, meant that the payments from Aramco to the Saudi government would be borne by the American taxpayer. Such terms were attractive to the U.S. companies and would soon become standardized throughout the entire Middle East.[124] In the case of Iran, however, the Saudi agreement with Aramco meant that the terms of the Supplemental Agreement, which did not guarantee a fifty-fifty division, were obsolete.

With the British offer discredited, pressure to nationalize became even greater. On 21 December, Ayatollah Kashani issued a declaration in *Ettel-aat*, a major daily paper, calling for immediate nationalization to "uproot English influence which has caused, during the last 150 years, all the evils from which we suffer today."[125] Using talking points prepared in consultation with the AIOC's Ernest Northcroft, Razmara's minister of finance delivered a speech to the Majlis defending the Supplemental Agreement on 27 December. The assembly shouted him down, particularly when he used AIOC's rhetoric to defend the legality of the 1933 concession.[126] Once again, the company's efforts to influence matters in Iran proved heavy-handed and ill-timed. On 11 January 1951, the Majlis officially rejected the Supplemental Agreement and began debate on a proposal from Mosaddeq to nationalize the oil industry. Two weeks later, a crowd of ten thousand met at a large mosque in Tehran to hear speeches in support of nationalization. In February, a leading cleric issued a *fatwa*, or decree, condemning any government that allowed the nation's wealth to be given away to foreigners.[127]

AIOC was forced to admit that the Supplemental Agreement was "dead."[128] Grasping for ways to prop up the flailing Razmara, AIOC offered Iran £25 million paid over ten months, with the promise of a fifty-fifty agreement at some point in the future.[129] AIOC tried more pressure tactics. Northcroft gave Razmara an ultimatum: he would receive financial aid if and only if he took a public stand against nationalization. Caught between his nationalist opposition and AIOC brinksmanship, Razmara had no choice but to agree. On 4 March, he addressed the Majlis, giving a speech that had been written with "considerable assistance" from Northcroft himself.[130] Razmara argued that Iran could not run the Abadan refinery without foreign technicians, and that nationalization would bankrupt the country and unleash economic chaos. While the reception from the Majlis was muted, both the British and Americans hoped that the prime minister's stand against nationalization would help salvage the situation.[131] Instead, it cost him his life.

On 7 March, Razmara was assassinated. Although his assassin, Khalil Tahmasabi, was a member of the *Fedayeen-e Islam,* a religious group with ties to Kashani, the CIA could not determine who was behind the killing.[132] There is some evidence to suggest that the shah was at least aware of the plot against Razmara's life and welcomed the fall of the powerful prime minister. The next day, the Majlis oil committee unanimously approved a resolution recommending nationalization. The loss of Razmara, the rejection of the Supplemental Agreement, and the failure to arrest the country's slide into economic depression had created a situation that the National Front would quickly exploit. The conservatives surrounding the shah seemed powerless, as were the U.S. and British governments, which remained divided on how best to resolve the issue of AIOC's concession. The failure to pass the Supplemental Agreement, Anglo-American divisions, and AIOC's stubbornness had produced a crisis. For Iran's nationalists, however, nationalizing AIOC represented an opportunity to undo decades of foreign exploitation. With Razmara gone, the momentum toward nationalization became unstoppable.

2 Crisis in Iran

In April 1951, Mohammed Mosaddeq became prime minister and Iran nationalized the Anglo-Iranian Oil Company. This act set off a struggle pitting Iran's new government against AIOC, which maintained that the nationalization was illegal. Each side approached the crisis with distinct interests in mind. For Mosaddeq's nationalists, taking over Iran's oil industry was an important step toward achieving national independence. The economic ramifications of disrupting the flow of oil were secondary to the political importance of freeing the nation from foreign influence. Though he faced opposition from the communist Tudeh Party and Iran's conservative elite, Mosaddeq enjoyed popular support and the backing of the shah, who was not prepared to oppose the National Front at a time when public approval for nationalization was so strong. The British government supported AIOC and hoped to halt the advance of Iran's nationalization and retain control over Iranian oil. The British tried to use their influence within Iran to organize Mosaddeq's removal from power. They contemplated military intervention as a last resort.

With the Korean War at its height, the United States wanted to avoid another crisis, and U.S. officials worried that nationalization and conflict with Great Britain would produce conditions that could lead to communist control of Iran. The United States sought to broker an agreement that would allow AIOC to remain in Iran, keep the oil flowing, and satisfy Iran's nationalists. Although the British and U.S. governments were intent on retaining Western control over Iranian oil, they differed on tactics. The early months of the struggle for Iran were characterized by Anglo-American disagreement, intensified polarization of internal Iranian politics fueled by British covert operations, and high-level negotiations that failed to overcome the fundamental clash of interests over who would control Iran's oil.

Conflicting Views

A caretaker government led by the shah's advisor Hossein 'Ala took power following the assassination of Prime Minister Razmara on 7 March, but the issue of oil nationalization continued to dominate Iranian politics. Led by

Mosaddeq and other National Front deputies, the Majlis oil committee passed a resolution recommending nationalization on 8 March. A key Mosaddeq ally, Ayatollah Abolqassem Kashani, organized a pro-nationalization demonstration of 15,000 people in front of the Majlis building, and other National Front leaders, including the head of the Toilers' Party Mozaffar Baqa'i, held demonstrations throughout the city. On 14 March, the British government issued a statement, "phrased with all the patronizing complacency which Foreign Office drafters are capable when they put their minds to it," which maintained that under the terms of its 1933 agreement with AIOC, Iran did not have the right to terminate AIOC's concession unilaterally. Instead of slowing the momentum toward nationalization, it further inflamed Iranian nationalism. On 15 March, the Majlis approved the nationalization proposal from Mosaddeq's oil committee by a unanimous vote. Five days later, the Senate—an upper house dominated by pro-shah figures—approved a single-article bill nationalizing the oil industry.[1]

The resolution passed on 20 March was vaguely worded. A compromise between the National Front deputies and the Majlis's conservative majority, it stated that the oil industry was now the property of the Iranian people, without offering any guidance on how the process of nationalization would be carried out. Conscious of the bill's limited scope, Mosaddeq drafted a new bill that laid out the "repossession" (*khal'-e yad*) of the oil industry in more specific detail, including provisions for the payment of compensation to AIOC.[2] While Mosaddeq's nationalists moved forward with their agenda in the Majlis, Iran's oil workers took action against AIOC, which was slow to adjust to the changing political climate. Despite pleas from the Abadan refinery's managers, AIOC's management instituted labor cutbacks in late March—part of a multiyear efficiency drive—and canceled extended pay provisions.[3] The measures, which were regarded by the British consul in Khorramshahr as unnecessarily provocative, sparked a series of demonstrations among Iranian oil workers on 22 March. The British government responded by dispatching warships to the Persian Gulf, and the government deployed troops, tanks, and armored cars in Abadan. During the unrest, soldiers fired into crowds, killing and injuring a number of Iranian and British company employees. 'Ala was forced to institute martial law throughout the oil-province of Khuzestan, as 50,000 Iranian workers went on strike. The demonstrations triggered similar actions in Isfahan, where the Tudeh Party organized solidarity protests.[4]

While some officials in London and at the British embassy in Tehran acknowledged the political and popular strength of the National Front,

British policy was deeply influenced by overriding economic concerns, interest in retaining its strategic position, preoccupation with preserving imperial prestige, and cultural prejudices.[5] Abadan was Britain's most valuable overseas possession. AIOC's operations contributed £170 million annually to the British balance of payments.[6] Estimates of the company's value ranged from £81 million (undepreciated book value) to £500 million (replacement cost). In addition, the Admiralty bought around 85 percent of its oil from AIOC at a substantial discount, paying roughly one-third of what the oil would cost on the commercial market.[7] According to one projection from the Foreign Office, the loss of Iran's oil would cost the sterling zone £100 million a year.[8] The British feared that if Iran's nationalization succeeded, other British assets, most notably the Suez Canal, would be threatened. Britain's "paramount objective" was retaining control of Iranian oil in British hands.[9]

The death of Razmara, Mosaddeq's nationalization bill, and the rising violence in the oil fields worried the Truman administration, which feared the mounting crisis would end with Iran turning toward communism—an outcome that seemed likely if nationalization interrupted the flow of Iranian oil, creating internal economic and political disruptions. The strategic and economic consequences of such a development would be severe. Loss of Iran, the National Security Council (NSC) warned on 14 March, would allow the Soviets to threaten the oil-producing areas of the Persian Gulf. Iranian oil production in 1950 had been 664,315 barrels per day (bpd), 37.8 percent of total Middle East production (1,756,786 bpd) and almost 6.4 percent of total world production (10,418,073 bpd). The refinery complex at Abadan supplied more than one-fourth of all refined products outside the Western Hemisphere. A National Intelligence Estimate from January calculated that the loss of Iranian oil, which was sold in sterling, would have to be made up by "dollar oil," increasing the dollar charge to Western Europe by $700 million. Loss of Iran's oil would retard European recovery and impose severe financial hardships on Great Britain. Loss of all Middle East oil would make the Western European rearmament program "impossible of accomplishment" and force "profound changes" in Western Europe's economic structure.[10]

The NSC recommended that the United States should "take all feasible steps to assure that Iran does not fall victim to communist control." These steps included accelerated and expanded military, economic, and technical assistance, and political support and covert financial and other assistance to pro-Western and anti-communist elements in Iran. In addition, the NSC recommended that the United States "press the United Kingdom to effect an early and equitable settlement of the Anglo-Iranian Oil Company dispute."[11]

With the stakes so high, officials in the Central Intelligence Agency recommended that the agency finance an "intensified propaganda campaign" in support of the shah and 'Ala. Kermit Roosevelt, chief of the Near East and Africa Division of the Directorate of Plans, argued that there was an "immediate" danger of losing Iran.[12] The State Department regarded the CIA suggestions as "hurriedly prepared," noting the difficulties in uniting the disparate non-communist groups inside the country.[13] Assistant CIA Director Allen W. Dulles shared Roosevelt's views, but saw little role for the agency while the State Department controlled policy. "The steps which the CIA alone can take," he wrote to CIA Director Walter Bedell Smith, would not be effective without "coordinated planning" with the rest of the United States government.[14] Much to Roosevelt's chagrin, an intensified covert campaign was not approved.[15] Nevertheless, with the State Department's approval, the CIA prepared emergency financial assistance for 'Ala's government.[16]

The central focus of American attention was securing an oil settlement that would preserve British control of the industry and contribute to Iranian economic well-being and internal political stability. Assistant Secretary of State for Near Eastern, South Asian, and African Affairs George C. McGhee, who was on a trip to the Middle East, flew to Iran and conferred with British embassy officials and the shah before heading to London, where he met with AIOC and government officials. McGhee stressed that Iran was the most vulnerable point along the Soviet periphery and a country the Soviets could conceivably take over without precipitating a third world war. With U.S. forces tied down in Korea, European defense arrangements still incomplete, and rearmament just getting underway, the United States wanted to avoid a crisis in Iran. The best course for AIOC to follow, McGhee advised, was to give formal recognition to the principle of nationalization while working out a "formula" for retaining effective control and dividing profits fifty-fifty. McGhee strongly recommended supporting the shah but warned that it was important not to weaken the shah by pressuring him to oppose nationalization openly.[17]

McGhee repeated these arguments in discussions with a British delegation in Washington in mid-April. McGhee urged the British to devise a deal that paid "lip service" to nationalization, assuaging Iranian nationalism without affecting "the actual control of the company's operations." The

British, however, did not believe it would be possible to make any real concessions to Iranian nationalism without losing effective control of Iran's oil. Control of oil—how much oil to produce, to whom it should be sold, and on what terms—was crucial because Iran could meet its foreign exchange needs at a much lower level of production and export than Britain needed to maintain the value of sterling. The most the British would consider was allowing Iranian participation on the board of a new British-owned company, which would hold the concession and AIOC's Iranian assets, operate the industry, and share profits equally with Iran according to the fifty-fifty principle.[18]

Rather than negotiate, the British focused on finding a suitable replacement for Razmara. British officials doubted the staying power of the National Front. The Foreign Office's Geoffrey Furlonge argued that the drive to nationalize could not maintain its "present pitch," and that most Iranians "did not share the extremism of Mosaddeq's supporters."[19] As a replacement for 'Ala, British Ambassador Sir Francis Shepherd pressed the shah to appoint Sayyed Zia, a veteran pro-British politician, as prime minister. While wary of the National Front's growing political support, the shah agreed to cooperate with Shepherd and back Zia at the appropriate time.[20] Before the British could arrange Sayyid Zia's appointment, Mosaddeq and the National Front deputies on the oil committee proposed a new bill calling for the liquidation of AIOC's assets and outlining steps to implement nationalization.[21] The bill passed the committee and came before the Majlis on 27 April.

After 'Ala abruptly resigned, Zia and the shah came up with a plan to fix matters in the Majlis. Conservative leader and Majlis Speaker Jamal Emami would propose Mosaddeq be named prime minister, assuming that Mosaddeq would refuse the premiership, as he had done in the past. This would clear the way for Emami to nominate Zia, who was waiting with the shah at the palace. Mosaddeq apparently learned of Emami's plan and, rather than reject the offer, addressed the Majlis and suggested the nationalization bill be put to a vote. If it passed, he would accept Emami's offer. The bill passed with a large majority and the Majlis named Mosaddeq prime minister on 27 April. The Senate confirmed his appointment the next day. The shah accepted Mosaddeq's nomination and signed the nationalization bill, now known as the Nine-Point Nationalization Law, on 1 May.[22] There was now a legal mandate to implement nationalization, and a government in place committed to carrying out that mandate.

Nationalization: U.S. and British Reactions

Mosaddeq had not expected to become prime minister. The job carried considerable risk—Razmara had been assassinated and no one had lasted more than a year in the office since Ahmed Qavam's tenure in 1946–47. Faced with the immense task of successfully carrying out nationalization, many expected Mosaddeq to fail and leave office in disgrace. Conscious of the need to retain the support of the conservative elite, Mosaddeq kept on many of 'Ala's cabinet members, including Finance Minister Ali Varasteh and Interior Minister Fazlollah Zahedi. Karim Sanjabi later noted that Mosaddeq's cabinet "would appear both radical and monarchical," thus preserving national unity at a time of crisis.[23] The National Front's progressive agenda, which included labor and welfare reforms, would have to wait. Mosaddeq also worked to maintain good relations with the shah, who told U.S. Ambassador Henry F. Grady that he "had no alternative" but to accept nationalization or risk being branded a national traitor.[24] Combining shrewd management of Iran's traditional players with his prestige and popular support, Mosaddeq came to office with more power than any prime minister in recent memory.

The British were hostile to the new government. According to Ambassador Shepherd, Mosaddeq was an irrational "lunatic" representing Iran's backward aristocratic class who had managed to stir up anti-British sentiment through demagoguery. Shepherd, an opinionated and somewhat delusional official who had served in the Dutch East Indies in the period immediately before its independence and earlier in the Belgian Congo and Haiti, wrote that Mosaddeq "looks rather like a cab horse . . . [and] diffuses a slight reek of opium."[25] Emami believed his nationalization campaign would fail. "Given a little rope," Emami told Shepherd in early May, "Dr. Musaddiq would hang himself."[26] Shepherd shared this view and believed Mosaddeq's government would soon collapse. British assessments of the National Front dripped with contempt, and most officials in the Labour government regarded Iranian aspirations to run the oil industry as ludicrous.[27] Foreign Secretary Herbert Morrison, the most aggressive member of Clement Attlee's cabinet, warned on 1 May that Britain was in danger of losing prestige, as well as property, if it mishandled the situation. Like Shepherd, Morrison supported a policy that would pressure Mosaddeq to accept British proposals.[28]

Although Attlee personally opposed the use of force, the British government had been considering military options since the beginning of the crisis. On 20 March, Morrison tasked the chiefs of staff to explore practical possibilities for taking military action against Iran. There was widespread support for some sort of military response within the government and the opposition, as well as among the public. Minister of Defence Emmanuel Shinwell warned on 23 May that "if Persia was allowed to get away with [nationalization], Egypt and other Middle East countries would be encouraged to think they could try things on: the next thing might be an attempt to nationalize the Suez Canal." The chiefs listed three options: a show of force in the Abadan area that would stop short of an actual invasion; intervention to protect lives and property in the Abadan area and evacuate British nationals; and an invasion and occupation of Abadan and the oil fields in Khuzestan. Britain could send additional warships to the area, but without the Indian Army, which had provided the troops for the 1941 invasion of Iran, it did not possess the necessary forces in the region to intervene swiftly and successfully. Although Britain possessed a powerful military, most of its units were tied up in Korea and Malaya or dedicated to the defense of Western Europe, and its forces in the Middle East did not have the training and equipment that would be needed for a successful intervention. There was also the problem of what intervention would accomplish. The Abadan refinery could be supplied with crude oil brought in from nearby Kuwait, but as AIOC's Chairman Fraser pointed out, its operation would be dependent on the cooperation of its 75,000 Iranian employees, which was highly unlikely if it were occupied by British troops.[29]

Although the United States and Britain did not agree on how best to approach the issue of Iran's nationalization and the country's new and assertive nationalist government, the United States, like Britain, had no intention of recognizing nationalization in any substantive form. In an interview published on 24 May, President Harry S. Truman told journalist Arthur Krock that the head of AIOC, Sir William Fraser, looked like a "typical nineteenth-century colonial exploiter," and that the British had dealt "ineptly and disastrously" with Iran. He cautioned, however, that "if the Iranians carry out their plans as stated, Venezuela and other countries on whose supply we depend will follow suit." Secretary of State Dean Acheson also criticized British policy, noting in his memoirs that "never had so few lost so much so stupidly and so fast," but he consistently worked to maintain Anglo-American unity.[30] George McGhee was harshly critical of AIOC and British government policies in Iran, but he feared permitting Iran to take over AIOC's concession and produce oil independently "would jeopardize oil concessions held by the USA, United Kingdom, and other firms around the world."[31] Paul Nitze, the influential head of the Policy Planning Staff, thought AIOC's leadership was incompetent and Mosaddeq "far preferable to the shah and his regime," but was also determined that nationalization "fail."[32]

In meetings with the British, U.S. officials urged conciliation and cautioned against applying pressure.[33] Acheson warned British Ambassador Oliver Franks on 27 April that opposition to the nationalist movement would provide an opening for the Soviets. The British, according to the U.S. ambassador in London, did not appreciate this "unhelpful needling," as it implied the United States might prioritize assisting Iran over protecting British commercial and economic interests.[34] The British suspected officials like George McGhee and Ambassador Grady hoped to undermine British oil interests, potentially at the behest of American oil companies, though Grady regarded Mosaddeq's act as "confiscation" and like McGhee saw nationalization as a threat to U.S. interests.[35]

There was some sympathy for the British desire to remove Mosaddeq, particularly at the CIA. Deputy Director Allen Dulles put it in blunt terms on 9 May: "Have the shah throw out Mosaddeq," he told CIA director Smith, "close the Majlis and temporarily rule by decree. At a later date a new premier could be installed with our help."[36] In contrast, CIA station chief in Iran Roger Goiran doubted the "feasibility and wisdom" of any covert action to remove Mosaddeq. He regarded the National Front as a potential bulwark against communism. In his opinion, the United States should support "legitimate indigenous liberal progressive movements," rather than back the aristocracy and elite, who were corrupt and ineffective.[37] A CIA report noted Mosaddeq's broad public support and concluded it was "unlikely" that Mosaddeq could be overthrown "except by violence or by the establishment of a semi-dictatorial regime under the aegis of the shah." Mosaddeq was not a communist and had shown hostility to the Soviet Union in the past.[38] U.S. officials also believed Mosaddeq would try to retain access to Western markets to avoid an economic collapse.[39]

Given these realities, the State Department recommended that the United States try to work with Mosaddeq, and perhaps even offer him financial and military assistance. Now that nationalization had taken place, American efforts focused on bringing the British and Iranians together in a mutually beneficial oil agreement.[40] The United States would not oppose nationalization publicly. To do so would inflame Iranian nationalism and potentially drive Mosaddeq and his supporters toward the Soviets. Britain was an important Cold War ally and shouldered a considerable portion of the Western defense burden. U.S. officials also recognized the economic importance of the AIOC concession and especially the Abadan refinery to Britain. "We have to remember that we are dealing with Britain's most important economic asset abroad," McGhee argued during a State Department–Joint Chiefs of Staff meeting on 2 May.[41]

The United States strongly opposed British plans to use military force, however. On 11 May, the Foreign Office instructed Britain's ambassador in the United States to ascertain the U.S. attitude on the possible use of force, noting that Britain was deeply concerned about the "world-wide consequences of our losing control of Persian oil, and the great danger of repercussions elsewhere in the Middle East if we tamely acquiesce in ejection from Persia."[42] After Ambassador Oliver Franks outlined British plans, Acheson replied that while the United States recognized Britain's right to use force to evacuate British citizens whose lives were in danger and would also support use of force in the event of open Soviet intervention or of a communist seizure of power, the United States had "grave misgivings" about the use of force in any other circumstances. Acheson also explained that the United States could not support any proposals by Britain that did not reflect acceptance of the principle of nationalization. In the U.S. view, a proposal that did not accept that principle would not resolve the crisis.[43]

Acheson told the National Security Council on 16 May that British plans to use force were "sheer madness," and that he was "unalterably opposed" to them. Other members agreed, but also argued that the United States "could not afford to be neutral" in the conflict between Britain and Iran because nationalization was likely to set a precedent that would lead other countries to take similar action. The situation was "highly contagious" and had to be contained. The United States should vigorously support British efforts to reach an "equitable settlement," short of assisting them in the use of force against the "present Iranian government." President Truman approved Acheson's recommendation the following day."[44] To make sure the British got the message, Acheson and McGhee reiterated their concerns about the use of force in meetings with British officials on 16 and 17 May and instructed the U.S. ambassador in London to take up the matter personally with Foreign Secretary Morrison.[45]

U.S. policy sought to balance British and Iranian interests. Given the potential impact of Iran's nationalization on other oil concessions, the United States also had to consider the interests of the major U.S. oil companies. On 14 May, McGhee told American oil executives that U.S. objectives (in order of importance) were to avoid war, keep Iran on the side of the West, maintain the flow of oil from the Middle East, and protect concession rights in the

Middle East and other parts of the world. The United States believed that nationalization had to be accepted as an accomplished fact. Public support for nationalization and hatred for the British ran so deep that "threats to boycott Iran" would be ineffective and could threaten access to refined products from the Abadan refinery, which were "irreplaceable" in the global oil economy.[46]

An official U.S. statement released on 18 May made it clear that while the United States would not oppose nationalization in principle, it backed the British position. The statement condemned "any unilateral cancellation of clear contractual relationships," and argued that the "efficient" operation of the Iranian oil industry would require technical expertise, capital, transportation, and marketing facilities. Elimination of AIOC would deprive Iran of these essentials, and the U.S. companies that possessed these capabilities had "indicated . . . that they would not in the face of unilateral action by Iran against the British company be willing to undertake operations in that country." The Iranians, who were planning to initiate discussions with the British on implementation of nationalization, saw the statement as proof of U.S. support for the British. The British, in contrast, objected to its tone and complained that it was excessively neutral. Reflecting the polarized atmosphere in the United States, *Life* magazine called for Acheson's dismissal for the imminent "loss of Iran."[47]

The Jackson Mission and the Shutdown of Iranian Exports

On 20 May, Finance Minister Ali Varasteh sent AIOC a letter declaring that Iran had nationalized the company's holdings "in accordance with the acts of 15 and 20 March." Varasteh invited the company to send a delegation to Iran to discuss plans to keep the industry operational, in a way that would retain "the experience and knowledge of the former oil company."[48] Under U.S. pressure, Morrison announced on 29 May that AIOC would send a delegation to Iran to begin discussions. While the British could not accept the right of the Iranian government to repudiate its contract with AIOC, they were prepared to consider a settlement that would involve some form of nationalization, "provided it were satisfactory in other respects."[49]

On 10 June, an AIOC mission headed by its Deputy Chairman Basil Jackson arrived in Iran.[50] Before leaving London, the AIOC team assembled briefs to inform Jackson's negotiating position. The briefs instructed Jackson to emphasize the inability of the Iranians to operate the industry, pointing out the "immense complexity" of the Abadan refinery. Jackson should note that 74 percent of Iran's exports went to AIOC affiliates and the Admiralty, while another 20 percent was sold to other major oil companies. If Iran proceeded with nationalization, it would lose access to this expertise and the markets, and be left with an unwieldy and expensive industry.[51] Presumably, once the Iranians realized they could not operate the industry successfully without British help, they would agree to British proposals that left control of the industry in AIOC's hands.

The Iranian negotiators insisted that AIOC had to abide by the terms of the Nine-Point Nationalization Law. AIOC should surrender all proceeds earned since 20 March, with 25 percent set aside in an account from which AIOC would receive compensation. The company's staff could continue to work as employees of the National Iranian Oil Company (NIOC), a new state-owned enterprise created by the 1 May nationalization law. Contracts, salaries, and benefits under AIOC would be honored by NIOC. Varasteh stated that he had no wish to "paralyze the Company's operations," and once the articles of the Nine-Point Law were executed, business would resume "under the same mechanism as had hitherto been in operation."[52] None of Jackson's arguments regarding the operation of the industry persuaded the Iranian negotiators. "The Iranian oil industry was a child which the Western World would fondly nurture in any circumstances," said Kazem Hassibi, Mosaddeq's oil expert. If operating the industry proved expensive initially, the losses would be made up quickly, as selling oil after nationalization would produce "eight or nine times" more revenue than Iran had received from AIOC.[53]

Jackson considered Iranian demands "wholly unacceptable" and refused to accept the Nine-Point Law as a basis for discussion. Jackson also rejected the Iranian position on British staff, arguing that they were accustomed to living and working under British management in a British-run company town and would never submit to Iranian supervision. On 19 June, AIOC made a counteroffer. It would establish a new company to operate the oil industry on behalf of NIOC, with profits shared on a fifty-fifty basis. AIOC would forgo compensation in exchange for a long-term contract to operate the oil fields and the Abadan refinery on behalf of Iran. AIOC would pay £10 million plus £3 million a month until permanent arrangements could be worked out.[54] In effect, the deal would produce the appearance of nationalization while allowing AIOC to continue in its current position. Ambassador Grady felt it to be a "most liberal offer."[55]

The Iranians rejected the British counteroffer and again insisted that talks had to be based on the Nine-Point Law. As discussions broke down,

Acheson pushed Grady to bring the shah into the fray, arguing that it was time for Iran's monarch to "exert his leadership." Grady met with the shah but found him depressed. The AIOC offer, the shah complained, had been "unfortunately phrased," and the British had failed to provide terms with which the National Front could agree.[56] Despite Grady's efforts to keep the AIOC negotiators in Tehran, the Jackson mission left on 22 June without reaching a settlement.[57] The company had assumed that Mosaddeq—once "educated" on his inability to operate the oil industry without British assistance—would capitulate. Once again, AIOC had misjudged the political strength of nationalization and squandered a potential opportunity to resolve the crisis.

The failure of the Jackson mission confirmed the British belief that it was fruitless to negotiate with Iran. Mosaddeq and his allies appeared determined to implement nationalization and place AIOC under Iranian control. Rather than pursue further discussions, the British decided to achieve their objectives through a combination of economic and political pressure. The British believed that cutting off Iranian oil exports would starve the Iranian state of revenues, thus demonstrating the dangers of nationalization by isolating Iran from the global oil market and preventing it from profiting from its action against AIOC.

A boycott of Iranian oil appeared feasible for several reasons. The British were confident the other major oil companies would show solidarity with AIOC and refuse to do business with Iran. Before nationalization, around 94 percent of the products and crude exported from Abadan were purchased by AIOC, its corporate subsidiaries, the Admiralty, or other large companies. Only 6 percent went to national companies operating in Western Europe or Latin America.[58] Further strengthening the British position, 73 percent of the world's 1,500 tankers were under charter with AIOC or other major oil companies. Communist countries and Argentina controlled most of the rest.[59] While the economic cost to AIOC of losing access to Iranian oil would be severe, the loss could be managed by increasing output in Kuwait, where AIOC held a 50 percent stake with U.S.-owned Gulf Oil, and from Iraq, where AIOC held 23.75 percent of the Iraq Petroleum Company. A boycott could be reinforced with economic sanctions enforced by the British government, including freezing Iran's sterling convertibility privileges and suspending shipments of strategic materials such as steel. Such actions might not prove "catastrophic" for Iran's economy, which the British felt could withstand an oil shutdown, but would place pressure on the government.[60]

Officials in the British government's Persian Oil Working Group recognized that a boycott would not be completely effective at ending Iranian oil exports. Peter Ramsbotham of the Foreign Office estimated on 25 June that Iran could produce around 265,340 barrels of crude and 102,054 barrels of products per day without foreign assistance.[61] Although Mosaddeq might find some customers by offering oil at reduced prices, the British did not believe Iran would sell enough oil to pay for nationalization or affect the global oil market. In any event, they believed the pressures from the boycott and sanctions would push Mosaddeq from power before damage to the global oil market or Iran's internal economy became too serious. There was widespread skepticism regarding Iran's ability to handle the industry, owing to culturally prejudicial notions of Iranian inferiority and lack of technical skill. Indeed, some felt that a few months of "inefficient operation" would cause such damage to the Abadan refinery that the Iranians would have no choice but to turn to Britain for aid.[62]

The second pillar of the British strategy was to create circumstances that would make it politically possible for the shah to replace Mosaddeq.[63] Ann Lambton, a British specialist on Iran with close connections to the Foreign Office, believed that Britain should undermine Mosaddeq, encouraging the prime minister's opponents to mobilize against him. Dr. Robin Zaehner, a British subject of Swiss origin who had headed a successful covert propaganda operation in Iran in 1944, was sent to Iran and tasked with managing political operations inside the country. Lambton regarded Zaehner, an Oxford professor of oriental studies who was fluent in Persian, as a "man of great subtlety" who could organize public opinion from the bazaars upward, drawing on British assets in the city, including a network of bribery and patronage run by the Rashidian family, a merchant group that the British had cultivated during the war.[64] Zaehner shared a room with Norman Darbyshire, an MI6 agent attached to the embassy. While Zaehner operated in a quasi-autonomous role, Darbyshire reported to Christopher Montague "Monty" Woodhouse, the local MI6 head of operations.[65] Neither Darbyshire nor Zaehner were to inform the ambassador of their activities, and very little of their clandestine operations are revealed in Foreign Office records.

Needing the shah's support to remove Mosaddeq, Ambassador Shepherd met with him on 30 June and urged him to replace the prime minister with a more pro-British figure.[66] Shepherd still believed that Mosaddeq lacked staying power. He had become prime minister through "parliamentary accident," and Shepherd felt that "respectable" political opinion did not support Mosaddeq and would revolt against him if granted the opportunity.[67]

While the British believed that the Iranian army would support the shah in a showdown with Mosaddeq, it would have to be clear that the shah was acting in Iran's best interests and was not pulling British chestnuts out of the fire.[68] There was relatively little British interest in continuing negotiations with the Mosaddeq government after Jackson's failure. Time and pressure, through cutting off Iran's access to oil revenue and the tactics of Shepherd, Zaehner, and Darbyshire, would eventually engineer Mosaddeq's removal from power.

As in May, some within the U.S. government supported the idea of ousting Mosaddeq. A memorandum drafted in the Office of Greek, Turkish and Iranian Affairs agreed with the British assessment that "no satisfactory compromise" could be reached with Mosaddeq, "[and] that it would therefore be most advantageous for that government to fall" as early as conditions permitted.[69] Max Thornburg, Razmara's former economic advisor and a friend of Allen Dulles at the CIA, told Acheson on 5 July that the shah should jail some of the "bad elements" and dissolve the Majlis. Eventually, Mosaddeq would be forced out.[70] In contrast, T. Cuyler Young, an American academic who advised the State Department on Iranian issues, argued that Mosaddeq was a historically popular figure with widespread support and warned that the United States would become unpopular if it sided openly with the British.[71]

Unlike the British, the United States had few concrete assets inside Iran that could be utilized to remove Mosaddeq. Gerald Dooher of the U.S. embassy had been in contact with the Qashqa'i, a confederation of armed tribesmen in southern Iran, since 1948. The Qashqa'i had historically held their own against the Iranian military and enjoyed a degree of autonomy within their territory. They were anti-communist, and in early 1949 Dooher had incorporated the tribes into a "stay-behind" plan, to be implemented in the event that Iran was invaded by Soviet forces or fell to a communist government.[72] On 25 June 1951, Dooher met with Qashqa'i leaders and suggested to other U.S. officials that a lump sum of $1 million would buy their support.[73] The Qashqa'i were pro-Mosaddeq. They were firmly opposed to Pahlavi rule, and they found Mohammed Reza "ridiculous." They would not support a policy that favored the shah.[74] The CIA focused on assembling an Iranian political force "for the propagation of U.S. views and policies to counteract the powerful influence of the Tudeh."[75] The CIA's actions were coordinated as part of Operation TPBEDAMN and focused on bolstering anti-communist forces, including the National Front, so their assets were poorly positioned to support a move against Mosaddeq's government.

A move against Mosaddeq appeared unwise due to divisions among existing pro-U.S. factions, the apparent weakness of the shah, and the strength of the National Front. The United States also worried about the impact of the cessation of Iranian oil exports and the shutdown of the oil industry. Closing the Abadan refinery and ending oil production would throw thousands of Iranians out of work, further exacerbating labor tensions and potentially producing a new opening for the Tudeh to organize oil workers. The loss of oil revenue could undermine the Iranian government's efforts to maintain order. Without funds the army and civil service would go unpaid, development work would stall, and the domestic economy would grow more depressed, producing the ideal ingredients for a communist takeover. The State Department argued that the security of Iran and its continued orientation toward the West were "clearly of paramount importance," and that any solution to the oil controversy had to take these objectives into account. McGhee recommended letting the British know that if the choice was between losing Iran or letting U.S. companies buy Iranian oil and/or supply technicians, the United States would choose the latter.[76]

Meanwhile, while negotiations stalled in Tehran, Mosaddeq established a committee to take over the oil industry and operate it on a provisional basis according to the Nine-Point Law. The committee, led by National Front orator Hossein Makki, arrived in Abadan on 19 June. Makki announced that the refinery and oil fields were now the property of the Iranian people before a massive crowd assembled in front of the company headquarters.[77] Two days later, National Front investigators raided the house of Norman Seddon, AIOC's chief representative in Iran, and discovered a trove of documents outlining the company's campaign to influence the Iranian press.[78] The following day Mosaddeq addressed the Majlis and declared that no negotiations would be possible unless the "former company" accepted the terms of the Nine-Point Law. As the assembly cheered his resolve, a crowd surged through Baharestan Square, tearing down AIOC billboards.[79] Mosaddeq, Grady reported, was "riding a wave" of nationalist fervor, and would no longer shy away from using "terrorism" against those who opposed him. Jackson's proposals had only fueled the "intense hatred" felt toward the British.[80]

On 25 June, Makki's provisional committee in Abadan announced that "Foreign Staff, who continue to stay in their posts and serve loyally, will enjoy the respect and affection of the Iranian people." Those who were not willing to work for NIOC were free to leave.[81] In response, AIOC threatened to shut down all operations. The Iranians countered with an anti-sabotage bill, which provided stiff penalties for interfering with oil operations, leading AIOC General Manager Eric Drake to flee to Iraq. Refusing to comply with the Iranian demand that tanker captains sign a receipt acknowledging NIOC's title to the oil they were loading, AIOC ceased loading oil for its affiliates, and AIOC's major customers began diverting their oil tankers elsewhere.[82] On 28 June, Foreign Secretary Morrison announced publicly that operations in Abadan could no longer continue.[83] By 1 July, exports of oil and oil products had ceased, though production continued at a declining rate while storage tanks remained unfilled in Abadan. When storage tanks were full, the refinery would have to shut down.

Harriman Comes to Iran

The United States believed that the British policy of pressuring Iran could lead to disaster. Ambassador Grady wrote on 1 July that Mosaddeq enjoyed the support of "95 to 98 percent" of all Iranians: "it is utter folly to try and push him out." If the British believed they could remove him through economic pressure, they were making a "tragic mistake."[84] The United States feared that the British might intervene militarily. Both sides, Acheson recalled, were "pressing their luck to the point of suicide." Alarmed by the situation in Iran, President Truman approved a National Security Council recommendation that the United States "bring its influence to bear" to effect a settlement between Iran and the British, "making clear both our recognition of the rights of sovereign states to control their natural resources and the importance we attach to international contractual relationships." Mosaddeq wrote to Truman on 28 June, stating his "readiness to enter into negotiations" on the basis of the nationalization law. Truman proposed sending veteran statesman Averell Harriman to Iran to find a formula that would allow Iran and Britain to resume negotiations.[85]

The British opposed the idea, arguing that negotiations be paused while they awaited a decision from the International Court of Justice (ICJ), where they had lodged a complaint in late May charging that the Iranian nationalization was illegal. An interim judgment from the Court on 5 July instructed each side to abstain from any actions until a ruling had been delivered. The British seized on the judgment as a way head off action by the United States, providing more time for British agents and supporters in Iran to destabilize the government and remove Mosaddeq from office. Ambassador Franks in Washington admitted to Acheson on 4 July that his government had no concrete plan for new discussions and was content to stall until Mosaddeq fell from power.[86] Nevertheless, the British agreed to let Harriman try to get talks started again. Truman wrote to Mosaddeq on 8 July, urging him to observe the ICJ decision while offering Harriman as a mediator "to talk over with you this immediate and pressing problem."[87] Mosaddeq agreed to receive Harriman, though he refused to accept the ICJ's competence to rule in a dispute between a sovereign nation and a private corporation.[88]

Averell Harriman, son of railroad baron E. H. Harriman, was an experienced diplomat who had served as ambassador to the Soviet Union from 1943 to 1946 and to Britain from April to October 1946. Acheson instructed Harriman to find some "common denominator" to unite the Iranian and British positions. To achieve their goal of a settlement that maintained AIOC's presence in Iran, the United States needed to bring the British around to recognizing the legitimacy of nationalization, while convincing the Iranians to abandon their plans to run the oil industry without British management. At the very least, talks could proceed slowly, giving time for "sensible" Iranians like the shah to pull Mosaddeq away from his rigid position and agree to a settlement that would allow Iranian oil to continue flowing.[89]

Harriman's first job was to get the British onboard. Stopping in Paris on his way to Tehran, Harriman met with Hugh Gaitskell, Attlee's chancellor of the exchequer, and assured him that the United States shared Britain's interest in retaining control of Iran's oil industry. The goal of negotiations would be to convince Mosaddeq that oil "could not be sold without British help." Harriman was prepared to make concessions to Iranian nationalism, but not at the expense of British economic interests or Western oil holdings elsewhere.[90] Most British officials expected Harriman's efforts would fail. Norman Seddon of AIOC guessed that Harriman would find Mosaddeq overly stubborn. When talks dragged out, "moderates" in the Majlis and elsewhere would rally against the National Front and force Mosaddeq from power.[91] The forthcoming talks were thus one part good-faith effort to bring Mosaddeq around to the British and American view and one part delaying maneuver designed to give Mosaddeq's opposition more time to organize against him.

Harriman arrived in Iran on 14 July. Accompanying him were oil expert Walter J. Levy and interpreter Colonel Vernon Walters, a career army officer whose linguistic abilities would take him on many similar "silent missions" in the future.[92] Conditions in Tehran were tense. On his way from Tehran's airport to the center of the city, demonstrators surrounded Harriman's car,

Averell Harriman (second from left) went to Iran in July 1951 at the request of President Truman (second from right), to act as mediator. In reality, he pushed for a deal that would benefit the British and tried to convince the shah to remove Mosaddeq as prime minister. Also pictured: Secretary of State Dean Acheson (first on left) and Secretary of Defense George C. Marshall (first on right). Truman Library, Accession No. 65-2759.

pelting it with stones and trash. Most of the crowd were Tudeh supporters, but some of the demonstrators were probably paid by CIA agents in a "false-flag" operation meant to draw the city's security forces into cracking down on communist activity. Toilers' Party chief Mozaffar Baqa'i's paper, *Shahed*, blamed the violence on AIOC and accused the company of working secretly with the Tudeh to sabotage the Harriman mission. Furious at the relative passivity of the police, Mosaddeq dismissed Interior Minister Fazlollah Zahedi and Tehran's police chief.[93]

Brushing off the initial violence of his arrival, Harriman met with Mosaddeq on 16 July. Mosaddeq was willing to concede Iran's inability to market oil on its own—despite frequent claims to the contrary, Mosaddeq had a fairly firm grasp of the international oil industry—but he refused to allow AIOC control over production. The problem with the Jackson proposal, Mosaddeq explained, was that it merely replaced AIOC with a new company. AIOC had offered Iran £10 million pounds "to shut up and be quiet."[94]

To Harriman, the situation in Iran appeared increasingly unstable. This was partially due to British intrigues against Mosaddeq. Court Minister 'Ala complained that British agents were running rampant, dispensing bribes and patronage, while the British military attaché went on "shooting trips" in order to meet with tribal leaders and organize unrest in the provinces.[95] Harriman was not impressed with Mosaddeq, whom he found "rigid" and consumed with anti-British animus. At the same time, however, the National Front appeared to enjoy broad public support. Harriman met with the shah and 'Ala to discuss the possibility of replacing Mosaddeq. They explained that this was politically impossible because the country was solidly behind Mosaddeq on the oil issue. With the opposition disorganized and the shah unwilling to provide leadership, there was no way to engineer Mosaddeq's removal. The only viable course was to settle the oil issue through negotiation, one that would protect British interests without openly contravening the principle of nationalization.[96]

Harriman and Levy worked to bring the Iranians around to proposals that would allow AIOC to remain in the country. Levy, an oil industry consultant who had worked with the Office of Strategic Services during World War II and as an advisor to the Marshall Plan, met with Kazem Hassibi, Mosaddeq's oil advisor. The British derided Hassibi as a "second-rate oil engineer," but he understood oil production and would not be misled by arguments emphasizing British technical proficiency.[97] Levy chose to focus on the integrated international market for oil. He argued that even if Iran could produce its own oil, without the cooperation of the major companies it had no way to transport or sell it for a profit. There was an oversupply of oil, Levy explained, and if Iranian oil was to "find a place," the Iranian government must be prepared to act "in a cooperative spirit." That meant coming to terms with AIOC.[98]

Harriman presented Mosaddeq with a formula that called for Iran to enter into negotiations with the British on the basis of the "principle of nationalization" in the 20 March resolution, a much broader and vaguer piece of legislation than the Nine-Point Law. Mosaddeq admitted on 23 July that Iran could not market oil without help from AIOC—a sign that Levy's pressure on Hassibi had been effective. If the British accepted the principle of nationalization, Iran would negotiate an agreement that promised "effective management" of the industry. Mosaddeq agreed to receive a British mission, provided they abide by Harriman's formula.[99]

The opening for new negotiations was narrow. Mosaddeq's ally Kashani warned Harriman that "blood would flow" if nationalization was impeded in any way.[100] Harriman recommended Britain send a "responsible and skillful" negotiator. In a swipe at Ambassador Shepherd, he noted that British reports from Tehran had not been "realistic," while AIOC had exercised "absentee management" and was giving the British government bad advice.[101] It was crucial that the language of negotiations and the final settlement conform "as far as possible to Iranian public sensibilities."[102] Recognizing the hatred most Iranian felt toward AIOC, Levy suggested a group of companies—organized into a consortium—could manage distribution of Iran's oil exports. AIOC would "dilute" its share of the industry to make room for these new partners. He warned that the Soviets could easily step in to supply Iran with a market, propping up Mosaddeq indefinitely and turning Iran into a "Yugoslavia in reverse," unless the British made concessions and allowed other companies into Iran.[103]

The British doubted Levy's proposals would work. They did not believe that private oil companies would put up the capital for a share of AIOC's operation, and they were skeptical that the Iranians would accept it: "It is questionable whether dilution, except with Persian blood, would be of any interest," one AIOC analysis concluded.[104] Moreover, the "dilution" idea ran counter to British interests, as it would limit AIOC's ability to manage the price and production of Iranian oil and reduce the Treasury's ability to maximize the positive benefits from Iranian oil to Britain's balance of payments.[105] Finally, British officials—again guided by Shepherd's advice—felt that the shah and his supporters would agree eventually to an arrangement similar to the Jackson proposal from June. If Britain stood firm, its friends in Iran would force Mosaddeq to accept the British offer or resign.[106] For these reasons, the British ignored Levy's recommendations. Instead of dilution, their offer to Mosaddeq would be based on the Jackson proposal, "dressed up" with some "sweetenings" to entice Mosaddeq into accepting it.[107]

The Stokes Proposal

The Attlee government selected Lord Privy Seal Sir Richard Stokes, a businessman with ties to the Labour Party but little knowledge of Iran, to head the mission. His mandate was limited: the British government was not prepared to entertain terms that went beyond Jackson's proposal from June. Stokes, a businessman more akin to AIOC's pugnacious Chairman Sir William Fraser than to the smooth diplomat Harriman, was not well suited

Richard Stokes, Lord Privy Seal (center), at London Airport shortly before his departure for Iran. On his right is Sir Francis Shepherd, British ambassador to Iran, and on his left Sir Donald Fergusson, Permanent Secretary of the Ministry of Fuel and Power. BP Archive 78147 © BP plc.

to his task. He was inclined to talk down to the Iranians, considered Mosaddeq "feminine" and irrational, and frequently used clumsy and insulting language during discussions.[108] Meanwhile, Prime Minister Attlee declared in the House of Commons on 1 August that Britain would never abandon Abadan, and the British kept a military option in reserve should negotiations fail.[109]

In his first meeting with Stokes on 5 August, Mosaddeq insisted that AIOC's relationship with Iran was over. The "former company" was entitled to compensation, which he was ready to recognize according to existing precedents, specifically the British Coal Nationalization Act of 1945. The two parties were "divorced"; all that remained was negotiating the terms of the separation. Stokes responded that this was more than "divorce": Iran sought to starve its "ex-wife" by making it impossible for AIOC to operate.[110] Stokes made his official offer on 13 August. AIOC assets would be transferred to Iran, in recognition of the principle of nationalization, but the industry would be operated by a "purchasing organization" set up to buy all Iranian oil for global distribution. An operating company set up by AIOC would take care of production and refining. Profits would be divided on a fifty-fifty basis, with compensation for AIOC included in operating costs. The board of the purchasing organization would include Iranian representatives, but the organization itself would function as a subsidiary of AIOC.[111] Stokes did not offer much beyond Jackson's proposals of June— the terms contained the appearance of nationalization with none of the substance. As one astute observer later wrote, "the British attitude was that, in return for their recognizing the principle of nationalization, the Persian government should forgo its insistence on that principle."[112]

Mosaddeq rejected Stokes's proposal. He felt the arrangement gave AIOC an effective monopoly over Iranian oil. Although Harriman admitted privately that the British plan could result in "camouflage for the complete return of British control" unless adequate safeguards were included in the final agreement, he lobbied vigorously for the plan.[113] Mosaddeq charged that the British offer failed to conform to the definition of nationalization stipulated by the law and by Harriman's formula. As talks continued, Stokes pushed back against Mosaddeq's presumption that Iran could manage the industry without foreign oversight. "No prudent businessman would dream of entering into long term contracts that are dependent on an industry run by Persians," he asserted. British control of the oil operations was an "essential safeguard."[114] Stokes seemed confident that the Iranians would accept his arguments. "Whilst [Iran] had the oil we had the know-how," he told a group of Iranian senators on 16 August; "they would kill themselves if they did not come to an arrangement with us."[115] Wary of antagonizing nationalist sentiment, the shah urged Stokes to accept a deal with Mosaddeq that would allow the British staff to work under NIOC management. Stokes rejected this idea. "None of the British staff," he said, "would stay unless they were under contractual obligations to a predominantly British controlled administration." Meanwhile, British officials discussed plans to evacuate the British staff from the oil fields to Abadan. Should Mosaddeq respond by canceling British residency permits, "the only means . . . of hanging on would be to use force."[116]

On 18 August, Iran submitted its counterproposal. NIOC would retain all oil assets and sell oil directly to AIOC and other customers, according to "ordinary commercial contracts." Iran recognized the need for foreign technicians, but rejected the purchasing organization, calling it a ploy "to restrict the sovereignty of Persia." AIOC staff were welcome to remain in Iran and work for NIOC.[117] Harriman felt the prime minister's counterproposal was "totally unacceptable."[118] In his opinion, the Iranian demands ran counter to "well-known commercial methods of the international supply and distribution of oil."[119] In other words, Harriman resisted the very idea of Iran attempting to sell oil on its own terms. Bringing Stokes and Mosaddeq together on 19 August, Harriman noted that the United States was anxious to help Iran; Mosaddeq had repeatedly warned that a Tudeh takeover was imminent without American assistance, but Harriman emphasized that the "whole principle of U.S. assistance . . . is to help other countries to help themselves."[120] The implication was clear: unless Mosaddeq agreed to Stokes's proposal, additional help from the United States would not be forthcoming.

Stokes and Harriman repeatedly urged the shah to intervene and to replace Mosaddeq, but the shah refused to move against his popular prime minister.[121] On 22 August, Stokes presented Mosaddeq with an ultimatum: either accept British management of day-to-day operations or abandon negotiations. Under mounting pressure from the shah and facing the united front of Stokes and Harriman, Mosaddeq offered some new concessions. He accepted Stokes's proposal that Iran's oil should be managed by a purchasing organization but continued to insist that British staff become employees of NIOC, pledging that he would guarantee their security.[122] Mosaddeq's shift represented a potential breakthrough. Stokes, however, had already abandoned hope for a settlement. As he wrote to Attlee: "I felt obliged to go as far as possible to meet Musaddiq, if only to convince Harriman and public opinion . . . I had made every effort." Stokes believed that if negotiations broke down, the failure should rest on "Persian insistence on management arrangements which neither the British staff in Persia nor any other staff . . . could possibly be expected to accept."[123] Stokes rejected Mosaddeq's final offer, and left Tehran on 23 August. At Harriman's insistence, Stokes's statement described the talks as suspended rather than broken off, phrasing that left the door open for further discussions.[124]

Harriman blamed Mosaddeq for the breakdown. In his report to Acheson, he complained that the prime minister had suggested he was open to having AIOC technicians remain in Iran, "and then completely refused to accept any arrangement which would make it possible for them to work."[125] For Harriman, the Iranian insistence on national control of the oil industry was absurd. For the British, the episode confirmed that Mosaddeq was an unreasonable and unreliable negotiator, and that American efforts to use "soft soap" and placate Iranian nationalism only encouraged his obstinacy.[126]

Playing on American concerns, Attlee wrote to Truman and argued that Mosaddeq's actions had left Iran more vulnerable to communist pressure. The United States should support Britain and force Mosaddeq to yield "to the logic of facts."[127] While Mosaddeq had bent somewhat to the Anglo-American terms, Stokes's refusal to go beyond the Jackson proposals doomed the August talks to failure. The United States, rather than act as a neutral mediator, had tried to push Iran closer to the British position. The result was a breakdown that set the stage for AIOC's ejection from Iran.

Scuttle

While Harriman and Stokes were seeking a negotiated solution, British agents and Mosaddeq's conservative opposition maneuvered to oust him. Zaehner made contact with the shah's Swiss tutor and confidant, Ernest Perron, who reported on 27 August that the shah was eager to remove Mosaddeq and replace him with Sayyed Zia, now that the Stokes mission had failed.[128] Zaehner wrote that the British would keep Zia "on the rails," and ensure that he offered AIOC suitable terms for remaining in the country.[129] According to Shepherd, Majlis deputies feared opposing the National Front in upcoming elections and wanted Mosaddeq gone before Iranians went to the polls in early 1952. Shepherd recommended Britain do nothing "which might contribute to [Mosaddeq's] survival," including participating in new negotiations.[130]

For the United States, the failure of the Stokes and Harriman missions made a bad situation even worse. The United States strongly opposed British military intervention, which might trigger a Soviet response and divide world opinion. The United States did not favor leaving Mosaddeq in power, however. According to McGhee, the United States could "explore every avenue leading towards a change in government in Iran," but should at the same time emphasize to Britain that the main goal was "to make sure Iran does not fall victim to communism."[131] Acheson also felt that Mosaddeq should not be propped up. He froze progress on the Export-Import Bank loan on 24 August.[132] Proceeding with financial assistance to Iran would place "undue strain" on Anglo-American relations.[133] When he met Attlee in London on 30 August, Harriman suggested they do everything possible to bolster the shah "to act when the situation permits."[134] The United States would neither support Mosaddeq nor support direct action to remove him from power.

With negotiations suspended, tensions between Britain and Iran continued to increase. On 5 September, Mosaddeq revoked the residency permits of AIOC personnel still in Iran. Unless they agreed to work under NIOC, all British nationals would have to leave by 4 October. Shepherd approached the shah, suggesting that the situation had grown "dangerous," and implying that "the use of force" might be necessary. The time had come to dismiss Mosaddeq, who had botched the negotiations and forced the oil industry to shut down, dooming the country's economy.[135] Facing an election in October and feeling mounting pressure from the Conservative Party led by a bellicose Winston Churchill, Attlee and Morrison sent four additional destroyers to the Persian Gulf, bringing the total number of British warships threatening Abadan to fourteen. The Bank of England suspended Iran's sterling trade privileges, revoked export licenses, and denied virtually all its dollar exchange. AIOC issued a statement warning it would pursue legal action against any company, government, or individual that purchased "stolen" Iranian oil. In the words of a Labour cabinet minister, "whoever bought Iranian oil bought a lawsuit with it."[136]

Shepherd believed that the opposition to Mosaddeq was "gradually summoning up [the] courage" to act, "if only the shah can be induced to take a strong line."[137] The State Department disagreed, and informed the Foreign Office on 22 September that while it was not U.S. policy "[to] discourage the shah from dismissing Musaddiq if he felt politically able to do so," they did not think this was the case.[138] Attlee wrote Truman on 25 September, warning that Mosaddeq's actions left him with the choice of submitting to the eviction of AIOC's British staff or intervening to secure Abadan. Submission to eviction would have dire consequences not only for British interests in the Middle East but for those of the United States as well, Attlee argued. It would be a blow to British and Western prestige and influence and would leave a vacuum in Iran which the Soviets would seek to fill. As an alternative to armed intervention, which Attlee (almost alone in his government) opposed, he implored Truman to back Britain in an urgent effort to convince the shah to replace Mosaddeq with a government with which Britain could negotiate on a "reasonable basis."[139]

The United States continued to strongly oppose military intervention. According to Secretary of Defense Robert Lovett, British thinking was based on "bad intelligence." If troops were landed in Abadan, they would find the situation unmanageable.[140] Although the British had improved their capability to intervene since July, Iran had strengthened its forces in the region.

In addition, if British forces attacked Abadan while AIOC personnel were still there, there was a high likelihood of significant civilian casualties, not to mention damage to the refinery. If they waited until AIOC personnel left, intervention would no longer have a humanitarian justification and would be seen as an exercise in gunboat diplomacy to protect property. In a larger sense, the British inability to utilize force to support its policy without U.S. approval and assistance was yet another indication of Britain's decline as a great power.[141]

Newly arrived U.S. Ambassador Loy W. Henderson and Shepherd met with the shah on 26 September and urged him to replace Mosaddeq to avoid a permanent shutdown of the oil industry.[142] Despite this pressure, the shah chose not to dismiss Mosaddeq from office. Doing so on the eve of AIOC's withdrawal and with British warships surrounding Abadan would have invited a fierce nationalist response. The shah also would be abandoning his public stance of supporting nationalization to side with the hated British, who were once again pushing their favorite Sayyed Zia for prime minister. Though he frequently consulted the British embassy, Mohammed Reza Pahlavi had a deep and bitter distrust of the British, who had overthrown his father in 1941. Ayatollah Hossein Borujerdi of Qom, the *marja-e taqlid* or "figure for emulation" for Shi'a Muslims and the most influential religious figure in Iran, published an open letter to the shah on 20 September declaring that all Iranians should stand together against the British invasion threat. On 28 September, 'Ala told Henderson that while the shah hoped to remove Mosaddeq, the time had not yet come to do so. The next day, the shah himself explained to Henderson his reasoning, pointing out that even his father—a much stronger ruler—had only taken action when he knew the nation was with him.[143]

Without the shah, and with the United States still firmly opposed to armed intervention, the British were left with no choice but to stand down. On 27 September, Attlee's cabinet agreed that withdrawal from Abadan was preferable to an open break in relations with the United States.[144] Iranian troops entered Abadan that same day and occupied the refinery without resistance. Mosaddeq delivered a victory speech to the thousands assembled in Tehran's Baharestan Square. When the crowd began chanting "Death to the British," he urged them to stop and "pray to God Almighty to lead the British to the path of justice [and] recognize our lawful rights . . . that God may open their eyes."[145] Henderson, however, found Mosaddeq privately defiant. The Iranian oil industry would now be operated by Iranian technicians, he said. If it could find no market, Iranian oil would remain in

The last of AIOC's staff departs Abadan on HMS *Mauritius*. BP Archive 64874
© BP plc.

the ground for future generations. Henderson's points regarding Iran's imminent loss of oil revenues had little effect.[146]

On 4 October, the British cruiser HMS *Mauritius* took on a raft of passengers from the port of Abadan. The few men, dressed in shirtsleeves and khakis, toted their belongings in a handful of valises and hastily packed suitcases. The *Mauritius* would take them fifty miles up the Shatt al-Arab to Basra in pro-British Iraq. In a last act of defiance, the passengers, accompanied by the ship's band, sang an unpublished and somewhat obscene version of the venerable marching song, "Colonel Bogey's March." It was, in the words of one *Times* editorial, "a humiliating defeat."[147] While only a few were aware of it at the time, an important turning point in global history had been reached. Iran had bested an imperial power, seized its assets, and ousted its nationals. According to Peter Ramsbotham of the Foreign Office, the retreat from Abadan—not Indian Independence—marked the real "end of empire" for Great Britain.[148] Months of negotiations, posturing, pressure tactics, and covert maneuvers had failed to save AIOC. The shah's decision to remain inactive and the U.S. refusal to back military action had forced the British to withdraw. Fifty years after the D'Arcy Concession, British control of Iranian oil had come to an end.

Conclusion

On 26 September, Henry Villard wrote his boss, Policy Planning Staff Chairman Paul Nitze, that the British were the single greatest obstacle to resolving the Iranian oil crisis. Mosaddeq might eventually prove flexible during discussions, but the British obsession with removing him would sabotage any chance of a settlement. Worse, it might permanently turn Iran against the West. "British intrigue," Villard warned, "is the surest way of increasing Iranian antagonism and preventing any sort of agreement."[149]

Villard's memorandum represented a strain of frustration running throughout the U.S. government. The U.S. position on Iran's nationalization mirrored that of Great Britain: Iran could not be permitted to seize control of its oil and had to be forced into an arrangement with AIOC or another major oil company preserving private control over its oil resources. British inflexibility and behind-the-scenes maneuvers to remove Mosaddeq were counterproductive. According to Henderson, the British position had grown "unrealistic," and their public statements indicated they lacked a "grasp of the situation."[150] From the U.S. point of view, the crisis of May had by October become a catastrophe, with the oil industry in Iran shuttered, the shah subdued, and Mosaddeq's National Front triumphant. An oil-less Iran faced economic cataclysm, while the continuing dispute with the British would aggravate anti-Western sentiment in the country and potentially strengthen the Tudeh Party. While the British focused on removing Mosaddeq, the United States still sought a solution that would restart the oil industry and preserve Iran from communist control while not endangering U.S. interests in the region. The struggle for Iran would continue.

· ·

The struggle for Iran came before the United Nations Security Council in October 1951, pitting British claims regarding the "sanctity of contracts" against Iranian arguments supporting the primacy of national sovereignty. The United Nations declined to intervene, leading the World Bank to become involved in the elusive search for a settlement. American officials also continued to seek an agreement with Mosaddeq that would resolve the oil dispute, preserve the position of Western corporations, stabilize conditions inside Iran, and prevent the country's fall to communism. A settlement remained out of reach for several reasons. Anglo-American differences grew deeper. The British believed that economic pressure from the oil boycott, combined with internal political intrigues, would force Mosaddeq from power. In contrast, U.S. officials feared that economic pressure would increase Iran's vulnerability to communist influence. Mosaddeq, meanwhile, fought to maintain his position, expand the mandate of the National Front through free and fair elections, and bring an end to the oil crisis without sacrificing Iranian national interests. Iranian conservatives sought ways to force Mosaddeq out of office, while the Tudeh continued to view him as a bourgeois nationalist. The shah maintained a middle ground, publicly supporting nationalization even as he conspired against Mosaddeq in private.

Mosaddeq at the United Nations

After abandoning the option to use military force in Abadan, the British government decided to take its case to the United Nations Security Council. The British believed the move offered potential strategic and legal advantages. It would allow Britain to argue against Iran in a public forum, appealing to global opinion and emphasizing the threat of Iran's actions to the sanctity of contracts. A show of diplomatic strength would offer Britain a face-saving maneuver to maintain prestige. Calling out Mosaddeq publicly would weaken his domestic support, while strengthening the resolve of the opposition and the shah. Finally, the Labour government, facing an election challenge from the Conservative Party in late October, was under immense pressure to maintain the diplomatic offensive against Iran in the wake of the humiliating "scuttle" from Abadan.

Although U.S. Secretary of State Dean Acheson had argued that a "new element" needed to be injected into the crisis, he believed the move to the United Nations was ill-advised. Acheson worried that Mosaddeq would present damaging evidence of AIOC interference in Iran, mismanagement, and political tampering before an international audience. In addition, the statements presented to the United Nations would harden each side's negotiating stance, making it more difficult to find a solution. Even if the British had the votes—an outcome few in Washington felt was likely, given the relative weakness of the British claim—the Soviet Union could veto a motion against Iran, producing an embarrassing scenario that allowed the Soviets to represent themselves as the champion of small nations. To make matters worse, Mosaddeq was planning to come to the United States to defend his country at the United Nations. A letter expressing sympathy and support from President Truman intended for British Prime Minister Clement Attlee had been mistakenly delivered to Mosaddeq, giving him the false impression that the U.S. government welcomed his visit.[1]

The apparent show of support from the United States came as the prime minister consolidated his political position inside Iran. Mosaddeq now enjoyed the support of the religious leadership in the wake of a call for national unity issued in September by the influential cleric Ayatollah Hossein Borujerdi. Ayatollah Abolqassem Kashani, a vocal anti-British cleric and an important member of the National Front coalition, demonstrated the power of his street organization by closing the bazaars on 30 September. The Majlis voted to table all criticism of Mosaddeq as he prepared to travel to New York City to argue Iran's case before the Security Council. According to a 5 October report from Tehran, the British position in Iran had "collapsed," with the shah rejecting British entreaties that he rally the opposition behind Sayyid Zia, the preferred British candidate for prime minister. Even the Tudeh temporarily ceased its press campaign against Mosaddeq. According to U.S. Ambassador Loy W. Henderson, Mosaddeq would remain in power for as long as the oil issue lay unresolved: neither the British nor Iran's old guard were in any position to challenge him.[2] Mosaddeq assembled his closest advisors, including his oil expert Kazem Hassibi and legal counselors Karim Sanjabi and Ali Shayegan. They agreed that Britain's case had no basis in international law because nationalization was between Iran, a sovereign nation, and AIOC, a private corporation.[3]

The Security Council discussion of the case began on 15 October. Sir Gladwyn Jebb, the British representative, argued that Iran had violated its contract with AIOC and through the confiscation of privately owned assets had shattered the basis upon which nations conducted business with one another. Drawing on all his oratorical skills, Mosaddeq condemned AIOC's record in Iran, pointing out that the company had withheld royalties, abused its workers, and meddled in Iranian politics. Finally, Mosaddeq called upon the United Nations, "the ultimate refuge of weak and oppressed nations," to stand by Iran as it escaped from "centuries of colonial exploitation" and took its place alongside other nations, including Pakistan and India, which had been granted their freedom from British colonial rule. Growing faint, Mosaddeq delivered the first half of his address in French before passing the rest to Allahyar Saleh, a National Front deputy.[4] The U.S. representative registered his support for the British side on 17 October, arguing that the case lay within the Security Council's competence. It was clear, however, that the British lacked the necessary votes, and the debate adjourned pending a ruling by the International Court of Justice, which was not expected until summer 1952.[5]

Mosaddeq's performance before the United Nations created an international sensation. According to Acheson, the Iranian prime minister had won the day, making his case "with great skill and drama," becoming a "television star" practically overnight.[6] More significant than Mosaddeq's sudden celebrity were the legal and political implications of the Iranian arguments. The Iranian case, meticulously prepared by Sanjabi, Shayegan, Saleh, and Mosaddeq, drew a clear connection between the cause of decolonization and the concept of permanent sovereignty over oil resources. The idea became a rallying cry for Third World leaders intent on achieving independence from European imperialism and the dominance of Western capital. In the United Nations General Assembly, a fierce debate began in 1952, culminating in a December resolution that declared "the right of peoples . . . to use and exploit their national wealth and resource" free from foreign interference.[7] Mosaddeq used his visit to the United States to emphasize the links between Iran's struggle against British imperialism and the U.S. War for Independence, illustrating the stark paradox in the American message of liberty and continued U.S. support of the European colonial powers. In Philadelphia, where he gave a speech tying Iran's fight for independence to the American Revolution, Mosaddeq passed his hands across the Liberty Bell.[8]

The Charm Offensive: The McGhee-Mosaddeq Discussions

As the Iranian drama played out before the Security Council, U.S. officials sought a new approach to the nationalization question. The key issue was whether the United States would assist Iran's government to prevent further economic or political instability, or side with the British and major oil companies and pressure Iran into submitting to a favorable oil agreement.

For months, the U.S. government had worried about Iran's ability to manage without an operating oil industry. A statistical picture assembled by the U.S. embassy's Economic Counselor Robert M. Carr in April 1951 concluded that Iran relied on the operations of AIOC for around one-third of its state budget and three-quarters of its foreign exchange balance. AIOC's departure and the boycott had placed immense financial pressure on Iran's state budget, while the lack of foreign exchange flowing into the country would soon have an impact on business activity and trade. Mosaddeq had various emergency financial measures in place to fill the budget gap, but it was unclear how long these would last before the government became insolvent.[9] There was a risk that Mosaddeq would turn to the Soviet Union for assistance in breaking the British boycott and relieving the pressure on his finances. A CIA study from March 1951 had concluded the Soviet Union could move 2.9 million tons of oil and products, both by sea and via rail links, bartering locomotives and rolling stock for oil.[10] In the wake of AIOC's retreat from Abadan, Henry Villard of the Policy Planning Staff suggested in a 9 October memorandum that the "main concern" should be to "keep Iranian oil moving in the interest of the West," both to offset the chances of a Soviet intervention and to prevent an Iranian economic collapse.[11]

From the point of view of the major U.S. oil companies, nationalization was a threat that could not be permitted to spread to other oil-producing areas. They framed their ongoing boycott on Iranian oil as necessary to preserve the "sanctity of contracts," echoing the language used by Britain at the United Nations. Meeting with Acheson on 10 October, the top executives of the five U.S. major international oil companies—Jersey Standard, Socony, Gulf, SOCAL, and Texaco—argued that losing Iran to the Soviets would be preferable to the instability that successful nationalization would create. The situation transcended the oil industry, for what was at stake was the "sanctity of contractual relations" upon which all U.S. investment abroad depended. Acheson, however, countered that the U.S. government also had to keep in mind the strategic and political consequences that would flow from the loss of Iran.[12]

The U.S. military argued that maintaining Iran's orientation to the West was more important than backing the British. In a report to the National Security Council on 18 October, the Joint Chiefs of Staff (JCS) warned that Soviet control of Iran would mean immediate loss of Iranian oil and eventual loss of all Middle East oil. Loss of Iran would also outflank Turkey and provide the Soviets with a springboard for the domination of the entire Middle East and the eastern Mediterranean. From a strict military point of view, maintaining Iran's pro-Western strategic alignment "transcend[s] in importance the desirability of supporting British oil interests."[13] The State Department countered that the cooperation of the international oil industry was essential for the efficient operation of Iran's oil industry and hence for Iran's prosperity and stability. Moreover, a settlement in Iran that undermined U.S. concessions and investments elsewhere in the world was not in the U.S. national interest. Thus, while the primary objective of U.S. policy was maintaining Iran as "an independent country aligned with the free world," the United States should not support a settlement that would seriously injure "the fabric of the world oil industry."[14] The central conflict affecting U.S. policy was the question of how to keep Iran from falling to communism without seriously undermining the international oil economy or causing major tension in Anglo-American relations.

As the Iranian drama played out before the Security Council, U.S. officials worked on a new approach to the nationalization question. George C. McGhee, assistant secretary for Near Eastern, South Asian, and African affairs, led the effort. A former oilman, McGhee had been instrumental in forming American oil policy and had helped engineer the Saudi Arabian fifty-fifty agreement with Aramco in December 1950. Trusting Ambassador Henderson's judgment that AIOC could not return to Iran and that any deal to resolve the crisis had to acknowledge Iranian nationalism, McGhee spearheaded a campaign in October to negotiate with Mosaddeq one-on-one. While he did not believe Iran should control its oil resources, he believed that some concessions to Iranian nationalism were necessary to reach a settlement and restart Iran's oil industry.[15]

The new approach to Mosaddeq concentrated on finding an amicable basis for discussions. There was no British involvement in McGhee's discussions with Mosaddeq, which lasted throughout the month of October. During this time, Mosaddeq received medical care at Walter Reed Hospital in Washington, D.C., and met with President Truman at Blair House, an honor accorded to visiting dignitaries of high standing. Urged to prolong his stay to facilitate further negotiations, he found time to visit McGhee's farm in

Virginia, where the two men discussed agricultural practices Mosaddeq might use on his own estates in Iran.[16] The "charm offensive" worked to establish a rapport lacking in previous discussions. McGhee found Mosaddeq "agreeable" and basically "pro-Western," with a "remarkable sense of humor." He later observed that Mosaddeq's habits—his tendency to hold meetings in bed in his pajamas, to weep during public speaking, or to suddenly break out into laughter—belied a "deep firmness, determination, and clarity of purpose."[17] Unlike previous interlocutors, McGhee made an effort to understand Mosaddeq's arguments and his approach to the oil issue.

McGhee and Paul Nitze, the influential head of the Policy Planning Staff who was brought into the talks to emphasize U.S. strategic concerns, stressed to Mosaddeq that oil was one of "the sinews of strength of the free nations of the world," and the United States was concerned with ensuring it flowed throughout the world, "in adequate quantities." They also repeatedly made it clear that Iran could not expect arrangements better than those received by other oil-producing countries. The United States had extensive overseas oil interests, and if Iran got an arrangement much better than any other, "it would upset the whole pattern of concessions worldwide."[18]

Three weeks of discussions produced a tentative plan, one that would offer Iran nominal control of its industry while ensuring the continued practical dominance of AIOC over production, refining, and marketing.[19] Iran would exclude the massive refinery complex at Abadan from nationalization and allow AIOC to sell it to a "neutral" foreign company, which was assumed to be Royal Dutch/Shell. The National Iranian Oil Company (NIOC) would control the oil fields and other facilities and be responsible for the production of crude oil. NIOC would be governed by a board composed of three Iranians and four foreign neutrals, with a general manager of a nationality designated by the Iranian government but appointed by and responsible to the board of directors. NIOC would contract with a "large oil company (Dutch) with international experience"—in other words, Shell—to manage the industry and ensure its efficient operation. AIOC would form a new purchasing subsidiary to buy, ship, and market most of Iran's oil on behalf of its former customers. Although NIOC would have the right to market crude oil in excess of that sold to the purchasing organization for the refinery or for export, the price of any direct sales could not be lower than prices in the long-term contracts of the purchasing organization.

McGhee's suggestion that AIOC "sell" the Abadan refinery to a different company was a way to resolve the question of compensation. To preserve the legality of nationalization, Iran would have to pay compensation for

Mosaddeq and George C. McGhee. The two met repeatedly during October
to discuss a possible solution to the oil dispute. Truman Library, Accession
No. 66-8022.

AIOC's nationalized assets. Initially, Mossadeq offered to pay AIOC compensation based on the stated value of the company's installations in AIOC's
annual statement, around £27 million. This was less than the market value
of the assets and did not include the value of oil left in the ground, which,
though legally belonging to Iran, AIOC could have been expected to produce and sell over the life of the concession. Selling the refinery complex to
another company greatly reduced the amount of compensation Iran would
have to pay AIOC. The remaining compensation Iran owed AIOC would be
offset by Iran's counterclaims against AIOC for past royalties and other
matters. Iran would sell a major portion of its output to the new purchasing organization set up by AIOC at prices that allowed AIOC to receive oil
on roughly the same terms as if it had retained its concession.

The price at which Iran would sell its oil to AIOC's purchasing organization became a sticking point. To preserve the principle of fifty-fifty
profit sharing, the United States insisted that Iran could not receive a higher
price for its oil than other producing countries in the Middle East. Mosaddeq

argued that Iran should receive the price (at that time around $1.75/barrel) at which production companies such as Aramco sold oil to their parent companies' marketing subsidiaries. In contrast, McGhee insisted that Iran should receive no more than $1.10/barrel, the price that producing companies paid to host governments. Mosaddeq believed that Iran deserved the same price that production companies received because Iran now owned its own production facilities. Although the United States mediators believed that Mosaddeq did not understand the complexities of oil pricing, the problem was really about the distribution of revenue. In cases like Aramco, the same parent companies owned both the production and marketing companies—a key feature of the vertical integration and joint-ownership arrangements that characterized the major companies' system of control of the international industry.[20] What Mosaddeq wanted would have interfered with this arrangement. In essence, the U.S. position on price denied Iran one of the fruits of nationalization by giving Iran no more for its oil than other countries received, even though Iran now owned the production company as well as the oil in the ground.

The Price of a Deal: Backing Mosaddeq or Siding with the British?

Mosaddeq was understandably reluctant to accept this reality of the international oil business. He had demanded in countless speeches that Iran should enjoy the full benefits of its oil, and on more than one occasion he had stated that if Iran could not get a satisfactory price for its oil, it would be better to leave it in the ground for future generations.[21] Given the profits derived from controlling the producing end of the business and the existence of alternative sources of supply, neither AIOC nor any other major oil company was likely to agree to a price high enough to be acceptable to Iran. Thus, the United States was faced with the decision whether to let Mosaddeq go home from his talks with McGhee without an agreement or break the line on price and acquiesce to Mosaddeq's terms.

In a study of the issue that echoed British concerns, the Policy Planning Staff (PPS) argued on 24 October that the consequences of yielding to Mosaddeq on price were more serious than the consequences that might flow from a failure to reach an agreement. Though it might help preserve Iran's pro-Western alignment in the short term by stabilizing the economy, allowing Mosaddeq to win such a victory would be seen as a sign of Western weakness and would encourage Iran to take further steps against the West, confident that the United States would bail them out of any difficulties resulting from "reckless, improvident, and irresponsible behavior." Surrendering to Mosaddeq's demands on price would also encourage other oil-producing countries to demand similar terms. The PPS study recommended that the United States permit the negotiations with Mosaddeq to end in failure. The United States should inform Mosaddeq that his position on price was "unreasonable," and that while the United States was concerned about Iran's security and welfare, it was more concerned about Anglo-American relations.[22] Although he was also concerned about upsetting the stability of Western oil concessions in the Middle East, McGhee believed he could eventually talk Mosaddeq into accepting U.S. views on price.[23] Acheson submitted McGhee's proposal for British approval on 30 October.[24]

Meanwhile, the British government had been reviewing its policy options. Sir Donald Fergusson, permanent undersecretary at the Ministry of Fuel and Power, was convinced that it would be impossible to reach an agreement with Mosaddeq that would not have "disastrous effects" on investments elsewhere. Though Iranian oil was important to Britain, it was not more important than all the rest of Britain's foreign investments, "on which the standard of living of the people of this country, and our ability to maintain our freedom and independence depend." A "bad" agreement with Iran could lead "foreign governments, and foreigners generally" to conclude that they could unilaterally repudiate contracts with British companies, seize British assets, and pay only as much compensation as they wished. Fergusson recommended that Britain stand firm on its rights until the Iranians "came to their senses" and replaced Mosaddeq with a more reasonable government.[25]

According to historian Wm. Roger Louis, Fergusson's views represented the mainstream of official British opinion, and they found an especially warm reception with the Conservative government that took power after general elections on 25 October.[26] The new prime minister, Sir Winston Churchill, and Foreign Secretary Sir Anthony Eden turned to permanent officials for advice on how to proceed after the Security Council fiasco. The British ambassador to Iran, Sir Francis Shepherd, argued that Britain should let the matter "simmer" and "encourage, so far as we properly can, a change of government in the near future." He warned that negotiating with Mosaddeq would "hamstring" the opposition and make Mosaddeq's victory in the forthcoming elections "practically certain." Shepherd felt that if Mosaddeq returned to Iran empty-handed, his position would weaken. Shepherd and the Treasury also opposed the exclusion of AIOC from operations in Iran. Allowing Shell or a group of American companies to manage Iran's nationalized industry would be a serious blow to British prestige, giving the impression that Britain was "under the Americans' thumb."[27]

Many Foreign Office officials believed that AIOC would not be able to return to Iran. Under-Secretary of State for Foreign Affairs Sir Roger Makins argued that AIOC was "bankrupt both in men and ideas." The company's irrational stance had cost Britain its most valuable overseas asset. It was time to recognize the political power of the National Front and do business with Mosaddeq before matters deteriorated further. The Foreign Office proposed a plan that called for the creation of a consortium of the major U.S. companies and AIOC to take over oil operation in Iran once suitable terms had been concluded with Mosaddeq. This approach would guarantee a U.S. commitment, satisfy anti-British Iranian nationalists, and ensure "efficient management" (a euphemism for foreign control) of the oil industry.[28] The Foreign Office argued that although the prospects of Mosaddeq's accepting any settlement were "slight," some new approach was necessary to keep the Americans "in play." Waiting for Mosaddeq to fall increased the risk of Soviet intervention and aided the Tudeh. There was also the danger of other oil interests entering Iran at AIOC's expense, or of Iran producing and marketing sufficient volumes of oil to make nationalization a success. It could do this on its own or with foreign technical assistance. In this regard, a survey of the world tanker fleet concluded that "in the long run," it would not be possible to prevent some tankers from lifting Iranian oil.[29]

The Foreign Office arguments failed to carry the day. The new Conservative government chose to continue the hardline stance Labour had taken earlier. Churchill himself later claimed a withdrawal from Abadan could have been avoided with a "splutter of musketry."[30] The British maintained that McGhee's terms failed to protect Britain's balance of payments position, undercut the fifty-fifty principle, and set compensation too low, which would allow Iran to carry out nationalization at little cost and encourage other oil-producing countries where British companies held concessions to do the same. Finally, the deal threatened other British assets, as it would seem to accept the Iranian confiscation of AIOC's assets as a fait accompli.[31] Accepting the deal, AIOC's Neville Gass argued during a meeting with the Treasury, would cause "other Mosaddeqs" to arise throughout the oil-producing world. "What would be left of the fabric of the oil industry to which the Americans professed to attach so much importance?"[32]

When they met on 4 November, Eden told Acheson that the U.S. proposal was "completely unacceptable." The best course of action was to wait for a "more amenable government" to come to power in Tehran.[33] He then presented Acheson with a memorandum outlining the British position. Any settlement with Iran had to provide for fair compensation for concessionary rights and properties, agreed through negotiation or arbitration. The amount could not be set unilaterally. Second, Iran had to be able to produce and sell sufficient volumes of oil to pay compensation. At a minimum, this meant that Iran would need to make a deal with a company possessed of "world wide markets" acting as distributor. Third, Iran could not obtain "a more favorable return" from its industry than other oil-producing nations. Fourth, British nationals could not be excluded from a reactivated Iranian industry.[34]

To Acheson, the meetings illustrated just how wide the gulf between the British and Iranians had become. Britain's new leaders were "depressingly out of touch with the world of 1951," anxious to preserve British prestige and unwilling to preside over "the complete dissolution of the empire." Allowing non-British companies such as the Royal Dutch/Shell to move into Iran without AIOC would, the British believed, be "like asking us to step aside in favor of Guatemala."[35] For Acheson, the British were being "incredibly light-hearted" about the risk of losing Iran to communism. "They are perfectly prepared . . . to take all the risks of doing nothing," he said, "having in mind the possibility . . . of drawing us in."[36]

Despite Acheson's frustration, there was no way to move forward with McGhee's plan without British cooperation. On 9 November, McGhee informed Mosaddeq that his proposal to the British had been rejected. Mosaddeq appeared disappointed, though in McGhee's recollection he accepted the news "quietly, with no recriminations."[37] The sticking points were financial, but in reality the issue was political. Mosaddeq would not agree to terms that renewed British dominance of Iran's oil industry, while Britain would accept nothing less than arrangements that would constitute a return to the status quo pre-nationalization. In addition, both the U.S. and British officials were unwilling to entertain Mosaddeq's proposal to sell Iranian oil at a higher price than what prevailed among the major international oil companies or in a manner that undermined the existing price structure. McGhee was willing to accommodate Iranian concerns by removing AIOC from the equation in favor of a different oil company, but the need to maintain Western control (or "efficient management," as U.S. and British officials termed it) remained paramount.

After leaving the United States on 18 November, Mosaddeq stopped briefly in Cairo, where thousands turned out to catch a glimpse of the famous Iranian who had stood up to Britain in the United Nations.[38] Yet, while his international prestige had reached its apex, Mosaddeq would be returning home without an oil settlement. U.S. efforts were at a standstill, the British oil boycott was holding strong, and Mosaddeq's political opponents in Iran were beginning to remobilize. Without a solution to the oil question, Mosaddeq faced renewed threats to remaining in power.

The Political Impact of the Oil Boycott

The political situation in Iran grew more uncertain following Mosaddeq's return from the United States. The conservative opposition, which included the country's traditional elites, Anglophile politicians who hoped for a resurgence in British influence, clerics who feared Mosaddeq was encouraging the growth of secularism, and bazaar merchants worried over the economic ramifications of the oil shutdown, resumed their activities in the Majlis and Senate, Iran's upper house. Behind the scenes, MI6 agent Robin Zaehner distributed money and bought influence in Tehran's anti-Mosaddeq political circles. Mosaddeq estimated that at least one-third of all Majlis deputies received bribes from the Rashidian family, the principal British agents, who controlled or influenced twenty newspapers and had numerous contacts within the army and police.[39]

Key figures in the opposition included Sayyed Zia, the most pro-British politician in the country; activist anti-Mosaddeq clerics including Ayatollah Sayyed Abdullah Behbahani; and anti-Mosaddeq members of the Majlis and the Senate. Ahmed Qavam, an aged though ambitious Iranian politician and a mainstay of the old guard who had held the premiership four times since 1920, was also involved. Acknowledging the weakness of Zia, whose British affiliations were well known, Zaehner and the Rashidians shifted their support to Qavam. In late 1951, Zaehner met with a Qavam supporter who assured him that once in power, Qavam would prioritize reestablishing ties to the British, rather than the Americans, "who were foolish and without experience" and would come to a quick oil settlement along lines the British would accept.[40]

In November, senators attempted to delay the forthcoming Majlis elections, under the belief that Mosaddeq would manipulate the results and return a house dominated by National Front deputies. On 6 December, a crowd of students from Tehran University broke the ban on demonstrations and clashed with police forces, while right-wing groups used the opportunity to stage counterdemonstrations, looting the offices of the Tudeh Party. Followers of Mozaffar Baqa'i, head of the Toilers' Party and an ally of Mosaddeq who had grown discontented with the prime minister's leadership, were also actively involved. Some of the more violent anti-Tudeh activists were led by Sha'ban "Brainless" Jafari, a popular figure among the *zurkhaneh* (wrestling houses) in the city, and a man known to be a thug for hire. In a thunderous address to the Majlis on 11 December amid a bitter assembly debate, Mosaddeq denounced the opposition. The Senate's attempt to postpone elections failed as the Majlis delivered a unanimous vote of confidence in the prime minister.[41]

Mosaddeq also faced a challenge from the Tudeh Party. While still technically illegal, the Tudeh expanded its organizing and media activities in the latter half of 1951, and by December had positioned itself to challenge the National Front in the forthcoming Majlis elections. The Tudeh was a "relatively small conspiratorial party . . . highly concerned about security," and the CIA lacked precise information on its leadership, size, and military capabilities. In the fall of 1951, the CIA estimated that it had around 4,000 active members and somewhere between 20,000 and 40,000 members and sympathizers. Although Tudeh rallies in the summer had drawn around 10,000–20,000 participants, recent Tudeh demonstrations in Tehran never had more than 5,000 participants and demonstrations in provincial centers had been "markedly smaller." The CIA emphasized the party would likely only become a "critical factor" in Iranian politics if it succeeded in taking over the National Front through success in the Majlis elections. By leveraging support in cities and the southern oil fields, the Tudeh could potentially gain up to twenty out of the total 136 seats and pursue a popular front strategy with the National Front, following the Soviet strategy in Czechoslovakia from 1945 to 1948. A direct takeover of the government lay outside the party's reach, as it lacked support within the military.[42]

Part of Mosaddeq's strength came from the continued reluctance of the shah to oppose him openly. Mosaddeq was very popular, and the shah believed he was the only politician who could bring the nationalization crisis to a successful conclusion. The pro-British affiliation of many opposition figures also repulsed the shah, who was deeply suspicious of the British. Conversely, the shah feared Mosaddeq's expanding political powers, and had historically sought to undermine powerful prime ministers. The shah remained above the fray, choosing inaction even as his advisors, including Hossein 'Ala, urged him to take action against Mosaddeq.[43]

Internal conditions in Iran created considerable concern among U.S. officials, who believed that economic distress increased the Tudeh threat.[44] Although Ambassador Henderson felt that Mosaddeq's nationalism represented "a real and potent force," he warned that changing circumstances could see nationalist support swing behind a pro-Soviet platform. The shah, usually regarded as a bulwark against communist influence, appeared to have "no confidence in his own influence" and was following Mosaddeq's lead. The security forces, though still loyal to the shah and influenced by U.S. advisory missions, were "weak reeds" to rely on. The lower ranks were "discontented and ill-paid," the junior officers "receptive to Commie propaganda," and the senior officers "often incompetent and corrupt." Although the British had been "shortsighted" at times, Henderson noted that British influence had been effective in the past in keeping the Soviets from gaining control of Iran. British influence had declined, but the British still had "powerful unseen support which might be effectively mobilized in certain circumstances." The best hope for Iran's future, he concluded, was to end the "running sore" of the oil dispute with Britain.[45]

Restarting the oil industry was essential to provide the resources necessary to keep Iran from falling into Soviet hands. According to the U.S. embassy in Tehran, oil provided "40 percent of [the] total budget," and a government capable of delivering economic development and lasting reforms "must have funds . . . the best source of income is from the country's vast oil resources." Henderson felt that Iranian nationalism remained an important factor to consider. If the economy disintegrated, however, he thought it likely that most Iranians would embrace communism rather than submit to Anglo-American pressure. It was possible that Iran "would fall victim to international communism without any overt intervention on the part of Russia."[46]

While Truman administration officials were compelled by a sense of urgency, the British were more sanguine. British officials argued that the Tudeh was not the only alternative to Mosaddeq. George Middleton, chargé d'affaires and ranking British diplomat in the country, told Henderson on 7 November that Iranian nationalism had been "artificially stimulated," and that if Mosaddeq failed to obtain an oil settlement, his government would be replaced by one led by a traditional old guard politician such as Sayyed Zia, the perennial British favorite. The British were less concerned about the economic effects of the boycott, believing financial pressure would push Mosaddeq out before it damaged Iran's primarily agricultural economy. While the United States hoped for a negotiated settlement,

Henderson noted that the British "seem to be placing their hope on remov[ing] Mosaddeq."[47]

Henderson bluntly informed to the shah on 7 December that the time had come to replace Mosaddeq, and on 22 December warned him that Iran "was headed towards destruction" if it failed to reach an oil agreement and suppress the Tudeh.[48] The shah, unsure about what course to take, wanted to wait to see the outcome of the forthcoming Majlis elections. If the elections went poorly for the National Front, Mosaddeq might resign, in which case he would be replaced by a trusted loyalist like 'Ala or an old guard figure like Zia or Qavam. It was likely that such a successor would face resistance from Mosaddeq, a proven master at opposition politics, and an invigorated Tudeh Party. The new government would need to rule by martial law.[49] Henderson, however, worried about the result of elections and felt there was a danger of "irresponsible elements" coming to power and dominating the Majlis, but he also feared that direct U.S. intervention would shatter American prestige, "regardless of whether or not . . . Mosaddeq's overthrow was effected."[50]

The British, as usual, were more optimistic. Middleton reported on 19 November that prospects for forcing Mosaddeq out through elections were "reasonably promising," and that Qavam had a chance of supplanting Mosaddeq, "if the Americans would give a little shove in the right direction."[51] Qavam's supporters were already approaching Henderson and arguing that it was time for "strong" leadership amid the growing risk of a Tudeh victory in the elections. Henderson was reluctant to back Qavam, a figure "so tricky [that] no one knew exactly what he would do if once in power." The shah, moreover, had told Henderson that he would only support his Court Minister 'Ala to replace Mossadeq; he considered Qavam "untrustworthy."[52] Any effort to remove Mosaddeq through parliamentary means would require the shah's cooperation, so there was little chance Qavam or a similar figure who the shah opposed would be able to take office, even with British support.

Before leaving the United States, Mosaddeq told McGhee he would ask President Truman for a loan of $120 million, and that he intended to pursue the long-delayed $25 million Export-Import Bank loan from 1950.[53] Based on estimates provided by Robert M. Carr at the U.S. embassy in Tehran, Iran needed $30 million in budgetary support and $30 million in development funding for 1952, with another $100 million in 1953.[54] Once back in Tehran, Mosaddeq hinted to Henderson on 14 December that if the British oil boycott was not lifted or if U.S. aid was not forthcoming, he would begin offering Iranian oil at a discounted price to any interested customers, including Eastern Bloc countries. Henderson felt that Iran might not have the capacity to send oil to the Eastern Bloc, but he did not doubt that the Soviets would place large orders "for propaganda purposes," to embarrass the British and position themselves as champions of Third World nationalism. Mosaddeq also began to question continued U.S. military aid to Iran, which he regarded as wasteful and undermining Iranian neutrality.[55]

Nitze and Acheson felt that large-scale aid for Mosaddeq would be a tactical mistake. Nitze warned on 21 November that U.S. aid would allow Mosaddeq to return to his people "as a hero, and we might never get him out."[56] Limited assistance, however, might mitigate the worst effects of the oil boycott without entrenching Mosaddeq. The United States had already pledged around $23 million for technical assistance projects in Iran through Point Four, the global technical assistance initiative President Truman had launched in 1949. Truman wrote to Mosaddeq, promising to give his requests for aid "careful consideration," Although limited aid would still infuriate the British and might encourage Mosaddeq to be more intransigent during negotiations, providing Iran with the "bare minimum" needed to keep its economy going, "so pressure to settle the oil dispute [would] not be relieved," appeared the best option. The $23 million Iran would receive in 1952 paled in comparison to the $300 million Britain received from the United States to help cover the increased dollar cost of replacing Iranian oil.[57]

Mosaddeq's request for aid, his threat to seek Soviet assistance, and his threat to end U.S.-Iranian military cooperation put the United States in a difficult position. Since coming to office, Mosaddeq had tried to exploit U.S. fears of communism to gain American support. If Mosaddeq chose to accept aid from Moscow, it would violate the terms of U.S. Mutual Security Act and force the United States to withdraw its aid and weaken the Iranian military, which the United States regarded as an important pro-Western force.[58] To prevent Iran from turning toward the Soviets, the United States might be forced to offer emergency assistance. Another option would be to break the British boycott and offer to buy Iranian oil or support a unilateral oil deal that excluded the British and allowed Mosaddeq's government to remain in power. Both entailed conflict with the British. There was, however, a third option.

The World Bank Intervention

The failure of the U.S. efforts to mediate an agreement left the way open for a third-party actor to enter the arena. During Mosaddeq's visit to the United Nations, Pakistani Ambassador Habibollah Isfahani suggested that the World Bank involve itself in the dispute. Robert L. Garner, vice president of the Bank, met with Mosaddeq on 10 November and proposed an interim arrangement whereby the Bank would operate Iran's oil industry and arrange for the distribution and sale of Iranian oil for a designated period of time. Profits would be split into separate accounts: Iran and AIOC would each receive a share, while a third account would be managed by the Bank, holding the funds pending a final settlement. Though vague, the idea appealed to Mosaddeq, and he suggested Garner approach the British. After consulting oil expert Walter Levy, Garner traveled to Rome on 26 November to pitch his plans to Acheson and Eden, who were attending a North Atlantic Council meeting. Both encouraged Garner to proceed. AIOC also felt there were "considerable possibilities" in the World Bank's interim proposals.[59]

Despite Garner's hopes, there were problems with his approach. First, the terms needed to match Mosaddeq's stated requirements, which included a prohibition on employing British nationals. Though he had initially offered AIOC staff the opportunity to remain in Iran in the wake of nationalization, after the company's withdrawal from Abadan, Mosaddeq had adopted a much firmer position, pressured in part by the left flank of the National Front coalition and partly because some British staff were in fact British intelligence operatives.[60] Readmitting British nationals to operate the oil industry was out of the question. Garner's proposal would have the Bank handle distribution of Iran's oil, which would be sold at a discount and the proceeds divided according to the fifty-fifty principle after a deduction for operating expenses. This would leave Iran $0.58/barrel, far below the price of $1.75/barrel which Mosaddeq had insisted upon during his discussions with McGhee. The British were also adamant that any interim settlement handled by the Bank could not prejudice their case before the International Court of Justice, which they hoped would determine AIOC's right to "full compensation" for the loss of its assets and its oil concession. The terms, in other words, were unlikely to please either side, though there was a chance that the Bank, acting as a neutral third party, would find room for a compromise.[61]

The World Bank was a commercial organization approaching a problem that was essentially political. Garner, a former executive for General Foods and a Wall Street banker, was no diplomat. He had some experience with Iran, which had attempted at several points between 1946 and 1951 to obtain loans from the Bank. During these negotiations, Garner blamed Iran's economic and political problems on the "habitual lethargy and weakness for action of the Iranians," and held firm to the Bank's conservative philosophy, refusing loans until the country had proven its creditworthiness.[62] According to Acting Secretary of State Robert Webb, Garner appeared "very sensitive" to how an Iranian settlement might affect "other oil arrangements," but seemed less aware of the "political risks" of reaching a bad deal with Mosaddeq.[63] Garner explained the Bank's motivations during a meeting of the Council on Foreign Relations in March 1952, citing concern over Iran's "collapse" without oil revenue, the global oil market's need for Iranian oil, and the worry that "some unscrupulous operator" might take over the Abadan refinery and oil fields "and upset the pattern of the industry." According to Garner, the Bank "was not interested in rewarding Iran" for ending its contract with AIOC but hoped to return Iran to "some semblance of stability" while preserving the global oil industry from further disruption.[64]

These problems were compounded by the fact that Garner, who was no oil expert, turned to the British for advice on what to offer Mosaddeq. Garner traveled to London and met with Eden and other officials on 30 November. The priority, according to Eden, was protecting other concessions: the terms offered by the Bank could not exceed those existing in other countries. Garner understood this and seemed convinced that the issue of management "did not preclude the employment of a considerable proportion of AIOC staff . . . provided that a neutral façade was maintained."[65] Eden was encouraged by Garner's ideas and recommended he seek further advice from AIOC. Garner dutifully met with the AIOC's Neville Gass on 1 December, and Gass explained how the "posted price" was a bit of accounting make-believe, "a somewhat arbitrary formula" designed to produce a figure that could then provide the basis for a fifty-fifty division. To calculate a practical price for Iranian oil exports, Gass suggested the Bank consider adding considerable production and depreciation costs, "in view of the precarious nature of the investment in a foreign country." He also argued that the value of the Abadan refinery was at least £250 million, based on annual output, and estimated Iran needed at least 1,100 foreign technicians to manage the oil fields and refinery—figures that were wildly at odds with other estimates.[66] While the British had hoped to delay the mission, the terms Garner intended to offer suited their interests, even if there was only a slim chance Mosaddeq would accept them.[67]

The British went along with the Bank's intervention because time appeared to be on their side. British strategy remained one of strategic patience and "masterly inactivity," running out the clock while keeping Anglo-American unity intact. During a series of joint government talks in early January, Churchill repeatedly emphasized the importance of strengthening the "special relationship," particularly in the Middle East, where Britain faced pressures related to the Iranian crisis, rising nationalism in Egypt, and a general decline in prestige. If only the United States "would stand solidly with the British," Churchill argued, "the Iranians would come to terms in short order." Acheson argued that if they continued down their present course in Iran, "we would be like two people locked in loving embrace in a rowboat . . . about to go over Niagara Falls."[68] He suggested they work with a plan put forward by Mosaddeq, whereby Iran would pay £100 million in compensation while waiving the £49 million owed under the Supplemental Agreement—money that Mosaddeq had previously argued belonged to Iran. This would put total compensation at around $400 million. The main drawback, Acheson admitted, was that once Iran had finished paying compensation, Mosaddeq might seek to disrupt the world oil industry by selling oil at cut-rate prices. The British, however, insisting on giving the Bank plan a "full run" before coming up with a new proposal.[69]

Try as he might, Acheson could not get the British to view matters in Iran from the U.S. perspective. Ambassador Henderson believed neither Mosaddeq nor the British were ready to negotiate on a realistic basis. "Iran is [a] sick country," he wrote, and Mosaddeq was "one of its most sick leaders." Discovering a solution to the crisis would require "patience even in the face of considerable provocation." The Bank's representatives, however, had come to Iran expecting a leader "who might be swayed by representations of logic and reason." Moreover, their proposals reflected "the unrealistic atmosphere . . . [that] still seems to be pervading London." The British did not seem to be negotiating in good faith, and Henderson felt it might soon be time for the United States to consider "whether it can afford . . . to defer to British leadership in this area."[70] According to Paul Nitze, who spent much of January and February meeting his counterparts in London, the British felt American assessments of the situation in Iran were "excessively catastrophic," and that Mosaddeq's incompetence, rather than economic factors, was the prime reason the Tudeh Party had grown more active.[71]

A Bank delegation arrived in Iran on 31 December 1951. The mission consisted of Hector Prud'homme, a loan officer with knowledge of Iran, and Torkild Rieber, former chairman of Texaco and a personal friend of Bank Vice President Garner. Rieber had earned notoriety for selling oil to Franco's Nationalists during the Spanish Civil War and was a controversial figure within the oil industry.[72] The Bank laid out its terms in a 28 December letter to Mosaddeq, which stated the Bank would offer a temporary solution to the crisis, one that would "restore large scale oil operations" in order to provide Iran a "steady stream of revenues, without prejudicing the rights of the interested parties." The Bank would have effective control over operations and would "engage non-Iranian personnel only to the extent it considered necessary."[73] Rieber felt there were grounds for a compromise. Prud'homme agreed. "The crucial part of the problem is not one of substance but all of approach." Mosaddeq was wheeling and dealing but could be made to see reason: "as [Rieber] says, an avowed crook is easier to deal with than an honest fanatic."[74]

Prud'homme and Rieber presented the Bank's proposals to Mosaddeq on 2 January. The discussions did not go well. Mosaddeq argued that "the Bank apparently desires [an] oil concession from Iran." He felt that essential questions of ownership, operations, and compensation had been settled in Garner's original proposal; all that remained was agreeing on a price. While he was open to a commercial discount for oil offered on the open market, any oil delivered to AIOC would have to be sold at the full posted price and credited toward compensation claims. He felt that the proposals revealed the Bank to be a "British tool."[75] Mosaddeq told Prud'homme that Iran did not need to produce 30 million tons, that 5 million tons a year were enough to cover its financial needs, and rejected the idea that AIOC act as distributor, suggesting instead he would sell to Eastern Bloc nations. Rieber thought this was an empty threat, noting that there were not enough "free" tankers available to move even small quantities of oil.[76]

After finding Mosaddeq unwilling to accept AIOC's terms, Prud'homme concluded that the prevailing logic in London was "unrealistic," as there was no way Mosaddeq would agree to distribution through AIOC or to employing British technicians.[77] Before leaving Iran, Prud'homme and Rieber visited the oil fields and the Abadan refinery. They were surprised to find the facilities in excellent physical condition, lacking only a few spare parts. Iranian engineers possessed the skill to operate most of the refinery's components, and foreign technicians were needed only for the most sophisticated processes.[78] Rieber later concluded that Iran possessed the technical means to produce 15–20 million tons of crude and 6 million tons of products a year without the assistance of foreign technicians.[79] Prud'homme suggested that the best course of action would be to let Iran "run its own show" and learn the difficulties of selling oil internationally firsthand; this would "teach the Iranians a lesson" and bring them back to the negotiating table.[80]

The End of the World Bank's Efforts

After the Bank's delegation left Iran to prepare fresh proposals, Mosaddeq met with Henderson and warned of a communist revolution within thirty days unless Iran received emergency financial aid.[81] To place added pressure on the United States, Mosaddeq continued to reject U.S. military assistance, which was formally suspended on 8 January. The following day, Mosaddeq delivered a speech in which he accused British consulates of tampering with Iran's upcoming elections. To prevent further interference, Mosaddeq had the British consulates in the provinces closed, leaving only the embassy in Tehran. He told Henderson that if no aid arrived by 18 January, he would reach out to the Soviets.[82] Henderson felt the time was right for emergency action and proposed a plan whereby Iran could sell the oil it held in storage at Abadan at a 30 percent discount while agreeing to a binding arbitration agreement with AIOC. Henderson felt that the British "would be lucky to get as much out of [the] AIOC wreck as this arrangement might give them."[83]

With the Bank's intervention stalling and instability inside Iran on the rise, U.S. officials once again considered unilateral aid. Henderson's recommendation received support from Defense Secretary Robert A. Lovett, who felt the United States should provide "substantial, immediate economic assistance to Iran." The British methods carried "extremely serious risks" of a communist seizure of power. Increased U.S. aid to Iran, he thought, would push the British toward a more flexible stance in oil negotiations.[84] A CIA analysis, however, concluded that emergency aid would do little to avert a crisis. Furthermore, it would alienate the British and discourage the shah and the opposition from moving against Mosaddeq, who would appear to have U.S. support. If no aid was forthcoming, Mosaddeq might turn to the Soviets, but the CIA now estimated that the Soviets lacked the tanker capacity to move more than a small amount of oil.[85] The U.S. embassy in London, which tended to take a pro-British view, rejected the idea of offering aid to an "irresponsible fanatic who has consistently jeopardized Western interests."[86] State Department officials were also hesitant to give in to Mosaddeq's demands, fearing that such a course would "open the door to demands by other small countries."[87]

The sense of urgency compelling U.S. policy had waned, for several reasons. First, the crisis in global oil appeared over by the end of 1951. Through the efforts of the Petroleum Administration for Defense (PAD), a special division within the U.S. Department of the Interior, as well as the major companies and the U.S. and British governments, major shortages of crude oil and products had been averted.[88] PAD had devised a plan that allowed U.S. oil companies to cooperate with AIOC to replace Iranian oil exports. Utilizing the power of the Defense Production Act (DPA), the Truman administration offered the companies immunity from antitrust action. Increased production in Kuwait, Saudi Arabia, and Iraq replaced Iranian crude oil, while construction of new refineries gradually replaced refined products previously supplied from Abadan. AIOC was able to maintain supplies to established customers, and while its profits before taxes fell from £84 million in 1950 to £47 million in 1952, net profits only declined from £33 million to £25 million as a result of lower British income taxes.[89] A paper from the World Bank completed on 28 January concluded that available supplies of crude oil "are more than adequate to meet expected demand," and that new refineries would meet demand for products, even if Abadan remained idle.[90] While the British faced a drain on their dollar reserves in the short term, overall the global oil economy would survive the loss of Iranian production.

Second, the United States was beginning to realize that pressure from the oil boycott would not trigger an immediate economic collapse inside Iran. Although some American officials exaggerated the importance of oil in Iran's economy, which they viewed "through the lens of an industrialized nation," most officials in Tehran, London, and Washington recognized that the Iranian economy was largely agricultural. Iran also possessed a large gold reserve and a strong currency, which would allow it to absorb a foreign exchange shock as a result of the shutdown.[91] It was becoming clear that Iran could go without oil for a length of time, perhaps indefinitely, depending on how effectively the government managed the transition. In October 1951, Robert M. Carr at the U.S. embassy in Tehran reported that Iran's economy appeared to be shouldering the impact of the oil shutdown, "due to its predominantly agricultural character," and had not yet shown the signs of rising prices, inflation, or slowing activity.[92]

By late January, the State Department had concluded that although "financial difficulties would provide an early and severe test" for Mosaddeq's government, they probably would not cause permanent damage to the Iranian economy.[93] Acheson began to realize that Mosaddeq's apocalyptic predictions were largely a negotiation tactic—that the Iranian economy could survive for "considerably longer" than he was intimating, and that the danger of a collapse (and subsequent communist takeover) was being invoked for tactical reasons.[94] On 17 February, Nitze admitted to British officials that Iran's economy seemed in better condition than they had initially assumed. Continued large budget deficits, however, were bound to cause problems for Mosaddeq eventually.[95]

Despite frustration over the British position and a clear lack of enthusiasm for the Bank proposal, the United States did not actively intervene in the dispute or break with the British. Acheson and Truman took no action on aid to Iran and allowed the Bank discussions to run their course. Henderson informed Mosaddeq of Truman's decision on 29 January and said that any U.S. aid would have to be tied to an oil agreement. Mosaddeq requested a clarification, which Truman sent on 11 February. The U.S. government could not justify a loan to Congress "at a time when Iran has an opportunity of obtaining oil revenues of a very great magnitude." The response was calculated to reach Mosaddeq just before Garner arrived in Iran to continue discussions on the Bank's proposal, a fact that was not lost on Mosaddeq, who charged that it was part of a ploy "to put him in such a position that he would have no choice" but to accept Garner's terms.[96] By refusing to offer Mosaddeq aid or urge the Bank to adjust its terms, the United States was, in effect, adopting the British position. The only plausible outcome of this policy was a breakdown in the oil negotiations, potentially leading to Mosaddeq's fall from power.

Acheson, Nitze, and the rest of the U.S. policymaking community did not think the Bank's proposals stood a chance of convincing Mosaddeq. Garner's terms were too inflexible, and his position too closely aligned with the British, for his mission to succeed.[97] Nevertheless, the U.S. embassy put on a show of support for Garner, who arrived in Iran with Prud'homme on 12 February. Henderson did his best to prepare the ground, urging Mosaddeq to set aside political questions and consider the Bank's proposals as "a business proposition."[98] Garner stuck to what had been offered to Mosaddeq in early January. The Bank would operate Iran's oil industry, ensuring "efficient management" and hiring foreign technicians. Oil would be sold at a discount to a distribution company owned by the Bank with profits split three ways—for AIOC, Iran, and an account for paying compensation.[99]

Garner's first meeting with Mosaddeq hit a snag immediately. Mosaddeq would not accept Garner's proposal to include British nationals among the technicians employed by the Bank to restart the oil industry. He also rejected Garner's proposed discount on the price, which after a fifty-fifty division would give Iran roughly $0.50/barrel. In addition, Garner rebuffed Mosaddeq's requests for economic aid. The Bank would only put forward the capital needed to restart the industry. If Iran needed financial relief, it would have to be realized through oil sales.[100] Talks broke down completely on 19 February, when Garner refused to accept an aide-mémoire drafted by Iran that indicated the Bank would be operating "on Iran's behalf," arguing that it placed the Bank on one side of an ongoing commercial dispute. Garner's inflexibility shocked both Prud'homme and Henderson, who noted that Stokes's proposal had accepted nationalization, "[and] Iran has apparently made surprising concessions," including allowing the Bank effective control over the industry.[101] For Garner, Mosaddeq's continued rejection of the British technicians "had no logical basis," and seemed grounded in "fear, resentment, and suspicion."[102] Garner left Iran on 20 February, though Prud'homme remained for several more weeks to keep talks going.

There was simply no bridging the gap between the Bank's proposals—which largely reflected British needs—and the political realities inside Iran. Mosaddeq would not permit British technicians to return to Iran, fearing it would allow AIOC to continue to meddle in internal Iranian politics. Nor would he allow Iranian oil to be sold at a discount that in his view disproportionately profited the British or other major oil companies. Prud'homme found the Iranian approach to the problem of restarting the oil industry "stubborn, difficult, and unrealistic," though privately he worried over the vagueness of the Bank's ideas: "We have not been able to give Iran a complete picture why we want British technicians and how many."[103] For Garner, the issue of the technicians remained one bound by commercial considerations. "The practical fact," he explained to Arthur L. Richards, the U.S. chargé d'affaires in Tehran, was that the Bank could see no alternative to hiring large numbers of British technicians, "who are available and know the property. This is not a matter within our control."[104] Garner believed that Iran faced a "breakdown" in five months without an oil agreement, claiming that Mosaddeq was already "selling the carpets in the government offices" and had put the army on half pay to cover his budget gap.[105] Nevertheless, he refused to change course and wrote to Mosaddeq on 1 April: "If Iran is to really benefit from its oil resources, the industry must be operated on a business-like basis," free from the influence of boards or committees "influenced by political rather than economic considerations."[106] With such priorities at the forefront of the Bank's considerations, Garner's approach was doomed to fail. On 3 April, the bank announced the end of its efforts.[107]

Conclusion

Throughout the search for a settlement in late 1951 and early 1952, the United States focused on Iran's internal political stability. The British, in contrast, were content to let matters drift as they prepared the ground for Mosad-deq's exit. As Harold Linder, Nitze's economic advisor, wrote to Acheson on 14 February, the British plan was to "go slowly, hoping for a break."[108] Despite their differing assessment of the strength of Iranian nationalism, both the British and the United States agreed that further nationalizations would be immensely disruptive and could threaten Western access to Middle Eastern oil. While the primary objective of U.S. policy was maintaining Iran as "an independent country aligned with the free world," the United States would not support a settlement that might threaten "the fabric of the world oil industry." The United States was not prepared for a general war with the Soviet Union in late 1951 and needed to retain British cooperation in the Middle East, the Far East, and elsewhere. Breaking with the British was not an option.

The threat of instability on the world oil market faded by early 1952, as did U.S. fears of an economic collapse inside Iran. Following the World Bank's failure, the struggle for Iran entered a period of "static trench warfare."[109] Negotiations in Tehran were suspended, and though discussions between the United States and Great Britain continued intermittently, the struggle turned into a war of attrition, with Mosaddeq and the British waiting to see who would crack first.

4 The July Uprising

Following the failure of the World Bank intervention, the United States and Great Britain stepped up their efforts to convince the shah to replace Prime Minister Mohammed Mosaddeq with someone willing to settle the oil dispute on terms that would preserve Western control of Iran's oil. Mosaddeq disrupted these plans when he unexpectedly resigned on 16 July after the shah refused to relinquish control of the armed forces to the Majlis. After the shah selected veteran statesman Ahmed Qavam, whom the United States and Britain favored, as Mosaddeq's successor, massive popular opposition to Qavam forced the shah to withdraw his support. Qavam resigned after only five days in office, and Mosaddeq returned to power triumphant and determined to enact a program of social, economic, and political reforms. The "Qavam debacle" and the July Uprising led the British to conclude that the only way to replace Mosaddeq was through a coup d'état. In contrast, the United States concluded that there was no acceptable alternative to Mosaddeq, and the best option was to stabilize his government without undermining the postwar petroleum order. The British sabotaged U.S. attempts to reach an interim settlement, but their efforts to promote a coup failed and Iran broke relations with Britain and expelled British diplomats in late October 1952.

Searching for an Alternative

The World Bank effort roughly coincided with elections for the Seventeenth Majlis, held between January and April 1952. The elections were an important test for the National Front, which had to vie with Tudeh challenges in the major cities and entrenched elite opposition, as well as British subterfuge and election tampering in the provinces. National Front candidates won all twelve seats in Tehran, a rare instance of direct democracy in Iranian history. Mosaddeq's faction also secured seats in several other cities, while the Tudeh failed to win a single seat. According to a Central Intelligence Agency report, the government manipulated elections in Tehran to prevent any Tudeh candidates from winning. The government did not tamper with elections in the provinces, where vote rigging and intimidation by the army and local elites remained the norm. In this case, Mosaddeq's commitment to free elections proved counterproductive to his political aims, as around forty-nine of the deputies elected were landlords or pro-British figures hostile to the National Front. After it became clear that his foreign and domestic opponents were conspiring to tip the Majlis balance against the government, Mosaddeq suspended voting. The Seventeenth Majlis would consist of only seventy-nine deputies—the minimum required to constitute a quorum. Mosaddeq could count on around twenty-five to thirty deputies who were aligned with the National Front, making him dependent on Kashani's ten supporters and "independents" to achieve a majority, though most deputies were hesitant to oppose him on the oil issue or on questions of foreign, especially British, influence.[1]

Despite his success in retaining a hold over the Majlis, Mosaddeq's position by the spring of 1952 was coming under considerable pressure. The breakdown in the World Bank talks ended hopes for an oil settlement. While Mosaddeq used emergency financial measures to plug the budget hole in 1951, available sources were nearly exhausted. A monthly deficit of 350–400 million rials could be met through deficit financing or drawing down the country's gold reserves, which were valued at over $100 million. The Majlis refused to provide Mosaddeq with the power to enact fiscal measures, however, and Iran's central bank warned that the government's credit would soon run out.[2]

A CIA estimate in late March concluded that opposition to Mosaddeq was growing stronger: "there appears to be at least an even chance that Mosaddeq will fall from power within the next two months." The keys were the shah, who would have to play a "significant role" in any change of government, and the armed forces, whose leaders were "almost exclusively" opposed to Mosaddeq.[3] The U.S. ambassador to Iran, Loy W. Henderson, disagreed, arguing on 10 April that Mosaddeq would most likely continue in office for "at least for several months." On 14 April, the CIA issued a revised estimate: while there had been a revival of anti-Mosaddeq agitation and activity by "more conservative elements," Mosaddeq would be able to gain Majlis support for measures to avert a fiscal breakdown through the summer, and the shah was unlikely to take any initiative to remove him.[4]

Aware that opposition forces were mobilizing against him, Mosaddeq agreed to allow U.S. military aid to Iran to continue, a move calculated to win favor with the shah and assuage the armed forces. After Eden complained that the aid agreement gave Mosaddeq a new lease on life and created the impression that the United States and Britain were divided over policy toward Iran, the United States assured the British that the action was taken to bolster the shah and the Iranian armed forces and that it was limited to military aid. In addition, the United States issued a press statement reiterating its policy of not providing additional financial aid to Iran while the oil dispute remained unsettled.[5]

Finally giving up on Sayyid Zia, the British tried to convince the opposition to rally behind veteran politician Ahmed Qavam, whose supporters, including the shah's mother, sister, and half brother, were "working like beavers" on his behalf. Qavam contacted British officials in early 1952. At a clandestine meeting in Monte Carlo, the former premier suggested he would reinstate the Qajar dynasty, which the shah's father had supplanted in 1925.[6] Qavam met with U.S. diplomats in Paris in March, hinting that he would soon be returning to Iran to form a new government, so long as he had U.S. support and assurances that the shah would not undermine him. Noting that Qavam, who was in his eighties, "appeared old but not extinct," a U.S. embassy official reported the former prime minister's desire to work with the United States to "save" Iran. After a meeting with Qavam's supporters at the end of March, Ambassador Henderson felt that of all the candidates who had been mentioned as a successor to Mosaddeq, Qavam would be the most effective, despite his age.[7] Qavam returned to Iran in April 1952 and began working through a network of former supporters in the Majlis and Senate. The British believed that Qavam was keen to reach an oil agreement and would be prepared to dissolve the Majlis and arrest dissident elements, including Mosaddeq and Kashani, if necessary.

To become prime minister, Qavam would need the support of the shah. Mohammed Reza Pahlavi distrusted Qavam, as well as the British, and argued that it would only be safe to replace Mosaddeq after he had been thoroughly discredited. Qavam and the shah had fought for control of Iran's government during the Azerbaijan crisis, and in 1948 the shah branded Qavam a traitor and banished him from the political scene. Although several of the National Front's leaders, including Hossein Makki and Mozaffar Baqa'i, had connections to Qavam's old political party, it was not clear whether they would support him. Ayatollah Kashani, Mosaddeq's most powerful supporter, hated Qavam with a passion. As prime minister, Qavam had ordered Kashani jailed for anti-British activity, and later exiled him to Lebanon.[8]

The increasingly uncertain political environment and mounting fiscal problems stemming from the ongoing British boycott raised questions about how long Mosaddeq would be able to remain in power. A joint appraisal of the financial, economic, and political situation in Iran by the U.S. and British embassies in early May concluded that while support for Mosaddeq had declined, "the most probable development" was that he would remain in power until after the International Court of Justice ruled on Britain's complaint against nationalization in June. Although "ultimate financial and economic collapse" was "inevitable in the absence of the restoration of oil income," the government could probably find sufficient funds to continue to function for several months. Mosaddeq's personal prestige remained high, the opposition was uncoordinated, and the shah, who Henderson had derided as a "Persian Hamlet," was "weak and vacillating." An opposition government would need the full support of the shah and the army, and it would be very difficult to convince the shah to act "unless considerable pressure were exerted" to convince him of the dangers of inaction and "the concrete advantages to Iran and to himself to be derived from his intervention." Even if the shah agreed to use the army to support a weak prime minister, a weak government would be short-lived, and the shah was "notoriously reluctant" to support a strong prime minister.[9]

The British and U.S. governments drew different conclusions from the joint appraisal. The British were encouraged that Mosaddeq's popularity was declining and downplayed U.S. fears of an economic collapse, arguing that Iran could meet its financial needs for several months by revising its currency rules. If Mosaddeq was unable to do this, his failure would lead to his removal by the shah as soon as it became impossible to pay the army. The British also tried to counter the joint appraisal's warning that Mosaddeq, "if driven into a corner," might turn to the Soviets for support. The British argued that Mosaddeq was unlikely to turn to the Soviet Union, and that any pro-Soviet or Tudeh moves would spur the shah to move against him. Both Britain and the United States agreed that there was little prospect of the Tudeh taking over because its appeal was limited to a few urban areas and because the army was still loyal to the shah. Nevertheless, the United States stressed that without a settlement of the oil dispute, Iran's financial and political situation could continue to deteriorate, and the Tudeh would gain in strength. The United States also pressed the British to develop a long-range solution to the oil dispute, warning that if the situation in Iran deteriorated to the point that U.S. interests and those of the "free world" were threatened, it might become necessary for the United States to extend financial aid to Iran.[10]

Despite this disagreement, both the United States and Great Britain wanted the shah to dismiss Mosaddeq. The question was who should replace him. On 16 May, the head of the State Department's Office of Greek, Turkish, and Iranian Affairs met with the delightfully named Launcelot Pyman, the outgoing oriental counselor at the British embassy in Tehran, to discuss possible candidates for prime minister should Mosaddeq resign or fall. Pyman suggested Qavam, a military figure like former general Fazlollah Zahedi, or a National Front figure like Hossein Makki. Noting Qavam's poor relationship with the shah, Pyman thought Zahedi would be a good choice. In addition to his appeal as a military strongman, he was an experienced politician and had connections with the National Front, having served as Mosaddeq's interior minister in 1951. He would also seek to settle the oil dispute on a "realistic" basis.[11]

Communicating with the shah through Court Minister Hossein 'Ala, Ambassador Henderson made it clear that the United States felt a solution to the oil dispute was impossible as long as Mosaddeq was prime minister. Although Henderson declined to recommend a successor, he let 'Ala and the shah know that he did not believe that Iran Party head Allahyar Saleh, who the shah was considering, was a suitable replacement. Saleh had cooperated with the Tudeh in the past, had been hostile to the Point Four program and U.S. military assistance, and held views similar to Mosaddeq on the oil question. While prepared to provide up to $60 million in additional aid to Iran to ensure the survival of a successor government, Henderson stressed that the United States would insist that any aid to Iran would be contingent on Iran's willingness to negotiate "realistically" on the oil question.[12]

Henderson met Qavam on 10 June. After the ambassador made it clear that the United States would not provide financial assistance unless it was convinced that Iran was doing everything possible to help itself, Qavam replied he would do "everything within reason" to reach an oil settlement with the British and emphasized that it was "extremely important" for him to know what the British wanted in a settlement. Impressed by the elderly leader's good health and by his determination to reach an oil settlement, Henderson briefed George Middleton, chargé d'affaires at the British embassy, and stressed that the shah as well as Qavam wanted to know if a new government would receive "friendly and reasonable" treatment from Britain.[13]

Two days after his meeting with Qavam, Henderson called on the shah. While his report was careful not to make this explicit, their discussion centered around the question of how to replace Mosaddeq as prime minister and thus resolve the oil dispute. Henderson explained that the United States was forced to deal with Mosaddeq as Iran's prime minister; rumors that the United States secretly supported Mosaddeq were without foundation. Henderson reminded the shah that on numerous occasions he had made it clear that the United States believed that Mosaddeq was leading Iran to ruin, and that the shah should face up to the responsibility for a change in government. The shah argued that he would be taking a great risk moving against Mosaddeq unless he had assurances that the new government would receive financial assistance from the United States or Britain. The British could not insist on impossible terms for an oil settlement because no government could survive unless it respected the nationalization laws. Henderson assured the shah that the United States would not let a pro-Western government fall if it were "energetically and sincerely" trying to settle the oil dispute. Henderson opposed Saleh or any National Front figure as a successor to Mosaddeq and informed the shah that he had met with Qavam, who had assured him that he was too old to have any personal ambitions.[14]

Along with his doubts regarding Qavam, uncertainty about what kind of oil settlement Britain would make with a new government was a key factor in the shah's hesitation to move against Mosaddeq. AIOC no longer needed Iranian oil as much as it had previously due to increased production in other countries. The company was building new refinery capacity to replace Abadan. In these circumstances, the British were determined not to jeopardize their other holdings just to reach an agreement that would stabilize Iran. According to the Foreign Office, if the Iranians wanted a settlement, they had to "face facts" and create conditions that would make Iranian oil attractive to potential purchasers.[15] Referring to the deadly British attack on an Egyptian police station in the Suez Canal Zone, Prime Minister Winston Churchill wrote Foreign Secretary Anthony Eden on 17 June that "if we had fired the volley you were responsible for at Ismailia at Abadan, none of these difficulties and great losses to our hard-pressed country would have occurred." Churchill told Eden that there was no need to be in a hurry to reach an oil settlement: "by sitting still on the safety valve and showing no weariness we are gradually getting them into submission." Britain could wait out Iran on the oil issue because "to us it is a fraction, to them it is their all."[16]

Middleton met with Qavam on 14 June and explained that Britain wanted an oil settlement that would not endanger its interests elsewhere. The economics of any settlement would be governed by the terms prevailing in the oil industry, so the best Iran could expect was a fifty-fifty profit-sharing arrangement. Qavam asked if Britain preferred a parliamentary or author-itarian government, to which Middleton replied that Britain wanted a sta-ble government able to exercise its authority. It was up to the Iranians to work out the details. After Qavam noted that he was counting on British help, Middleton replied, "God helps those who help themselves."[17]

Although the British believed that Qavam would be the best alternative to replace Mosaddeq, the shah continued to resist, reportedly telling Hasan Emami, the *Imam Jum'eh* or Friday prayer leader of Tehran, that it was fine to bring Qavam to power, "but how are we going to get rid of him when we want to do so?"[18] After meeting with the shah on 16 June, Middleton con-cluded that Britain could expect no assistance from him unless the United States applied additional pressure. Even then, Middleton warned, "a joint appeal might have to be accompanied by virtual threats that he must bear the consequences if he does not follow the advice given him."[19] Henderson agreed and informed the State Department on 27 June that even though the shah realized that the time had come to take action, he (Henderson) had "considerable doubt" that the shah had the "hardihood to do anything really constructive."[20]

The United States did not expect Mosaddeq to fall before August, but it wanted the British to be ready to negotiate quickly and reasonably if the shah should move against Mosaddeq. An acceptable settlement plan was not only necessary to ensure the survival of the government that replaced Mo-saddeq; the prime minister's enemies, including the shah, were reluctant to act until they knew what kind of deal they would receive from the Brit-ish. In ministerial talks in London, the British agreed, in the event of a change in government in Iran, to offer Iran a long-term settlement based on a non-British firm composed of several oil companies under contract to the National Iranian Oil Company (NIOC) managing Iran's oil industry. AIOC, under a different name, would purchase the bulk of the oil produced. Although AIOC could not return to its former position in Iran, there had to be British participation at the managerial as well as the technical level in the managing agency. Most importantly, Iran would have to compensate AIOC not only for physical assets but also for the loss of its concession. The British were not prepared to go beyond this broad outline. Neither the United States nor Great Britain expected any further progress on the oil issue while Mosaddeq remained in office. "He would have to be pushed," Eden argued on 28 June, "and the one person who could do this was the shah."[21]

Mosaddeq's Resignation and the July Uprising

While the British, Americans, and Iranian opposition were preparing for his eventual fall from power, Mosaddeq traveled to The Hague, where the International Court of Justice was hearing Britain's May 1951 petition that the court rule nationalization of AIOC violated Iran's treaty obligations to the United Kingdom and was therefore illegal. At the public hearing on 9 June, Mosaddeq made an impassioned political and moral argument defending nationalization. He returned to Iran, leaving the legal case to renowned Belgian lawyer Henri Rolin. Iranian newspapers carefully followed the case, and enthusiastic crowds greeted Mosaddeq on his return to Tehran.[22] Acutely aware of the political sensitivity of the case, the shah wanted to postpone a decision on replacing Mosaddeq until the Court had ruled. If the decision went against Iran, it would be easy to remove Mosaddeq. If the Court found in favor of Iran, Mosaddeq would be a hero and it would be dangerous to oppose him.[23]

Despite evidence of his continued popularity, the National Front prime minister faced an atmosphere of mounting crisis. On 18 June, *Ettelaat* ran an interview with Mosaddeq's finance minister, who admitted the government faced a 3 billion rial deficit.[24] On 1 July, the Majlis elected Hasan Emami, a popular cleric and conservative supporter of the shah, as its speaker. Though the assembly's attitude seemed to be turning against Mosaddeq, the shah hesitated to intervene directly, instead indicating he would wait for the Majlis to push Mosaddeq out through a vote of no confidence.[25] Henderson was not certain Mosaddeq would fall as a result of financial pressure, as the British hoped. On 14 July he reported that Mosaddeq "should be able to print enough bank notes to finance the government for months to come." Until circumstances improved, he warned the next day, any attempted intervention by Britain and the United States "might do more harm than good."[26]

The situation took a dramatic turn on 16 July when Mosaddeq presented his new cabinet list and program to the shah for royal approval. To deal with the fiscal crisis and enact his social and economic agenda, Mosaddeq requested six months of emergency powers and full authority over the fields of justice, finance, economics, administration, and personnel. What shocked the shah most of all was Mosaddeq's request that he take the portfolio of minister of war for himself. Traditionally (though not constitutionally), the shah controlled the War Ministry and appointed his own chief of staff of the armed forces, acting in his capacity as commander-in-chief. Mosaddeq's request threatened the shah's dominance over the military, the chief source of his power and influence within politics. The shah refused Mosaddeq's request. Finding the monarch implacable, Mosaddeq resigned from office at 8:00 P.M. on 16 July. In a statement published the following day, Mosaddeq announced he would step down "and permit someone who enjoys royal confidence to form a new government. . . . In the present situation, the struggle started by the Iranian people cannot be brought to a victorious conclusion."[27] Mosaddeq withdrew to his estate at Ahmadabad and refused press interviews or public appearances.

It is not clear if Mosaddeq's resignation was premeditated or if he acted on impulse. According to Baqa'i, "absolutely no one knew" in advance about the prime minister's choice to resign. In his memoirs, Mosaddeq regretted his decision. Homa Katouzian, the memoirs' editor, argues that Mosaddeq's resignation "unwittingly played right into the shah's hands." Alternatively, the U.S. embassy believed that Mosaddeq, recognizing his position was becoming untenable, manufactured the crisis so he could leave office on a suitable pretense, one that would "place the responsibility for his fall on the Shah rather than on his own policies."[28] This seems the most likely answer: knowing he would need full control over the government to resolve the fiscal crisis and preserve his political position, Mosaddeq chose to gamble.

Despite pressure from Kashani to agree to Mosaddeq's demands, the shah accepted the prime minister's resignation and instructed the Majlis to choose a successor. Although Mosaddeq's supporters boycotted the closed session of the Majlis held on 17 July, thus denying it a quorum, forty of the forty-three remaining deputies voted in favor of Qavam. After Speaker Emami calmed the shah's fears that Qavam's selection would lead to a revolution, the shah, without waiting for the Senate's approval, issued a *firman* appointing Qavam prime minister. Qavam learned of his election during a meeting at his home in north Tehran with the chief of police and the military governor of Tehran, whom he expected "to maintain complete law and order." Discussing the situation with the shah over the telephone, Qavam received assurances of trust and loyal cooperation. Qavam also sent a message to the U.S. embassy that stressed his desire to "gradually bring Iran into full and unequivocal alignment with the West," and that he needed U.S. financial assistance to "save" Iran.[29] The following morning, Radio Tehran issued the new prime minister's first address. Qavam emphasized a commitment to "law and order," denounced "black reaction and outdated superstition," and vowed to keep religion out of politics.[30] Qavam also denounced the Tudeh and the National Front, particularly Kashani's wing of the coalition, which he expected would be in ascendance now that Mosaddeq had withdrawn from the scene. While it was calculated to please conservatives and reassure Mosaddeq's opponents, the speech enraged National Front supporters.[31]

The sudden turn of events apparently caught Britain and the United States by surprise. Both had been pressing the shah to remove Mosaddeq, but neither expected matters to come to a head before August at the earliest. MI6 operative C. M. Woodhouse had already decided that a coup would be necessary to remove Mosaddeq but was apparently still "working out the details." Woodhouse writes in his memoirs that he and his CIA colleague were out of Tehran fishing at the time of Mosaddeq's resignation.[32] Henderson met with Middleton, and together they prepared a joint recommendation calling for U.S. financial assistance to Qavam's government. Assistance would be necessary, Henderson wrote, to allow Qavam "to remain in power and work out [an] agreement with [the British]." Assistant Secretary of State for Near Eastern, South Asian, and African Affairs Henry A. Byroade explained that Qavam was showing "strength of character and determination" and was "sticking his neck out" to reach an oil settlement. It was important for the United States to support him without delay. The U.S. government quickly approved the joint recommendation.[33]

British officials argued that aid had to be contingent on an oil agreement. "We regard this as an opportunity for settling the oil dispute," Roger Makins of the Foreign Office told the U.S. ambassador in London, "and [are] determined to seize it."[34] Although the British in late June had agreed to an arrangement that called for a new company to run Iran's oil industry under contract with the NIOC, AIOC was unwilling to accept any plan that did not allow it to dominate Iran's oil industry. AIOC's obstinacy, backed by the Ministry of Fuel and Power and the Treasury, infuriated Foreign Secretary Eden, who had been pressing unsuccessfully for a reorganization of the company and the replacement of AIOC head Sir William Fraser. Fraser, who Eden complained was "in cloud cuckoo land," apparently saw the sudden turn of events in Iran as a vindication of his policies and as an opportunity to get AIOC back into Iran. Despite the Foreign Office's efforts to seize the opportunity for a settlement, Fraser continued to hold up agreement on a settlement plan.[35]

While the British quarreled over what terms to offer Qavam's new government, the political situation in Iran rapidly spun out of control. In Tehran, National Front–affiliated bazaar guilds shut down the market and suspended commercial activity as the coalition's leaders organized protests.

"Mosaddeq or death!" was a common slogan. Kashani delivered a blistering tirade against Qavam, "a traitor and gangster," and declared jihad, or holy war, against the new government. At a press conference, Kashani invited all opposition groups, including those associated with the Tudeh, to unite against Qavam, whom he regarded as an "imperialist tool." *Shahed* and *Bakhtar-e Emruz* published statements by the National Front imploring the police and soldiers not to use force against demonstrators. "The acts of Ahmed Qavam," declared Kashani in *Kayhan*, "must not be carried out through you and must not make you responsible for the shedding of blood and injustice."[36]

On 19 July, Qavam met with Henderson and complained that agitators were hiding behind parliamentary immunity "to break down law and order," and noted that he might be forced to dissolve the Majlis. In a carefully worded response, Henderson said that world opinion would not expect the government "to tolerate [a] situation in which it was paralyzed." Qavam pointed out that it might be necessary to undertake "certain strong measures," and that he might have to proceed in an "undemocratic manner . . . in order to save democracy." Henderson registered no objection, suggesting Qavam could act with "firmness and restraint" while maintaining his "reputation" in the eyes of the West. Henderson also clearly and carefully linked U.S. aid to Qavam's willingness to settle the oil dispute. Qavam assured Henderson that he intended to move as quickly as conditions permitted to solve the oil problem on a "reasonable and fair basis."[37]

Though Qavam was ready to use force to preserve his government's position, the extent of the opposition to Mosaddeq's removal gave the shah pause. Some of the demonstrations in Tehran and other cities began to take on a revolutionary flavor, assuming an anti-monarchical as well as an anti-foreign and anti-Qavam attitude, and the shah feared backing Qavam could threaten his throne. On 19 July, the shah refused Qavam's request to dissolve the Majlis and permit him to rule by decree for three months. Long suspicious of Qavam's designs against the Pahlavi dynasty, the shah further feared granting Qavam such sweeping powers lest they be turned against the monarchy. Lacking what he considered the necessary powers to deal with an increasingly difficult situation, and with no nationwide organization to counter the National Front, Qavam lapsed into inaction.[38]

At dawn on 21 July 1952—30 *Tir* 1331, according to the Iranian calendar—Tehran was silent. All stores and workshops were closed, as the bazaar guilds held a general strike of all commercial activity. By midmorning, both the National Front and Tudeh marshaled their street organizations. Hours of street combat ensued as the police and armed forces used live ammunition to suppress the crowds. According to British accounts, the crowds were chanting "Down with the shah" as well as "Death to Qavam." At least one statue of the shah's father was torn down. Mehdi Azar, a doctor in Tehran, recalled leaving his shift at the hospital and seeing mounted police "galloping towards the crowd" and fighting them off, only for the crowd to surge again and drive the security forces as far as Baherastan Square. The shah's brother narrowly escaped with his life after his chauffeur mistakenly drove his car into a National Front demonstration. A Majlis deputy who called for calm was pelted with stones, and 600 detainees broke out of the city's jails to join the protesters. Twenty-nine people died and hundreds were injured as National Front and Tudeh demonstrators battled the city's police and military garrison.[39]

Qavam went to the royal palace early on 21 July intending to request emergency authority to put down the crowds with brute force. The shah, who was meeting with representatives from the National Front to negotiate an end to the demonstrations, refused to see him. Qavam returned to his house and "a state of complete passivity," according to Henderson. Middleton and Henderson tried to convince the shah to support Qavam, arguing that the Tudeh was backing Mosaddeq and if Mosaddeq got back into power with their support, the authority of the government and the position of the monarchy would be "fatally impaired." According to Middleton, Henderson gave the shah "categorical and forceful advice" not to be too "scrupulous" and allow concerns about the constitution to keep him from authorizing necessary measures.[40]

The shah refused to back Qavam. After some army units ceased their efforts to resist the protesters, the shah ordered all soldiers to return to their barracks. Qavam submitted his resignation, which the shah accepted at 5 P.M. Before the shah could name a replacement, news that the International Court of Justice had ruled in Iran's favor arrived. By a vote of nine to five, the Court ruled that the 1933 concession represented "a contract between a government and a foreign corporation," and did not constitute "treaties and conventions," which fell under the Court's jurisdiction. The British judge ruled with the majority, while the American judge sided with the minority.[41] Although the British government declared that its legal position was unchanged and did not relax its efforts to prevent the sale of Iranian oil, the Court's decision was hailed as a personal victory for Mosaddeq.[42]

When the Majlis reconvened on 22 July, sixty-one of the sixty-four deputies present voted in favor of Mosaddeq. Left with little choice, the shah signed the *firman* confirming Mosaddeq as prime minister.

The events of July 1952 marked an important turning point in the struggle for Iran. As Middleton wrote on 28 July, for decades Iranian politics had been dominated by a small elite, with the shah acting as "umpire." That elite was now marginalized.[43] Qavam, a thirty-year veteran of Iranian politics, fled Iran and died in obscurity in 1955. Richard Cottam, a CIA officer at the time and later a scholar of Iranian history, wrote in 1988 that the uprising was "one of the really great outpourings of popular sentiment" in Iranian history.[44] At the time, however, the events of July 1952 apparently led the CIA to conclude that control of "the street" was the key to power in Iran.[45] The events displayed the organizational prowess of the Tudeh. A faction within the party's leadership advocating for greater cooperation with the National Front won out over hard-line Marxists who had rejected Mosaddeq as a bourgeois "American tool."[46] Most significantly of all, however, was the precipitous decline in the prestige and influence of the shah. Once he returned to office, Mosaddeq won control of the War Ministry (which he renamed the Defense Ministry) and the freedom to select his own chief of staff. The shah still held influence in the armed forces, but his practical authority (which, according to Iran's constitution, was fairly limited) drastically declined in the wake of the July Uprising.

Considering a Coup: Anglo-American Positions after the July Uprising

Firmly back in power after the events of 21 July, Mosaddeq met with Middleton on 25 July and suggested a fresh attempt to resolve the oil dispute. Mosaddeq argued the two sides should settle the remaining outstanding issue—compensation for AIOC's lost assets—through arbitration. Iran and Britain would each appoint an arbitrator, with a third arbitrator to be chosen jointly. Iran would remain in full control of its industry. While Iran would work with AIOC and other companies on the distribution of its oil, foreign companies would not be allowed to operate in Iran, which would sell no more oil than was necessary to balance its budget and pay compensation. Mosaddeq reminded Middleton that Iran faced severe financial difficulties and would need immediate assistance from Britain. Unless oil revenues were restored, Mosaddeq warned, Iran's drift toward a communist revolution would be difficult to halt.[47]

Mosaddeq's move put the British on the spot. The offer to Middleton upheld the principle of negotiated compensation and might open the door to the return of AIOC and other oil companies to Iran if arbitration set compensation at so high a level that Iran would need outside help in selling enough oil to pay. On the other hand, Mosaddeq's proposal did not get Iranian oil flowing again in large quantities or provide for "efficient management," the favored British euphemism for foreign control, and thus did not ensure substantial oil revenues, a key U.S. concern. It also did not necessarily provide large quantities of sterling oil for Britain. Negotiating with Mosaddeq would further discourage the opposition and strengthen Mosaddeq's hold on power. Nevertheless, Middleton argued that outright rejection of the proposal would only prolong the deadlock and thereby increase the danger of a communist seizure of power. Although Foreign Secretary Eden initially agreed that Britain had to consider Mosaddeq's proposals, "vague and unpalatable" as they were, the British did not respond to Mosaddeq's offer.[48]

The United States believed that Mosaddeq's proposal represented the last opportunity for Britain to salvage a settlement of the oil dispute that offered compensation and a role for AIOC in the distribution of Iranian oil. Moreover, failure to respond favorably to the offer would strengthen the extremists in the National Front and the Tudeh. After an "exhausting and depressing" meeting with Mosaddeq on 27 July, Henderson lamented that a "person so lacking in stability and clearly dominated by emotions and prejudices should represent the only bulwark left between Iran and communism." Nevertheless, Henderson argued that Mosaddeq and the National Front, despite their faults, represented the only political force, "aside from the small likelihood of a military coup," that could successfully challenge the Tudeh. Henderson warned that the National Front would succumb to the better-organized communists if Britain and the United States did not work to keep Iran on a friendly basis with the West. In the U.S. view, the alternatives in Iran were either reaching a settlement with Mosaddeq, a gradual breakdown of the oil boycott, or continued deadlock with an increasing trend to the left and a great risk of a communist takeover. Henderson believed that the overriding policy objective of saving Iran from communist domination took precedence over "business" considerations.[49] State Department counselor and noted Soviet specialist Charles Bohlen emphasized the folly of the British policy in Iran to one Foreign Office representative, arguing that the obsession with avoiding an unsatisfactory oil settlement blinded the British to the risk of losing Iran and the entire Middle

East to communism. In that event, the region's oil resources would be lost forever. It was therefore more important to keep Iran in the Western camp. Commercial concerns were secondary.[50]

Mosaddeq had demanded that the British reply to his proposal by 28 July. When the British failed to respond, he withdrew the offer and informed Middleton that Iran would pay compensation according to the Nine-Point Nationalization Law, which only covered physical assets. Mosaddeq's move angered the British, who had hoped to link arbitration with arrangements for controlling Iran's oil industry. In any event, the British were following a different path. With Zaehner's departure, covert operations in Iran were now led by Sam Falle, a junior officer fluent in Farsi.[51] Falle concluded that the conservative, pro-British parliamentary opposition to Mosaddeq had been routed, and that the only solution was a "coup d'état with or without the consent of the shah." On 27 July, Falle and Middleton met with Fazlollah Zahedi and proposed a "coup d'état" against Mosaddeq, drawing on support from the army and "among the mullahs." Explaining his reasoning, Middleton maintained that Mosaddeq's "record, his character and capacity as a statesman and the balance of forces which keep him in power all lead me to believe that he is unlikely to prove a very effective barrier to the growth of Communist strength in Persia." The only thing to stop Iran from falling into communist hands, Middleton argued, was a coup d'état, though he could not "at present see anyone who might play the role of strong man."[52]

In addition to discussing the possibility of organizing a coup with General Zahedi, Sayyid Zia, the Rashidian brothers, and other opposition elements, the War Office instructed the British military attaché in Iran to assess the loyalty of the armed forces to the shah, which side the armed forces would take in a confrontation between the government and the shah, and the extent of Tudeh penetration of the armed forces. The War Office also wanted an assessment of the capability of the armed forces to mount a successful coup given the morale of senior officers, Tudeh penetration of the lower ranks, and possible opposition in the military to a coup.[53]

Although the United States was not yet ready to sponsor a coup against Mosaddeq, Byroade noted that "unorthodox measures" might be necessary to prevent Iran's fall to communism. He agreed that the U.S. and British embassies in Iran, in addition to discussing means of reaching an oil settlement with Mosaddeq, should explore the option of removing Mosaddeq, including recommendations as to possible alternatives, what methods might bring such alternatives to power, and the type of encouragement and support that would be necessary for an alternative leader to be successful. According to Secretary of State Dean Acheson, the United States believed that no "constructive alternative" to Mosaddeq existed but felt that "every possibility should be re-explored."[54]

On 31 July, Henderson informed the department that he and Middleton had concluded that it was not likely that any alternatives to Mosaddeq could be brought to power, and neither he nor Middleton knew of any military leader who had the "strength, standing, or intelligence necessary for assuring success" of a coup, or for governing Iran if the coup succeeded. According to a joint U.S. and British assessment, the shah's "indecision" had been the prime reason for Qavam's failure in July.[55] Henderson felt a coup would need to be carried out in the shah's name, but it would have to happen without his knowledge, since the shah "would probably not have the stamina to see it through and might at [a] certain stage weaken and denounce its leaders." Moreover, a successful coup would "almost certainly" result in Tudeh control of the nationalist movement, and a military dictatorship would find it very difficult to control the country and enact a constructive program. According to Henderson, Middleton agreed with him that "neither British nor American government should undertake to encourage or support a coup d'état and that our two Embassies should not become involved in any way."[56] Since Middleton was involved in such activities, it appears that he was not being candid about his government's policy. The CIA agreed that there were no figures "around whom a coup could be engineered" who were not already aligned with Mosaddeq. The agency had assets including the Qashqa'i, a powerful tribal confederation in southern Iran, but the Qashqa'i supported the National Front, were fiercely anti-British, and did not trust the shah.[57]

While the British continued to try to organize a coup, the United States moved in the opposite direction. The United States believed that it was highly unlikely that the shah and conservative elements would regain political power and concluded that providing limited financial support to Mosaddeq and the National Front was the only viable option for preventing economic chaos and the danger of the Tudeh eventually coming to power. Support would have to be designed so that it would preserve the principle of compensation for the nationalization of AIOC. It would also have to be acceptable to public opinion in the United States and Britain and would have to provide for the resumption of oil revenues to Iran.

With these criteria in mind, the United States proposed a plan whereby it would provide Iran with $10 million in grant assistance, out of the $26 million the United States had planned to make available to Qavam; AIOC would buy the oil in storage at Abadan at a "suitable discount"; Mosaddeq would agree to submit the question of compensation to international arbitration; and negotiations on permanent arrangements for distributing Iranian oil would be undertaken promptly. Neither the U.S. grant nor the British purchases would be held up pending the arbitration, and the British boycott of Iranian oil would end. The United States believed that these were the minimum conditions that Mosaddeq was likely to accept, and the best the British could get given the circumstances. If the British refused to work with the United States to negotiate a settlement, Acting Secretary of State David Bruce told the National Security Council on 6 August, the United States "might have to go it alone" and prop up the Mosaddeq government with unilateral aid or oil purchases.[58] Meanwhile, Mosaddeq published a note on 7 August demanding AIOC return all unpaid royalties to Iran, end the boycott, and begin discussions with Iran on a compensation award. The note contained strong language denouncing the British record in Iran and hinted that failure to negotiate might result in severing diplomatic relations.[59]

Keeping the Americans "in Play"

The British were not pleased with the shift in U.S. policy. While it did not appear possible to unseat Mosaddeq in the near term, the British believed that he would never accept their terms on compensation and continued their efforts to organize a coup. They opposed providing Iran with financial assistance since this would bolster Mosaddeq's position. The British position in Iran had weakened in the wake of the July Uprising. Though the embassy remained open, consulates in the provinces had been closed in January and Zaehner's intelligence network was in tatters.[60] Since a fresh attempt to dislodge Mosaddeq would require U.S. assistance, Falle suggested a change in tactics. Rather than emphasizing the oil issue, Britain should take a "slightly self-sacrificing line" and instead emphasize the risk of Iran falling to communism if Mosaddeq remained in power.[61]

The British also argued that there were alternatives to tolerating Mosaddeq. Drawing on the reports from Falle and Middleton, Eden argued there was a chance that a "local Neguib" could be found, a reference to the recent military coup in Egypt that suggested a military leader might succeed in overthrowing Mosaddeq.[62] Whereas Henderson had reported that the army was inclined to back Mosaddeq as long as he did not challenge its authority or that of the shah, Eden claimed that the army's morale remained strong, and if army commanders challenged the government, the Majlis would rally to its side.[63] Worried that the United States might ignore their objections, the British decided to go along with the U.S. plan, "if only to gain time" while they worked with Zahedi to mobilize another attempt to oust Mosaddeq.[64]

The issue of compensation took center stage in oil negotiations. Mosaddeq argued that compensation should only cover AIOC's physical assets, pointing out that oil in the ground legally belonged to Iran. The British opposed such terms, arguing that accepting them would allow Iran to profit from its nationalization, thus establishing a precedent that might encourage other countries to nationalize their own oil industries. Instead of physical assets, the British insisted on compensation terms covering the future profits AIOC would have earned under the 1933 concession, which was to remain in force until 1993. In 1951, AIOC calculated that the profits from the remaining concession years would equal at least £1 billion, whereas physical assets were valued at only £26 million.[65] The British also insisted that AIOC should receive compensation for the "loss and damage caused to the company" by nationalization.[66] The British demand for broad arbitration terms covering compensation reflected a shift in their tactics away from questioning the legality of nationalization and toward bringing about a settlement that would saddle Iran with a heavy compensation obligation, thereby requiring a resumption of Iranian oil exports handled either by AIOC or a group of Western oil companies, or by a reversal of nationalization.

The British knew that Mosaddeq would probably reject such harsh terms. Middleton pointed out that the proposed terms would "fatally prejudice the chances of Persian acceptance."[67] British tactics were not meant to produce a settlement, though the British were open to negotiations if their goals could be accomplished. As one Foreign Office official noted, "we cannot insist in the presence of third parties that Musaddiq is 'unnegotiable,' even though we may ourselves think that he is."[68] Meanwhile, the British pushed Falle's "self-sacrificing line," emphasizing Mosaddeq's weakness as a barrier to communist control. Ambassador Oliver Franks met with Acheson over dinner and argued that Mosaddeq's recent alliance with the Tudeh "lessened his power to be a bulwark against Communism." Franks also argued that Henderson's reports "did not exclude the seizure of power by someone else, as happened not too infrequently in Middle Eastern countries."[69] The apparent openness to negotiations was yet another British stalling tactic, designed to preserve Anglo-American unity and prolong the oil crisis until Mosaddeq could be forced from power.

The British approach irritated the United States. President Truman complained of "this type of usual delay on urgent problems" and stated that "if it proved impossible to get together with the British on Iran, we would have to see what we could do unilaterally."[70] Acheson told Ambassador Franks on 11 August that the only resemblance he could see between the U.S. proposal and the British reply "was that they were both written on paper with a typewriter." In contrast to the British claim that Mosaddeq might be replaced by a "better" government, the United States believed that any change that might occur, "by coup or otherwise," would not produce an Iranian government that could accept proposals as stringent as the British had outlined.[71]

Mosaddeq seemed ready to negotiate. He met with Middleton on 14 August in what the diplomat described as "the most hopeful and productive meeting I have yet had." Mosaddeq explained that his 7 August note had been phrased to satisfy Iranian public opinion. As the American had surmised, Mosaddeq was feeling pressure from Kashani and others intent on punishing the British, and he was anxious to reach an oil settlement that would allow him to deal with Iran's domestic problems. He was therefore willing to send the issue of compensation to arbitration through the ICJ, provided Iran secured financial relief in the short term. He suggested that arbitration terms remove any mention of the 1933 concession or the Nationalization Law.[72]

To provide an incentive for the British to negotiate, Mosaddeq had invited W. Alton Jones, president of Cities Service, an Oklahoma-based oil company, to come to Iran to inspect the production facilities and the Abadan refinery and offer advice on how to restart the industry. There was little the U.S. government could do to prevent private citizens from doing business with the Iranian government, the recognized owner of the nation's oil industry. On 13 August, Jones told President Truman, Secretary of the Interior Oscar L. Chapman, and Acting Secretary of State David Bruce that he planned to offer Mosaddeq advice and would stress the need for Iran to reach a deal with AIOC.[73] Nevertheless, if independent and state-owned oil companies began buying and distributing Iranian oil, the resulting revenues would strengthen Mosaddeq's government and eliminate the need for an oil settlement. Britain's entire position would collapse.

Acting as his own foreign secretary while Eden recovered from surgery, Churchill warned Truman on 16 August that allowing Jones to enter Iran and turning AIOC's oil over to American oil interests would deeply damage Anglo-American relations. Truman assured Churchill that the United States did not wish "to profit by your present difficulties," and urged him to accept

Iran's nationalization law and moderate his position on compensation. "If Iran goes down the Communist drain," Truman wrote, "it will be of little satisfaction to any of us that legal positions were defended to the last." The best way to prevent oilmen like Jones from flocking to Iran and shattering the British boycott was to negotiate with Mosaddeq.[74]

In an effort to keep the Americans "in play," Churchill suggested to Truman on 20 August that they make a joint proposal to Mosaddeq. "We are dealing with a man on the very edge of bankruptcy, revolution, and death," he wrote, displaying his talent for rhetorical flourish, "but I still think a man. Our combined approach might convince him." Churchill proposed framing compensation for AIOC in terms of the losses caused by "the nationalization of the enterprise . . . and the termination of the 1933 Concession Agreement, having regard to the claims and counter-claims of both parties." In any event, the terms must not prevent Britain "from maintaining . . . the validity of the 1933 Concession and claiming damages for its unilateral abrogation."[75] Churchill insisted on a joint approach. "I thought that it might do good," he wrote to Truman, "if we had a gallop together such as I often had with F.D.R."[76] Churchill leaned on the legacy of the wartime alliance, but his overture was motivated by the British need to prevent the United States from any action that would interfere with Britain's plans to organize Mosaddeq's downfall. According to one Foreign Office official, it was crucial "that we should not lose momentum. . . . At any minute Musaddiq or the State Department may have another bright idea."[77]

U.S. officials were under no illusions as to why Churchill suggested a *joint* proposal. Secretary of Defense Robert A. Lovett noted the danger of "being tied to the umbilical cord of the British Empire" at a time when the British position in Iran had collapsed and their prestige throughout the Middle East seemed to be in free fall. Rather than a joint message, Lovett suggested the United States and Britain send *parallel* messages, delivering the same proposal through separate means.[78] To preserve Anglo-American unity, however, Truman agreed to a joint offer that called for Iran and the AIOC to sign a sales agreement allowing AIOC to handle Iranian oil exports. Compensation would cover "the nationalization of the enterprise of the AIOC in Iran."[79] If Mosaddeq agreed to these terms, he would receive $10 million in interim aid from the United States, a figure the U.S. embassy calculated would cover Iran's budget expenses for about one month.[80]

The Foreign Office believed that these terms would safeguard British interests in the unlikely event Mosaddeq accepted the offer. Even if Iran succeeded in selling oil outside of its deal with AIOC, other producers would

British Prime Minister Sir Winston Churchill (center) and Foreign Secretary Sir Anthony Eden (left) spearheaded an effort in August 1952 to keep oil talks going while covert assets were organized to oust Mosaddeq. Truman Library, Accession No. 2013-2147.

remain deterred "by the heavy compensation which Persia would have to pay."[81] Meanwhile, Jones, who arrived in Iran on 23 August, told Mosaddeq that for Iranian oil to flow once more, a cooperative arrangement with AIOC would be necessary. The Foreign Office thought he conducted himself "sensibly and helpfully."[82] British fears dissipated. "I have had a try with Truman over Persia," Churchill wrote to a convalescing Eden, and the attitude at Whitehall was "quite content."[83]

Mosaddeq received the Truman-Churchill joint proposal on 27 August and found many problems. He recognized that the opening paragraph, which stipulated that AIOC should receive compensation for its "lost assets and concession," opened the way to a settlement covering the company's future profits under the 1933 concession. Against the threat of a crushing compensation burden, the U.S. offer of $10 million was wholly inadequate: Mosaddeq also suspected the money would come "with strings attached," guessing that further aid would be contingent on an oil deal that favored the companies over Iran's needs. Iran wanted only money that belonged to it "by right," and he demanded that AIOC hand over the £49 million shown on the company's balance sheet as being due to Iran under the never-ratified 1949 Supplemental Agreement.[84]

While Churchill argued the proposal should stand, Truman suggested a redraft allowing the ICJ to determine compensation terms, with neither party questioning "the validity of the nationalization laws," to make them more palatable to Mosaddeq.[85] The British had to be careful not to overplay their hand. Middleton reminded Eden of the need to compromise with the Americans to keep negotiations going. Mosaddeq knew that "we are on the horns of this dilemma and feels that he is in a strong bargaining position." Falle's work with Zahedi was still in its early stages, and a concrete plan for a military coup was nowhere near completion. "I place no reliance whatsoever on . . . intervention by the shah," Middleton wrote, noting that there were "all kinds of anti-Musaddiq plots" popping up in the capital, "[but] I do not consider them significant."[86] In Washington, Ambassador Franks continued to warn against actions that might fray the Anglo-American alliance: "There is considerable risk that the Americans will say that the joint operation is finished . . . [and] go off on their own."[87]

Nevertheless, British leadership refused to agree to any changes to the 27 August joint proposal. Eden accused Mosaddeq of using "blackmail tactics," and Churchill declared, "[w]e have decided to offer what is right and fair. Let the world judge." Eden instructed Franks to tell the Americans that any change would constitute "weakness in the face of Persian pressure."[88]

The United States relented, and Middleton and Henderson resubmitted the proposal to Mosaddeq on 30 August and released the text to the press the same day.[89]

Mosaddeq was outraged, but probably not surprised. Once again, the British were trying to force Iran to agree to compensation terms that would prevent Iran from gaining economically from nationalization. The sales agreement seemed a front to return AIOC to its former position in control of Iranian exports. "Iranians were not donkeys," he told Henderson. The only reason the United States offered such terms was that they sought "to get rid of him and bring in another government." While he regarded the terms as wholly inadequate, Mosaddeq suggested he would have the Majlis consider them when it convened in September.[90]

Eden believed the joint proposal had served as a "valuable demonstration" of Anglo-American unity. Pending further developments, he instructed Franks to point out "that there is still no evidence that financial difficulties have played any part in the increased Communist threat to Persia," as a way to dissuade the United States from taking unilateral action.[91] Complaining that Mosaddeq seemed incapable of "rational thought," Middleton argued that the next few weeks would be decisive, as Mosaddeq would be forced to deal with his mounting political challenges without the benefit of an oil settlement. "I only hope we have not missed any tricks."[92] The British government had not yet abandoned hope of altering the political circumstances inside Iran and remained opposed to any terms that would imperil other oil concessions. Vigilance would be necessary to maintain Anglo-American unity and prevent the United States from making offers of its own.

Zahedi's Coup Plans and the British Expulsion

While he negotiated with the Americans and the British over the oil issue, Mosaddeq consolidated his control over the government in the wake of the July Uprising, drawing on the emergency powers he had secured from the Majlis. These powers gave him the authority to select cabinet ministers and enact legislation without a Majlis vote—though Mosaddeq, as a staunch constitutionalist, continued to permit open debate and a free press. He nevertheless used his new authority to adjust the makeup of his government. After July 1952, the government was dominated by a larger progressive contingent, with a mandate to undertake sweeping reforms to Iran's labor laws, justice system, military, and land tenure. Control over the Majlis and the central bank also allowed Mosaddeq to cover the government's budget deficit by issuing new banknotes, part of new "oil-less" economic strategy designed to help the economy withstand the effects of the British boycott.[93]

Despite his success at retaining power, Mosaddeq faced new challenges from within his original circle of supporters. A diverse coalition of political figures and groups, the National Front had never been particularly cohesive. Its unity before July 1952 stemmed from its commitment to nationalization and its members' loyalty to Mosaddeq. After the July Uprising, that loyalty began to crack. Mozaffar Baqa'i, Hossein Makki, and other National Front leaders grew frustrated with Mosaddeq, who they believed was hoarding power to himself. Some were opposed to Mosaddeq's reform legislation, which threatened the power of the entrenched elite. The prominence of Iran Party members within the post-July government produced "anger and jealousy" among the original National Front coalition, particularly Makki, Baqa'i, and Kashani.[94] At the same time, the rise of the Tudeh Party as a force in politics and the simultaneous decline of the shah and the conservative opposition left a vacuum in politics that formations like Kashani's street network or Baqa'i's Toilers' Party were eager to fill.[95]

On 7 August, Kashani left Tehran, ostensibly embarking on a hajj pilgrimage to Mecca. Middleton reported it was due to "serious disagreements" over Mosaddeq's cabinet appointments.[96] Rumors reached Henderson in late August that the cleric was planning a coup against the government once he returned from his pilgrimage.[97] Facing unrest within his coalition, Mosaddeq also had to contend with challenges from the left and right. On 18 August, a few days after Mosaddeq ended martial law in the capital, fighting broke out between the Tudeh, right-wing demonstrators, and religious groups, forcing Mosaddeq to reinstate martial law on 20 August.[98] On 23 August, he used his authority as war minister to retire 136 high-ranking and pro-shah military officers, many of whom then joined the ranks of Zahedi's supporters in the Retired Officers Association and the Devotees of the Shah, two groups established by the former general to organize anti-Mosaddeq opposition within the military.[99]

The plotting continued as talks over the joint proposals reached an impasse in September. Baqa'i, who had contacted Zahedi in July, met with CIA agents and discussed a break between his Toilers' Party and Mosaddeq.[100] According to one account, the CIA encouraged Baqa'i to distance himself from the prime minister and even offered him money.[101] Baqa'i also sought support from the Rashidians.[102] Kashani continued to marshal street support through the bazaar guilds, clerical organizations, and within the Majlis. Rumors suggested he was also making inroads with the Qashqa'i, or possibly even the Tudeh.[103] Further reports of a possible Kashani-Tudeh alliance came from the CIA and Point Four mission chief William E. Warne.[104]

Though he was successful at warding off political challenges and stabilizing the government's financial position, Mosaddeq continued to regard the resolution of the oil issue as his chief objective. On 16 September, Mosaddeq sent a message to the Majlis via Finance Minister Baqer Kazemi stating he was willing to agree to arbitration by the ICJ for compensation covering AIOC's former assets, with payment of compensation "based on any law followed by any country for nationalization" that AIOC found acceptable. Discussions would depend on the payment of the £49 million AIOC owed Iran. If Britain did not accept these terms, "the continuance of diplomatic relations will be of no use to either party." The deputies declared their support, denounced the joint offer, and delivered a vote of confidence for Mosaddeq by sixty votes to one.[105]

Mosaddeq formally rejected the joint proposal on 24 September. Acheson still felt that a change from Mosaddeq "could only be a change for the worse." Truman agreed, and he turned down Churchill's offer of another joint message. Further pressure on Iran, he warned, "will hasten [Iran's] disintegration and loss."[106] On 5 October, Henderson and Middleton submitted their respective governments' response to Mosaddeq's statement separately. Mosaddeq pointed out that both messages lacked any mention of his request for funds and declared "it is all finished." There was no point in further negotiations: "It was no good negotiating with a dead man and without money Persia would soon be dead."[107] Mosaddeq still wanted AIOC to send representatives to Iran to begin new discussions.[108] Eden, however, believed "a breach of relations" was preferable to abandoning the joint offer, which had maintained AIOC's claim to compensation for future profits. Dragging their feet, the British did not respond to Mosaddeq's request until 14 October, dismissing the £49 million as a "fictitious debt" and insisting again on compensation for the "unilateral termination of the 1933 Concession."[109]

With the joint proposal discussions going nowhere, Mosaddeq chose to strike directly at the opposition forces arrayed against him. On 13 October, he had the Rashidian brothers and a notable pro-British general arrested on charges of conspiracy. Zahedi, Kashani, and Baqa'i were also involved, but escaped arrest due to their parliamentary immunity. Foreign Minister Hossein Fatemi announced to the press that the conspirators had been working with a "foreign embassy." Available sources suggest that Falle and Middleton encouraged Zahedi, though they did not rate his chances of success very highly.[110] Falle had met with Zahedi on 12 October, finding him "bubbling with optimism" at the thought of working with Kashani and Baqa'i. The degree of Falle and Middleton's support of Zahedi is not known, but Falle noted after this meeting that Zahedi, "whatever his chances of success," was performing a "useful task in uniting the discouraged and dispersed opposition." Baqa'i had been meeting with the CIA as well as opposition figures, but there is no evidence of any formal U.S. participation in the incipient October coup, though local agents may have been involved under the umbrella of the TPBEDAMN program.[111]

On 15 October, Zahedi addressed the Senate, denouncing Mosaddeq's "dictatorial government," while extolling his own credentials as a military commander and former minister of the interior.[112] Since Zahedi was a senator and immune from arrest or prosecution, Mosaddeq chose not to take action against him. On 22 October, however, he made good on his threat from 7 August and ordered the British embassy to close and all British citizens to leave Iran. The next day, the National Front deputies in the Majlis ordered the Senate to dissolve, arguing that the body had exhausted its constitutional term.[113] In a single stroke, the prime minister crippled Britain's ability to interfere in Iran's internal politics and neutralized another source of opposition.

Conclusion

The break in relations and the closing of the British embassy were a direct result of the British efforts to force Mosaddeq from power. After October 1952, London would play a much smaller role in Iranian affairs. Already expelled from their dominant position astride the Khuzestan oil fields and the Abadan refinery, the British found themselves in a position of secondary importance to the United States, now the preeminent power in Iran.

Securing American cooperation had always played an important role in British strategy, and the loss of their position in Iran forced the British to rely even more on U.S. help. The British nevertheless held fast to the principles laid out in the joint offer. AIOC had to receive compensation for loss of the concession as well as physical assets, and any agreement had to include provisions that enabled Iran to earn sufficient revenue to pay compensation, which in practice meant a continued role for AIOC. The British also continued to insist that Mosaddeq was dangerous, unreliable, and ought to be replaced. Following Falle's "self-sacrificing line," they argued that leaving Mosaddeq in power would lead to communist control, in the hope that this would galvanize the United States into action.

The events of July–October 1952 forced a change in U.S. policy. A report filed by the CIA on 14 October just hours after Mosaddeq disrupted the Zahedi coup attempt estimated that the prime minister would remain in power "at least for the next six months." He had subordinated the shah and controlled the army, but his position was precarious, and should he fall from power he would almost certainly be replaced by Kashani or the Tudeh.[114] Neither of these outcomes was acceptable, and with the situation in Iran deteriorating, the United States decided to take a more active role in the search for a settlement to the oil dispute. According to Acheson, he and his colleagues concluded that the British were so determined on a "rule or ruin" policy in Iran that the United States would have to take independent steps to salvage the situation, or risk losing Iran to communist control and putting the rest of the Middle East and its oil in danger.[115]

5 The Final Attempt

. . . .

Following the British withdrawal from Iran in October 1952, the United States launched another effort to resolve the oil dispute. Analysis of the situation convinced U.S. policymakers that any attempt to remove Mosaddeq through a coup would probably fail due to the weakness of the opposition and the unreliability of the shah. Even if it were possible to oust Mosaddeq, the most likely beneficiary would be Ayatollah Abolqassem Kashani, who U.S. analysts believed would follow policies that increased the chances of a Tudeh takeover. In its final months in office, the Truman administration hoped to boost Mosaddeq's financial position enough to keep him in power and agree to an oil settlement. The U.S. plan called for reviving the Iranian oil industry through an arrangement that left production and refining under Iranian control but allowed AIOC and the other major oil companies to distribute Iranian oil to international markets, thus providing Iran with sufficient revenues to stabilize its economy and pay AIOC compensation. The plan hinged on Britain and Iran reaching agreement on the compensation issue.

According to Secretary of State Dean Acheson, the negotiations "came very close" to a final settlement.[1] Progress during the grueling and complex discussions was slowed by British intransigence on the issue of compensation. The British insisted that AIOC had to be compensated not only for physical assets but also for the profits the company would have earned had its concession been allowed to run until 1993. The British knew that Mosaddeq would never accept this condition, but they stuck firmly to their position. British intransigence on the compensation issue ensured that oil negotiations would fail. In addition, an Iranian political crisis in late February 1953 revealed deep divisions between Mosaddeq and the shah, with many of Mosaddeq's former supporters turning against him. U.S. interest in finding a negotiated solution faded away amid a growing belief that only intervention and regime change could solve the stalemate over oil and preserve the position of the monarchy. The changing calculus surrounding Iranian oil and the Iranian political situation were crucial in producing the U.S. decision in early 1953 to support a coup to remove Mosaddeq from power.

Looking for Alternatives, September 1952

In mid-September 1952, as the prospects for a negotiated settlement faded, U.S. policymakers concluded that a change in policy was necessary to prevent the loss of Iran. The British strategy of applying economic and political pressure to force a change in government had failed. Rather than replacing Mosaddeq, British policy had increased the influence of Iranian nationalism, undermined the position of the traditional elite and the shah, and strengthened the Tudeh. The likely outcome of such policies would not be Mosaddeq's capitulation, but the collapse of his government and a Kashani succession, followed closely by a Tudeh takeover. Given these circumstances, the United States began exploring alternative ways to prevent the loss of Iran to communist control.[2]

One option was to back the shah. On 22 August, Ray Allen, director of the Psychological Strategy Board, had met Max W. Thornburg, former advisor to the Iranian government, and discussed Thornburg's views about a coup. An oilman who had worked for SOCAL during the 1930s and the State Department during World War II, Thornburg had enjoyed a lucrative tenure as economic counselor to the shah's government before nationalization.[3] Arguing that the oil question "could not be settled until there were a government in Persia that wanted to settle it," Thornburg contended that the way forward would be to remove Mosaddeq and replace his government with one committed to economic development. As oil was the only sizable source of income from which Iran could fund such projects, the new government would be compelled to enter into an agreement that would restart the flow of Iranian oil along terms the British and major companies would find acceptable. "The most promising figure around whom a responsible government can be built," Thornburg concluded, "is the shah."[4] Thornburg believed the shah should exercise dictatorial powers, closing newspapers, arresting dissidents, declaring martial law, and ruling by decree. With backing from the United States, the shah would become the critical actor in Iran, "regardless of who is his Prime Minister."[5] What Thornburg was advocating was a return to Iran's pre-1941 regime, an authoritarian government run by the shah and backed by the army.

Thornburg had powerful supporters, most notably the deputy director of the CIA, Allen W. Dulles. A State Department Middle East specialist before the war, Dulles served as an agent for the Office of Strategic Services (OSS) during World War II. After the war he worked as a lawyer for the firm Sullivan and Cromwell alongside his brother John Foster Dulles. He worked briefly with Thornburg's company in Iran, Overseas Consultants Inc., in 1949.[6] According to an internal CIA history of the agency's operation in Iran, Dulles tended to rely on "personal acquaintances" like Thornburg for analysis of the situation in Iran, rather than intelligence specialists in the CIA or State Department. Dulles regarded Thornburg as an expert on Iranian affairs, even though Thornburg had never studied Iranian history, culture, or language, and he encouraged Thornburg to draft a longer "think piece" outlining the ideas he presented in August.[7]

Thornburg's ideas found little support elsewhere in the U.S. government. John H. Leavitt, chief of the CIA's Iran Branch, believed that it was "extremely unlikely" that the shah would agree to support such an operation, due to his personal indecision and the risks involved. Leavitt, who believed that a functional democracy would not emerge in Iran for many years, recommended that the CIA should build a network "dedicated to maintaining the loyalty of the Army to the Shah," before attempting to push Mosaddeq from power through a military coup.[8] Donald Wilber, a former OSS operative and scholar of Persian architecture who worked with Leavitt, also felt that the shah's "record for indecision" meant he could not be trusted to support a military coup.[9] Arthur L. Richards in the State Department's Office of Greek, Turkish, and Iranian Affairs also found Thornburg's faith in the shah "ill-informed and unrealistic."[10]

The British tried to convince the Americans that a coup was necessary to save Iran, and on 8 October sent the State Department a paper, "The Communist Danger to Persia." Instead of emphasizing the threat of nationalization to British interests, the paper focused on the communist threat and argued that since Mosaddeq had been prime minister the Tudeh had greatly expanded its influence, while the influence of the shah and the army had been "seriously undermined." Should current trends continue, the Tudeh would inevitably come to power. This outcome could be prevented by backing a military government to supplant Mosaddeq. "Absolute Anglo-United States solidarity" was essential, for without such unity Mosaddeq would be able to play the United States and Britain against each other.[11] Assistant Secretary of State for Near East, South Asian, and African Affairs Henry A. Byroade worried that the paper did not "come to grips with the true nature of the Iranian problem." The British view of Mosaddeq as "the worst possible Premier Iran could have" was significantly at odds with the views of U.S. officials, who believed that Mosaddeq's nationalist government "at least [had] a chance . . . to combat Tudeh rule," as there was no better alternative in sight.[12]

Other options also faced obstacles. Kermit Roosevelt, chief of the CIA's Near East Division, put great stock in the CIA's ability to train and arm guerrillas from the Qashqa'i tribe, part of the "special political measures" cited in a National Security Council policy statement draft circulating in early October.[13] The CIA recognized that such plans were "insufficient to prevent a Tudeh coup," and an internal assessment concluded that the CIA was "not in a position to influence the Iranian government" in any meaningful direction.[14] Short of a military invasion, the United States did not have the means to change the government inside Iran, according to the Joint Chiefs of Staff.[15]

Another option was to stabilize Iran by restoring Iranian oil exports. Although the British-led boycott, coupled with the limited number of oil tankers available outside the control of AIOC and the other major oil companies, had effectively shut down exports, the International Court of Justice decision from July 1952 had weakened the legal foundation of the boycott. Most U.S. experts believed that it would become progressively more difficult to prevent independent and state-owned oil companies from buying Iranian oil.[16] A State Department analysis estimated that Iran would be able to sell around 100,000 to 150,000 barrels of oil per day to independent and state-owned companies. The alternative to allowing Iranian oil back into world markets, Director of the Policy Planning Staff Paul Nitze argued on 22 September, was the "inevitable loss of Iran to the free world," as the financial pressure would eventually force Mosaddeq to turn to the Soviets for help or facilitate his fall and the rise of a new Tudeh-led government.[17]

Independent oil companies were very interested in Iran. Cities Service head W. Alton Jones traveled to Iran in mid-August, met Mosaddeq and other prominent Iranians, and toured oil facilities. Although Jones recommended to Mosaddeq that Iran settle with AIOC, he also made it clear that Cities Service was ready to supply technicians to help Iran run the Abadan refinery and to buy Iranian oil if it were clear that no settlement between AIOC and Iran were possible.[18] Byroade recommended that the United States cease discouraging U.S. oil companies from getting involved in Iran. While the reappearance of Iranian oil in world markets would lead to price competition, Byroade argued that such a policy would not encourage other companies to nationalize foreign oil concessions. The psychological damage had already been done, and the amounts Iran would be able to sell were significantly less than what the other major Middle Eastern producing countries were selling, thus lessening incentives to follow Iran's example.[19]

The British vehemently objected to the U.S. government giving a "green light" to purchasers of Iranian oil in the absence of a settlement on compensation. The major U.S. oil companies were very concerned about the threat of renewed Iranian exports to the oil price structure, and they also opposed the plan. In addition, selling oil in small volumes to independent and state-owned companies at steep discounts would not deliver sufficient financial relief for Iran or leave it with enough money left over to pay "adequate" compensation to AIOC. What was needed was a way to allow Iran to export more oil without disrupting pricing arrangements. In light of these problems, the State Department put the idea of relying on independent oil companies to revive Iranian oil exports on hold.[20] Warning that the situation in Iran had become critical, Nitze argued in early October that it was crucial to find a "road to a solution" or face "a further dramatic turn towards eventual Communist control of Iran."[21] He therefore began work on a new plan to get Iranian oil flowing again.

The Consortium Approach: Breaking with the British

Nitze's plan, which he and other U.S. officials presented to the British in a series of meetings in mid-October, called for the formation of a consortium of the major international oil companies, including AIOC, to purchase and distribute Iranian oil. The consortium would purchase 25 million tons of oil from Iran over the course of fifteen years at a price that would result in a fifty-fifty division of profits. To meet Iran's immediate needs, the plan initially called for the consortium to advance Iran $100 million against future purchases of oil. Subsequent versions of the plan called for the U.S. government to make the $100 million advance against future deliveries of oil through the Defense Materials Procurement Agency. The plan addressed the compensation issue by proposing that AIOC receive 10 million tons of "free oil" per year for three years, which worked out to be around $420 million. AIOC would pay Iran £20 million (approximately $56 million) to settle counterclaims. The consortium would manage marketing and distribution, while Iran would remain in control of production and refining. The British did not like these terms. They especially objected to idea of a lump sum of $420 million for compensation, which they argued was far too low. They continued to insist that compensation be set through arbitration, with terms of reference that included compensation for lost profits.[22]

Problems of a different sort arose with the U.S. Department of Justice. President Truman, over the objections of the State Department, had authorized the Justice Department to begin a grand jury investigation of the major international oil companies in June 1952. Utilizing a report by the

Federal Trade Commission, the Justice Department charged that the largest companies acted as a cartel and controlled the world oil industry through a series of agreements to divide markets, fix prices, control production, and monopolize reserves.[23] After Secretary of State Acheson outlined Nitze's plan during a meeting on 8 October, Attorney General James McGranery argued that it would be "most difficult" to pursue the consortium approach (which would require cooperation between the major companies) and Justice's antitrust action at the same time. Secretary of Defense Robert Lovett thought the antitrust investigation was "a mistake," while General Omar Bradley, chairman of the Joint Chiefs of Staff, warned that pushing the antitrust investigation risked access to overseas reserves of iron and oil by making the major companies seem like "criminals." Acheson argued that Nitze's plan recognized the realities of the world oil economy. "One of the concrete problems" in bringing Iranian oil back into the market "is determin[ing] whom it is we can count on. . . . The independents are not in position to give us any real help." Only the majors, including AIOC, were capable of moving Iranian oil in the volume necessary to deliver financial relief to Mosaddeq's government.[24]

The situation in Iran prompted Secretary Lovett to recommend on 24 October that the United States provide Iran with immediate economic assistance and help Iran start up its oil industry and find markets for its oil. Such action would be "tantamount to the extension of the Truman Doctrine to Iran," and should be taken independently of the British "if necessary." To minimize the risk of damaging relations with the British, Lovett recommended that the United States should do its best to ensure that AIOC received "reasonable compensation for the loss of their properties."[25] Acheson replied on 4 November that Britain was "the most important element" in the Western alliance, and unilateral action by the United States "could do deep and lasting harm" not only to relations with Britain but to relations with the other NATO allies as well. Therefore, the objective of U.S. policy had to be "to save Iran without unnecessarily damaging our relations with the United Kingdom." Lovett agreed but contended that the United States, "with or without British approval," needed to be ready to take action in Iran before a military intervention became necessary—a situation, Lovett noted, "for which we are not prepared."[26]

Acheson informed President Truman on 7 November that the State Department plan required the cooperation of the major U.S. oil companies. The president would have to authorize their participation under the Defense Production Act to protect them from antitrust action. President

Truman approved the plan the same day.[27] Acheson and Truman met with President-Elect Dwight D. Eisenhower on 18 November to brief him on the situation. Acheson explained that both sides in the oil dispute had proven intransigent, requiring the United States to develop a new plan to break the deadlock. The new plan was dependent on British cooperation because AIOC would be needed to provide markets for large volumes of Iranian oil. Allowing U.S. companies to take over AIOC's former markets would bring them into "violent competition and conflict" with the British, disrupting world oil markets and undermining Anglo-American unity.[28] Although the United States was prepared to pressure the British to cooperate, in the final analysis, the United States would have to acquiesce if the British refused to change their policy.

Despite U.S. plans to provide financial assistance to Iran, it would be a mistake to characterize U.S. policy as anti-British or pro-Mosaddeq. Although the United States did not support the British plan for a coup d'état, Acheson continued to prioritize maintaining Anglo-American unity. U.S. reluctance to back a coup at this time was not due to lack of will but rather to strong doubts that a coup would succeed. Moreover, military options to intervene in Iran were limited. General Omar Bradley warned the National Security Council on 19 November that the United States could not move troops to Iran without disrupting commitments in other areas, including Korea, pointing out that a "substantial augmentation" of U.S. forces (likely requiring a draft) would be necessary to maintain all commitments.[29] Finally, the U.S. government did not want to restart Iranian oil exports in a way that would disrupt the major companies' control of global oil markets and regarded the antitrust laws as an inconvenient obstacle to resolving the crisis.

The National Security Council approved Nitze's plan on 20 November in a policy statement that highlighted rising instability in Iran and the need for U.S. intervention. The National Front had vanquished all opposition other than the Tudeh Party, and while it appeared likely that Mosaddeq would retain power through 1953, "present trends in Iran were unfavorable to the maintenance of control by a non-communist government for an extended period of time." The failure of Mosaddeq's government to restart the oil industry was "likely to produce a progressive deterioration of the economy." Since it was clear that Great Britain no longer possessed the capability of maintaining stability in Iran, the United States had to intervene and do what was necessary to prevent the loss of Iran to communism, including "special political measures" (covert action) if the communist threat became more acute.[30]

Moving swiftly to implement the policies approved by the National Security Council, Acheson informed British Foreign Secretary Anthony Eden on 21 November that the United States was planning to undertake "a new and more vigorous effort" to salvage the situation in Iran. While the United States would always consult with Britain and try to find a solution acceptable to the British government, "in the last analysis . . . the US government may have no alternative but to move forward in a manner best designed in its opinion to save Iran."[31] Acheson later recalled that "the first and [most] pressing problem" was getting money to Iran; resolving the Anglo-Iranian oil crisis on terms that would be acceptable to the British was the second concern.[32]

The British viewed the U.S. decision to proceed with a new oil proposal as a setback. Conversations with President-Elect Eisenhower and his Secretary of State–Designate John Foster Dulles gave the British hope, however, that Republican sympathy for big business and concern for U.S. overseas investment, coupled with a desire to show some quick successes against communism, would lead the new administration to take a strong line with Mosaddeq. On the other hand, the British were concerned about the influence of independent oil companies on the new administration and whether "Mr. Dulles' somewhat tortuous mind" would reach the correct conclusion on how to deal with Mosaddeq. It would be necessary to "keep the Americans in play" until the policies of the new administration could be assessed, one British official noted.[33]

The Treasury and Ministry of Fuel and Power continued to stress the importance of the compensation issue and warned that surrendering to Nitze and Acheson's lump sum idea would leave the door open "to other countries to follow Persia's example in breaking their concession contracts."[34] The British government remained determined to hold the line on the oil issue, waiting out the Truman administration's final effort. Worried about losing U.S. support, Eden agreed to the rest of the plan on the condition that Mosaddeq accept suitable terms for compensation. Though he continued to regard Mosaddeq as a "reckless fanatic," Britain, he promised, would not stand in the way of U.S. discussions with Mosaddeq.[35]

The British also stepped up their efforts to convince the Americans that removing Mosaddeq was both possible and necessary "to save Iran." Since their embassy in Tehran had been closed, the British would need extensive American cooperation in the effort to unseat Mosaddeq. On 22 October, British officials met with Roosevelt of the CIA and John Jernegan of the State

Department. The British argued that the greatest danger did not lie in Iran's "bad financial situation," but in Mosaddeq's "unwillingness to take measures to check the growth of communist strength." According to the memoirs of former MI6 Tehran station chief Christopher Montague ("Monty") Woodhouse, emphasizing communism was a premeditated tactic for gaining American support for the British coup plan, codenamed Operation Boot. Unfortunately for them, it was not very effective. To the British arguments that Mosaddeq could survive financially, the U.S. officials countered that if the army went unpaid, "it would in time disintegrate and thus destroy the last concrete barrier against the Tudeh." Mosaddeq could cover his budget deficit by printing new notes and raiding Iran's gold reserves, but U.S. officials were wary of allowing Iran's economy to slowly disintegrate, arguing that financial assistance or a deal to restart the oil industry and renew the flow of revenues to the Iranian state was necessary to arrest Iran's slide into communism.[36]

When Woodhouse and Sam Falle, an MI6 operative and former oriental counselor of the British Embassy in Iran, arrived in Washington in November to discuss potential operations, they found support in the CIA, where Deputy Director Allen Dulles, head of covert operations Frank Wisner, and Near East and Africa Division chief Kermit Roosevelt all responded favorably. The State Department, however, remained skeptical. Byroade felt that the British plan was "full of dangers and uncertainties," which would not end even after the successful execution of a coup. Moreover, the United States was preparing a "new approach" for reaching a settlement. Therefore, Byroade told the British that while the United States did not want to dismiss their plan entirely, it would not consider such a course of action until "at least one more effort" had been made to reach an oil agreement.[37]

Getting the Companies on Board

The key assumption behind the U.S. plan was that of the limited options available, Mosaddeq was the best barrier to the spread of communist influence inside Iran. The U.S. plan did not offer Mosaddeq carte blanche regarding the oil issue. Iran would not be permitted to sell oil freely. Rather, the plan, known as the "package proposal," sought to tie Iran back into the global oil economy dominated by U.S. and British oil companies. AIOC would take at least half of Iran's oil exports and distribute them through its global commercial network. Before receiving $100 million in U.S. aid,

In late 1952, Paul Nitze, head of the Policy Planning Staff, devised a new plan to resolve the oil dispute. Truman Library, Accession No. 83-171.

Mosaddeq would have to accept third-party arbitration to resolve compensation for AIOC on terms the British could accept. Though in many respects a favorable deal, the plan did not grant Iran the freedom to sell its oil in quantities and at prices of its own choosing. To pay compensation at the level the British demanded, Iran would have to work with AIOC and the other major international oil companies to sell large quantities of oil and would probably have little left over for its own needs. The package proposal continued the pattern initially set by the offers of the Jackson, Harriman, and Stokes missions in 1951: it recognized the principle of nationalization without actually allowing Iran full control of its oil industry.

Nitze met with the companies on 21 and 29 November, while Acheson joined him for discussions on 4 and 9 December. According to Acheson, these discussions "were perhaps the longest and most difficult" of the entire oil crisis.[38] The companies refused to cooperate without written protection from the attorney general shielding them from antitrust action. Nitze promised protection under the Defense Production Act. Acheson focused on the broader strategic concerns. The goal was "to save Iran from going

Communist." Although Acheson disparaged the Iranians, claiming that they were led by "emotions" and the "foment of nationalism," he insisted that Iran was poised on the brink of a "real revolution," and it was necessary to restart the flow of oil to stabilize its economy and government. The oil executives worried that the terms of Nitze's plan would undermine fifty-fifty contracts, warning that if Iran received terms better than those in Saudi Arabia or Kuwait, it would have "cataclysmic results" for U.S. oil concessions. The oil executives regarded the "sanctity of contracts" as the primary issue and argued that Iran should seek a new concessionary agreement with AIOC and pay adequate compensation. Acheson "recognized that this was not a very attractive business," but stressed that the United States required their assistance to get Iran "out of the danger zone."[39]

The meetings revealed the issues separating the American policymakers from their counterparts in the oil industry. While Nitze and Acheson were willing to make certain concessions to restart Iran's oil industry, the companies were resistant to upsetting the pre-nationalization status quo. The Foreign Office learned that the companies were "intensely" opposed to the State Department's proposal and would cooperate "only as instructed."[40] Like the British, the companies were preoccupied by the question of compensation. Meeting privately with Nitze, Eugene Holman, head of Jersey Standard, argued that compensation would have to include "some consideration for losses" beyond physical property, including "rupture of contract."[41] Overall, the companies seemed more interested in defeating nationalization and punishing Iran for its challenge to the global oil order than preventing eventual communist control. Nevertheless, the companies agreed to Nitze's plan for AIOC to take 10 million tons of oil from Iran in the first year, with U.S. companies taking another 10 million tons. The volumes were necessary to provide for repayment of the $100 million aid package, while leaving enough revenues available for Iran to cover compensation for AIOC, which would be determined through arbitration.[42]

As it prepared for negotiations to start again, the United States made tactical maneuvers designed to increase its leverage over the British in case they dragged their feet on the package proposal. On 6 December, the State Department announced that it no longer objected to U.S. companies purchasing oil from Iran.[43] On 10 December, Henderson met with the chairman of the Export-Import Bank, suggesting it would be "extremely helpful" if the Bank reconsidered the $25 million loan originally offered to Iran in 1950.[44] The British were categorically opposed to offering new aid to Mosaddeq, and Eden protested any move to extend loans while Mosaddeq kept to his "rigid" negotiation stance.[45] Another factor in compelling British co-operation was Alton Jones, the independent oilman who had visited Iran in the summer, and who was a friend of President-Elect Eisenhower. Jones began making plans to visit Iran again in early 1953. The State Department agreed to delay further discussions with the Export-Import Bank but was prepared to move forward on the loan if the British proved uncooperative.[46] If negotiations failed, a possible backup plan proposed supplying Mosaddeq with enough aid to keep his government afloat for the next twelve to fifteen months.[47]

With only a few weeks left in office, the Truman administration was determined to bring the talks to a successful conclusion. While the cooperation of the companies and the British would be needed to make the package proposal work, negotiations to secure Mosaddeq's agreement to the plan were also necessary. Ambassador Henderson briefed the senior staff of the National Security Council and members of the incoming Eisenhower administration, including future Secretary of State John Foster Dulles, on 2 December. The Iranians, he contended, were "emotional to an almost suicidal degree," and it was nearly impossible to guess how the situation in Iran would evolve. The shah was now a "negligible influence," while General Fazlollah Zahedi, the leader in October's unsuccessful military coup, did not have "any real following" in the army. Continuing oil discussions appeared the only acceptable path forward.[48] According to an analysis from John Stutesman in the State Department, Mosaddeq was firmly in control but had come under pressure from the "irrational political and psychological attitudes of his nationalist supporters." It was vital that a new offer be made soon, before the prime minister buckled under this pressure and either succumbed to the wishes of his leftist supporters or stepped down to make way for Kashani.[49]

The Package Proposal: "Finding the Right Words"

The package proposal assembled in late 1952 was the most detailed attempt to resolve the oil crisis. The United States was prepared to concede Iran's ownership of its oil industry, Iranian management of oil production and refining, and even Iran's right to sell oil independently, provided it entered an agreement to sell a large amount of oil to a consortium of the major international oil companies, including AIOC, and agreed to pay adequate compensation to AIOC. The terms offered to Mosaddeq were more conciliatory than any that had come before, but on the key issue of compensation, the

United States and Great Britain continued to insist that payment could not be limited to physical assets but also had to cover lost future profits. The British insisted on making this condition explicit in the agreement, but U.S. policymakers worried that stating such terms would doom an agreement with Mosaddeq, who was understandably wary of any deal that might saddle Iran with a heavy debt burden.

Henderson returned to Tehran and met with Mosaddeq on 25 December. The meeting was secret. Mosaddeq agreed to meet with Henderson without any of his advisors present, and no news was leaked to the Iranian press. Henderson laid out the terms of the package proposal. The United States would offer Iran $100 million in exchange for 20 million tons of oil, to be distributed by the major companies through a sales agreement with the National Iranian Oil Company (NIOC). Iran would be left "master of its own oil industry." In return, Mosaddeq would agree to third-party arbitration to settle AIOC's compensation award, using Britain's 1945 Coal Nationalization Act as a basis. The use of this law was intentional. In a message to Mosaddeq on 3 December, Henderson had pointed out that the Coal Act took into account earnings the owners of the nationalized property "might reasonably be expected to earn in the future." Using the law was thus a tactic meant to bring Mosaddeq into an agreement that would allow Britain to claim compensation for the value of its concession and its lost future profits.[50] Henderson asked Mosaddeq if he realized that the Coal Act had covered compensation for loss of future profits. Mosaddeq replied that if the arbitrator decided to use that law as the basis for determining compensation, "he would not object." Henderson stressed that "practically the whole business world" would reject terms of reference that limited compensation to only physical assets. Although Henderson believed he had tricked Mosaddeq into agreeing to British demands, Mosaddeq had a doctorate in international law and probably knew that the Coal Act would not guarantee AIOC compensation for loss of future profits. The Coal Act provided for compensation for lost profits to the owners of the nationalized assets. In the British case, private companies owned the coal reserves. In contrast, AIOC had a concession to produce and export Iranian oil, but *ownership* of subsoil oil reserves remained in the hands of the Iranian government.[51] Mosaddeq therefore accepted the Coal Act on the belief that it would not undermine Iran's position on compensation or offer extra benefits to the British.

Acheson felt the discussions with Mosaddeq were a "constructive step."[52] Mosaddeq's willingness to conduct them in secret was evidence of his desire to come to an agreement. Acheson wrote to Eden that it was imperative they take advantage of the "change in [Mosaddeq's] attitude."[53] On 2 January Mosaddeq agreed to enter into talks with a group of major companies including AIOC for a sales agreement once he had received U.S. financial aid.[54] The British regarded Mosaddeq's tactics as blackmail.[55] They were determined to have payments to Mosaddeq linked to a long-term contract with AIOC, one that would guarantee British control of the flow of Iranian oil and ensure Iran possessed the means to pay compensation.[56] The British government, which had already stated its willingness to let Iran sell oil once the arbitration agreement was in place, also argued it was absolutely necessary that both be concluded simultaneously.[57] The British insisted that Mosaddeq explicitly commit to arbitration terms based on the Coal Act, including provisions for compensation "on the loss of future profits."[58]

Henderson grew impatient with the "leisurely" pace in London. Like Acheson, Henderson thought it encouraging that Mosaddeq kept details of his meetings out of the press. Tehran dailies like *Ettelaat* and popular weekly magazines like *Tehran Musavvar* could only speculate as to the substance of the oil negotiations.[59] "His tenacity in maintaining this secrecy under pressure," wrote Henderson, "is an indication to me of his real desire for an oil settlement."[60] Calling on the prime minister on 8 January, Henderson found him depressed, anxious, and suspicious of British delays. He expressed his readiness to return Anglo-Iranian relations to a "friendly" basis and stated once again his commitment to a suitable commercial agreement, as the oil problem "would not be solved if Iranian oil did not return to world markets."[61] The prime minister promised swift Majlis ratification for their agreement once he received concrete terms outlining how compensation would be handled.[62]

The British remained focused on the protection of their commercial interests. Moreover, they continued to believe that Mosaddeq could be removed from power. As a result, discussions in London proceeded slowly. Henry A. Byroade, leading the U.S. team in London, insisted to Eden that Mosaddeq would not accept terms that explicitly covered loss of future profits. The utility of the Coal Act lay in its vagueness, which Mosaddeq could use as a shield against Iranian public opinion.[63] The British, however, had begun to back away from the Coal Act, complaining that it was "a badly drafted law filled with ambiguity." They now insisted on adding new wording that would provide a "proper basis" for determining compensation.[64] The Foreign Office's legal counsel pointed out on 13 January that the Coal Act did not cover a concession to exploit a natural resource, but rather "the physically enumerated assets, including the coal deposits themselves owned by private companies" that had been nationalized. Therefore, the British would have to insist that any agreement on arbitration had to include explicit language acknowledging AIOC's right to claim compensation for the loss of its "rights and interests" in Iran as well as for loss of property.[65] Otherwise, an arbitration ruling might find that the nationalized assets did not include future profits, AIOC would get a smaller compensation award, and other countries might consider nationalizing their own oil industries. The stakes for Britain were thus very high and hinged on the specific language used in the compensation terms.

British officials handed Byroade a draft on 11 January indicating the Coal Act would provide the "principle," rather than the "basis," for determining compensation. Byroade recognized that the change was "designed to give loose and more vague terminology [to] the terms of the reference."[66] Henderson, kept informed of discussions in London, felt this would be unacceptable to Mosaddeq in light of the "public relations" problems he would face selling the deal to his supporters.[67] Though he agreed with Henderson, Acheson was sympathetic to British concerns and suggested that arbitration terms be crafted to offer the British "an even broader and more comprehensive formula." If the terms were not acceptable, Acheson suggested, Henderson could pursue a lump sum compensation deal that bypassed arbitration, even though this was an approach the British previously opposed.[68]

The threat of unilateral U.S. action forced the British to come up with new terms. According to Archibald Ross of the Foreign Office, the terms had to satisfy Mosaddeq "and still leave no doubt . . . that claims for loss of future profits are admissible."[69] After discussions with Eden on 13 January, Byroade agreed to terms that provided for compensation for AIOC's "loss of enterprise," with the arbitration tribunal employing the "principles" of any British law nationalizing any industry in the United Kingdom. A British note emphasized that these new terms would include consideration for future profits, "without mentioning the UK Coal Act."[70] Byroade accepted this formula. The U.S. desire to keep the British on board trumped their worries over Mosaddeq's "public relations" problems. Although based in extensive research in British records, previous accounts of the negotiations do not discuss the British shift from reliance on the Coal Act to insisting on accompanying terms that explicitly included loss of future profits.[71] They thus give the erroneous impression that it was Mosaddeq rather than the British who backtracked and reinforce the conceit that he did not understand the issues.

The wording would prove decisive. For the British, American acceptance of "loss of enterprise" constituted an important victory. Eden wrote to Churchill, then in Jamaica, that the final terms "contain no disagreeable departure from our previous plans." Should Mosaddeq accept them, the terms offered a satisfactory conclusion "both financially and politically on this long and troublesome business."[72] With the final barrier removed, the proposal was sent to Henderson on 14 January, with Byroade wishing him "Good luck!"[73]

Meanwhile, in Washington, the Truman administration took action to provide U.S. oil companies with protection against the Department of Justice antitrust suit. In a 6 January report to the National Security Council, drafted with the assistance of Aramco lobbyist James Terry Duce, the Departments of Defense, State, and the Interior argued that the security and prosperity of the United States and its allies depended on maintaining access to foreign oil. The major international oil companies provided this access, and "they alone" were capable of maintaining and expanding access in the future. The antitrust case threatened national security by harming the reputations of the major companies and increasing the risk that they would be expelled from the major foreign oil-producing countries. The Department of Justice countered with the argument that cartelistic activities by the major companies were a greater threat, as they promoted ill feeling among producing nations and accelerated the trend toward nationalization.[74]

The National Security Council discussed the issue on 9 January, and three days later President Truman, apparently convinced by General Bradley's warning that a criminal case against the companies was a "serious threat to national security," ordered Attorney General McGranery to drop the criminal case in favor of a civil suit.[75] On 14 January, the National Security Council requested antitrust protection for U.S. companies "to participate in an international consortium to purchase oil," reactivate the Abadan refinery, "and provide therefore to the friendly government of Iran substantial revenues on terms which will protect the interests of the Western world in the oil resources of the Middle East."[76] The package proposal needed the support of the major companies, which would be responsible for moving and marketing Iranian oil, delivering the financial aid Iran needed, and they would not cooperate without protection from the antitrust laws. The U.S. decision not to proceed with antitrust action was thus closely linked to the Iran oil crisis. Much, however, hinged on whether or not Mosaddeq would accept the new British compensation terms.

"Loss of Enterprise": Oil Negotiations, January–February 1953

Mosaddeq understood that "loss of enterprise" was a legal construction designed to ensure AIOC received a massive compensation award, a move that would limit the success of nationalization and threatened to restore the pre-nationalization status quo. Such an outcome was intolerable. From the very beginning, nationalization had been primarily a political project, rather than an economic one. While Mosaddeq was not opposed to selling oil to foreign companies, he prioritized Iran's independence from foreign control over the perceived economic rewards that might come from cooperating with the major international oil companies. He tried to convince Henderson that such terms were impossible for him to accept, but he was in a precarious political situation and did not want discussions to end prematurely, as continued talks allowed him to claim U.S. support for his government.

Mosaddeq wanted to maintain U.S. support for a number of reasons. Though he prioritized the political aspects of the oil issue, Mosaddeq needed financial relief. While his "oil-less" economic reforms had been somewhat successful at boosting exports, cutting imports, and preserving the country's stock of foreign exchange, the government had been covering its budget deficit by printing new currency. Like most of his contemporaries, Mosaddeq feared the return of wartime inflation, when Iran's currency had depreciated by more than 1,000 percent. Selling Iran's nationalized oil on terms deemed acceptable to his supporters would constitute a major victory and solidify Mosaddeq's political position while bolstering the country's finances and cooling rising labor tensions in the oil fields. Although the Tudeh Party had supported his return in July 1952, Mosaddeq maintained his distance from Iran's communists. He also avoided a closer relationship with the Soviet Union, which continued to regard him as a bourgeois nationalist, denying a Soviet request to renew their fishing concession in the Caspian Sea.[77] His willingness to negotiate a new oil deal, and his evident eagerness to secure new U.S. aid, demonstrated his desire to cement ties with the West, though he still wished to preserve Iran's independence according to the principles of negative equilibrium.

Mosaddeq had to balance the demands of the conservative and progressive elements of his coalition. He drew support from a small group of advisors, his deputy and foreign minister Hossein Fatemi, and the army, which remained loyal to the government so long as the prime minister maintained cordial ties with the shah.[78] Mozaffar Baqa'i and Ayatollah Kashani feigned allegiance to Mosaddeq while plotting behind his back, but other National Front leaders such as Majlis deputies Abdolhossin Haerizadeh and Hossein Makki were openly critical of the government. While there were ideological disagreements, personal politics were also at play as these luminaries chafed under Mosaddeq's domination and hoped to carve out their own positions of influence. On 26 December, an angry row had broken out in the Majlis, with Makki accusing Mosaddeq of passing him over for a position atop the NIOC hierarchy.[79] Makki resigned from the NIOC council the following day.[80]

Mosaddeq's reform programs aimed at improving conditions for workers and peasants but shied away from sweeping social or economic changes advocated by his more progressive supporters. Third Force leader Khalil Maleki, a key Mosaddeq supporter, advocated for women's suffrage throughout December 1952, which Mosaddeq declined to support for fear of attracting the opposition of Iran's clerical leadership.[81] Kashani demanded stricter religious laws and called for state persecution of the Baha'i, a religious group which Shi'a clerics had been trying to suppress since the nineteenth century.[82] Karim Sanjabi later recalled how Kashani's two sons, who were both politically active, would demand new regulations on dress and consumption, "which were either impractical or illegal."[83] The differing interests and objectives of Mosaddeq's rivals and allies threatened to undermine the government's effectiveness.

As he negotiated in secret with Henderson, Mosaddeq maneuvered to retain his position. On 5 January, he gave a blistering speech in the Majlis, in which he denounced his enemies as "foreign hirelings." He secured a vote of confidence from sixty-four supporters, with one abstention, out of the seventy-person assembly. Four days later, Mosaddeq surprised the Majlis and his own advisors by requesting a twelve-month extension of his emergency powers, which were set to expire on 9 February. Kashani, the Majlis speaker, declared the request unconstitutional, and debate raged over whether the prime minister's request was lawful.[84] Mosaddeq's supporters organized a week of strikes in Tehran, as crowds chanted "Mosaddeq or death!" in front of the Majlis building. Kashani relented, and on 21 January Mosaddeq secured twelve more months of emergency powers.[85] The announcement brought condemnations from the opposition press, including the Tudeh papers.[86] While the vote was a victory for the prime minister, it marked his first major public break with Kashani.[87]

In this tense and fractious political environment, Henderson presented Mosaddeq with the complete package proposal on 15 January. It provided for U.S. aid for Iran in exchange for acceptance of the British arbitration terms, coupled with a commitment to enter into talks with a consortium of oil companies, including AIOC, at a later date. Mosaddeq examined the proposal in detail. He objected to Great Britain acting as a party in the dispute, insisting that only Iran and AIOC were involved, but then insisted he would not enter into an agreement with AIOC, as from his point of view the company had been nationalized and "did not exist." According to Henderson, the prime minister "reached the zenith of his emotions" when he came to the British terms of reference governing arbitration, which included a suggestion that compensation cover "loss of enterprise." He suggested a simpler phrasing, with the arbitration tribunal determining compensation in accordance with any British law governing nationalization. When Henderson responded that the British would reject such terms as "inflexible," Mosaddeq responded that "inflexibility" was his intention. He did not want the British "to take advantage of flexibility of wording in order [to] broaden basis for determining compensation."[88] While making small concessions on the issues of price, interest payments, and the formation of the arbitration panel, Mosaddeq refused to budge on the terms of arbitration, and refused to accept paying compensation for AIOC's "loss of enterprise."[89]

While the British had succeeded in bringing the United States closer to their position on compensation, Mosaddeq's efforts had the opposite effect. Henderson left the 15 January meeting very discouraged. The prime minister's comments were a "confused, meaningless mass of disjointed statements," and his objections—which were as minute and technical as the British comments—were "of such petty character as not to be worth detailed mention."[90] Despite his frustration, Henderson could see that the British terms of reference were "the most acute problem," and suggested they be abandoned.[91] The British resisted any change to the terms, revealing their recent reservations regarding the reliability of the Coal Act, which was "ambiguous" on the question of compensation for an oil concession. The British believed that Mosaddeq clearly understood their concerns and despite U.S. entreaties to alter the wording refused to back away from the phrase "loss of enterprise.[92] Henderson therefore tried to convince Mosaddeq to accept the British phrasing, spending an hour on 19 January arguing that "loss of enterprise" ought to be included within the arbitration terms and warning Mosaddeq that rejection would lead to a breakdown in negotiations. Mosaddeq countered that the British were using the issue as an excuse to avoid a settlement.[93] Henderson reported to Washington that Iran was trying to avoid "a hundred years" of compensation payments to the

British.[94] Given British intransigence on this issue, Henderson doubted whether an agreement with Mosaddeq would be possible.[95]

The British were optimistic that the new U.S. administration, which took office on 20 January, would be less willing to "give away" aid to Mosaddeq.[96] In a lengthy note to the new secretary of state, John Foster Dulles, Foreign Secretary Anthony Eden argued that Mosaddeq was using the negotiations to extort "more attractive proposals" from the United States.[97] Initially, Dulles deferred to Byroade, who was trying to persuade the British to withdraw "loss of enterprise" from the arbitration terms. Byroade believed it was "inconceivable" that an impartial body would not rule in the company's favor regarding compensation for future profits: "[the] legal case is clearly on side of the British."[98] Sir Roger Makins, the new British ambassador to the United States, noted that the United States shared British concerns about the impact on oil concessions outside of Iran, and recommended patience "so as to be sure that we carry the Americans wholeheartedly with us at this crucial point."[99]

American enthusiasm for negotiating with Mosaddeq had begun to ebb. On 24 January, Henderson laid out his thoughts on the situation for the new secretary of state in a long telegram that highlighted commercial issues rather than the strategic risks of losing Iran to communism. Delivering aid or buying oil without a suitable arbitration agreement would allow Iran to profit from its oil and flout "the principles on which stable international economic relations must be based." It would mean "deserting the firm ground of principle for a morass" in which the U.S. would become "deeply entangled." Henderson recommended that the United States remain "firmly and calmly on the rock of principle," exploring remaining options through negotiation but rejecting additional unilateral aid.[100] Secretary Dulles found his message "timely and very helpful."[101]

On 28 January, Mosaddeq categorically rejected the idea of compensation for lost future profits. If future profits were included, he argued, Iran would be forced to pay £150 million each year for thirty-two years.[102] Though he was clearly frustrated with Mosaddeq, Henderson knew the prime minister could not agree to a compensation settlement with payments stretching "indefinitely into the future." An Iranian government that agreed to those terms "would not be likely to survive long."[103] Mosaddeq sought to bolster his position on 4 February, telling Henderson that he would prepare a bill for the Majlis empowering the government to sell oil "to any customer who might come."[104] Henderson, however, responded by recommending that the 15 January proposals be dropped and the negotiations terminated.[105]

On 1 February, Makins assured Eden that they could endure the "twists and turns," and eventually "bring the state Department along with us," given sufficient time.[106]

In June 1952, Royal Air Force fighters forced the *Rose Mary*, a ship carrying 1,000 tons of Iranian oil bound for Italy, into a port in British-controlled Aden. The cargo was impounded and in January 1953 a British court ruled that the oil still belonged to AIOC. Despite this outcome, efforts by independent oil companies to buy and transport Iranian oil continued, raising concerns that the British boycott was weakening.[107] A former corporate lawyer who was very familiar with the international oil industry, Dulles felt it was an "inescapable fact" that a large number of tankers would soon come on the market as long-term contracts with the major companies expired. This would enable Iran to sell large quantities of oil with little difficulty and without the assistance of the major international oil companies.[108] Though Nitze and Byroade wanted the United States to make one final offer, with a few minor changes to the 15 January proposals, there were clear concerns that any action that destabilized the world oil market "might in the long run have even more serious consequences" than failing to aid Mosaddeq.[109] On 14 February, during a meeting with Henderson, Mosaddeq stated that if the British offer on compensation did not improve by 21 February, he would make a speech to the Majlis announcing plans to sell oil at a 50 percent discount.[110] The CIA concluded that Iran could sell 3–3.7 million tons a year by making use of available tankers and by offering oil at cut rates to Argentina, Italy, or the Eastern Bloc nations.[111]

British officials worried that if the package proposal failed, the United States would give up on negotiations and "pursue its own policy with little reference to the United Kingdom."[112] Dulles discussed the possibility of buying oil from Mosaddeq or allowing the American oilman Alton Jones, a personal friend of Eisenhower, to travel to Iran with a team of technicians to restart the Abadan refinery.[113] The British did not think Mosaddeq's threats to sell oil were credible, but their chief concern was that the United States would give in to Mosaddeq's ultimatum and offer him aid.[114] Rather than break with the British, Dulles suggested they resubmit the proposal of 15 January, with some minor changes. "We believe the British . . . have now come to a point where we can no longer press them," and he suggested that Mosaddeq might yield to "sustained firmness," a line of reasoning that mirrored the position the British had taken since May 1951.[115] Dulles also sent Henderson a British note for delivery to Mosaddeq that maintained the prime minister was being "unreasonably suspicious." The offer that had been made was "just and equitable" and constituted the final offer Britain and the United States were going to make.[116] Byroade was not certain the British approach would work, but he told Henderson to deliver the terms however he chose.[117] The State Department was done making concessions to Iran.

Henderson delivered the message to Mosaddeq on 20 February. It contained the same terms of reference related to compensation for AIOC's "loss of enterprise," and though Mosaddeq said they were unacceptable, he declined to reject them entirely, telling Henderson he would consult his advisors before making a final decision.[118] Although negotiations were officially on hold, for all intents and purposes, the package proposal was a dead letter. The British were pleased that the Eisenhower administration policymakers had adopted "a much more robust attitude" than their Truman administration predecessors.[119] The British strategy of delaying discussions and holding hard to their line on compensation had worked and the Americans were moving away from the idea of offering Mosaddeq aid.

9 *Esfand*: The Shah and Mosaddeq Break

As the oil negotiations reached their denouement, a major political struggle was developing between Mosaddeq, the shah, and former members of the National Front. Months of infighting and mounting frustration with Mosaddeq's leadership culminated in a split in the original National Front coalition. On 6 February, a group of National Front deputies—including Haerizadeh and Baqa'i—left the group's Majlis faction, protesting the dominance of "subversive elements" over the government. Mosaddeq retained support from the Third Force and Iran Party, as well as key bazaar trade guilds. However, according to Mosaddeq loyalist Ali Shayegan, by mid-February the National Front no longer existed.[120]

While Baqa'i had lost much of his former political power, he retained his paper *Shahed*, which became a platform for anti-Mosaddeq rhetoric. The Tudeh-inspired press also attacked the government, focusing on Mosaddeq's willingness to negotiate an oil deal and his retention of the U.S. military advisory mission. Mosaddeq, committed to maintaining a free press, did nothing to suppress this criticism.[121] In addition to the parliamentary opposition, some clerics and bazaar groups were coming out against the government, arguing that Mosaddeq's economic policies were harming their interests. Mosaddeq fortified his position in Tehran, replacing the pro-Kashani chief of police with his own loyalist, Lieutenant General Mahmud

Afshartus. Stung by his failure to prevent Mosaddeq from renewing his emergency powers, Kashani gravitated toward the conservative circle of clerics surrounding Fazlollah Zahedi. Other National Front figures, such as Makki and Haerizadeh, had also begun to align themselves with Zahedi.[122]

The opposition lacked a uniting figure or force around which politicians, disgruntled military officers, bazaar merchants, and Shi'a clerics could rally. Their natural leader was the shah, Mohammed Reza Pahlavi, whose political influence had declined precipitously since July 1952. Though Mosaddeq continued to confer with the shah and maintained amicable relations with the court, the shah no longer met with foreign officials and played an incidental role in public affairs. According to one biographer, the monarch passed his time playing poker, listening to music, and driving his Packard convertible to his estate on the Caspian Sea.[123]

On 14 February, Bakhtiyari tribesmen ambushed an army column in the oil fields of Khuzestan. The attack left forty-two officers and enlisted men dead. Though the British were no longer officially present in Iran, the CIA reported "British intrigues" among the tribes—evidence of Rashidian involvement—and warned that the situation in Iran was "highly dangerous."[124] The attack infuriated Mosaddeq, who told Henderson on 18 February that the British were coordinating "tribal elements, fanatical religious groups . . . reactionary elements in [the] army and bureaucracy, discarded politicians and Communist front organizations" to remove him from power. He stopped short of accusing the shah, who was connected to the Bakhtiyari through his wife, Queen Soraya.[125]

At a press conference, Deputy Prime Minister Hossein Fatemi stated that Mosaddeq was suffering from exhaustion and had been mandated bed rest by his doctors. Mosaddeq feared assassination and seldom left his home, a gated compound a short walk from the shah's palace and the Majlis chambers.[126] Rumors now spread that Mosaddeq suffered from "acute nervous disorder."[127] Henderson worried that Mosaddeq's mental condition was "deteriorating," and even the prime minister's advisors like Baqer Kazemi felt that his resignation was only "weeks away."[128] On 22 February, Ardeshir Zahedi, the son of the opposition leader and an assistant to the Point Four technical advisory mission, told Commander Eric Pollard, naval attaché at the U.S. embassy, that Kashani and most of the old National Guard leadership had rallied behind his father, who expected to be named prime minister within a few days by the shah and Majlis after Mosaddeq was forced out.[129]

As in July 1952, Mosaddeq chose to act first, rather than wait for the opposition to make their move. On 20 February, as he received the final proposal from Henderson, Mosaddeq demanded the shah end his political intrigues, surrender control of his estates, and subordinate himself to the government. According to Sanjabi, both Court Minister Hossein 'Ala and the shah were astonished by Mosaddeq's threat, which had also caught his allies off guard.[130] At a lengthy meeting on 21 February, 'Ala told Mosaddeq that the shah would end his intrigues in the army, but offered only to negotiate on surrendering his financial prerogatives.[131] Mosaddeq told Henderson on 23 February that he would not discuss his dispute with the shah, which Henderson guessed was the reason why he had delayed issuing any response to the 20 February oil proposals.[132] The shah, eager to avoid a serious break, offered to leave the country, remaining abroad "until [Mosaddeq] requested his return."[133] During a four-hour meeting on 24 February, Mosaddeq told the shah it might be appropriate for the shah to leave "temporarily," undertaking a religious tour of Iraq and then a brief sojourn in Spain, returning to Iran when the political situation had stabilized. In his memoirs, Mosaddeq wrote that it was the shah who first proposed leaving the country, and that he told the shah that leaving during a time of crisis was not advisable. He acquiesced once the shah continued to insist it was necessary, in part because the shah and Queen Soraya hoped to consult medical professionals in Europe.[134]

These meetings sent shock waves through political circles in Tehran. Seizing on reports that the shah would soon leave the country, the Tudeh and elements of Iran's left-wing intellectual community called for an end to the monarchy and the creation of a republic. Conservatives worried that the shah's departure would fatally undermine the monarchy, and Kashani and Makki urged the shah to hold firm against Mosaddeq's demands. To preempt a potential coup, Mosaddeq had Police Chief Afshartus arrest Zahedi on 25 February. The CIA concluded Mosaddeq was demonstrating his "complete control of the government," both to bolster his position against opponents and to prepare the country for his rejection of the package proposal, which still remained under consideration.[135]

The shah's willingness to leave the country appeared genuine. In her memoirs, Queen Soraya recalled that the shah had grown "very depressed," and viewed his presence in the country as a "form of support for [Mosaddeq's] policies." 'Ala told Henderson the shah was "delighted" to leave and was open to having one of his half brothers appointed regent in his absence. According to 'Ala, the shah had succumbed to a "nervous breakdown." His departure was tantamount to a formal surrender. To Henderson, it was nothing less than the first step toward "the abolition of the monarchy."[136]

Ambassador Loy W. Henderson intervened in February 1953 to defend the shah against Mosaddeq. Truman Library, Accession No. 76-119.

The U.S. ambassador was an ardent anti-communist. Like most U.S. officials, he was inclined to support Iran's monarchy as a pro-Western and anti-communist institution. He had intervened during the July 1952 crisis, attempting to influence the shah into taking direct action. He did so again in February 1953. "I dislike remaining inactive," Henderson wrote in a telegram that remained classified for more than fifty years, "when [the] monarchical institution . . . regarded as stabilizing influence [in the] country is in grave danger." Henderson sent a message to the shah urging him to remain in the country. In the meantime, embassy officials would "discreetly" try to determine if there were sufficient forces left in the country to oppose Mosaddeq "in the name of the shah."[137]

After receiving Henderson's message, the shah told him that he did not "really intend" to leave but was "pretending for [Mosaddeq's] benefit."[138] One of the shah's biographers contends that the shah believed Mosaddeq was engineering the end of the monarchy, despite the fact that the prime minister had come around to the idea of the shah's departure only after their meeting on 24 February.[139] Another account contends he fully intended to leave, because he was "no longer sure of his standing with the people."[140] According to his own account, the shah decided to leave temporarily "to have a little respite from [Mosaddeq's] intrigues."[141] 'Ala reported that the shah planned to fly to Baghdad with his wife and a small entourage, before departing for Spain. Henderson suspected his travel plans were genuine.[142]

On February 27, Henderson went to the palace "to effect cancellation or at least postponement" of the shah's departure, claiming that a "very important personage" wanted the shah to remain in Iran.[143] When he learned that the shah was still determined to leave, Henderson, in a breach of protocol, told the shah that he had received no orders from his government, "but I knew U.S. government policies sufficiently well" to be confident that no one in Washington would support his departure "so hastily in present circumstances." He argued that the shah's flight would weaken the forces in support of the monarchy. The shah insisted that he must go to prevent Mosaddeq from issuing proclamations against him and his family. 'Ala confessed to Henderson in private that the situation was hopeless.[144]

Kashani seized the opportunity provided by the rift between Mosaddeq and the shah. Working with another activist cleric, Ayatollah Mohammed Behbehani, who possessed a large following in Tehran, Kashani summoned gang leaders, including notable figures like Sha'ban "Brainless" Jafari and Tayyeb Haj Reza'i, to his house and gave orders to close the bazaar and gather a crowd outside the shah's palace. Zahedi's retired officers' association worked in his absence to coordinate with the cleric-affiliated mobs.[145] On the morning of 28 February, or 9 *Esfand* according to the Iranian calendar, Baqa'i and Kashani each addressed the Majlis and spoke in support of the shah. A group of deputies marched to the palace to deliver a message of support.[146] At the same time, a high-ranking general sent a separate message to the shah claiming that a mass resignation of officers would follow his departure.[147] Ardeshir Zahedi was present outside the palace as the opposition's crowd began to gather. Included in the throng were students, disgruntled government workers, bazaar traders, followers of Kashani and Behbehani, and street toughs.[148] By midday, the crowd outside the palace had grown to between 1,000 and 3,000 people. Mosaddeq arrived to meet with the shah for a farewell lunch before the shah departed. The crowd then grew violent, and Mosaddeq left through a passage at the rear of the palace.[149]

Once home, Mosaddeq received Henderson, who had requested a meeting. Mosaddeq warned that if the shah did not leave, the government would be forced to issue a statement accusing the court and the royal family of interfering in internal affairs. Henderson stated his concerns and delivered a note regarding minor changes to the 20 February package proposal. As he left, Henderson saw "groups of persons in a surly mood" collecting outside Mosaddeq's house.[150] These were the street thugs hired by Kashani and Behbehani, and shortly after Henderson left they attacked the house, crashing a jeep into the gate and attempting to storm the compound. Soldiers guarding the prime minister's residence tried to disperse the mob but were unsuccessful. According to Henderson's report, Mosaddeq fled the scene by climbing over the wall into the Point Four headquarters next door. Mosaddeq went first to Army Chief of Staff Taqi Riahi, then to the Majlis, where he rallied the National Front deputies and began organizing counterdemonstrations. That night, the shah issued a statement announcing that he had decided not to leave the country, citing the "sincere wish of the people" that he remain in Iran.[151]

Conclusion

The events of 9 *Esfand* constituted an important turning point in the struggle for Iran. Kashani and Behbehani demonstrated their ability to summon hundreds of street toughs and organized crowds, in conjunction with Zahedi's retired military network. The shah, though a marginal figure in the day's proceedings, had demonstrated his value as a rallying point. The fragile unity of the National Front had been shattered. Mosaddeq remained in power but was more isolated from his former supporters and in open conflict with the monarchy. The events caught many off guard. Anthony Eden found reports of Kashani's evident support of the shah against Mosaddeq "puzzling."[152] The Tudeh Party had demonstrated against the shah, joining the pro-Mosaddeq forces as they had done in July 1952, and the CIA worried that loss of Kashani's "street machine" could potentially force Mosaddeq to lean on further support from the Tudeh in the future.[153]

By the end of February, the struggle for Iran had reached a critical juncture. The attempt to reach a settlement looked dead and Secretary Dulles had decided against breaking with the British on the oil issue. Mosaddeq's opponents tried to remove him but failed. Ambassador Henderson had intervened in Iran's internal affairs and backed the shah against Mosaddeq, in effect choosing monarchy over representative government. The State Department concurred with Henderson's actions during the crisis, "believing that risk involved was worth taking."[154] Although the shah remained in Iran and on the throne, the power and influence of the monarchy appeared to be in decline and in danger of disappearing. The Eisenhower administration now faced the choice of whether to continue efforts to prop up Mosaddeq or commit to a covert operation that would remove him from power.

6 28 *Mordad*

The Coup against Mosaddeq

. . . .

Financed, guided, and supported by U.S. and British agents, the anti-
Mosaddeq opposition successfully overthrew the National Front government
on 19 August 1953 (28 *Mordad*, according to the Iranian calendar) in a violent
coup d'état combining indigenous forces with foreign actors. U.S. policymakers had long believed that without the substantial oil revenues that the international oil companies could provide, Iran would descend into economic and
political chaos, leading eventually to communist control. In March 1953, U.S.
policymakers became convinced that Mosaddeq would never accept a "reasonable" oil settlement with the British and that allowing him to remain in
office would lead to disaster. From April to August 1953, the United States,
Great Britain, and their Iranian allies worked to weaken Mosaddeq in prep-
aration for a coup d'état. Great Britain had been attempting to organize
Mosaddeq's ouster since he first came to power and eagerly supported the
American effort. Internal opposition to Mosaddeq, particularly military officers led by General Fazlollah Zahedi, sought out and accepted foreign assistance. The final and key element was the shah, who reluctantly agreed to
participate once he received assurances of U.S. and British backing.

The Coup Decision: March 1953

Mosaddeq's rejection of the "final" offer in February 1953 convinced many
officials in the Eisenhower administration that further oil negotiations with
his government would not succeed, and that without an oil agreement, Iran
would edge closer to collapse. Moreover, the February crisis and its aftermath exacerbated concerns that Mosaddeq intended to undermine the shah,
who U.S. officials viewed as the main guarantor of Western interests in
Iran. The Eisenhower administration was also concerned that Mosaddeq's
threat to sell oil at cut-rate prices would destabilize the global oil market.
These concerns featured heavily in reports and meetings and produced the
decision to remove Mosaddeq by covert action. Recently declassified U.S.
documents made it possible to trace this process in detail.

President Dwight D. Eisenhower (left) and Secretary of State John Foster Dulles (right) made the decision to overthrow Mosaddeq at some point in spring 1953. National Archives of the United States.

In a report to the president on 1 March, Central Intelligence Agency Director Allen W. Dulles stated that the possibility of a communist takeover had increased in the wake of Mosaddeq's showdown with the shah. Although Mosaddeq would probably remain in power, his position had weakened. Ayatollah Abolqassem Kashani, who an earlier CIA report had described as "dangerous and irresponsible," had emerged as a serious threat to the prime minister. If Mosaddeq was removed, Kashani could come to power, which would increase the chances of the Tudeh gaining control. Although the crisis had shown that the institution of the monarchy "may have more popular support than expected," Dulles concluded the shah's record "does not suggest that he will act."[1]

Secretary of State John Foster Dulles was even more pessimistic. Briefing notes for Dulles warned that Mosaddeq "appeared to be winning the struggle" against the shah. Ambassador Loy W. Henderson, with the State Department's approval, had been working to convince the shah to remain in Iran. Although the Tudeh had not created the February crisis or played a decisive role in its outcome, it was actively supporting Mosaddeq to get rid of the shah, whom they had opposed for years.[2] According to Dulles, Mosaddeq was becoming increasingly dependent on Tudeh support. Although many military and civilian leaders were loyal to the shah and would act if he gave them "positive leadership," the shah was maintaining a policy of "complete inaction." As a result, these "substantial and relatively courageous opposition groups" were afraid to act. Dulles thought it "likely" that Mosaddeq would retain power; "this would mean early disappearance of

[the] shah from [the] Iranian political scene, rapid deterioration in relations between Iran and West and greatly increased possibilities of Communist takeover."[3]

Briefing the National Security Council on the situation in Iran on 4 March, CIA Director Dulles lamented that "the shah had once more missed an opportunity to take control." Dulles predicted that Mosaddeq would curtail the shah's power, resulting in a dictatorship with Mosaddeq in command. This would not be a threat so long as Mosaddeq remained in power, but if he were assassinated or otherwise removed, the resulting power vacuum would provide an opening for the Tudeh to seize power. Dulles warned that if Iran were lost to the Soviets, there was little doubt that the rest of the Middle East, with around 60 percent of world oil reserves, would quickly fall under communist control. Secretary Dulles then laid out three options for dealing with the situation. The United States could recall Ambassador Henderson, who had openly backed the shah over Mosaddeq during the February crisis. The United States could try to improve its position in Iran by "disassociating" itself from British policies, though breaking with the British in Iran risked losing essential British support in other parts of the world. Finally, the United States could provide Iran with financial assistance to deal with its budgetary problems, purchase large amounts of Iranian oil for its own use, and allow U.S. oil companies to buy Iranian oil and provide technical assistance to Iran to revive its oil industry.[4]

In the discussion that followed, President Eisenhower noted that unlike earlier offers, the latest British proposals had been "wholly reasonable." The United States needed to respect the "enormous investment" the British had in Iran. After discussing the difficulties involved in defending Iran from a Soviet attack, Eisenhower stated: "If I had $500,000,000 of money to spend in secret, I would get $100,000,000 of it to Iran, right now." The National Security Council recommended that the United States explore a solution with the British, one that would allow the United States to put the Iranian oil industry back into operation "without prejudice to an ultimate settlement of the Anglo-Iranian controversy" and look into providing limited economic assistance "to strengthen Mosaddeq's position."[5]

While the assessments in Washington seemed gloomy, reports from the U.S. embassy in Tehran were more mixed. On 2 March, Ambassador Henderson noted that while there was no evidence that Mosaddeq had aligned with the Tudeh, he was capable of doing so to stay in power. Reconciliation between the shah and Mosaddeq would only happen if the shah capitulated to Mosaddeq's demands.[6] Two days later, Mosaddeq told Ambassador

Henderson that if the United States was really interested in preventing Iran from falling to the communists, it would stop supporting the British blockade of Iranian oil and buy oil from Iran without insisting that Iran agree to British demands on compensation. Henderson rebuffed Mosaddeq's request, explaining that the United States had to support the sanctity of international agreements like the AIOC concession contract.[7] Henderson reported on 6 March that Mosaddeq continued to consolidate power, arresting military officers thought to be loyal to the shah. Although the shah was allegedly in contact with the opposition, he had chosen temporary passivity for fear of moving before the time was right.[8] There was "still some possibility" that the shah's authority had not "disappeared." Though many army officers were disturbed by the shah's continued inaction, they had not given up on the idea of making a move on his behalf, according to Henderson.[9]

Dulles met with Foreign Secretary Anthony Eden on 6 March to gauge British interest in some new approaches to the oil issue. According to the Foreign Office, the Americans appeared to be "in one of their periodic panics" about what to do in Iran.[10] Dulles told Eden that the authority of the shah had "disappeared" and that Mosaddeq would remain in power. Although the United States did not contemplate providing Iran with large-scale financial assistance or purchasing large volumes of Iranian oil, it would consider minor measures, such as allowing technicians from Cities Service to assist Iran in restarting the Abadan refinery, to keep Mosaddeq "barely afloat." Eden stressed that any aid the United States provided Iran should not include purchases of oil or reactivation of the refinery. Even a few Americans in Abadan would do considerable harm to Anglo-American relations. Dulles countered that the United States had no desire to reward Mosaddeq but had to take action to prop him up and "avoid the disastrous possibility of the Communists replacing him."[11] Following the meeting, the British government issued a communiqué declaring its intention to stand by its offer of 20 February, which the U.S. government regarded as "reasonable and fair."[12] Eden concluded that the United States and Britain should focus on finding "alternatives to [Mosaddeq] rather than trying to buy him off."[13]

Eden raised the possibility of supporting Kashani as an alternative to Mosaddeq in a meeting with Under Secretary of State and former CIA Director Walter Bedell Smith and State Department official Henry A. Byroade on 9 March. The British claimed that while Mosaddeq was "unnegotiable," Kashani had "less history behind him" on the oil issue, and it might be possible to negotiate a deal with him once he became prime minister. Byroade responded that the United States was no longer thinking in terms of any urgent need to find a successor to Mosaddeq.[14] Turning to the oil dispute, Byroade stressed that the United States was very concerned about the increasing number of independent oil tankers and the fall in tanker rates. Countries like Italy and Argentina and smaller U.S. oil companies might take advantage of the situation and start buying oil, especially since Mosaddeq was offering a 50 percent discount. Large-scale deals would have a "very serious impact on the world oil situation." Smith also assured Eden that the United States would stand with Britain on the 20 February proposals.[15]

U.S. officials believed that resolving the nationalization crisis, ending the British boycott, and restarting the flow of Iranian oil were all crucial to ensuring Iran's stability and continued pro-Western alignment. Yet a negotiated solution appeared unlikely, largely due to American unwillingness to break with the British. On 9 March, Mosaddeq told Henderson that he would reject the 20 February proposals, citing the British stance on compensation. Once again, he asked Henderson if the U.S. government would aid Iran by buying substantial quantities of oil. Henderson argued that the British had made "important concessions" during the latest round of talks, a point that Mosaddeq denied.[16] The following day, Henderson warned that Mosaddeq was preparing to move against the shah, "whom he regards as the weakling son of an upstart tyrannical imposter." The shah, though passive, was "holding his ground."[17]

On 11 March, in advance of another meeting of the National Security Council, Henderson reiterated his strong opposition to the United States providing Iran with financial assistance if Mosaddeq rejected "a fair and reasonable settlement" of the compensation problem, claiming that American public opinion would reject a deal that appeared to reward Iran's nationalization.[18] The State Department had already recommended that the United States adopt the approach Henderson suggested in late January and provide only limited economic and military aid to Mosaddeq, rather than oil purchases. Forsaking the principle of compensation for lost future profits would "undermine United States commercial interests abroad" and damage relations with Britain.[19] A CIA report on 11 March concluded that it was "extremely unlikely" the opposition would be able to remove Mosaddeq on their own. On the bright side, the National Front government appeared to have the Tudeh under control.[20]

On 11 March, the National Security Council concluded that the United States should reject Mosaddeq's request for aid. Purchase of Iranian oil without a compensation agreement would be "a terrific blow to the British,"

Secretary Dulles argued. In addition to the compensation issue, the British were concerned about their prestige, having suffered "terrific" blows in Egypt, Sudan, and elsewhere. Secretary of Defense Charles E. Wilson agreed that the United States had to say "no" to Mosaddeq's proposals, in order to defend the "sanctity of contracts." President Eisenhower doubted that the United States could work out a deal with Mosaddeq, and even if it did it would harm U.S. oil concessions in other parts of the world. Robert Cutler, Eisenhower's assistant for national security affairs, warned of what would happen if Iran, "as it easily could," slashed the price of its oil to entice buyers. Unlike the situation in 1951 and 1952, there were plenty of oil tankers available for hire. Such a move would upset markets and affect the major companies' ability to supply the West with oil.[21]

On 13 March, Dulles instructed Henderson to halt all negotiations with Mosaddeq. The United States would not buy Iranian oil, though limited aid would continue "as evidence of our continued interest in [the] welfare of Iran."[22] This would include the Point Four technical cooperation mission and the military advisory mission. Cities Service's head and Eisenhower's friend Alton Jones did not go to Iran.[23] Although there was no obvious choice to replace Mosaddeq, the CIA decided on 18 March that it should preserve any assets that could be rallied to support a replacement.[24] Mosaddeq formally rejected the package proposal on 20 March but left the door open to further negotiations provided the British stated their maximum aims regarding compensation. The British had already rejected such an idea.[25] A 20 March report to the National Security Council continued the alarmist strain from earlier in the month, warning that a communist takeover could occur imperceptibly over a long period of time, and recommended intensifying operations aimed at counteracting Tudeh influence.[26]

While closing the door to further progress on the oil issue, the United States continued to pay close attention to the position of the shah and the anti-Mosaddeq opposition. On 5 March Mosaddeq had appointed a committee of eight Majlis deputies to study the constitutionality of the shah's control of the army. The Committee of Eight concluded on 12 March that the shah should accept his position as constitutional monarch "for the conduct of all civil and military affairs." Opposition in the Majlis prevented the report from receiving a full hearing and a vote.[27] The shah confided to a CIA source (possibly his secretary, Ernest Perron) that his "duty to his people was making him a virtual prisoner," and that his true desire was to leave Iran and live "like a human being." The agency concluded that the shah's departure would bring about a tribal "dog-fight" that would incapacitate

Iran's internal security forces and precipitate a Tudeh seizure of power.[28] On 30 March the shah's Minister of Court Hossein 'Ala told Henderson that the rift between the shah and Mosaddeq was too great to be closed. Leading opposition figures believed that General Fazlollah Zahedi was the best candidate to replace Mosaddeq. After 'Ala said the opposition wanted to know the U.S. attitude about their plans, Henderson assured him that the United States was not supporting Mosaddeq and stressed that while the United States could not be associated with a coup, if "patriotic Iranians" believed a coup was necessary to save Iran, they should act.[29]

The United States preferred the shah and had tolerated Mosaddeq in the absence of any viable alternative. It strongly opposed Kashani. The State Department Office of Intelligence and Research argued in a 31 March report that replacement of Mosaddeq by Kashani would be "disadvantageous to Western interests." Should Kashani come to power, it would cause greater internal instability and potentially push Iran closer toward communist rule, because Kashani did not possess Mosaddeq's prestige and would be forced to lean on Tudeh support. Kashani had supported nationalization of the oil industry, wanted to eliminate British influence in Iran, and hoped to displace the traditional governing groups. He also supported violent political methods, including assassination, to achieve his ends. The report conceded that "power to choose the Prime Minister resides in the Majlis," and it was unlikely that the shah would risk another "Qavam incident" by appointing anyone "who did not have controlling Majlis support."[30]

Available evidence suggests the Eisenhower administration began planning to remove Mosaddeq from power in April 1953, even if it had not yet fully committed to doing so. The reasons were linked to the failure of the package proposal, concerns that Iran's internal political situation teetered on the brink of collapse and would lead to a Tudeh government in the absence of U.S. action, and the desire to resolve the oil crisis and restart the flow of Iranian oil. Faced with a breakdown in oil negotiations and unwilling to push the British any further or offer Mosaddeq financial aid, the United States began exploring covert means of removing Mosaddeq. Drawing on Max Thornburg's argument in February that the solution to the crisis was to "bolster up a government" in Iran that would reach an oil agreement, the covert operation that began in April was meant to create conditions that would allow such a government to take power.[31] According to Donald Wilber, who played a key role in planning the coup, the central idea was to force the Iranian people to choose between the shah and the monarchy and Mosaddeq and an unknown future.[32] Although Wilber was referring only to Iranians, U.S. leaders and the shah should also be included among the people who were being forced to choose.

Setting the Stage: Assets and Actors in TPAJAX

In mid-March, CIA Deputy Director Frank Wisner reached out to British intelligence and suggested discussions on tactics. The Foreign Office agreed to begin these discussions by mid-April.[33] Clearance for "psychological measures" and special political operations outlined earlier in NSC 136/1 were approved on 3 April.[34] The following day, the CIA released funds for an operation to remove Mosaddeq. An internal history of the operation by Donald Wilber, a scholar of Persian architecture and agency operative, suggests the initial budget was $1 million.[35] By mid-April, Wilber and other CIA operatives were producing reports on how best to marshal assets to be used for a coup, "upon the premises that U.S. interest and policy requires the replacement of [Mosaddeq]."[36]

The CIA's Directorate of Plans had warned on 3 March that the agency's assets in Iran, though not inconsiderable, were "far from sufficient in themselves" to prevent a Tudeh assumption of power. Moreover, the key assets in Iran were poorly positioned to take on the Mosaddeq government.[37] In a 16 April report entitled "Factors Involved in the Overthrow of Mossadeq," Wilber echoed these conclusions, noting that "agency assets in Iran are not by themselves capable of overthrowing Mosaddeq's Government" and that an alliance of Iranians and foreigners would be needed to unseat the still popular prime minister.[38] In Tehran the CIA relied on two assets, Ali Jalali and Faruq Keyvani, code-named "Nerren" and "Cilley," who had received training on covert operations in the United States. They organized crowds and instigated street demonstrations against the Tudeh as part of the agency's TPBEDAMN operation.[39] They received $600,000 out of a total budget of $1 million (about 1 percent of the CIA's total budget for clandestine operations in 1952) and employed around 130 subagents including newspaper editors, publishers, and activists.[40]

The United States possessed some influence within the Iranian military through the advisory mission headed by Brigadier General Robert A. McClure. Iran's army was approximately 125,000 strong and consisted of eight divisions, nine independent brigades, and one military police brigade. The army's primary task was ensuring internal stability, and for that reason most units were in major cities, including the capital Tehran, while troops were stationed in Khuzestan to secure the oil fields, pipelines, and Abadan refinery. Additional troops were positioned in the southern provinces to keep an eye on the Qashqa'i and Bakhtiari tribes. Most divisional commanders and much of the officer corps were believed to be pro-shah even though Mosaddeq had removed some of the shah's loyalists and placed his own supporters in positions of authority after taking control of the War Ministry in July 1952.[41] Many officers within Iran's security forces were on the CIA payroll. The CIA had also cultivated anti-Tudeh forces in the south, mainly among the Qashqa'i tribe, as part of a stay-behind operation. By early 1953 the agency had enough weapons to outfit a Qashqa'i army for six months.[42] British assets in the country included the Rashidian family and its network of agents, who were well represented in the bazaar guilds, clergy, street gangs, and newspaper publishers. The British also possessed an informal network of supporters in the army, inside the Majlis, and among the political elite. These assets lacked formal direction, however, due to the closing of the British embassy in October 1952.[43]

The acknowledged leader of the opposition was retired Major General Fazlollah Zahedi. Known to be ambitious and unscrupulous, Zahedi had been arrested during the war for pro-German activities and had a history of anti-British politics. He served as Mosaddeq's interior minister until his dismissal in July 1951, at which point he began organizing anti-Mosaddeq opposition forces, concentrating on former military officers Mosaddeq had cashiered or forced out. Following the fall of Qavam in July 1952, Zahedi became the favored British choice to succeed Mosaddeq. By early 1953 he had emerged as the de facto head of the opposition.[44] Reports on his activities reached the U.S. embassy via Zahedi's son Ardeshir, who worked for the U.S. Point Four technical cooperation mission and often met in secret with Commander Eric W. Pollard, the embassy's naval attaché.[45]

From the point of view of the British and Americans, Zahedi represented the best of limited options. Sam Falle of MI6 regarded Zahedi as "comparatively strong . . . in this country of weak men."[46] The fact that he had been imprisoned for anti-British activities during the war made him attractive, as he would not be labeled as a British tool. Wilber wrote that Zahedi was "the only major personality in undisguised opposition to Mossadeq."[47] Although Henderson felt that Zahedi "might be no improvement over Mosaddeq," citing the former general's ambition and incompetence, he accepted that risks were necessary "since [Mosaddeq] seems persistently to be leading Iran towards disaster."[48]

Most of the anti-Mosaddeq opposition had rallied around Zahedi by the spring of 1953, including nearly half the Majlis, led by house Speaker

Kashani, who regarded himself as the real power behind Zahedi and clearly had ambitions to succeed Mosaddeq as leader of the country.[49] Some smaller groups with anti-Tudeh orientation were also counted among CIA assets. These included the Pan-Iranist Party and SUMKA, Iran's national socialist party. The country's senior Shi'a cleric Ayatollah Borujerdi remained neutral, though members of the opposition attempted without success to elicit his cooperation. 'Ala told Henderson on 31 March that he had met with Borujerdi two days before to gauge the cleric's support for Zahedi. Borujerdi "had not committed himself, but reportedly had seemed sympathetic."[50]

The opposition argued that Mosaddeq had failed to resolve the oil issue, that he was destroying the economy, that he was too permissive toward the Tudeh, and that he acted as a dictator through his use of emergency powers.[51] The opposition worked to stymie the government's parliamentary agenda. Kashani used his position as Majlis speaker to launch investigations into Mosaddeq's programs, while deputies absented themselves to deny the Majlis a quorum.[52] When the Majlis Committee of Eight recommended the shah give up his power over the military, Kashani organized the deputies to block the committee's resolution.[53] As part of the plotting against Mosaddeq, Kashani and Zahedi drafted a *firman*, or royal decree, dismissing Mosaddeq from office and appointing Zahedi in his place.[54] The shah refused to sign, however, even after 'Ala warned him that Mosaddeq's supporters might succeed in stripping him of his power by passing the Committee of Eight resolution.[55] The shah's caution reflected his distrust of Zahedi and the others, who he felt were using him to advance their own agendas. Court Minister 'Ala told Henderson on 15 April that the shah suspected Great Britain was plotting against him, and he did not wish to be a "cat's paw."[56] In contrast, American officials interpreted the shah's caution as evidence of indecision and cowardice. Wilber's April report characterized him as "vacillating, hesitating and indecisive."[57]

On 15 April a Tudeh mob attacked an American technical assistance headquarters in Shiraz. The opposition press used the incident to emphasize the government's alleged alliance with the Tudeh. Mosaddeq declared martial law in Shiraz and sent a letter to William E. Warne, head of the technical assistance mission, reaffirming his desire for friendly relations with the United States.[58] Despite this violence, which was chiefly directed at the U.S. presence, the Tudeh avoided directly opposing the government. The party's leadership was divided over whether to openly back the prime minister or adopt a more neutral position. According to CIA reports, "the Party does not yet deem circumstances favorable for [the] seizure of power," suggesting their alignment with Mosaddeq was tactical.[59] Although Mosaddeq permitted the Tudeh to begin demonstrating publicly, his Minister of the Economy Ali Akbar Akhavi explained to Warne that the prime minister knew that the Tudeh were enemies, "but right now they are not fighting him."[60] Should the party threaten the government, Mosaddeq and his allies felt it could be suppressed quickly—an assessment that was proven to be accurate after the coup, when the shah's military crushed the Tudeh with relative ease.[61]

While the shah remained hesitant, the successful stymieing of the Committee of Eight's resolution compelled the conspirators toward bolder action. On 23 April, Tehran's police chief and important Mosaddeq supporter Mahmud Afshartus disappeared. Four days later his body was found in the slums of south Tehran. According to MI6 operative Norman Darbyshire, Afshartus was shot by one of the officers who kidnapped him, allegedly for making anti-shah comments. However, the press reported the cause of death to be strangulation.[62] A government investigation uncovered a conspiracy to kidnap several high-ranking officials, including Army Chief of Staff General Taqi Riahi.[63] Although the Afshartus affair demonstrated the opposition's ability to challenge Mosaddeq, they failed to capitalize on the situation. Baqa'i was implicated in the kidnapping, but his immunity as a Majlis deputy prevented the government from prosecuting him. Zahedi took shelter in the Majlis building, protected by Kashani.[64] The CIA station speculated that the outcome of the month's events "may signal the end of Zahedi as an immediate threat" to Mosaddeq's government.[65]

Disturbed by the public elimination of a powerful supporter, Mosaddeq put more pressure on the shah. He removed 'Ala as court minister and replaced him with Abolqassem Amini, a well-connected courtier with ties to the Qajar dynasty and the Qashqa'i whose brother, General Mahmud Amini, was head of the gendarmerie.[66] Meeting with Henderson in early May, Amini argued that the government faced a "serious financial crisis" and would have to "make radical changes" if it hoped to remain in power. Amini's ideas included patching things up between Mosaddeq and the shah, placing members of his own family in positions of power, and eliminating the influence of the Iran Party and its allies, including Army Chief of Staff Riahi. It was clear to Henderson that Amini had his own agenda and could possibly move against Mosaddeq if he sensed an opportunity to do so.[67]

Approaching the Shah

While the opposition maneuvered in Tehran, Anglo-American coup planning reached an advanced stage. In late April, Wilber traveled to Cyprus, where he met Norman Darbyshire, head of the Iran branch of MI6. Expelled from Iran in October 1952, the British lacked the means to influence matters there directly. According to Wilber's report, Darbyshire was "perfectly content" to follow the CIA's lead and agreed to pass control of the Rashidian network and other MI6 assets over to the CIA. Without such coordination, it is doubtful that the Rashidians—who were pro-British but skeptical of the United States—would have agreed to cooperate.[68] The British also backed Zahedi, and by June had paid him 4–5 million rials (roughly $50,000) through the Rashidian network.[69] Zahedi made contact with the U.S. embassy in mid-May. He promised embassy officials that once he became prime minister, he would pursue an oil settlement with the British, crush the Tudeh, and pass social and economic reforms. Zahedi stressed that he needed U.S. support, "because Iranians cannot save themselves."[70]

While Wilber coordinated with Darbyshire in Nicosia, Kermit Roosevelt, chief of the Near East and Africa Division of the CIA's Directorate of Operations, managed operations.[71] Grandson of President Theodore Roosevelt, Kermit Roosevelt had a background in covert affairs and was familiar with Middle Eastern politics, having written a book on the subject in 1947.[72] Impetuous and self-important, with a highly tuned sense of the dramatic, Roosevelt viewed his work from the romantic vantage of the adventurer-spy. Unlike Wilber and Darbyshire, he did not speak Farsi.[73]

Efforts to settle the oil dispute continued, though they produced no substantive outcome. Discussions around the oil issue revealed a sense of hesitancy among some U.S. officials regarding the wisdom of the coup plan. On 5 May, the British government rejected a proposal sponsored by Secretary of the Treasury George M. Humphrey that called for a group of U.S. oil companies to buy AIOC's interests in Iran. President Eisenhower noted in a letter to Prime Minister Churchill on 8 May that the British seemed to believe the situation in Iran was "absolutely hopeless" and preferred to risk losing the entire Middle East to Soviet domination than to try a new approach. The tone of the letter suggested Eisenhower was not yet fully committed to ending negotiations with Mosaddeq. While assuring Churchill that the United States appreciated British concerns about the sanctity of contracts, Eisenhower stressed his concern that the situation was a "potential disaster for the Western world."[74]

Henderson was reluctant to embrace the coup plan and instead suggested "one more energetic effort" in early May to resolve the nationalization crisis through a lump sum compensation award for AIOC, rather than an agreement sending compensation to arbitration. A lump sum agreement, he argued, would mollify Mosaddeq's fears of an open-ended compensation award for AIOC. "I do not believe the problem can be solved merely by attempts to unseat Mosaddeq," he wrote.[75] Walter Levy, the oil expert who had accompanied Averell Harriman to Iran in 1951, also suggested that the United States approach Iran with a lump sum compensation offer, proposing the 1947 settlement between Britain and Mexico over Mexico's 1938 nationalization of British oil interests could be used as a basis.[76]

Henderson repeated his concerns about supporting a coup during a meeting with Secretary Dulles in Karachi on 19 May. The chief factor pushing Iran toward communism was the "absence of an oil settlement." An attempt to change the government "by foreign intrigue" was very risky, and there was no figure who could rival Mosaddeq's prestige.[77] This was probably when Henderson learned of the coup operation. Henderson's arguments failed to convince Dulles, who had already concluded that it was no longer necessary to press for an oil settlement with Mosaddeq.[78] Dulles was particularly interested in seeing a pro-Western government placed in Tehran as part of new strategy emphasizing a "northern tier" of Middle Eastern states containing the spread of Soviet influence, now that nationalists had assumed control of Egypt and planned to prevent the use of the Suez Canal Zone as a base for Western forces.[79] State Department officials waited almost a month to reject Levy's idea, arguing it would be "unfortunate" to give the prime minister "any ammunition which would strengthen his political position."[80]

Levy and Henderson's ideas for a lump sum agreement were incomplete solutions to the key problem facing the United States: how to restart the flow of oil revenues to the Iranian state. While a lump sum agreement would have solved the problem of compensation, it did not address the problem of returning large volumes of Iranian oil to world markets, nor did it provide Iran the revenues the United States believed were necessary to meet the country's economic needs. Henderson's doubts about the viability of a covert operation stemmed from his lack of confidence in the shah, who in mid-May had not backed the opposition but was instead suggesting Mosaddeq was "desperate" for a deal that would allow him to retain U.S. support.[81]

On 20 May, Mosaddeq told Henderson that it was clear that the British were not interested in an oil settlement, and he asked Henderson to convey a request for aid to Secretary of State Dulles. Mosaddeq pledged to "do [his] utmost" to preserve good relations with the United States but warned a negative U.S. response on aid would harm Iran politically and economically. After Henderson delivered a noncommittal reply on 26 May, Mosaddeq asked him to stress Iran's difficulties in "maintaining political and economic stability in an effort to stave off chaos, Communism, and British control" during the ambassador's upcoming visit to the United States.[82] In a letter to Eisenhower, Mosaddeq emphasized his ongoing economic problems and his belief that further "disintegration" could only be halted through oil sales or emergency aid from the United States "if the American government is not able to effect a removal" of the boycott.[83]

Mosaddeq's requests for aid fell on deaf ears. The Eisenhower administration's focus was now fixed on the coup plan then in progress. On 30 May Henderson met with the shah. Henderson considered this conversation so sensitive that he did not send it as a telegram or embassy dispatch, instead filing it as a confidential memorandum.[84] Henderson was clearly familiar with the coup operation by this point, and he tried to determine what would be needed to secure the shah's cooperation. Knowing that the shah's reticence stemmed from his suspicion that the British were plotting against him, Henderson told the shah that British Prime Minister Churchill offered his personal assurance that the British government supported the monarchy.[85] When asked if General Zahedi was acceptable as a replacement for Mosaddeq, the shah replied that Zahedi would be acceptable on three conditions: he would have to come to power through legal means, not through a coup; he would have to have broad popular support; and the U.S. and British governments would have to offer their support to the new government, including substantial financial aid. Henderson reassured the shah that the British and U.S. governments would welcome a new government headed by Zahedi and would give it their full support.[86]

Backtracking, the shah qualified his conditions, saying that he would support Zahedi even if the general came to power through a coup if it was clear Zahedi had a "strong array of political leaders as well as considerable popular support" behind him. Henderson suggested that it might be "extremely difficult" for Zahedi to be brought to power by "ordinary Parliamentary methods," and pointedly asked the shah what he would do if a majority of Majlis members requested Zahedi through a petition, but the National Front blocked Majlis action through a boycott, preventing a quorum. The shah refused to commit himself in advance and repeated his belief that Mosaddeq was still best positioned to reach an oil settlement. Given the dangerous economic situation in Iran, it would be best for the United States to provide Iran with aid even if this temporarily strengthened Mosaddeq's position. Finally, the shah suggested that he might leave Iran because it was "too humiliating" for him to remain. Henderson warned the shah that leaving the country would be seen as "a sign of weakness and defeat," and reassured him that the U.S. government regarded him as a force for stability and did not want him to leave.[87]

On 31 May, Henderson made it clear to Mosaddeq that the United States would not provide financial and economic assistance unless Iran settled the compensation issue on a "realistic" basis, in line with what the British had asked for in February. Henderson reported that the talk left him more pessimistic than before about the possibility of an oil settlement so long as Mosaddeq remained in power.[88] Talk of new oil negotiations went nowhere, as none of the options appeared favorable to U.S. officials, who were unwilling to break with the British. Focus remained fixed on removing Mosaddeq through a coup d'état.

Planning and Politics, June–July 1953

Wilber's discussions with Darbyshire in Nicosia produced an outline of an operational plan on 1 June.[89] The outline emphasized the need for psychological warfare to prepare public opinion and laid out a scheme whereby an organized crowd overwhelmed the Majlis and forced its members to approve a vote of no confidence against Mosaddeq. Once the vote passed, the shah would sign *firmans*, or royal decrees, removing Mosaddeq and appointing Zahedi. If this "quasi-legal" method failed, a military coup would follow "in [a] matter of hours."[90]

The CIA consulted Henderson upon his arrival in Washington in early June. Fresh from his 30 May meeting with the shah, Henderson believed it would be very difficult to convince the shah to take part. He suggested that if the shah refused to participate, planners should consider "replacing . . . [him] with one of his brothers."[91] Henderson stressed the importance of providing the new government with "immediate budgetary and economic support in substantial quantities" once the coup was complete. This would allow it to suppress further dissent and maintain government spending until an oil agreement could be concluded.[92] Henderson also suggested approaching Court Minister Amini, who had ties to the army through his brother and was known to be in contact with members of the National Front. However, Henderson later told the British ambassador to the United States that he did not trust Amini, noting that Amini and his brother were "just as likely to doublecross us as the Shah and [Mosaddeq]."[93]

While the precise contours of the coup plan remained in the planning stages, the United States took public steps to distance itself from the Mosaddeq government. After a month of silence, Eisenhower replied to Mosaddeq's request for aid. Drafted by Henderson, the president's reply argued that "it would not be fair to the American taxpayer to extend any considerable amount of economic aid" since Iran could have access to large oil revenues if it would reach a "reasonable" agreement with Britain on compensation. There was "considerable sentiment" in the United States that compensation only for the loss of physical assets would undermine international trade and investment. The State Department released the president's letter to the press, publicizing the U.S. rejection of Mosaddeq's plea to isolate the prime minister in advance of the coup operation.[94]

Following meetings in Beirut in mid-June, Wilber and Roosevelt traveled to London to meet former MI6 Tehran chief Christopher Montague ("Monty") Woodhouse and Darbyshire.[95] The group produced a "London Draft" of the operation that outlined three stages. First, the CIA would distribute propaganda undermining Mosaddeq, tying his government to the Tudeh and alleging he was planning to rule as a dictator. Second, hired mobs would converge on the Majlis and force its members to vote Mosaddeq out of office. Third, pro-shah military units would seize control should Mosaddeq, as was expected, refuse to step down. The shah would sign two *firmans*: one dismissing Mosaddeq and the second appointing Zahedi in his place.[96]

It is difficult to determine precisely when the United States officially approved the plan, code-named TPAJAX. In his account, Roosevelt describes a meeting on 25 June where the plan was supposedly discussed in detail, but no record of such a meeting has been found.[97] A chronology found in CIA records indicates Secretary Dulles gave his approval to the operation on 11 July. No written authorization from President Eisenhower has been found and presumably does not exist. According to one CIA history, "[t]he President knew what was going on but preferred to keep himself out of all formal deliberations. His orders and briefings were given orally with no record kept." Churchill approved the plan by 1 July.[98]

The coup plan required a critical mass of anti-Mosaddeq deputies in the Majlis, and the Rashidians had begun distributing bribes to deputies. Although Kashani lost reelection as speaker to a Mosaddeq ally, opposition deputies were able to elect Hossein Makki as special overseer of the government's budget, which enabled them to paralyze activity in the Majlis.[99]

Outside the assembly, Mosaddeq's allies rallied large crowds in support of the Committee of Eight recommendation to limit the shah's powers. "The shah must reign, not rule" was the most popular slogan. The opposition continued to block a vote on the committee's resolution; had it passed, the shah likely would have left the country and the conspiracy against Mosaddeq would have collapsed.[100] Before the opposition could fully mobilize against him, Mosaddeq acted. On 14 July, all National Front deputies resigned, leaving the Majlis without a quorum.[101] The move effectively dissolved the assembly. Mosaddeq planned to ask for the people's support for the Majlis's dissolution through a referendum, despite concerns from some of his supporters that such an action was unconstitutional.[102]

Mosaddeq's move was a response to the mounting conspiracy against him. In his view, his actions were legal according to Iran's 1906 constitution, which had vested executive power in the Majlis, because foreign intrigues and the shah's interference had rendered the current body dysfunctional. His opponents in 1953, however, denounced both the Majlis dissolution and the planned referendum as violations of the constitution and evidence of Mosaddeq's tyranny.[103] On 22 July the Tudeh and National Front held demonstrations to commemorate the one-year anniversary of Mosaddeq's return to power. The embassy estimated the crowd exceeded 50,000 people. *New York Times* correspondent Kennett Love claimed it numbered 100,000 and was primarily communist, an exaggeration that supported the opposition's claim that Mosaddeq was becoming more dependent on the Tudeh.[104] According to the U.S. embassy's ranking officer, Chargé d'Affaires Gordon H. Mattison, Mosaddeq was erecting a leftist dictatorship "with little remaining [of] outward democratic forms."[105] Mosaddeq's maneuver in the Majlis, while necessary to maintain his government's hold on power in light of foreign and domestic subterfuge, became ammunition in the coup plan to discredit him and tie his government to communism. With CIA propaganda depicting him to be a communist sympathizer, the need to remove him to prevent Iran's fall to communism constituted a self-fulfilling prophecy.

The Coup Plan, July–August 1953

While it helped strengthen the opposition's argument for his ouster, Mosaddeq's dissolution of the Majlis presented a problem for the coup planners. The London Draft included a Majlis vote against Mosaddeq, facilitated by pressure from paid crowds. This vote would give the coup a gloss of legality and provide cover for the military coup that would follow if Mosaddeq did not acquiesce to the vote. More importantly, a Majlis vote would help the conspirators secure the support of the shah, who was reluctant to move against Mosaddeq without Majlis support. Mosaddeq's success at retaining power despite mounting foreign pressure and internal intrigue added urgency to these efforts, and agents began distributing propaganda on 22 July, accusing Mosaddeq of holding communist beliefs, acting as a secret British agent, and concealing Jewish ancestry.[106] This campaign aimed at isolating and weakening Mosaddeq and turning average Iranians away from the government, thus mitigating the chances of a violent street response to Mosaddeq's fall, as had occurred in July 1952.

A second element of the plan focused on securing the support of pro-shah military officers, particularly in units stationed inside Tehran, who could lead troops against the government forces. George Carroll, a paramilitary expert at the CIA fresh from active duty in Korea, arrived in Iran on 21 July. After Carroll "painfully confirmed" that Zahedi's claims to influence within the military had been wildly exaggerated, he drew up a list of military figures who might be willing to take part in the operation.[107] Zahedi had not established a military secretariat, so Carroll and Roosevelt set one up for him. They focused their attentions on Colonel Ne'matallah Nassiri, commander of the shah's Imperial Guard, and other officers stationed within the city.[108]

Eventually, Roosevelt and Carroll produced a list of officers who were prepared to participate, brought them into contact with Zahedi and his deputies, and confirmed their participation. As soon as the *firmans* dismissing Mosaddeq and appointing Zahedi were delivered, military units would seize key points, including the radio station, army headquarters, and the prime minister's residence, and arrest Mosaddeq, other government officials, and pro-Mosaddeq officers.[109] Timing would be crucial: "success might depend," Wilber later noted, "upon whether or not General Riahi, the army's chief of staff, succeeded in arresting our friends before we arrested his."[110]

The shah's cooperation was essential. The shah's signature would be needed to validate the *firmans*, which were necessary to give the operation a shred of legality, and military forces would probably not act without his support. The shah continued to move cautiously, in part because he believed he could not directly command any military units, since he was no longer in the chain of command.[111] The shah would occasionally threaten to leave Iran, though Mattison guessed he was "telling different stories to different people" in order to conceal his real motives.[112] He had been encouraged by

Eisenhower's letter denying Mosaddeq aid and had resolved to remain in the country.[113] Allen Dulles told his brother the secretary of state on 24 July that shah was an "unaccountable character" and might "pull out at the last minute."[114]

Arthur L. Richards of the State Department believed there were two key criteria that would have to be met before the plan proceeded. First, the United States would have to be ready to offer Iran substantial aid, in the range of $60 million, to stabilize the post-coup government. Second, the British would have to provide a firm commitment to be flexible in subsequent negotiations to resolve the oil issue. "No commercial concessions," concluded Richards, "or special political privileges should be asked of Iran."[115] The British accepted these terms on 23 July, though they insisted that any future oil agreement had to include a provision covering compensation through arbitration and could not "provide a reward for the tearing up of contractual obligations."[116]

The coup planners hoped that a series of visits from notable representatives would convince the shah to take part in the coup. The first envoy was the shah's twin sister Ashraf. Exiled in 1951 and barred from returning to Iran by Mosaddeq, Ashraf took up residence in France. Approached by Darbyshire and Colonel Stephen Meade of the CIA in June, Ashraf agreed to undertake a trip to Iran, provided the United States guaranteed her brother an income if the coup failed.[117] She arrived on 25 July and met with the shah four days later. Though their meeting was "stormy," Ashraf delivered a letter preparing the shah for further visits by Asadollah Rashidian and Brigadier General H. Norman Schwarzkopf, who had headed the U.S. mission to the Iranian gendarmerie during World War II. Rashidian visited the shah on 30 and 31 July and assured the suspicious monarch that the British were not conspiring against him and that the United States and Britain were working together against Mosaddeq and the communists.[118]

Schwarzkopf's mission was to acquire *firmans* dismissing Mosaddeq and appointing Zahedi, as well as a letter requesting all military officers remain loyal to the crown.[119] According to Wilber, Schwarzkopf took to his task "with relish" and met with the shah on 1 August.[120] The shah feared audio surveillance, so they spoke at a small table in the middle of a grand ballroom. Arguing that he could no longer depend on the army's loyalty, the shah refused to sign the *firmans*. He also insisted that he had to approve a full cabinet in accordance with the constitution and not simply a prime minister. If Mosaddeq held his referendum, however, then the shah believed he would have the authority to dismiss him.[121]

The referendum took place on 3 August. Mosaddeq defended his decision in a radio address, asking the people to choose between him and the "moribund" Majlis.[122] The opposition boycotted the vote and ballot boxes were strategically placed to ensure a positive result for the government. The outcome was as Mosaddeq intended: 99 percent of those voting approved dissolving the Majlis. According to the CIA, support from the Tudeh was crucial to the success of the vote. A report warned that the prime minister "may already be reassessing his policy toward the United States," though it offered little evidence to support this conclusion.[123] While there had been some communication between Mosaddeq and the Soviet ambassador, Soviet records suggest Moscow continued to view the prime minister as pro-American and remained aloof.[124]

The United States took further steps to isolate Mosaddeq and emphasize the communist danger in Iran in advance of the coup operation. On 28 July, John Foster Dulles gave a press conference where he made several prepared comments alluding to the "growing activity of the supposedly illegal Communist party" in Iran, "which appears to be tolerated by the Iranian government."[125] President Eisenhower suggested that Mosaddeq's referendum to dissolve the Majlis was "supported by the Communist party" during a public event on 4 August and declared that the United States would not sit "idly by" while Iran fell to communists. As with Dulles's comments on 28 July, the president's statement had been drafted ahead of time with CIA assistance and was designed to illustrate U.S. displeasure with Mosaddeq's government while hinting at the rising threat of a communist uprising.[126] The CIA also planted a story in *Newsweek* warning of the danger of a communist takeover in Iran.[127] The *New York Times* ran an editorial on 15 August characterizing the prime minister as a "ruthless demagogue . . . trampling over the liberties of his own people."[128] Despite intelligence reports that concluded the Tudeh remained too weak to attempt a takeover of the government, actions by the coup planners and rhetoric from U.S. leaders had manufactured a communist threat in order to justify an extreme response.

The First Attempt

Following his meeting with Schwarzkopf, the shah met with Kermit Roosevelt several times, but he still refused to sign the *firmans*. Though Zahedi was ready to act, the military attachés at the U.S. embassy warned that army units would obey orders from Mosaddeq, "[who] has political and actual control of the army," unless they received contradictory instructions from the shah, to whom they owed their allegiance. Riahi, the current chief of staff, was a Mosaddeq loyalist, but his officers would back a replacement "in the name of the shah."[129] An Iranian colonel involved in the operation provided the shah with a list of forty military officers who had sworn allegiance to the monarchy rather than to Mosaddeq. Still, the shah hesitated.[130] On 12 August the shah left Tehran for his retreat on the Caspian Sea.[131] Colonel Nassiri of the Imperial Guard joined him that afternoon. According to Nassiri's account, the shah did not sign the *firmans* but rather two blank sheets of paper, on which the *firmans* were later printed.[132] This implied that the shah did not himself write the *firmans*, thus rendering their constitutional authority suspect.[133] In any event, signed documents were in Zahedi's possession the following day. "*Al Homdulillah*," cabled Roosevelt: Arabic for "Praise Be to God."[134]

According to Roosevelt, he turned over control of the operation to Zahedi once the *firmans* were in hand. Zahedi and the coup's military participants held clandestine meetings between 11 and 13 August. The original plan was to deliver the *firmans* to Mosaddeq and seize control of the city on the night of 14 August, but Zahedi delayed a day, giving rumors of the impending coup time to circulate throughout Tehran.[135] Zahedi revealed details about the operation to General Mohammed Daftari, who may have leaked the information.[136] The Tudeh Party probably learned of the coup through their network inside the Iranian armed forces and published a warning in *Shojat*, a party daily, on 13 August. The party's senior leadership called Mosaddeq and offered their assistance in combating the coup.[137]

Forewarned of the operation, Mosaddeq strengthened his position. Riahi put troops on high alert and stationed a large contingent at the prime minister's residence. When Nassiri led a heavily armed convoy to the prime minister's home, arriving there around 2:30 A.M. on 16 August, he met a superior force and was arrested.[138] A column of Zahedi's allies arrived to take over the army headquarters but found it too heavily defended and retreated. The attempt collapsed in a matter of hours.[139]

Radio Tehran reported at 5:45 A.M. that an attempted coup had taken place.[140] The Tudeh daily *Shojat* published a report arguing (accurately) that it had been a U.S.-supported plot to replace Mosaddeq.[141] The government arrested several of the military officers involved in the coup attempt and initiated a citywide manhunt for Zahedi. Government forces arrested Court

Minister Amini, the shah's personal secretary Ernest Perron, and dozens of others.[142] Foreign Minister Hossein Fatemi gave a press conference at which he denounced the opposition and the shah: "the people . . . want to drag you from behind your desk to the gallows," he declared.[143] Riahi gathered the general staff and reaffirmed the army's loyalty to the people, "[who] came before Shah or any particular government." He refused to comment on whether the *firmans* existed.[144] Under interrogation, several of the coup participants divulged more details on the scope of the plot, including its connections to foreigners.[145]

Mattison felt the operation had failed due to "Iranian incapacity for large-scale organized effort[s]."[146] Wilber later blamed leaks from within the coup's "inept" military contingent."[147] The operation had failed, in other words, because Iranian participants failed to maintain operational security. Roosevelt later admitted he only learned of the failure at 5:50 A.M. on 16 August when he heard the announcement over the radio.[148] He then drove to Shimran in north Tehran to meet with Zahedi. They agreed the situation could be salvaged, provided public opinion could be turned against Mosaddeq.[149]

The shah did not share their confidence. Upon learning of the operation's failure, he flew his wife on a private plane to Baghdad in neighboring Iraq, ruled by the pro-British Hashemite monarchy, arriving at 10 A.M. the morning of 16 August. His departure was not planned: "he just took off," Roosevelt later reported.[150] The U.S. ambassador to Iraq, Burton Berry, found the shah tired from three sleepless nights, "utterly at a loss to understand why the plan failed." He was now making plans to take his family to Europe, where he would be "looking for work . . . he has a large family and very small means outside of Iran." Berry told the shah never to reveal that "any foreigner had had a part in recent events," and the shah agreed.[151] The shah spoke to the Arab press on 17 August and argued that Mosaddeq remained in office illegally. Taking no chances, he then left for Rome.

Some National Front leaders interpreted the shah's flight as an abdication and argued that the throne was now vacant. The Tudeh called for the end of the monarchy and the establishment of a republic.[152] Denunciations of the shah and calls for a republic also ran in left-leaning papers like *Mardom-e Iran*.[153] In the evening of 16 August, National Front groups rallied outside the Majlis building to hear speeches from Fatemi and others. The rally was large but orderly, suggesting the government still retained considerable support from major bazaar trade unions. The rally ended with a resolution to form a regency council. Behind closed doors, Mosaddeq rejected Fatemi's call for a republic, reminding Fatemi that he had taken a vow on the Qu'ran to uphold the monarchy.[154]

Mosaddeq's insistence on retaining the monarchy stemmed, in part, from personal conviction; he supported the institution and did not wish to see it eliminated. It was also based on his evaluation of what the Iranian people would and would not accept.[155] Moreover, Mosaddeq's position seemed secure. He had vanquished his opponents, the shah had fled, and the army appeared loyal. He looked ahead to new Majlis elections and the consolidation of power by the loyal remnants of the National Front, possibly with some involvement of the Tudeh Party. What he and his supporters did not anticipate was further aggression from the conservative opposition. Apparently, neither Mosaddeq nor his advisors realized that a second coup attempt was underway.[156]

The Hybrid Coup: Planning a Second Attempt

Roosevelt was not ready to abandon the operation. He proposed a new narrative, that of a royalist countercoup. According to Roosevelt, by rejecting the *firmans* and remaining in office, Mosaddeq had carried out a coup against the shah. Pushing this narrative would force Iranians to choose between Mosaddeq, and by extension the Tudeh Party, and Iran's monarchy. The key, Roosevelt believed, was a strong indication from the shah that Mosaddeq was no longer the legitimate prime minister.[157] To disseminate this version of events, Ardeshir Zahedi met with Kennett Love of the *New York Times* and a journalist from the Associated Press on 16 August and passed them copies of the *firmans*, complete with the shah's signature. The *New York Times* published the *firmans* and ran a version of Roosevelt's countercoup narrative that argued Mosaddeq was no longer the legal prime minister.[158] The plan was to inspire opposition to Mosaddeq, particularly within the military, where pro-shah sentiment was believed to be strong. Roosevelt argued that the shah also had the support of the clerical community and proposed a second military coup attempt if popular opposition could be rallied.[159]

Roosevelt suspected skeptics in the State Department would be eager to begin new oil negotiations. "Past Dept. of State policy can only end in loss of Iran," he warned.[160] Both the CIA and State Department hesitated to support Roosevelt's recommendations. State Department guidance noted that unless there was a "real and significant possibility of decisive action in Iran, the Department does not wish to become associated with the reckless backing of a hopeless cause."[161] Similarly, the CIA's Office of National Estimates concluded that Mosaddeq's non-communist opposition had been dealt "a crippling blow."[162] The British also had doubts. Ambassador Roger Makins told Under Secretary Smith that it might be necessary "to cultivate good relations with Musaddiq" in order to keep Iran from going communist.[163] Smith suggested in a note to the president that the United States might have to "snuggle up" to Mosaddeq now that the coup had failed.[164] On the morning of 18 August, the CIA cabled Roosevelt: "all operations against Mosaddeq should be discontinued."[165] It is not clear if Roosevelt ignored this instruction or if new orders were sent later that day or the following morning. He later admitted during his debriefing that he declined to communicate further with CIA headquarters, focusing instead on continuing the operation.[166] In any event, Roosevelt, Zahedi, and others within the opposition had already set in motion a second coup attempt scheduled for 19 August.

The failure of the conservative opposition to oust Mosaddeq apparently encouraged the Tudeh Party to take action to advance its agenda. As a result, the party made tactical errors that ultimately benefited the opposition.[167] The Tudeh-affiliated press began calling for the declaration of a republic on 16 August. That night, Tudeh crowds appeared throughout the city, throwing stones at mosques and tearing down statues of the shah's father, Reza Shah. Some of these crowds were infiltrated by people organized by CIA assets Jalali and Kayvani at a cost of about $50,000.[168] The night's violence, Fatemi's denunciation of the shah, and the news that the government would soon be holding elections for a new Majlis created a confused and volatile situation in Tehran and laid the groundwork for the events of 19 August.[169]

After meeting in a "council of war" on 18 August, Zahedi, Roosevelt, Carroll, and the Rashidians agreed that a second attempt would be made the following day.[170] According to Wilber, the plan would be for "soldiers and the people to rally in support of their religion and their throne." The Rashidians and CIA assets Jalali and Keyvani would assemble crowds with help from the coup's clerical allies. Organized mobs would march on the city center chanting pro-shah and pro-Islamic slogans. They would be joined by pro-shah military units, which would then move against government forces, using the crowds as cover.[171] The planners also contacted military units outside of Tehran led by commanders believed to be loyal to the shah. These forces would march on Tehran and assist local units.[172] As historian Ali

Rahnema notes, the plan was a hybrid model, combining the military element of the first attempt with the "street" forces mustered by the Rashidians, CIA assets Jalali and Keyvani, and the coup's clerical allies.[173]

The coup organizers hired street toughs from the city's wrestling houses (*zourkhaneh*) and instructed them to organize mobs the following morning. The thugs were paid in cash or promised valuable import licenses once the coup was successful.[174] The propaganda arm of the coup operation dispersed materials designed to turn more of the city against the government. These included an interview allegedly given by General Zahedi, though in fact given by his son Ardeshir to *New York Times* correspondent Kennett Love, arguing the *firmans* made Mosaddeq's government illegitimate, as well as copies of the *firmans* themselves, which were printed in large numbers and distributed throughout the city by Jalali and Keyvani.[175] According to Roosevelt, these activities had "a tremendous effect," particularly in the army.[176] To muster more force behind the demonstrations, Ayatollah Behbehani solicited support from Ayatollah Borujerdi, requesting he issue a *fatwa* denouncing communism and Mosaddeq's rejection of the *firmans*. There is no record that Iran's most important cleric responded. Although Borujerdi released a decree calling for all Iranians to support the shah after the coup had succeeded, it appeared too late to influence the events of 19 August.[177]

After the failure of the first attempt, Henderson, who had been in Beirut awaiting the outcome of the operation, returned to Iran and participated in the planning for a second attempt to remove Mosaddeq. In an hour-long meeting with Mosaddeq the evening of 18 August, Henderson complained about reports of violence against Americans in Tehran and elsewhere. Mosaddeq reportedly replied that such attacks were "almost inevitable," leading Henderson to threaten to withdraw the U.S. military advisory and Point Four missions from Iran unless the government took action to protect American citizens. According to Henderson, Mosaddeq agreed to ensure the safety of U.S. citizens and take the necessary steps to restore order. Mosaddeq explained the Majlis had been dissolved because at least thirty deputies "had been bought outright by the British." Dissolving the assembly was the only way to prevent further British interference. Henderson then asked about the effort "to replace him with General Zahedi." Mosaddeq replied that the British had prompted the shah to send Nassiri to arrest him. Mosaddeq said he had seen no *firmans*, but in his view the existence of such documents was immaterial because the shah's powers were "ceremonial." The meeting ended with a tense exchange over the presence of "political refugees" at the U.S. embassy.[178]

Henderson later claimed that the prime minister phoned the chief of police and ordered the streets cleared of demonstrators during their meeting. Other accounts confirm that the order came after or during their meeting, implying that Henderson's threats convinced the prime minister to move against the Tudeh.[179] Whether Mosaddeq acted in response to Henderson's threats is difficult to determine, but the prime minister ordered the streets of Tehran cleared that night. Henderson later reported that police and military units fanned out across the city, using brutal methods against anyone chanting pro-Tudeh, pro-republic, or anti-shah slogans. Tehran was engulfed in clouds of tear gas, as security forces clashed with the Tudeh.[180] In his debriefing, Roosevelt called the action "a spontaneous thing" that gave the operation "tremendous encouragement," and argued that it demonstrated the depths of anti-Tudeh and pro-shah sentiment within the security forces.[181] Ironically, Mosaddeq's decision to crack down on the Tudeh, which illustrated his anti-communism and his desire for U.S. support, helped seal his fate and allowed the coup to succeed.

The Second Attempt

On the morning of 19 August, the center of Tehran was quiet. Neither the Tudeh nor the National Front was present, both having suffered from the previous night's crackdown. The opposition, meanwhile, mobilized its street assets. In the south of the city, crowds gathered under the direction of thugs hired by the coup planners. Later in the morning a prison break released hundreds of other ruffians, including popular zourkhaneh fighter Sha'ban "The Brainless" Jafari. The Rashidians and Jalali/Keyvani contributed to these crowds, which included elements of the Pan-Iranist and SUMKA parties, groups the CIA had infiltrated during TPBEDAMN operations.[182] The crowds numbered between 1,000 and 2,000 individuals. Precisely who led the organizing is not clear. It is likely that all the coup's participants worked together to amass the mobs, with some encouragement (material and otherwise) from British and American agents.[183]

These groups were initially "disorganized and milling about aimlessly" until people with prior knowledge of the coup began directing crowds toward targets in the city's center.[184] Around 9 A.M. Riahi ordered troops to disperse the crowds, but most of the officers in charge of the effort were reluctant to act. "We had no dispute with the protesters," explained one commander, who dismissed his troops rather than proceed with aggressive action.[185]

Tehran's chief of police also declined to put down the demonstrations, which began to swell in size by midday, chanting *"Marg bar Mosaddeq! Zendebad shah!"* [Down with Mosaddeq! Long live the shah!]. Meeting no police or military resistance, the crowds marched on the center of Tehran.[186] They were joined by units that distributed weapons, allowing the crowd to occupy government buildings. Trucks and jeeps brought reinforcements from south Tehran, and by 10:00 A.M. police and soldiers joined the crowds, allowing them to overpower government forces guarding the ministerial offices.[187]

Aided by military units and meeting very little resistance, the crowds set to work destroying anything associated with the Mosaddeq government. They ransacked the offices of *Bakhtar-e Emruz*, the Third Force, and the Iran Party.[188] By noon the crowds and military units moved toward more heavily guarded targets, including Mosaddeq's residence.[189] Intense fighting ensued as royalist forces clashed with government troops. Tehran Radio, a crucial prize necessary to solidify the coup's success outside of Tehran, fell at 2:12 P.M. The station had been playing music and reporting on grain prices all morning, but after the takeover it began broadcasting pro-shah messages, including a reading of the *firmans*.[190]

At this point Roosevelt traveled from the embassy to Zahedi's safe house.[191] He assisted the general in finding a suitable escort to the radio station. Zahedi left on a tank and arrived at the radio station in the afternoon.[192] At 5:25 P.M., Zahedi delivered an address that included a message to pro-shah units outside the capital. Colonel Teymur Bakhtiar in Kermanshah had mobilized his armored brigade and made for Tehran, passing through Hamadan and breaking up a Tudeh rally then in progress.[193] Roosevelt sent a cable to the CIA: "overthrow of Mossadeq appears on verge of success."[194] The embassy reported "truckloads of soldiers, civilians, and six tanks seen roaming the city."[195] Other accounts put the number of royalist tanks at twenty-four, while the government mustered only five.[196]

Within several hours the remaining National Front positions collapsed. Riahi surrendered in the late afternoon. Though they initially repulsed the royalists, heavy fire from Sherman tanks forced the troops guarding Mosaddeq's residence to surrender.[197] Mosaddeq escaped as the mob ransacked his house, but the police captured him and several of his advisors the next day.[198] By the evening all the major government institutions were in the hands of the coup's participants and Zahedi appeared to be in "definite control" of Tehran.[199] Estimates put the day's casualties at around 100–300 dead and injured.[200]

Accounting for Success and Assigning Agency

How did the coup attempt on 19 August—28 *Mordad*, according to the Iranian calendar—succeed after the failure three days earlier? Who overthrew Mosaddeq: was it foreign agents, indigenous Iranian actors, or a combination of both? In memoirs and interviews, Ardeshir Zahedi contended that the events of 19 August were the result of spontaneous action without any foreign element.[201] Darioush Bayandor, a former diplomat and official in the shah's government, argues that the 16 August operation constituted the end of U.S. involvement.[202] Historian Ray Takeyh admits that Mosaddeq's Iranian opposition conspired with Anglo-American agents, but emphasizes local agency over the foreign contribution, concluding "it was more an Iranian plot than an American one."[203] The United States denied official involvement in the coup. In a telegram on 20 August that summarized the previous day's events, Henderson avoided any mention of U.S. involvement, probably to provide a sanitized official record.[204]

While it is clear that the coup would not have succeeded without the active participation of Mosaddeq's Iranian opposition, accounts that ignore or minimize the role of U.S. and British covert operatives are not credible.[205] The United States contributed significantly to the coup before, during, and after the operation. This includes the production and distribution of propaganda designed to undermine Mosaddeq and exaggerate the Tudeh threat, as well as involvement in organizing the crowds that contributed to the violence of 17–18 August.[206] The United States used its contacts within the Iranian military and information provided by the British to establish a military secretariat for Zahedi, enlisting officers believed to hold pro-shah or anti-Mosaddeq sentiments.[207] Roosevelt ensured that copies of the shah's *firmans* were delivered to press correspondents, published in Tehran's newspapers, and publicized abroad. Zahedi and others were given sanctuary at American residences. Had Zahedi been discovered and captured, the coup probably would have fallen apart, because the *firmans* signed by the shah named Zahedi as prime minister and could not be altered.[208] The shah would not have participated in the coup had the United States not been involved. Without the direct participation of the shah, it is unlikely either Zahedi or Kashani would have succeeded in removing Mosaddeq, as neither possessed sufficient popular backing to manage such an operation without the shah's support.

The British also played an important role. Their network in Iran, which they passed to the CIA in spring 1953, was broad and included elements from the clergy, the bazaar, the Majlis, and the military. The precise extent of this network is difficult to determine since the British government has refused to declassify documents related to intelligence operations. American coordination ensured that British assets were used along with CIA forces, while visits from U.S. proxies reassured the shah of U.S. and British support, thus ensuring his cooperation in the first coup attempt. Events like the 18 August "council of war" illustrate the U.S. role as an organizing agent that could bring together the clerical, military, and civilian components of the coup operation. Plans for the military mobilization had been "thoroughly laid" before 19 August, indicating the "multifaceted nature" of the operation.[209]

Once news of the coup's success reached Washington on 19 August, the United States moved immediately to support Zahedi's regime with economic aid.[210] Zahedi received $5 million in cash from the CIA and $45 million in emergency aid in September. The United States would dispense nearly $1 billion in economic and military aid to Iran over the course of the next decade.[211] To not count this expense as part of the total cost of the operation ignores the significance American policymakers placed on such aid. While it is possible, though highly improbable, that the coup would have succeeded without U.S. involvement, it is unlikely the Zahedi government would have survived without the assistance of the U.S. government.

Foreign actors worked with Iranian elements to bring about the overthrow of Mosaddeq's government. They were assisted in this venture by a combination of skill, luck, and miscalculations by their opponents. The Tudeh Party's demonstrations on 17–18 August resulted in a violent crackdown by Tehran's police and the military that put the party out of action.[212] After the failed coup of 16 August, Mosaddeq, Riahi, and others did not anticipate another attempt. According to Sanjabi, Mosaddeq refused to call out National Front or Tudeh demonstrators, fearing it would lead to civil war.[213] At an October 2003 conference at Georgetown University, Nasser Jahanbani, a relative of Mossadeq and son of one of the shah's military supporters, confirmed that Mosaddeq rejected requests by Tudeh leaders to provide them with arms to resist the coup.[214] The diverse nature of the 19 August operation—essentially a military coup that used the mobs created by Kashani, Behbehani, the Rashidians, and Jalali/Keyvani as cover—caught the Mosaddeq government by surprise. Mosaddeq's decision to clear the streets on 18 August may have been due, at least in part, to pressure from Henderson, who was aware of plans to launch a second effort to overthrow the government.

Regardless of whether the U.S. or British involvement in the coup determined its outcome, that outcome was precisely what the United States and Great Britain had intended. Mosaddeq was gone, replaced by a military regime tied to the shah. While fears of Iran turning communist or collapsing into anarchy played a part in motivating the coup, the immediate goal of the operation was to end the oil crisis. American policymakers worried that without a functioning oil industry and the benefits of revenues generated through the operations of the major oil companies, Iran would succumb to internal instability and eventually collapse. Once Mosaddeq was out of power, the American and British governments set about bringing the long-running nationalization crisis to an end, completing the victory they achieved on the streets of Tehran on 28 *Mordad*.

7 Oil and Autocracy

. . . .

Although the 28 *Mordad* coup successfully removed Mosaddeq, it did not mark the end of the struggle for Iran. The new government had to establish itself and deal with pressing economic and political problems, most importantly settling the oil dispute and consolidating its position against the Tudeh and remnants of the National Front. In addition, the shah was determined to reassert his control over the military and play a much larger role in the government than before the crisis.[1] An oil settlement faced many other obstacles including British determination to get the best deal possible for AIOC, U.S. and British efforts to protect their oil interests in other nations, the state of the global oil economy, and the influence of the major oil companies.

Just as the shah and his allies had needed U.S. help in ousting Mosaddeq, they needed U.S. support to overcome both internal and external obstacles in the wake of the coup. The United States used its leverage to accomplish its own agenda. U.S. officials wanted a stable, prosperous, and Western-aligned Iran as a barrier to the expansion of Soviet influence in the Persian Gulf. Rejecting the movement toward constitutional democracy, the United States backed an authoritarian government and helped the shah and Zahedi manipulate elections to ensure a compliant Majlis. In exchange, the shah and Zahedi accepted an oil agreement that effectively reversed nationalization. Although the United States forced the British to moderate their demands, it also insisted on an oil settlement that supported the interests of the international oil companies and was compatible with the privately managed postwar petroleum order. The result was an agreement that ensured Western control of Iran's oil for another two decades while providing the basis for an authoritarian state dominated by the shah and the military.

A New Regime Takes Over

For the Eisenhower administration, the first step toward stabilizing Iran was to provide the new government with economic assistance. Henry A. Byroade, the influential head of the Bureau for Near Eastern, South Asian, and African Affairs, recommended that the United States move rapidly to

Ambassador Loy Henderson (second from left) sits with General Fazlollah Zahedi (second from right) in the aftermath of the August coup. Seated with them are William E. Warne (first on right), head of the Point Four technical cooperation mission to Iran, and Norman Paul (first on left) from the Foreign Operations Administration. Photo by William Arthur Cram.

provide "substantial" aid to the new government.[2] Conceding that Iran needed economic assistance, the British warned that generous or long-term aid would remove incentives for the Iranian government to reach an oil settlement.[3] U.S. Ambassador Loy W. Henderson and other U.S. officials argued that Iran did not need elaborate social or economic programs before an oil settlement was concluded. They wanted the government to focus on suppressing the Tudeh, the National Front, and other sources of dissent, to ensure it would be able to pass an oil agreement.[4]

Zahedi sent a formal request for assistance to President Dwight D. Eisenhower on 26 August, assuring the president that his government would settle disputes with other countries "in accordance with accepted principles of international intercourse," a veiled reference to the oil dispute. Eisenhower carefully repeated this assurance in his response the same day. Drawing on a study completed before the coup and recommendations from CIA officials, the United States rushed $45 million in interim emergency aid to Iran, an amount that, in addition to existing aid plans, was calculated to keep the government going for around a year in the absence of an oil settlement. The aid would be disbursed in monthly packages of $5 million.[5]

The new regime moved swiftly to suppress the Tudeh. The party had not mobilized its members on 19 August, but after the coup it had begun to collect weapons and hold meetings among its leadership.[6] Government security forces raided party cells and shut down party publications. By late September the government had arrested some 1,300 Tudeh members and discharged around 3,000 government workers suspected of harboring Tudeh sympathies.[7] The new government also took action against the National Front, arresting and imprisoning prominent figures such as Khalil Maleki, Ali Shayegan, Kazem Hassibi, and Karim Sanjabi. Foreign Minister Hossein Fatemi evaded capture for several months but was eventually found and executed in November 1954.[8] Former National Front figures Hossein Makki, Mozaffar Baqa'i, and Ayatollah Abolqassem Kashani, who had broken from Mosaddeq and cooperated with the coup, remained active in politics, though the military's crackdown on street activities blunted Kashani's principal source of power, and his influence within Iran's political system declined rapidly.[9]

The staunchly pro-Mosaddeq and well-armed Qashqa'i tribe represented a key source of potential opposition to the new regime. While the Qashqa'i lacked the strength to march on Tehran, a major uprising in the southern provinces would require a military response and might motivate uprisings elsewhere. On 3 September, Zahedi sent Makki to meet with the tribe's leaders in the southern city of Shiraz and negotiate a truce.[10] The director of the U.S. technical cooperation mission in southern Iran also met with the Qashqa'i chiefs and assured them of U.S. support.[11] The U.S. embassy concluded that the tribe would not take action against the new government "unless they are subjected to punitive action."[12] On 23 September, Qashqa'i leaders relayed a message to the CIA station. If the shah pardoned Mosaddeq or allowed him to peacefully retire to his estate, the Qashqa'i would be prepared to support the new government. Despite frequent rumors of a Qashqa'i alliance with the Tudeh, the tribe took no action against Zahedi or the shah.[13]

Mosaddeq posed a particular difficulty for the new regime. The shah wanted to have the deposed prime minister tried for treason, but he and Ambassador Henderson worried about putting Mosaddeq back in the spotlight and making him a martyr for the nationalist cause.[14] In contrast,

Kermit Roosevelt believed that delay in bringing Mosaddeq and his advisors to trial was encouraging the Tudeh and National Front remnants to mobilize against the government.[15] Roy Melbourne, first secretary and counselor of the U.S. embassy, argued that the government should "convict Mosaddeq and his advisors of their crimes as soon as possible" as a way to combat growing public support for Mosaddeq.[16] The shah eventually decided that Mosaddeq should stand trial before a military tribunal, though his trial did not begin until November.[17]

The shah and Zahedi were unsure of what to do with the Majlis. A rump parliament of only twenty-one members remained from the Mosaddeq era, and the shah would need to dissolve the assembly, hold elections, and convene a new Majlis to pass legislation, including, eventually, an oil deal. Although Henderson warned that the government could run into problems if elections were not held quickly, the shah argued that it would be "dangerous" to hold elections without a substantial economic development program underway. Concerned that the shah's argument was a ploy to secure more financial assistance, Henderson stated that the United States would not provide more aid until an oil agreement had been reached and ratified by the Majlis. Henderson suggested that that "an undemocratic independent Iran" would be preferable to a "permanent undemocratic Iran behind [the] iron curtain."[18]

Byroade noted that the shah was "deeply distrustful" of strong leaders and would probably undermine Zahedi.[19] Despite Henderson's advice, the shah worked actively to constrain Zahedi's authority, particularly in military matters, and lobbied constantly for more military aid, arguing that "his" army should be strong enough to resist a Soviet invasion.[20] Some U.S. officials worried that a rift between the shah and Zahedi would imperil the new government's shaky hold on power.[21] Although he recognized that the shah was subordinating Zahedi, Secretary of State John Foster Dulles believed it was important for the shah to cement his "personal hold over the people."[22] In general, U.S. officials like Henderson and Dulles focused on stabilizing Iran and did not oppose the shah's efforts to reimpose a form of autocracy modeled after his father, Reza Shah.

Restarting Oil Negotiations

While the U.S. assisted with the shah and Zahedi's consolidation of power within Iran, discussions between the United States and Britain focused on how best to resolve the oil dispute. At a meeting of the National Security

Council on 27 August, the CIA deputy director said there was "real hope" for stability in Iran. The most urgent problems facing the new government were economic and financial, and the best way to address them was through settlement of the oil dispute. Secretary Dulles believed that the coup had given the United States a "second chance" in Iran and suggested that the president appoint a special representative to take charge of finding a solution to the oil dispute.[23]

The British presented a paper to the State Department on 11 September outlining their position. Any settlement of the oil dispute had to include compensation to AIOC not only for physical assets but also for loss of its contractual rights under the concession—the "loss of enterprise" principle that the British had insisted upon during the package proposal talks of the previous winter. The British also insisted that Iran should not receive better terms than its neighbors, which had signed fifty-fifty profit-sharing agreements with the major companies. In addition, any new arrangement must not damage AIOC markets or Britain's foreign exchange position, which in practice meant guaranteeing AIOC rights to buy a large portion of Iranian exports. Drawing on a Foreign Office study, the paper suggested that the February 1953 proposals, which provided for "adequate" compensation and access to Iranian oil without the complications and costs of restarting the industry, offered the best starting point for negotiating a settlement. Henderson agreed that it would be "fatal" for Zahedi to accept anything that appeared "less advantageous" than the offers made to Mosaddeq.[24]

Herbert Hoover Jr., son of the former president and a prominent oil consultant, who the State Department selected to lead U.S. efforts to facilitate a settlement between Iran and Britain, opposed using the February proposals as a basis for a settlement.[25] In response to the British paper, Hoover argued that when those proposals were drafted, alternative sources of oil and refinery construction programs were not fully developed and the oil industry wanted access to substantial amounts of oil from Iran. World markets now faced an oversupply of oil, and the "complete cooperation of the entire petroleum industry" would be needed to fit substantial amounts of Iranian oil into world markets without causing massive disruption. Hoover's solution was the establishment of a new company, half-owned by the major U.S. companies and half-owned by Shell and AIOC, with AIOC's share no larger than 25 percent, to operate the Iranian industry. The other companies would pay AIOC for their share, thus eliminating the need for compensation payments by Iran to AIOC. The new company would exercise "effective management" of all operations and control all producing and refining facilities. Iran would receive 50 percent of profits after the deduction of operating expenses and depreciation. Hoover estimated that the new company could probably find markets for around 400,000 barrels of oil a day (bpd) the first year, which would provide Iran with around $100 million in revenue.[26]

Hoover's recommendations were based not only on the "realities" of the world oil market, but also on concerns about the security of Western investment in raw materials in the Global South. He told a British delegation in Washington that U.S. oil companies believed the February proposals, which accepted Iranian control of the oil industry if Iran paid acceptable compensation to AIOC, would have "extremely serious repercussions" on operations elsewhere in the world and would lead to nationalization of most Middle Eastern and South American sources of oil "within a relatively short time." Although he recognized that his proposal entailed at least a "partial negation of nationalization," it was "highly doubtful" that the oil companies would accept a settlement that "placed a premium upon nationalization" and threatened the loss of concessions elsewhere.[27]

The British were open to Hoover's idea of setting up "an international syndicate" to run the Iranian oil industry. They had agreed to the February proposals only under pressure from the United States, in the belief that they would be rejected by Mosaddeq due to their insistence on compensation for lost profits. Under Secretary of the Ministry of Fuel and Power Victor Butler, who led a British delegation visiting Washington, noted that AIOC "in its heart of hearts" recognized that it could not regain its previous position in Iran. Bringing in other companies would provide additional markets for Iranian oil and spread the cost of renovating the Iranian oil industry, an important consideration since such investment would entail substantial dollar costs.[28] At the Foreign Ministers Conference in London on 17 October, Dulles told Foreign Secretary Anthony Eden that if the shah's government collapsed, the West would not get another chance in Iran. Eden agreed that Hoover should go to Iran to explore possible solutions but insisted that the immediate aim should be to restore relations between Britain and Iran so that Britain could negotiate directly with Iran.[29]

Hoover arrived in Iran on 17 October and briefed Zahedi on the global oil supply and demand situation. His presentation, which he also made to the shah and to an oil commission appointed by Zahedi, made it clear that Iran had limited leverage and would have to defer to the major international oil companies. There was a "substantial surplus" of oil in the Middle East; any one of the other three main producers in the region—Saudi Arabia,

Middle East and World crude oil production, 1950–1955 (barrels per day)

	Iran	Iraq	Kuwait	Saudi Arabia	Total Middle East*	United States	Total World
1950	664,315	136,235	344,443	546,704	1,755,786	5,407,052	10,418,073
1951	338,389	178,416	561,397	761,542	1,919,569	6,158,112	11,733,504
1952	21,369	386,575	749,131	827,016	2,083,832	6,273,523	12,379,756
1953	25,753	576,076	861,895	844,641	2,423,934	6,457,759	13,146,438
1954	58,904	625,841	959,772	961,213	2,736,802	6,342,433	13,747,780
1955	330,306	688,235	1,103,882	977,161	3,247,997	6,806,652	15,413,838

*Total also includes Bahrain, Qatar, and Turkey.

Source: DeGolyer and MacNaughton, *Twentieth Century Petroleum Statistics: Historical Data.*

Kuwait, and Iraq—had sufficient reserves to meet any foreseeable demand for Middle East oil "entirely by itself." No company would pay Iran more than it paid other countries in the Middle East. If Iran wanted to export "an appreciable amount" of oil, it would have to work with the large companies that already had stakes in Middle East oil fields, because smaller companies did not have large outlets available. In contrast, the major companies could provide markets for around 20 to 40 million tons annually (between 408,219 and 816,438 bpd) within three years, which would provide Iran with around $100 million to $200 million a year at prevailing prices. Although the Abadan refinery, the largest in the world, was a source of pride for Iranians, it was outdated, and the trend in refining had been toward refineries located close to consumption centers rather than in producing countries, so that the demand for refined products from the Middle East, and consequently the income from refinery operations there, would decline.[30] Hoover and Ambassador Henderson stressed that Iran could not expect to receive additional aid from the United States and warned that failure to reach a settlement of the oil issue "within next few months" would bring disaster to the country.[31]

Though it was dependent on U.S. support, the Iranian government was intent on securing the best possible terms. On 1 November, Foreign Minister Abdullah Entezam gave Hoover an unsigned statement outlining Iran's position. The opening paragraph excoriated AIOC for "its uniformly colonial aims in Iran" and concluded that it was "impossible for the former company to return to Iran." The statement endorsed the idea of working with a "group of large international companies having previous experience" in the region to transport and distribute Iranian oil purchased from the National Iranian Oil Company (NIOC), which would oversee production. AIOC could participate but would not be permitted to dominate the group, while total British participation could not exceed 50 percent. The companies purchasing Iranian oil would be responsible for paying AIOC compensation, and "no claims for loss of profits should be taken into account." Finally, the statement sought to finesse the question of fifty-fifty profit sharing by stipulating that the Iranian government's income "should at no time be less that the maximum accruing to others," in effect making fifty-fifty a floor rather than a ceiling.[32]

Hoover arrived in London on 4 November and briefed the British government and AIOC on his talks in Iran. The British regarded the Iranian memorandum as "entirely unacceptable." The British proposed a limited bilateral settlement that left Iran in control of its oil industry in return for heavy compensation and British handling of Iranian exports. Echoing Ambassador Henderson, Hoover warned that any attempt at a bilateral settlement would lead to disaster for the Iranian government and the shah, as it would prompt an immediate public response. He also warned that allowing Iran control over production and refining would give an "irresistible impulse" to nationalization in other oil producers and repeated his earlier proposal for a consortium of companies to run Iran's oil industry. Hoover argued that neither the Iranian government nor public opinion in Iran would accept more than 25 percent for AIOC or more than a total of 50 percent participation by British companies, but the British insisted that 51 percent British participation in any consortium was the minimum they could accept. Otherwise, it would establish a precedent for countries to dispossess one foreign company and transfer its rights to a foreign consortium of their own choosing.[33] Hoover pointed out that Zahedi had refused deals with U.S. independents and Italian and Japanese companies, but he might change his mind if he could not reach a settlement with AIOC.[34] There were dangers, therefore, in pushing Iran's government too far past the point that public opinion would accept.

Although AIOC and British officials often stated that the best solution would be for AIOC to regain its previous position in Iran, they knew this was not possible. They recognized they could achieve their key goals through a consortium with the major U.S. oil companies, though they insisted that AIOC have a 50 percent share. The other consortium members could help finance the heavy capital expenditures needed to reactivate the oil industry and modernize the Abadan refinery and would have to pay AIOC for their share in the consortium, which would help ensure fair compensation for AIOC's original concession. They possessed existing marketing networks needed to handle Iranian exports, and they could reduce production in their other holdings to make room for Iranian output.[35] The British insisted that a resumption of diplomatic relations had to precede any substantive oil talks. While there was strong opposition to resuming relations, particularly from former National Front leaders like Kashani, the United States convinced the shah and Zahedi that no progress could be made on the oil issue until diplomatic relations were resumed. The Iranians acquiesced, and Iran and Britain resumed diplomatic relations on 5 December.[36]

Returning to Autocracy

By late October, U.S. officials had become concerned that pressures were building on Iran's new government. Earlier in the month, a group of former National Front members had organized a brief boycott of the Tehran bazaar in opposition to Zahedi, and pro-Mosaddeq remnants of the National Front had organized a new coalition, the "National Resistance Movement," focused on petitioning for Mosaddeq's release.[37] Kermit Roosevelt warned that the shah's position was "by no means secure," pointing to the "squall of opposition" from disgruntled elites and the remnants of the Tudeh.[38] Tensions with the Qashqa'i also flared up, prompting Zahedi to send representatives to negotiate a new accord with the tribe's leaders near Shiraz.[39]

A National Intelligence Estimate produced on 16 November concluded that despite these problems, the chances of a "relatively moderate government" remaining in power in Iran throughout 1954 were good. While confrontations between Zahedi and the shah had become fierce, they had not yet impaired the military's ability to suppress the Tudeh or maintain internal security. Zahedi's cabinet was dominated by the "old ruling class," however, and the government was unpopular and incompetent. The oil issue was still explosive, and no Iranian regime could survive if it appeared to be compromising the provisions of the oil nationalization law or retreating far from Mosaddeq's key demands. Henderson argued that although an authoritarian regime could force through an unpopular oil settlement, it would not last long if it did so. From the U.S. point of view, a satisfactory oil settlement was the single most important element in stabilizing Iran.[40]

After conversations with the shah about military assistance, Henderson recommended that the United States provide more aid so that Iranian police and military forces would be capable of delaying enemy forces in the event of an invasion as well as maintaining internal order. Roosevelt agreed, noting that increased aid would "cement the loyalty of the strengthened Army" and bolster the shah, "the one element . . . we feel is unequivocally committed to the West."[41] Drawing on these recommendations, the CIA and the State Department in mid-November called for a change in U.S. policy to facilitate the rearming and reorganization of the army so that it would be capable of "strong withdrawal-delaying action" should Iran be invaded by "the armed forces of international Communism." These changes would also "increase the prestige, influence and actual power of the Shah," who the United States considered "the most effective instrument for maintaining and strengthening Iran's orientation toward the West and resisting pressures from within or without by international Communism."[42]

After many weeks of delay, Mosaddeq's trial began on 8 November. He was charged with treason, illegally printing currency and destroying the economy, subverting the constitution, and leading his followers into insurrection.[43] Mosaddeq used his oratorial skills and expert knowledge of Iran's constitution to discredit the government's case against him, turning the trial into a public circus. "Throughout my whole life I have had only one aim," he declared, "that the people of Iran enjoy independence and dignity." He went on to add that his struggle against foreign powers and the major oil companies "has broken, and will break, the chain of colonialism in the Middle East."[44] The trial ended on 21 December, and rather than follow the spectacle with a severe punishment, the shah chose to have Mosaddeq sentenced to three years in prison, followed by house arrest on his estate in Ahmadabad.[45]

The shah used the occasion of Mosaddeq's sentencing to issue a *firman* dissolving the Majlis and calling for new elections. He assured Ambassador Henderson that the elections would be carefully managed so that government-supported candidates won their seats.[46] Though he complained Zahedi supported candidates whose only qualification seemed to be loyalty to him, the shah was also "pulling strings" to ensure the election of people he trusted.[47] Henderson concluded that it might be necessary for the embassy to "make certain moves" toward getting more suitable candidates on the ballot.[48] The CIA station in Tehran was "very active" in selecting candidates, and was confident the agency could produce a Majlis "favorable to our purposes."[49]

With the Majlis dissolved, former deputies such as Makki, Kashani, and Baqa'i lost their parliamentary immunity. The shah threatened to arrest them if they became too critical of the government.[50] The Qashqa'i sent a delegation to Tehran in December to make their peace with the new government, and in early January agreed to swear oaths of loyalty to the shah.[51] On the other hand, CIA head Allen W. Dulles warned the National Security Council at the end of December that while the government had arrested some Tudeh leaders and many party members, it had made little or no progress on crucial economic and social reforms. Although the Iranian economy was doing reasonably well due to U.S. aid, long-term stability hinged on achieving an oil settlement that allowed Iran to receive substantial revenues from its oil industry.[52]

Getting the Companies and the British on Board

In late November and early December, Hoover met with British officials. He warned that the Iranian government would exhaust U.S. emergency aid by the end of March and was likely to be overthrown if it could not show progress on an oil settlement. Hoover again pointed out that independent and state-supported oil companies were trying to gain access to Iranian oil. So far, Zahedi had rebuffed them, but at some point, Iran could make deals with such companies. In meetings with Hoover, Eden conceded that AIOC probably would not be able to regain its previous position in Iran and that discussions about setting up a consortium should begin.[53]

The major U.S. companies claimed that they did not want to participate in a consortium to run the Iranian oil industry and insisted that they would only do so at the request of the U.S. government. The U.S. companies probably preferred that AIOC resume its exclusive position in Iran, which would leave AIOC responsible for cutting production in its other holdings and making the investments necessary to modernize the Abadan refinery. The U.S. companies had access to plenty of oil from other sources and did not need oil from Iran, nor were they interested in investing the capital needed to restart Abadan, a refinery which changes in the industry had made obsolete. On the other hand, they recognized that Iran was unlikely to allow restoration of AIOC's original position and were concerned that without a settlement, Iran could cut prices and sell enough oil to threaten the price structure and force them to cut back production in their holdings in the region. A settlement with Iran that came with short-term costs was better than the alternative of leaving Iranian oil outside their control. Given this danger, they were willing to participate.[54]

The U.S. companies were also concerned that joining an international consortium to control Iranian production would strengthen the Justice

Department's case in its antitrust suit. In mid-November, Hoover had informed the Department of Justice that the only solution to the oil dispute that would provide revenues sufficient to stabilize Iran would involve operating and offtake agreements among the major international oil companies to integrate Iranian oil into Eastern Hemisphere markets. Although this could raise antitrust concerns, Hoover argued that forcing Iranian oil into Western Hemisphere markets, which independent companies were likely to do, would result in "severe economic and political repercussions."[55] After AIOC's chairman William J. Fraser sent a letter to the heads of the major oil companies—Royal Dutch/Shell, Jersey Standard, Socony, SOCAL, the Texas Company, and Gulf—on 3 December inviting them to come to London for discussions, the companies demanded assurances that participation would not expose them to legal problems. The State Department argued that a solution to the Iranian problem was in the national interest and that participation in the proposed consortium was essential. The Justice Department acquiesced, though it reserved the right to rule on the legality of any agreement that might result.[56]

Joined by principals from the French-owned Compagnie française des pétroles (CFP), the heads of the major international oil companies met in London for three days of talks beginning 14 December. Hoover attended as the U.S. government representative. Fraser informed the assembled executives that AIOC intended to insist on a 50 percent share in the consortium. In addition to compensation from the other companies, Iran would have to pay compensation to AIOC. The other companies did not comment on Fraser's demands but insisted that the consortium had to control production and refining as well as distribution and marketing of Iranian oil to protect their investment and ensure adequate production to meet their needs. To deter other countries from nationalizing their industries, they insisted any agreement's terms should not be more favorable than those in place in other countries. The U.S. companies insisted that the U.S. government officially request them to participate so they would have some cover against U.S. antitrust laws.[57]

In a 23 December report to the National Security Council on his trip to Iran earlier in the month, Vice President Richard Nixon praised Zahedi as a "strong man," but argued that things would be better if the shah exercised more leadership. Nixon directed his sharpest criticism at the British, who were "showing the same intransigence as before." The chances of getting an oil settlement were slim "unless somebody topside in Britain puts the screws on."[58] The Department of Defense and the Department of the Treasury urged "independent action" by the United States if the British stood in the way of an oil settlement. Harold Stassen, director of the Foreign Operations Administration, argued that if a settlement were delayed beyond April or May of 1954, the United States would risk the stability it had built up through its assistance to Iran.[59]

A National Security Council paper in early January underlined the urgent need for an oil settlement that would allow Iran to receive substantial revenues from its oil resources. Without such revenues, the Iranian government would lurch from crisis to crisis, increasing the likelihood of a communist takeover. Although continuing substantial U.S. economic and military assistance might allow the Iranian government to survive, it could also make Iran less interested in an oil settlement and encourage other countries to emulate Iran and nationalize their oil industries. The United States believed that foreign control of Iran's oil industry was necessary to meet Iran's revenue needs and stressed that a settlement must not establish a precedent harming the international oil industry and U.S. foreign investments in natural resources. While the United States would maintain full consultation with Britain and avoid "unduly impairing" relations, it should not permit Britain to veto any action the United States considered essential. The president possessed the authority to grant exceptions to antitrust laws in the interest of national security. The report also recommended increased U.S. military assistance to Iran to improve the ability of Iran's armed forces to maintain internal security, offer some resistance to external aggression, and eventually participate in regional defense plans. Increased military aid would also increase the power and prestige of the monarchy. The shah was the "most effective instrument for maintaining Iran's orientation toward the West," and the military was his "only real source of power" remaining in the country.[60]

With the United States urging action and a consensus forming around Hoover's consortium proposal, the British government awaited a report from Denis Wright, head of the Economic Relations Department at the Foreign Office, who had been sent to Iran in mid-December to assess the prospects for an oil settlement. Zahedi, Foreign Minister Entezam, and Minister of Court Hossein 'Ala, who spoke for the shah, told Wright that it would be impossible for AIOC's position to be restored. Consultation with other members of the diplomatic community in Tehran revealed near-unanimous agreement that AIOC could not reclaim its previous position without triggering massive Iranian backlash. While he recognized that foreign assistance would be necessary for production as well as marketing, Zahedi argued that it would be necessary to "camouflage" foreign control in some way. Probed about British compensation demands, Wright declined to discuss specific figures but assured Zahedi that Britain had "no desire to bleed Persia white."[61]

Wright reported on 7 January that if the Iranian government agreed to restore AIOC's control of Iran's oil industry, it would be "courting disaster." He recommended that the British government accept a settlement based on an international consortium composed of AIOC and the other major oil companies. The cabinet accepted Wright's recommendation immediately and decided to pursue discussions about a consortium, provided AIOC's share was not "materially less than 50 percent." Fraser told Eden on 8 January that it would be a "very serious step" to abandon AIOC's claim for full restitution. Eden, who no doubt had been briefed by the Foreign Office that Fraser recognized that AIOC could not regain its previous position in Iran but was maintaining the fiction to strengthen his bargaining position, asked Fraser if AIOC really wanted to go back into Iran alone rather than sharing risks and costs with the other major companies. Fraser admitted that he would prefer the "consortium route."[62] With Hoover's assistance, Fraser drafted an invitation to the other majors and CFP to resume talks on a consortium in London.[63]

With things moving ahead in London and Tehran, the major companies renewed their argument for antitrust protection. Meeting with the secretaries of state, defense, and the treasury on 6 January, company heads warned that further progress toward a settlement could be hindered if the U.S. government did not offer full support and protection from antitrust action.[64] Hoover explained to the National Security Council on 21 January that it was necessary to allow the five major U.S. oil companies to participate in a consortium to restore the Iranian oil industry because they were the only companies besides Shell that were able to reintegrate Iranian oil into world markets without disrupting them.[65] After Hoover's presentation, Chairman of the Joint Chiefs of Staff Admiral Arthur W. Radford stated that it was "almost impossible to overstate the importance of an Iranian settlement from the point of view of national security." Attorney General Herbert Brownell had given them "full clearance" to participate in the consortium on 20 January, and President Eisenhower directed that the record state that the "so-called cartel case" was "an entirely separate matter from the Proposed Iranian Consortium Plan." The National Security Council agreed to advise the attorney general that "the security interests of the United States" required U.S. companies to participate in a consortium in Iran.[66]

Battling the British

Although AIOC's demand that it be restored to its previous exclusive position was largely a ploy to relieve the company (and Fraser) of responsibility should the final deal prove unsatisfactory, AIOC clearly wanted to dominate the consortium. In talks with Hoover and other U.S. government officials and with representatives of the other major companies in late January, AIOC, with the support of the British government, insisted that it have at least a 50 percent share in the consortium. Officials in the U.S. government and the other companies felt that 50 percent was too much. A long-term solution required the settlement be "defensible" to Iranian public opinion, and such a large share for AIOC would allow Iranian nationalists to claim the consortium was "indistinguishable" from the old AIOC concession. Hoover also warned that AIOC's demand that Iran make direct compensation payments to AIOC risked Iran claiming that the payments constituted purchase of the concession. In any event, AIOC would receive compensation from the consortium members for their shares in the consortium.[67]

The British were concerned that the distribution of shares in the consortium should not result in U.S. companies replacing AIOC in Iran "in fact or in the eyes of the public."[68] In private, however, AIOC and the British government were prepared to accept a 40 percent share "as a last resort," so long as AIOC was the largest single shareholder.[69] On 15 February, the State Department recommended rejecting AIOC's demand for a 50 percent share because it would give opponents of the Iranian government a "powerful weapon" against a settlement. Dulles assured Eden on 17 February that U.S. companies were not trying to gain shares in the consortium at the expense of AIOC and agreed that the overall U.S. share in the consortium should not be larger than AIOC's share. Eden agreed that 50 percent for AIOC was "probably unobtainable," but insisted that the overall British share—AIOC plus Shell—be around 50 percent.[70]

The United States issued an aide-mémoire to the British ambassador on 19 February, stating that negotiations would halt unless the British position changed. After further bargaining, the United States told the British that it would accept a division of 40 percent for AIOC and the five U.S. companies, with most of the remaining 20 percent going to Shell.[71] On 2 March, the AIOC board agreed to continue negotiations to form a consortium on this basis. Reflecting close ties between AIOC and CFP and AIOC's long-standing rivalry with Shell, AIOC offered CFP an 8 percent share, thus reducing Shell's share to 12 percent. Shell was not pleased but accepted the offer to help keep Iranian oil out of "undesirable hands." Angry at AIOC's unilateral action, the United States made it clear that it would not accept such a large share for CFP. Shell needed crude oil and products more than the others and giving it a large share would benefit the position of sterling. CFP, on the other hand, had access to plenty of oil through its share in the Iraq Petroleum Company, and French authorities had been discriminating against U.S. companies in West Africa to gain more outlets for CFP. After the British government agreed to cooperate in assuring working out a "suitable" distribution of shares between Shell and CFP, negotiations between the consortium members resumed, focusing now on the issue of compensation.[72]

Despite the agreement on relative shares, AIOC almost brought talks to a standstill again with its compensation demands. Fraser argued that the other members should pay AIOC approximately £280 million (around $784 million) for their 60 percent share in the "oil resources Anglo-Iranian has proved and developed." Fraser also wanted compensation from Iran, suggesting that Iran provide AIOC with 110 million tons of "free" oil over a twenty-year period, which at current prices (but not costs) would amount to about £530 million ($1.484 billion). The U.S. companies and Shell argued that AIOC's price for shares in the consortium was "fantastically unrealistic and completely unacceptable." They also pointed out that a key assumption behind the consortium plan was that if Iran signed an operating agreement giving the consortium control over production, refining, and distribution with fifty-fifty profit sharing, AIOC was not entitled to compensation from Iran for loss of future profits. In effect, AIOC was demanding to be paid twice, once by its partners and then by Iran. Such a solution would not be "fair or durable."[73]

Ambassador Henderson felt that Fraser's demands were "so fantastic and lacking in realism" that they were probably a maneuver to force the British government to intervene, thus sparing him the blame for not obtaining higher compensation for AIOC.[74] In response to Hoover's request that the U.S government give Britain a "full and frank statement" of the U.S. position, Dulles told the British ambassador that the United States was "deeply troubled," and warned that unless there was a "drastic change" in Fraser's attitude the U.S. government would not oppose U.S. companies breaking off negotiations. Such a development might ultimately force the United States "to review the whole scope of our Middle East relationships." Secretary of Defense Charles E. Wilson was so angry at the British that he thought the United States should pull out of the talks and take $100 million out of U.S. aid to Britain and use it to keep Iran going. The British ambassador warned the Foreign Office that if negotiations broke down American public opinion would blame the "obstinacy and unreasonableness" of AIOC and would support a much more independent U.S. policy in the Middle East.[75]

A National Security Council working group report endorsed the decision to "use exceptional pressure" to force the British toward an early settlement. The working group rejected other "independent actions" such as the U.S. government purchase of Iranian oil, purchase of Iranian oil by private U.S. companies, and continuing to subsidize the Iranian government by providing economic aid. In addition to the "almost insurmountable" problem of disposing of large amounts of oil, U.S. government purchase of Iranian oil would reward nationalization, undermine U.S. investments abroad, and seriously harm U.S. relations with Britain. The major U.S. oil companies with the capacity to handle large amounts of Iranian oil would not do so because it would reward nationalization without compensation. Although some U.S. independent oil companies were interested in buying Iranian oil at discounted prices, even as a group they would not be able to buy sufficient oil to meet Iranian budget needs. In addition, their main market would be the United States, and domestic oil companies would strongly oppose large-scale imports. Subsidizing the Iranian government would remove a key incentive for it to reach an early settlement, and Congress would object to continuing aid without an oil settlement. After complaining about Churchill's "Victorian" attitude, President Eisenhower approved the working group's recommendation at a National Security Council meeting on 18 March.[76]

Faced with Dulles's threat that further obstinacy might force the United States to "reconsider" its cooperation with the British in the Middle East, Eden told Fraser to reach a compromise with the other companies. On 20 March, Fraser told the U.S. companies and Shell that AIOC would agree to its consortium partners paying AIOC a little over $600 million (£214.4 million) for their 60 percent share in the concession, provided that the British and Iranian governments could reach a "satisfactory" settlement on compensation from Iran. Arguing that Iran should be required to pay compensation for the difference between what AIOC's enterprise in Iran was worth in 1950 and "the value now put on it by the American companies," they suggested that £100 million ($280 million) was "eminently reasonable."[77] Getting AIOC to back down on its demands for compensation from Iran proved difficult, in part because the British government believed that heavy compensation was necessary to deter other countries from nationalizing.[78]

The U.S members of the consortium and Shell refused to commit to such a settlement. Ambassador Henderson pointed out that that Iran would accept an agreement that left the oil industry "in effect" in foreign hands so long as they were not also required to pay "any appreciable amount" of compensation to AIOC. Secretary of the Treasury Humphrey complained on 22 March that nationalization had been a "complete failure," and forcing Iran to pay damages was "rubbing salt in the wound." The State Department informed the British on 23 March that it could not accept asking Iran to pay AIOC £100 million in compensation. Dulles later informed Humphrey he had told the British that AIOC should be satisfied with getting 40 percent of the consortium and $600 million from its consortium partners for the other 60 percent, which was a lot more than it had before the coup, "which was nothing," adding "if they don't change their tune, they will get nothing."[79]

As the disagreement dragged on, doubts grew among the British over the wisdom of driving a hard bargain. Ambassador Roger Makins warned the Foreign Office that "the hand having been played the way it has been we are in a fix" and pointed out that if the U.S. companies and the U.S. government pulled out of the negotiations, AIOC would get nothing. Eden reluctantly agreed that compensation would be set somewhere between £100 million as a maximum and the value of facilities to be turned over to Iran as a minimum. Asked what would happen if AIOC refused to accept such a settlement, a British official told Hoover on 25 March that "[Fraser] will have had his fun and will be through." Hoover felt that the British proposal was the best solution under the circumstances, and the State Department agreed to support it. The Foreign Office informed the State Department on 25 March that the British government would handle the compensation negotiations, which would be separate from the negotiations on the consortium.[80]

Inter-company talks concluded on 9 April with the signing of a memorandum of understanding that provided for the formation of a consortium with AIOC holding 40 percent of the shares, Shell 14 percent, 8 percent each for the five U.S. companies (making the share held by U.S. companies equal to that of AIOC), and 6 percent for CFP. Shell's 14 percent share assuaged Britain's concern that British interests hold an overall majority in the consortium while allaying Iranian concerns that Britain would control it directly through AIOC. To avoid congressional criticism, the U.S. companies would be permitted to transfer a portion of their shares in the consortium to other established U.S. oil companies if the British and Iranian governments did not object. The other companies would pay AIOC £32.4 million (around $90.7 million) in the first year and an overriding royalty of $0.10 a barrel for the oil they received from the consortium until they had paid an

The Iranian oil consortium

Company	Share	Nationality
British Petroleum (AIOC)	40	UK
Royal Dutch/Shell	14	UK-Dutch
Standard Oil Company (New Jersey)	7	U.S.
Standard Oil Company of California	7	—
Socony-Vacuum Oil Company	7	—
Gulf Oil Corporation	7	—
The Texas Company	7	—
Iricon*	5	—
Compagnie française de pétroles	6	French

* A group of nine American independents that joined the consortium in 1955: Richfield Oil Corporation, American Independent Oil Company, Standard of Ohio, Getty Oil Company, Signal Oil and Gas Company, Atlantic Refining, Hancock Oil Company, Tidewater Oil Company, and San Jacinto Petroleum Company.

Source: Painter, Oil and the American Century, 196.

additional £182 million ($509.6 million), which put the total price for their 60 percent share in the consortium at £214.4 million ($600.3 million).[81] As Daniel Yergin points out, Fraser's tenacity paid off. AIOC "came out surprisingly well" from the nationalization crisis. "It was the best deal Willie Fraser ever made," a high Shell official later noted. "After all, Anglo-Iranian actually had nothing to sell. It had already been nationalized."[82]

Negotiations with Iran

The next stage of negotiations took place in Iran. In one set of talks, consortium and Iranian government representatives sought to define the nature and degree of control the consortium would exercise over Iran's oil industry. At the same time, the new British ambassador to Iran, Sir Roger Stevens, negotiated compensation with the Iranian government and British Treasury representatives worked out currency arrangements between Iran and the United Kingdom. Running negotiations for Iran was Minister of Finance 'Ali Amini, a well-respected aristocrat with ties to the National Front (he had served in Mosaddeq's first cabinet) and a knowledge of the oil industry.[83]

How the consortium would be managed emerged as one of the most important points of conflict. Company representatives insisted that the consortium have "full control" of production and refining operations as principals, not as agents. The companies wanted the consortium to have lease rights to extract oil, with title to the oil passing to the consortium when it left the ground, as under the AIOC and other concessions. Amini insisted that the companies operate as agents of Iran. The companies feared that agreeing to an agency-type agreement would be an "open invitation to nationalization," because other countries would demand similar treatment. Having a property right to extract oil was also important to the U.S. companies so they could claim U.S. tax credits for taxes they paid to Iran on their profits.[84]

The nationality of the two operating companies, one for production and the other for refining, the nationality of the top management of the cooperating companies, and the location of consortium headquarters also proved to be contentious issues. Supported by the British government, AIOC demanded that the companies be registered in Britain and led and staffed mainly by former AIOC employees. AIOC also wanted consortium headquarters to be in AIOC headquarters at Britannic House in London. The British insisted on these points not only for reasons of prestige, but also because they involved management control of the consortium. British-registered companies would be subject to British financial and tax regulations. The taxes the companies would pay would be a boost to the British budget, and their financial activities and procurement of goods would be easier to control. U.S. registration was out of the question for currency reasons as well as prestige.[85]

Discussions with Iranian officials revealed the depth of opposition to the consortium's proposals. Minister of Court 'Ala, who was generally pro-Western, complained to Ambassador Henderson on 22 April that AIOC was trying to get back its old position in Iran "behind the mask of the consortium." 'Ala feared that AIOC, with the support of "British-controlled Shell" and "British dominated" CFP, would control the consortium and warned that "every patriotic Iranian" would oppose the consortium's proposals. If the consortium refused to reach a satisfactory deal, Iran would sell or barter its oil to other purchasers. The shah and the Iranian negotiators pointed out that any agreement had to conform to the Nine-Point Nationalization Law, the essence of which was that Iran should control its oil industry. What the consortium partners proposed was unacceptable, and the shah warned on 26 April that unless the companies changed their proposal there would be no agreement.[86]

The Iranians also insisted that it would be impossible to accept British nationality for the operating companies. The shah complained that this proposal was "particularly preposterous" and illustrated the consortium's ignorance or callousness regarding Iranian views. Ambassador Henderson pointed out that since the consortium insisted that it had to have management control, the agreement had to provide "some facade" that would make it possible for the Iranian government to claim that it did not violate the nationalization law. Location of company headquarters outside Iran would create the appearance that Iran's oil industry would be run "by remote control" from a foreign country.[87] Amini indicated that Iran might accept the operating companies being based in a neutral location such as the Netherlands. Although the other consortium partners had initially agreed to support AIOC on the nationality issue in return for receiving certain sterling operating privileges from the British Treasury, they and U.S. officials were concerned that incorporating the operating companies in Britain, staffing them with former AIOC employees, and locating the consortium headquarters in London would be so objectionable to Iran that even if the shah accepted such terms, they would undermine the Iranian government and would not be viable in the long run.[88]

Faced with Iranian opposition, the British agreed that the two operating companies could be incorporated in Iran, but still wanted the holding company to be incorporated in Britain to provide consortium members with protection in case of a dispute with the Iranian government. Ignoring that they had proposed that the operating companies be incorporated in Britain, the British now argued that Dutch incorporation of operating companies was "absolutely unacceptable," since it would be inappropriate for the operating companies to be incorporated in one of the consortium's member states. The British also opposed incorporation in a neutral country, arguing it would not provide sufficient diplomatic protection in case of a dispute with Iran. The U.S. companies, however, opposed Iranian registration of the operating companies, though they believed that their headquarters should be in Iran.[89]

The British government, which had taken over the compensation negotiations from AIOC, conceded that Iran would not have to compensate AIOC for the loss of future profits, but insisted that Iran pay compensation for losses incurred by AIOC as a result of being deprived of access to Iranian oil. The British estimated that after Iranian counterclaims were considered, Iran should pay AIOC around £100 million ($280 million), a figure that included the Naft-e-Shah oil field, the Kermanshah refinery, and internal distribution facilities, including oil in storage for domestic use, which would be turned over to Iran. The Iranians countered that loss of access to Iranian oil was the company's fault, pointing out that they had offered

to continue to deliver oil to AIOC after nationalization, but AIOC had refused due to Iran's demand that AIOC sign receipts recognizing nationalization. The Iranians also argued that their counterclaims for damages
resulting from the AIOC-led boycott of Iranian exports and other actions
were as great, if not greater than the losses suffered by AIOC.[90] The consortium partners agreed with the British government that all payments for oil,
including taxes, refining fees, and local expenditures should be in pounds
sterling. The Iranians reluctantly agreed that the consortium conduct its
business in sterling but insisted that Britain agree to convert sterling freely
into other currencies as needed by Iran to purchase items from non-sterling
countries.[91]

Convinced that the shah's support would be needed for an agreement
to be approved, Henderson and Hoover warned in mid-May that anything
other than an agency agreement would bear too close a resemblance to
the former AIOC concession to be acceptable to the Iranian public. "Effective
management by private industry" was of "infinitely greater importance"
than the legal and tax concerns the companies had about an agency agreement. The Iranians were willing to give the consortium the same degree of
management control under an agency agreement as would be inherent in
a concession, and the Treasury Department could work out ways for U.S.
companies to receive the same tax advantages they would receive under a
concession. Failure to reach a settlement would lead to political and economic chaos in Iran. Even if loss of Iran to the Soviets could be avoided, Iranian efforts to sell as much oil as possible on almost any terms would have a
very serious effect on world oil markets. The Iranians had already made
commitments to sell as much as 3 million tons a year to various countries.
The State Department agreed that the "very great political, strategic and
economic consequences" that might result from failure outweighed possible
legal precedents stemming from an agency agreement.[92]

The heads of the major U.S. oil companies met with officials from the
Treasury, State, and Defense Departments on 21 May and agreed that they
could accept an agency-type contract provided that it met certain "minimum
indispensable" conditions, including full and effective management control;
fifty-fifty profit sharing, with taxes constituting the main portion of the
money paid to Iran; duration approximately the same as the former AIOC
concession; monopoly of production and distribution of oil produced in the
contract area, though Iran could sell the small amount of "royalty oil" it
received; and Majlis approval of the essential parts of the agreement. The
companies expected the U.S. government to "exert maximum pressure"

on Iran to accept these requirements and to put pressure on the British on the questions of the nationality of the operating companies and their management.[93]

The threat of the Iranian government making deals with independent oil companies to handle Iranian oil exports increased pressure to reach a settlement. The companies likely to make such deals lacked markets in the Eastern Hemisphere and would either need to cut prices to sell their oil or try to sell it in the United States. More Iranian oil in Eastern Hemisphere markets would also force Venezuelan oil into the U.S. and other Western Hemisphere markets.[94] Oil imports were a contentious issue in American politics because even small quantities could upset the system that supported U.S. oil prices. Net U.S. imports rose from 116.2 million barrels (2.4 percent of demand) in 1948 to 230.9 million barrels in 1953 (8.17 percent of demand). The rise in imports led the Texas Railroad Commission (the agency managing oil output in Texas) to cut the level of production allowed in Texas oil fields from 100 percent to 65 percent between 1948 and 1953.[95] Further cuts or policies supporting greater imports would trigger a political response in the United States.

Hoover and other U.S. officials also feared that these deals in the aggregate could provide Iran with an alternative to reaching an agreement with the major oil companies. In addition to putting pressure on the existing price system, the deals could strengthen Iran's negotiating position. Confident that Iranians would not be able to run their oil industry efficiently, the British had previously played down the impact of letting Iran try to produce and market oil on its own. By the spring of 1954, the British also began to be concerned that Iran might be able to export sufficient oil on its own to make nationalization a qualified success and a settlement with AIOC unnecessary. Successful nationalization would threaten British investment throughout the Middle East, and indeed worldwide, an unwelcome development for a nation dependent on foreign investment income.[96]

The extent of British Treasury control over conversion of sterling into dollars also caused problems. Although the Treasury had offered to convert 40 percent of consortium earnings into dollars for the use of the Iranian government, it wanted Iran to agree to use the dollars provided only to purchase goods and service that were not available in the sterling area to limit the dollar drain caused by loss of monopoly control of Iranian oil and to avoid problems with Kuwait and Iraq, which also operated in sterling. The British insisted that they could not justify giving Iran more favorable treatment than other sterling area oil producers, "particularly in light of past Iranian actions." The U.S. companies, strongly supported by Secretary of the Treasury Humphrey, argued that any discrimination against the dollar was unnecessary and unfair to U.S. companies. The disagreement led to a series of heated exchanges between Humphrey and the British ambassador, but there was little the United States could do to pressure the British, because the bulk of Iranian oil would have to be sold in sterling markets. Sending it to the United States would disrupt the U.S. oil market and lead to congressional action to limit oil imports. Since Iranian oil would have to be sold in the sterling area, the British Treasury would have a degree of control over convertibility. Having lost the battle over nationality of the operating companies, the British refused to change their policy on sterling convertibility, though they assured Humphrey that there was no way they could force Iran to abide by an agreement limiting its dollar expenditures and that they had no intention of doing so.[97]

The final issue to be resolved was Iran's compensation payment to AIOC. The British ambassador apparently told Amini on 28 June that Iran had to pay substantial compensation regardless of the merits of Iranian counterclaims, and on 4 July the British presented Iran with calculations claiming to show that AIOC had suffered £263.5 million in damages and losses due to nationalization. The compensation issue was a dangerous problem for the Iranian government, and Ambassador Henderson warned that anything more than £15 million would "provoke serious consequences."[98]

Final Agreement

After weeks of arduous negotiations, consortium representatives and the Iranian government signed an agreement in principle on 5 August outlining the arrangements between Iran and the consortium.[99] According to the terms of the agreement, NIOC retained title to Iran's oil industry. In return for Iranian assurances that the consortium would have the same degree of management control as it would under a concession arrangement, the companies agreed that the consortium would act as an agent of NIOC, thus rendering Iranian control largely symbolic. Two operating companies, one for exploration and production and another to handle refining, operated the industry. Similarly, though legally exercising their powers on behalf of NIOC, the operating companies were given "full and effective" management control of all operations, and their rights and powers could not be modified during the twenty-five-year term of the agreement. The operating companies would be incorporated in the Netherlands, with top management drawn largely from Shell. Their headquarters would be in Iran, and most of their staff would reside there. The operating companies would be owned by a holding company incorporated in Britain and headquartered there, though Iran had the right to name two of each company's directors. In a symbolic slap at Iran, a member of AIOC's board of directors, H. E. Snow, was named head of the holding company. A service company in charge of supplying operations in Iran would also be incorporated and located in Britain.[100]

Pricing provisions were complicated, but in effect allowed the operating companies to set prices based on prevailing posted prices in the region. The complicated tax provisions were similarly designed to result in fifty-fifty profit sharing, and royalties and taxes were adjusted so that U.S. companies could count their payments to Iran as tax credits against their U.S. income taxes, as Aramco did in Saudi Arabia. The agreement placed the vitally important matter of the production level in the hands of the consortium partners, though they promised to increase offtake from Iran in accordance with supply and demand for Middle East oil and increased target production levels slightly. According to estimates by U.S. intelligence agencies, these volumes should bring in revenues of around $60 million in the first year, $150 million in the second year, and $175 million in the third year. Beginning in 1957, production levels would be determined by a complicated formula that ensured that the growth in Iranian production would not come at the expense of their other holdings in the Middle East. The agreement covered around 100,000 square miles and would remain in force for twenty-five years with provisions for three five-year extensions. After the initial twenty-five years, the consortium would have to give up 20 percent of its total area with each five-year extension.[101]

With support from the U.S. government, Iranian and British Treasury representatives reached a compromise agreement on the currency issue. The final agreement provided that the consortium would operate in sterling, but the British Treasury promised to convert up to 40 percent of total sterling receipts (the percentage U.S. companies held in the consortium) to dollars without limits. After the 40 percent limit had been reached, the British government would consider Iranian requests to convert additional amounts into dollars and other currencies on a case-by-case basis.[102]

Under strong pressure from the United States, the British government agreed to limit compensation from Iran to AIOC to £25 million ($70 million); £10 million for the properties Iran retained, the Naft-e Shah oil field located north of the main fields in Khuzestan, a small oil refinery at Kermanshah that served the field, and internal distribution facilities; and £15 million for the losses and damages suffered by AIOC from 1951 to 1954. Iran would pay the interest-free amount in ten equal annual installments beginning on 1 January 1957, in the form of free oil to AIOC. In a bit of creative accounting, the British were able to include in the final compensation total an additional £50 million ($140 million) that Iran had demanded under the never-ratified 1949 Supplemental Agreement, a debt the British government had previously termed "fictitious" and never paid. In addition to making total compensation seem closer to the British goal of £100 million, this provision lowered AIOC's British tax liability by approximately £25 million.[103]

Ambassador Henderson reported on 15 August that prospects for Majlis approval of the oil settlement appeared good. The shah supported approval and government-controlled newspapers branded opposition to the agreement as communist inspired.[104] Under pressure from the State Department and the CIA, the shah agreed to allow Zahedi to remain in office until the agreement had been ratified.[105] The uncovering of a Tudeh network in the army in August and the subsequent arrest of hundreds of suspected Tudeh members dealt the party a sharp setback and gave the government a needed boost. The Tudeh "ring" in the army was confined to espionage, which suggested that the party had decided to limit its efforts to developing assets rather than attempting to seize control of the military.[106] Despite these positive developments, the CIA warned that the shah's long-term prospects were threatened by the persistent low standard of living among ordinary Iranians, pervasive corruption, government repression, and "nationalist resentment of foreign influence" over government affairs.[107]

The consortium agreement undermined the Justice Department's antitrust suit against the major companies. Informed by Hoover of the completion of the oil agreement, Attorney General Brownell wrote President Eisenhower that he had reviewed the agreement and concluded that in light of the determination by the National Security Council that the security interests of the United States required that U.S. oil companies participate in the consortium, it did not constitute a violation of the antitrust laws.[108] This decision changed the focus of the antitrust suit from production control to price-fixing and marketing agreements. Both had become superfluous to the companies' management of markets, because once the vertically integrated majors were in control of almost all large foreign oil reserves, production, refining, and transportation, they could effectively control markets and set prices without fixing them directly. Not enough "free" oil was available to challenge their control.[109]

Recognizing that it was essential that any oil agreement have the "unequivocal support" of the shah, the United States, on Hoover's recommendation, had withheld the additional military assistance desired by the shah until he gave his support.[110] In September, General Robert A. McClure, chief of the U.S. military mission to the Iranian army and chief of the U.S. Military Assistance Advisory Group, recommended that financial support for Iran's military be increased from $30 million per year to $360 million spread over three years. Ambassador Henderson supported the proposal. During a 12 October meeting, State Department officials argued that the imminent conclusion of an oil agreement offered the United States an opportunity "for advancing our objective of sewing Iran up firmly with the West," which could be accomplished through an expanded program of military and economic aid. The following day the department confirmed an aid package for Iran of $120 million.[111]

The final draft of the oil agreement was completed on 17 September, and Minister of Finance Amini presented the agreement to the Majlis on 21 September.[112] Unsurprisingly, the carefully chosen members of the Majlis and the Senate approved the agreement: the Majlis vote on 21 October was 113 in favor, five opposed, with one abstention, and the Senate vote a week later was forty-one votes in favor, four opposed, and three abstentions. The shah, who had lobbied hard for an increase in military assistance, signed the bill on 29 October. The next day tankers, already dispatched to Abadan in anticipation of the agreement's approval, began loading Iranian oil for export, with an AIOC tanker at the head of the line.[113]

Conclusion

A National Intelligence Estimate in early December 1954 concluded Iran would remain a "basically unstable country" for quite some time. The shah had emerged as the most powerful force in political affairs through his control of the armed forces, which swore loyalty to him personally rather than to the nation. Despite the resumption of oil exports, which together with U.S. interim aid promised to provide Iran with substantial income, the shah and his allies had failed to achieve widespread popular support and were staying in power through the extensive use of authoritarian means such as martial law, strict press censorship, and use of the security forces to control demonstrations and suppress and imprison opponents of the regime. The shah and traditional conservative ruling groups would probably be able to retain control for the next few years through authoritarian means, but they would remain vulnerable unless they made progress addressing Iran's problems. Although the armed forces were a "fairly reliable instrument" for dealing with disorder, they were not immune from the grievances that mobilized civilians, and a sharp decline in popular acceptance of the ruling group could undermine their reliability.[114]

In February 1953, oil consultant Max W. Thornburg advised his friend Allen W. Dulles, who had just been named head of the CIA, that the question in Iran was not how to make an oil agreement that would bolster the government in Iran, but rather how to bolster a government in Iran that would reach a satisfactory oil agreement.[115] Although his remarks were aimed at convincing Dulles that the United States should oust Mosaddeq and back the shah, they also offer an insight into U.S. policy toward Iran after the coup. The oil settlement reintegrated Iranian oil into world markets and provided Iran with substantial and growing oil revenues. It also reversed nationalization and strengthened, at least temporarily, control of the world oil economy by the major international companies. These "successes" came at the cost of the Iranian people, as the settlement entrenched and strengthened authoritarian rule under an increasingly autocratic shah, dependent on support from the United States.

History and Contested Memories

· ·

The Iranian crisis of 1951–54 was a pivotal chapter in the history of the post–World War II world. The crisis, which began with the nationalization of the Iranian oil industry in the spring of 1951 and ended with the reversal of nationalization following the overthrow of nationalist Prime Minister Mohammed Mosaddeq in August 1953, was also a crucial turning point in the global Cold War. The United States feared losing Iran and possibly the entire Middle East and its oil to the Soviets, and the U.S. role in the ouster of Mosaddeq, a constitutional nationalist opposed to communism and Western imperialism, became a model for future interventions in Latin America, the Middle East, and Asia.

The outcome of the crisis, which returned Iran's oil to foreign control, confirmed the dominance of Western corporations over the resources of the Global South for the next twenty years. The crisis also marked a milestone in the process by which the United States replaced Great Britain as the guarantor of Western interests in the Middle East, though it did not fully take over that role until the 1970s. Although the Anglo-Iranian dispute demonstrated in vivid detail the weakness of Britain as a great power, the British nonetheless drew the lesson that they could rely on U.S. acquiescence and assistance in removing rulers in countries traditionally under their influence. These conclusions put Britain on the slippery slope to the Suez debacle of 1956. Finally, the crisis was a major turning point in the history of modern Iran, a moment when liberal democracy and constitutional government overcame the authoritarian impulses of Iran's monarchy, only to be dashed by foreign intervention. After the coup, U.S. assistance helped entrench monarchical power, altering the course of Iranian development and entrenching an autocratic regime that would endure until it collapsed amid the Islamic Revolution of 1978–79.

Given its importance, it is not surprising that the history of the crisis remains contested. The ongoing debate is partly the result of the uneven and delayed declassification of vital U.S. records, the British ban on releasing material dealing with intelligence operations, and the relative dearth of archival material on Iranian and Soviet policies and actions. It is also due to the efforts of the U.S. and British governments, the shah and his supporters, and the major oil companies to erect self-serving narratives surrounding the events of 1951–54.

In the West, cold warriors depicted the August 1953 coup as a victory over communism. The U.S. and British governments and the oil companies laid the groundwork for this interpretation during the crisis by feeding stories to the Iranian and Western press depicting Mosaddeq as an incompetent tyrant who was either wittingly or unwittingly paving the way for a communist takeover of Iran. After the coup, U.S. and British newspapers held this line, and former U.S. and British officials often argued in interviews and memoirs that the threat of a communist Iran precipitated and justified Mosaddeq's overthrow.[1]

No one worked harder to disseminate this narrative than Loy W. Henderson, a storied U.S. Foreign Service officer who served as ambassador to Iran from late September 1951 to the end of December 1954. In interviews and letters over the subsequent decades, Henderson argued that although Mosaddeq was not a communist, his refusal to settle the oil dispute was creating conditions that sooner or later would have led to the loss of Iran to communism, and that his ouster was therefore necessary.[2]

Henderson was generally careful to deny U.S. involvement in the coup and characterize the events of August 1953 as a spontaneous anti-communist uprising. In an interview in 1973, Henderson tried to prove his point by arguing that "no matter how skilled the CIA might be, it could not have engineered the overthrow of Mossadegh if the people of Iran had not overwhelmingly been in favor of the return of the Shah."[3] Writing to Bruce Riedel in 1975, Henderson claimed that the Tudeh had "controlled the streets" in the three days before the 19 August coup attempt, and the "overwhelming majority" of Iranians "spontaneously" joined demonstrations calling for the shah to return.[4] Henderson maintained in separate correspondence that it was "impossible" for Iran to "survive as a democracy" when it lay so close to the Soviet Union, and contended that scholars who claimed the United States played a role in Mosaddeq's ouster "[had] no sympathy for the Shah's way of trying to modernize his backward country."[5]

This interpretation became so dominant that U.S. officials often expressed it in private until publication of Kermit Roosevelt's 1979 memoir *Countercoup* exposed the falsity of such claims.[6] Internal histories of the operation by the CIA similarly argued that the coup was necessary to prevent Iran's "collapse" into communism.[7] No serving American official publicly acknowledged U.S. involvement in Mosaddeq's ouster until Secretary of

State Madeleine Albright admitted in a speech in 2000 that "the United States played a significant role in orchestrating the overthrow of Iran's popular prime minister." Even though she conceded that the coup was "clearly a setback for Iran's political development," she maintained that the Eisenhower administration "believed its actions were justified for strategic reasons."[8]

In addition to not calling into question the morality of U.S. actions or undermining the legitimacy of the shah, the United States had larger reasons for concealing its role in the crisis. The success of the coup suggested covert action could be deployed as a cheap and effective tool of Cold War statecraft. President Dwight D. Eisenhower noted in his diary on 8 October 1953 that if the facts of the U.S. involvement became public, "our chances of doing anything of like nature in the future would almost certainly disappear."[9] The United States subsequently deployed the covert tactics used in Iran in a host of operations throughout the Global South.[10]

Beyond the coup, American interference in internal Iranian affairs during the nationalization crisis period was kept secret, with CIA actions and Ambassador Henderson's activities hidden from view through the withholding of sensitive material or careful editing of declassified documents. The extent of such censorship became evident with the publication in 2017 of a retrospective *Foreign Relations* volume on the crisis that contained hundreds of previously censored documents.[11]

Mohammed Reza Pahlavi claimed that the coup was a "national uprising" that proved his popularity among the Iranian people and had the anniversary of the coup celebrated each year. The shah refrained from having Mosaddeq executed, for fear of making him a martyr. Instead, the former prime minister was sentenced to a three-year prison term followed by internal exile to his family estate in Ahmadabad, 100 kilometers from Tehran.[12] He died there in 1967, "a living legend, and the most popular unperson in the country," according to historian Homa Katouzian.[13]

Interpretations of the settlement after the coup also reflected the different needs of the parties who had agreed to the consortium deal in 1954. For the oil companies and the U.S. and British governments, the success of the boycott and the reversal of nationalization confirmed the dominance of the major international oil companies and served as a warning to countries seeking control of their resources. "Oil without a market, as Mr. Mossadeq learned many, many years ago, does not do a country much good," U.S. President Richard M. Nixon told reporters, somewhat ironically in retrospect, in September 1973 on the eve of the 1973–74 oil shock.[14] Although the companies' defeat of nationalization set back the cause of national sovereignty over natural resources for years, Mosaddeq's example inspired a generation of resource nationalists in the Global South.[15]

Iranians opposed to the shah's rule viewed the failure of nationalization and reform as emblematic of Iran's subjugation to foreign powers, symptoms of the country's "Westoxification" under the Pahlavi regime.[16] Toppling the shah from power in 1979, the new Islamic Republic of Iran denounced the United States as the "Great Satan" and decried its intervention in Iranian affairs. While the 1953 coup still warrants a mention at state events and in speeches and editorials written by regime officials, Iran's post-1979 leadership do not fully embrace Mosaddeq, a secular nationalist, and choose instead to de-emphasize his role in the nationalization in favor of his clerical allies.[17]

Recovering the History of the Crisis

Myths and misperceptions, many originally propagated to justify opposition to nationalization and legitimize the coup, have long distorted understanding of the crisis. Some of the most common include the argument that U.S. policy throughout the crisis was driven by security concerns and had little or nothing to do with protecting the interests of U.S. and British oil companies; that the United States acted as an "honest broker" between Iran and Great Britain during negotiations to resolve the nationalization dispute; that Mosaddeq had a poor grasp of the international oil industry and his approach to oil issues was "irrational"; that Mosaddeq's intransigence was the main reason why negotiations failed; that Mosaddeq's policies were leading to communism; and that the coup was carried out mainly by Iranian "patriots" acting independently rather than supported and directed by Anglo-American agents.

No one who has been through U.S. records for this period would deny that national security concerns played a very important role in U.S. policy. That said, the historical record does not support the notion that the United States was more concerned about containing communism than combating nationalization, a myth propagated by the British at the time and accepted by many scholars since. This view is also conceptually flawed because it fails to understand the broad definition of national security held by American leaders. Ideas about national security are not given, but rather are shaped by the structures of power and influence in the society they are meant to defend. As Melvyn P. Leffler points out, the U.S. conception of national security has included preservation of such "core values" as "private property, free enterprise, open markets and the rule of law as well as the safety of American lives, national sovereignty and territorial integrity."[18]

After considering a larger role for the government in international oil matters during World War II, in the postwar period the United States reverted to its traditional policy of relying on private oil companies to secure and maintain U.S. access to foreign oil supplies and markets.[19] Reliance on private corporations as vehicles for the national interest fundamentally shaped the way the United States approached the Iranian crisis. A report to the National Security Council by the secretaries of state, defense, and the interior in January 1953 argued that the major international oil companies "provided the ingenuity, capital, and technology" that had developed the oil resources of Venezuela and the Middle East, and that "they alone" were capable of maintaining and expanding production from those areas to meet the rising demand for oil. If the companies' assets were nationalized, "the oil from those areas would to a serious extent be lost to the free world."[20]

Relations between the government and the oil industry were even closer in Great Britain, where the interests of the government and the Anglo-Iranian Oil Company were often the same. Anti-communism and opposition to nationalization were directly connected, not mutually exclusive. When Mosaddeq nationalized Iran's oil industry in 1951, the U.S. and British governments and major oil companies regarded it as a threat against Western control of oil resources in the Global South. U.S. officials believed that losing Iran to communism would result in losing control of its oil. They also feared that successful nationalization would threaten Western control of raw materials, including oil, in the Global South, and limit Western access to these vital resources. The British shared these concerns and were also acutely aware of the economic consequences of Iran's action. As Steve Marsh and Steven Galpern have shown, British leaders believed that control of Iran's oil was crucial to Britain's aspirations to remain a great power.[21]

Control of oil was a significant source of U.S. power and influence, and U.S. oil policy was integrally linked to Cold War strategic calculations. Control of oil helped the United States contain the Soviet Union; end destructive political, economic, and military competition among the core capitalist states; mitigate class conflict within the capitalist core by promoting economic growth; and retain access to the raw materials, markets, and labor of the periphery in an era of decolonization and national liberation. Maintaining access to oil became a key priority of U.S. foreign policy and led to U.S. involvement in the oil-producing areas of the Global South, often in ways that distorted development in those areas.[22]

An independent non-communist Iran was of critical importance to the United States because of its strategic position and oil resources. Iran played a key role in the forward defense of the eastern Mediterranean and Persian Gulf area by blocking Soviet access to the Persian Gulf oil fields, which were of increasing importance to Western Europe and Japan. An oil settlement that would maintain Western control and access but also allow Iran to receive sufficient revenues from its oil resources to consolidate a pro-Western government was an essential step in keeping Iran in the free world and strengthening the U.S. position in Europe, the Middle East, and South Asia.[23] The stakes were high and, according to influential oil consultant Walter J. Levy, the crisis in Iran raised the question "whether in a situation where a vital national power position of the United States is at stake, it can afford to apply fully the normal and traditional laws of sovereign self-determination to the control of underdeveloped countries over the oil in their soil."[24]

The historical record also makes it clear that characterizing U.S. policy during the crisis as that of an "honest broker" is inaccurate. The oil nationalization dispute was a complex affair, but at its heart was the issue of who would control Iranian oil and the wealth produced by the sale of that oil on the global market.[25] For most Iranians, nationalization meant sovereign control of the oil industry. Though American and British officials frequently complained that Mosaddeq's stance shifted or changed during discussions, Mosaddeq held firm to his belief that Iran should manage the production and refining of its oil, that it should play a role in how that oil was sold, and that it should not be burdened by an onerous compensation obligation to AIOC. The U.S. and British governments as well as AIOC and the other international oil companies refused to accept any settlement of the dispute that would allow Iran to control its oil industry. Yet critics of Mosaddeq still claim that negotiations failed due to his stubbornness and irrational attachment to unrealistic expectations.

Between April 1951 and March 1953, the United States promoted multiple attempts to bring Britain and Iran to an agreement that recognized nationalization but left control in the hands of the oil companies. No agreement was possible because the British refused to relinquish even the semblance of control and demanded punishingly high compensation for the loss of their "enterprise" in Iran. Convinced of the correctness of their position, the British used talks as a stalling tactic to buy time for the economic impact of their boycott of Iranian exports and covert actions inside Iran to remove Mosaddeq from power. The British also repeatedly sabotaged discussions whenever they believed they might lead to a settlement that would threaten their interests. Despite pressure from the United States to take Iranian concerns into account, the British consistently maintained their position throughout the crisis.

Although the United States was somewhat more flexible over how to respond to Iranian nationalism, U.S. policymakers eventually concluded that Mosaddeq would never agree to a settlement that left control of Iran's oil in the hands of the major international oil companies, which was the only kind of settlement the United States would support. U.S. officials feared that failure to find a settlement to the oil dispute, which they mainly blamed on Mosaddeq, would lead to economic and political chaos and undermine the position of the shah, whom the United States had long seen as the key guarantor of Western interests in Iran. U.S. officials also worried that the British boycott of Iranian oil exports was breaking down and Iran would soon be able to sell enough oil to independent and state-supported oil companies to make nationalization a qualified success—a prospect that could threaten Western investment throughout the region and the world. Independent oil sales also threatened the postwar petroleum order established by the major Anglo-American oil companies by undermining their control of reserves and production outside the United States and the Soviet Union. After the coup, the U.S. government took the lead in setting up an international consortium to run the Iranian oil industry and reintegrate Iranian oil into the global oil market. Although the United States prevented the British from forcing Iran to pay extravagant compensation, the settlement effectively reversed nationalization and protected the interests of AIOC and the other major international oil companies.

The idea that Mosaddeq's policies were leading to communist rule, much less the notion that he would surrender Iran to the communists, is not a fact, but a myth created in the build-up to the coup and repeated for years after to justify his ouster. It is true that assessments produced by the coup planners during the operation emphasized the communist threat to Iran and the need for immediate action. In addition, the coup's operation plan stated explicitly that the replacement of Mosaddeq was necessary "as the alternative to certain economic collapse in Iran and the eventual loss of the area to the Soviet orbit."[26] Richard Cottam, a CIA analyst in Washington during the coup, believed that fears of communism in Iran were "widespread" and "sincerely held," even if they did not seem to be supported by intelligence.[27] Influential State Department official Henry A. Byroade admitted that evidence proving Mosaddeq's association with the Tudeh was lacking.[28] Intelligence estimates and reports from the U.S. embassy in Tehran consistently concluded that the Tudeh was not prepared to seize power. A draft National Intelligence Estimate from 12 August 1953, written by analysts uninformed about the coup operation, concluded that "the odds still favor Mossadeq's retention of power at least through the end of 1953." These reports suggested that a general economic collapse from inflation or a fall in business activity was many months away, though American views of Iran's long-term economic outlook were generally pessimistic.[29] Moreover, available evidence from Soviet archives indicates that the Soviet Union was preoccupied with events closer to home and was not interested in intervening in Iran, in part because Soviet officials viewed Mosaddeq's government with suspicion.[30] Rather than proving that he was "soft" on communism, Mosaddeq's policy toward the Tudeh reflected his belief in democracy and free speech, while the slight softening of his approach to the party in the months before August 1953 was a tactical ploy to shore up his position against pressure from conservative elements marshaling behind Zahedi and the Anglo-American coup operation.

The drive to oust Mosaddeq meant that contrary analysis was often ignored. CIA Director Allen Dulles relied on advisors like former oil executive Max W. Thornburg and General H. Norman Schwarzkopf, who had headed the U.S. advisory mission to Iran's gendarmerie during World War II, instead of his agency's analytical division when considering political conditions within Iran.[31] Tehran CIA station chief Roger Goiran had reservations regarding the wisdom of the coup operation.[32] Ambassador Henderson also had concerns regarding the shah's suitability as leader of Iran and doubted a coup would succeed, but once the decision was made he fully cooperated with the operation. Furthermore, British and American covert activities inside Iran between April and August 1953 were designed to exaggerate the communist threat and convince the shah and other Iranians that overthrowing Mosaddeq was necessary to save Iran from chaos and communism and to preserve the monarchy.[33] In a textbook example of a self-fulfilling prophecy, U.S. and British actions to undermine Mosaddeq helped produce the conditions they were ostensibly designed to combat.

In recent years, pro-shah Iranians and others have attempted to revise the history of the coup. They downplay the significance and efficacy of U.S. and British involvement and attribute the coup's success to Mosaddeq's Iranian opposition rather than Anglo-American support and involvement.[34] The claim that the United States played a minor role in the downfall of Mosaddeq is difficult to maintain in the face of the evidence. American financial and organizational support was decisive to the coup's success on

19 August, though luck and the errors by the coup's opponents in the government and Tudeh Party were also significant. British support for the coup was important. British agents, specifically the Rashidian family and British contacts within military and clerical circles, provided the United States with the tools needed to organize Mosaddeq's downfall. In addition to coordinating and funding the coup plan, the single most important American contribution to the operation was securing the active participation of the shah. Without his involvement, it is unlikely the coup would have succeeded. As for the claim that the coup was a popular uprising, Iranian scholar Ali Rahnema and others have demonstrated that the coup's success resulted from carefully planned and well-executed military maneuvers and mercenary mobs. U.S. and British influence in the Iranian military was extensive, and it is probable that U.S. military advisors in Iran played an important role in the coup, though records regarding their activity are still classified, assuming they still exist.[35] There is little dispute that American money paid for the mobs whose emergence set the stage for military action against Mosaddeq's government.

The result of the coup was an authoritarian state dominated by the shah and the military. This outcome reflected Anglo-American preferences—the shah was seen to be pro-Western, anti-communist, and willing to acquiesce in continued foreign domination of the oil industry—yet it also reflected dominant prejudices regarding Iran's ability to flourish as an independent, democratic, and constitutional society.[36] Western leaders ultimately did not trust Mosaddeq or the National Front to safeguard Western interests in Iran. Rather than allow Iranians to determine their own destiny or control their own resources, the United States and Great Britain intervened to erect an order conducive to their interests. The ramifications of their intervention are still felt seventy years later, reflected in the bitterness affecting Iran's relations with the West and the complicated legacy of Mohammed Mosaddeq, Iran's first and last nationalist prime minister dedicated to ruling according to the 1906 constitution.

This study draws on previous scholarship, a wide range of primary sources, and the additional evidence that has become available in recent years to reexamine the origins, course, and consequences of the struggle for Iran between 1951 and 1954. It also draws on the methods historians use to make sense of the past—a stress on context, sensitivity to both continuity and change, an emphasis on the interconnectedness of all aspects of the human experience, and close engagement with primary sources and scholarly studies.[37] It argues that the history of the crisis is more complex than existing narratives and myths suggest. The United States as well as Great Britain opposed nationalization because they saw it as a threat to Western control of the oil resources of the Global South. The coup took place not only because U.S. and British leaders feared Iran's imminent loss to communism, but because they desired a change in government to reverse nationalization, restart the flow of Iranian oil to world markets, and forestall a "collapse" that would bring about internal political instability and potentially the rise of a communist-controlled government. Their intervention halted the progress Iran had been making toward representative government. Autocracy was the outcome.

History is not just about the past. Learning how the world got to be the way it is and the forces that govern its evolution is essential to understanding the present and preparing to face the future. As Michael H. Hunt and Steven I. Levine point out: "without historical perspective we flounder in mid-ocean, the shore from which we came already out of sight, the land we seek well beyond the horizon."[38] We now know much more about the Iranian crisis than we did only a few years ago. There is no guarantee that a more accurate understanding of this history will help us deal more effectively with the present and think more creatively about the future. Clinging to myths about the past, however, distorts our understanding of the present and hinders our ability to create a better future.

Notes

Note on Sources

Volumes in the U.S. State Department's *Foreign Relations of the United States* series are cited with the volume number, year, document number, and a brief description. All volumes cited are located at the Office of the Historian (https://history.state.gov /historicaldocuments). Reference to the Central Decimal File (Record Group 59) in the General Records of the Department of State comes in the form of the decimal number (888.2553, 788.00, etc.) along with a brief description of the specific document.

Abbreviations in the Notes

BET	British Embassy, Tehran
BEW	British Embassy, Washington
CAB	Records of the Cabinet, Great Britain
DDEL	Dwight D. Eisenhower Library
DEFE	Records of the Chiefs of Staff Committee, Great Britain
DIA	*Documents on International Affairs*
DSB	*Department of State Bulletin*
FO	Foreign Office, Great Britain
FIS	Foundation for Iranian Studies
FRUS	*Foreign Relations of the United States*
GTI	Office of Greek, Turkish, and Iranian Affairs
HIOHP	Harvard Iran Oral History Project
HSTL	Harry S. Truman Library
JCS	Joint Chiefs of Staff, United States of America
LC	Library of Congress
MemCon	Memorandum of Conversation
NSC	National Security Council
PAD	Petroleum Administration for Defense
POWE	Ministry of Fuel and Power Records, Great Britain
PPS	Policy Planning Staff
PREM	Prime Minister's Office Records, Great Britain
PSF	President's Secretary's File
TelCon	Memorandum of Telephone Conversation
TPF	Tehran Post File, Located in RG 84.
WBGA	World Bank Group Archives

1. Odd Arne Westad, *The Global Cold War: Third World Interventions and the Making of Our Times* (New York: Cambridge University Press, 2005); Odd Arne Westad, *The Cold War: A World History* (New York: Basic Books, 2017); Lorenz M. Lüthi, *Cold Wars: Asia, the Middle East, Europe* (Cambridge: Cambridge University Press, 2020); David S. Painter, *The Cold War: An International History* (New York: Routledge, 1999); Robert J. McMahon, ed., *The Cold War in the Third World* (New York: Oxford University Press, 2013). "Global South" is a social, economic, and political term used to refer to the less-developed countries of Asia, Africa, and Latin America. It is not a geographical concept; most countries included in the concept are located above the equator.

2. Charles Bright and Michael Geyer, "For a Unified History of the World in the Twentieth Century," *Radical History Review* 39 (1987): 82–84; David S. Painter and Melvyn P. Leffler, "Introduction: The International System and the Origins of the Cold War," in *Origins of the Cold War: An International History*, 2nd ed., edited by Melvyn P. Leffler and David S. Painter (New York: Routledge, 2005), 1–12.

3. David S. Painter, "Explaining U.S. Relations with the Third World," *Diplomatic History* 19 (Summer 1995): 525–48; Robert E. Wood, "From the Marshall Plan to the Third World," in *Origins of the Cold War*, edited by Leffler and Painter, 239–49.

4. Hedley Bull, "The Revolt against the West," in *The Expansion of International Society*, edited by Adam Watson and Hedley Bull (New York: Oxford University Press, 1985), 217–28; S. Neil MacFarlane, *Superpower Rivalry and Third World Radicalism: The Idea of National Liberation* (Baltimore: Johns Hopkins University Press, 1985).

5. Bruce Podobnik, *Global Energy Shifts: Fostering Sustainability in a Turbulent Age* (Philadelphia: Temple University Press, 2006). Oil did not displace coal. Coal production and consumption continued to grow, but oil, and later natural gas, production and consumption grew faster and raised their share of global energy consumption, which increased sharply in the postwar period. Joel Darmstadter and Hans W. Landsberg, "The Economic Background," in *The Oil Crisis*, edited by Raymond Vernon (New York: W. W. Norton, 1976), 12–22.

6. David S. Painter, "Oil and the American Century," *Journal of American History* 99 (June 2012): 24–39.

7. Vladislav M. Zubok, "Stalin, Soviet Intelligence, and the Struggle for Iran, 1945–53," *Diplomatic History* 44 (January 2020): 22–46; Vladislav M. Zubok, "Soviet Intelligence and the Cold War: The 'Small' Committee of Information, 1952–53," *Diplomatic History* 19 (1995): 453–72; Artemy Kalinovsky, "The Soviet Union and Mosaddeq: A Research Note," *Iranian Studies* 47 (2014): 401–18.

8. *Foreign Relations of the United States, 1952–1954*, vol. 10: *Iran, 1951–1954* (Washington, DC: U.S. Government Printing Office, 1989) (hereafter FRUS 1952–1954 10); William B. McAllister et al., *Toward "Thorough, Accurate, and Reliable": A History of the Foreign Relations of the United States Series* (Washington, DC: U.S. Government Printing Office, 2015), 261–76.

9. Malcolm Byrne, "When History Meets Politics: The Challenging Case of the 1953 Coup in Iran," in *United States Relations with China and Iran*, edited by Osamah F.

Khalil (London: Bloomsbury Academic, 2019), 121–40; Bruce R. Kuniholm, "Foreign Relations, Public Relations, Accountability, and Understanding," *Perspectives* 28 (May–June 1990), http://www.historians.org/perspectives/issues/1990/9005/9005NOTE1 .cfm; McAllister, et al., *Toward "Thorough, Accurate, and Reliable,"* 277–303.

10. Donald N. Wilber, *Overthrow of Premier Mosaddeq of Iran, November 1952–August 1953, CIA Clandestine Service History,* https://nsarchive2.gwu.edu /NSAEBB/NSAEBB28/l.

11. *Foreign Relations of the United States, 1952–1954, Iran, 1951–1954,* 2nd ed. (Washington, DC: U.S. Government Printing Office, 2018) (hereafter FRUS 1952–1954 Retro).

12. FRUS 1952–1954 Retro, iii–iv.

13. Gregory Brew, "The 1953 Coup d'État in Iran: New FRUS, New Questions," Wilson Center, *Sources and Methods,* 30 October 2017, https://www.wilsoncenter .org/blog-post/the-1953-coup-detat-iran-new-frus-new-questions; Gregory Brew, "A Review of *Foreign Relations of the United States, Retrospective: Iran, 1951–1954*," *Passport: The Society for Historians of American Foreign Relations Review* 48 (January 2018): 53–55, David S. Painter, "Overthrowing Mosaddeq," *Diplomatic History* 42 (June 2019): 492–95.

14. Wisner to Dulles, 20 August 1953, No. 11, Iran Collection, National Security Archive.

15. FRUS 1952–1954 Retro, xv.

16. "Iran—Mosaddeq Overthrow, 1953," National Security Archive, https:// nsarchive.gwu.edu/events/iran-mosaddeq-overthrow-1953.

17. Transcripts from interviews for the Granada television documentary series *End of Empire* are now open to scholars at the Bodleian Library at the University of Oxford.

18. Wilber, *Overthrow of Mosaddeq*; Richard Cottam, review of *Countercoup* by Kermit Roosevelt, *Iranian Studies* 14 (Summer–Autumn 1981): 269–72; Hugh Wilford, "'Essentially a Work of Fiction': Kermit 'Kim' Roosevelt, Imperial Romance, and the Iran Coup of 1953," *Diplomatic History* 40 (November 2016): 922–47.

19. Michael H. Hunt, "Internationalizing U.S. Diplomatic History: A Practical Agenda," *Diplomatic History* 15 (January 1991): 1–11; Daniel Bessner and Fredrik Logevall, "Recentering the United States in the History of American Foreign Relations," *Texas National Security Review* 3 (Spring 2020): 38–55; H-Diplo Roundtable XXI-42 on Bessner and Logevall, "Recentering the United States," 25 May 2020, https://hdiplo.org/to/RT21-42; Brad Simpson, "Explaining Political Economy," in *America in the World,* 3rd ed., edited by Frank Costigliola and Michael J. Hogan (New York: Cambridge University Press, 2016), 58–73.

20. Bruce Cumings, *The Origins of the Korean War,* vol. 2: *The Roaring of the Cataract, 1947–1950* (Princeton, NJ: Princeton University Press, 1990), 3–32; Painter, "Explaining U.S. Relations with the Third World"; Steven Hurst, *The United States and Iraq since 1979: Hegemony, Oil, and War* (Edinburgh: Edinburgh University Press, 2009), 1–23.

21. Malcolm Byrne, "The Road to Intervention: Factors Influencing U.S. Policy toward Iran, 1945–1953," in *Mohammad Mosaddeq and the 1953 Coup in Iran,* edited

by Mark J. Gasiorowski and Malcolm Byrne (Syracuse, NY: Syracuse University Press, 2004), 201–26.

22. For U.S. national security policy in this period, see Melvyn P. Leffler, *A Preponderance of Power: National Security, the Truman Administration, and the Cold War* (Stanford, CA: Stanford University Press, 1992); Melvyn P. Leffler, "The Emergence of an American Grand Strategy," in *The Cambridge History of the Cold War*, vol. 1, edited by Melvyn P. Leffler and Odd Arne Westad (New York: Cambridge University Press, 2010), 67–88; Robert J. McMahon, "U.S. National Security Policy from Eisenhower to Kennedy," in *The Cambridge History of the Cold War*, vol. 1, edited by Melvyn P. Leffler and Odd Arne Westad, 288–303.

23. U.S. Senate, Select Committee on Small Business, *The International Petroleum Cartel*, Staff Report to the Federal Trade Commission (Washington, DC: U.S. Government Printing Office, 1952); David S. Painter, *Oil and the American Century: The Political Economy of U.S. Foreign Oil Policy, 1941–1954* (Baltimore: Johns Hopkins University Press, 1986); John Blair, *The Control of Oil* (New York: Pantheon Books, 1976); Anthony Sampson, *The Seven Sisters: The Great Oil Companies and the World They Shaped* (New York: Viking, 1975).

24. David S. Painter, "The Marshall Plan and Oil," *Cold War History* 9 (May 2009): 159–75.

25. FRUS 1951 5, doc. 102, NIE-14, "The Importance of Middle East Oil to Western Europe under Peacetime Conditions," 8 January 1951; FRUS 1952–1954 10, doc. 403, NSC-5402, "United States Policy toward Iran," 2 January 1954.

26. Gregory Brew, "The Collapse Narrative: The United States, Mohammed Mossadegh, and the Coup Decision of 1953," *Texas National Security Review* 2 (November 2019): 38–59; Gregory Brew, *Petroleum and Progress in Iran: Oil, Development, and the Cold War* (New York: Cambridge University Press, 2022).

27. Robert L. Beisner, *Dean Acheson: A Life in the Cold War* (New York: Oxford University Press, 2006), 335, 344–45.

28. Vladislav M. Zubok, *A Failed Empire: The Soviet Union in the Cold War from Stalin to Gorbachev* (Chapel Hill: University of North Carolina Press, 2007), 62–93; Geoffrey Roberts, *Molotov: Stalin's Cold Warrior* (Washington, DC: Potomac Books, 2013), chap. 4; Zubok, "Stalin, Soviet Intelligence, and the Struggle for Iran," 28–33; Zubok, "Soviet Intelligence and the Cold War"; Kalinovsky, "The Soviet Union and Mosaddeq."

29. Maziar Behrooz, "The 1953 Coup and the Legacy of the Tudeh," in *Mohammed Mosaddeq and the 1953 Coup in Iran*, edited by Mark J. Gasiorowski and Malcolm Byrne, 102–25.

30. Mark J. Gasiorowski, "U.S. Perceptions of the Communist Threat in Iran during the Mosaddeq Era." *Journal of Cold War Studies* 21 (Summer 2019): 185–221.

31. Steven G. Galpern, *Money, Oil and Empire in the Middle East: Sterling and Postwar Imperialism, 1944–1971* (Cambridge: Cambridge University Press, 2009).

32. Peter Ramsbotham, Interview with David S. Painter, Winchester, UK, 17 July 1991.

33. Steve Marsh. "Anglo-American Crude Diplomacy: Multinational Oil and the Iranian Crisis, 1951–53," *Contemporary British History* 21 (2007): 25–53.

34. Truman to Grady, 27 November 27, 1952, Grady Papers, Harry S. Truman Library (HSTL).

35. FRUS 1952–1954 Retro, doc. 171, NSC Meeting, 4 March 1953.

36. Ali Ansari, *The Politics of Nationalism in Modern Iran* (Cambridge: Cambridge University Press, 2012), 124–51; James A. Bill, *The Eagle and the Lion: The Tragedy of American-Iranian Relations* (New Haven, CT: Yale University Press, 1988), 94–97; Homa Katouzian, *Musaddiq and the Struggle for Power in Iran* (London: I. B. Tauris, 1990); Homa Katouzian, *The Political Economy of Modern Iran: Despotism and Pseudo-Modernism, 1926–1979* (London: Macmillan, 1981); Homa Katouzian, *Khalil Maleki: The Human Face of Iranian Socialism* (London: One World Academic, 2018); Ervand Abrahamian, *Iran Between Two Revolutions* (Princeton, NJ: Princeton University Press, 1982); Fakhreddin Azimi, *Iran: The Crisis of Democracy: From the Exile of Reza Shah to the Fall of Musaddiq* (London: I.B. Tauris, 2009); Sussan Siavoshi, *Liberal Nationalism in Iran: The Failure of a Movement* (Boulder, CO: Westview Press, 1990); Gholam Reza Afkhami, *The Life and Times of the Shah* (Berkeley: University of California Press, 2009); Abbas Milani, *The Shah* (New York: Palgrave Macmillan, 2011).

37. Douglas Little, *American Orientalism: The United States and the Middle East since 1945*, 3rd ed. (Chapel Hill: University of North Carolina Press, 2008), 9–42; Melani McAlister, *Epic Encounters: Culture, Media, and U.S. Interests in the Middle East*, 2nd ed. (Berkeley: University of California Press, 2005), 1–39; Matthew Jacobs, *Imagining the Middle East: The Building of an American Foreign Policy, 1918–1967* (Chapel Hill: University of North Carolina Press, 2011), 12–27; Osamah F. Khalil, *America's Dream Palace: Middle East Expertise and the Rise of the National Security State* (Cambridge, MA: Harvard University Press, 2016).

38. Mary Ann Heiss, "Real Men Don't Wear Pajamas: Anglo-American Cultural Perceptions of Mohammed Mossadegh and the Iranian Oil Nationalization Dispute," in *Empire and Revolution: The United States and the Third World since 1945,* edited by Peter Hahn and Mary Ann Heiss (Columbus: Ohio State University Press, 2001): 178–91; Ervand Abrahamian, *The Coup: 1953, the CIA and the Roots of Modern U.S.-Iranian Relations* (New York: New Press, 2013), 98–108.

39. George F. Kennan, *The Kennan Diaries*, edited by Frank Costigliola (New York: W.W. Norton & Company, 2014) entry for 23 January 1952, 305–08. Kennan made similar comments about Venezuela in February 1950; *Kennan Diaries*, 245.

40. FRUS 1952–1954 Retro, doc. 65, "The Rise of an Iranian Nationalist," Tehran Desp. 878, 16 February 1952.

41. Piero Gleijeses, *Shattered Hope: The Guatemalan Revolution and the United States, 1944–1954* (Princeton, NJ: Princeton University Press, 1991); W. Michael Weis, *Cold Warriors and Coups d'Etat: Brazilian-American Relations, 1946–1964* (Albuquerque: University of New Mexico Press, 1993); Bradley R. Simpson, *Economists with Guns: Authoritarian Development and U.S.-Indonesian Relations, 1960–1968* (Stanford, CA: Stanford University Press, 2008); Tanya Harmer, *Allende's Chile and the Inter-American Cold War* (Chapel Hill: University of North Carolina Press, 2011).

42. Robert J. McMahon, "Eisenhower and Third World Nationalism: A Critique of the Revisionists," *Political Science Quarterly* 101 (Fall 1986): 453–73.

43. Douglas Little, "Mission Impossible: The CIA and the Cult of Covert Action in the Middle East," *Diplomatic History* 28 (November 2004): 663–701; David F. Schmitz, *Thank God They're on Our Side: The United States and Right-Wing Dictatorships, 1921–1965* (Chapel Hill: University of North Carolina Press, 1999); Nathan J. Citino, *From Arab Nationalism to OPEC: Eisenhower, King Sa'ūd, and the Making of U.S.-Saudi Relations*, 2nd ed. (Bloomington: Indiana University Press, 2010); Robert Vitalis, *America's Kingdom: Mythmaking on the Saudi Oil Frontier* (New York: Verso, 2009); Victor McFarland, *Oil Powers: A History of the U.S.-Saudi Alliance* (New York: Columbia University Press, 2020); Brandon Wolfe-Hunnicutt, *The Paranoid Style in American Diplomacy: Oil and Arab Nationalism in Iraq* (Stanford, CA: Stanford University Press, 2021); Stephen G. Rabe, *The Road to OPEC: United States Relations with Venezuela, 1919–1976* (Austin: University of Texas Press, 1982); Bethany Aram, "Exporting Rhetoric, Importing Oil: United States Relations with Venezuela, 1945–1948," *World Affairs* 154 (Winter 1992): 94–106.

44. John Stephen Zunes, "Decisions on Intervention: United States Response to Third World Nationalist Governments" (PhD dissertation, Cornell University, 1990).

Chapter 1

1. L. P. Elwell-Sutton, *Persian Oil: A Study in Power Politics* (London: Lawrence and Wishart, 1955): 10–25; Mostafa Elm, *Oil, Power, and Principle: Iran's Oil Nationalization and Its Aftermath* (Syracuse, NY: Syracuse University Press, 1992), 6–7; R. W. Ferrier, *The History of the British Petroleum Company*, vol. 1: *The Developing Years, 1901–1928* (Cambridge: Cambridge University Press, 1982), 15–88.

2. Mostafa Fateh, *Panjah sal naft-e Iran* (Tehran: Entesharat-e Payam, 1979), 235–36, 267.

3. Bruce Podobnik, *Global Energy Shifts: Fostering Sustainability in a Turbulent Age* (Philadelphia: Temple University Press, 2006), 38–67; Daniel Yergin, *The Prize: The Epic Quest for Oil, Money, and Power* (New York: Simon & Schuster, 1991), 62–63.

4. Marian Jack, "The Purchase of the British Government's Shares in the British Petroleum Company, 1912–1914," *Past & Present* 39 (1968): 139–68; Anand Toprani, *Oil and the Great Powers: Britain and Germany, 1914–1945* (New York: Oxford University Press, 2019), 38–49; Ferrier, *History of the British Petroleum Company*, vol. 1, 158–201; Volkan S. Ediger and John V. Bowlus, "A Farewell to King Coal: Geopolitics, Energy Security, and the Transition to Oil, 1898–1917," *Historical Journal* 62 (June 2019): 427–49.

5. Ariane M. Tabatabai, *No Conquest, No Defeat: Iran's National Security Strategy* (Oxford: Oxford University Press, 2020), 23–35; Firuz Kazemzadeh, *Russia and Britain in Persia, 1864–1914: A Study in Imperialism* (New Haven, CT: Yale University Press, 1968).

6. Ferrier, *History of the British Petroleum Company*, vol. 1, 343, and appendix 0.1, "World Crude Oil Production, 1900–1932"; Elm, *Oil, Power, and Principle*, 18.

7. George W. Stocking, *Middle East Oil: A Study in Political and Economic Controversy* (Nashville, TN: Vanderbilt University Press, 1970), 19–20; John Blair, *The Control of Oil* (New York: Pantheon, 1976), 49.

8. Vanessa Martin, *The Qajar Pact: Bargaining, Protest, and the State in Nineteenth-Century Persia* (London: I. B. Tauris, 2005); Shaul Bakhash, *Iran: Monarchy, Bureaucracy and Reform under the Qajars, 1858–1896* (London: Ithaca Press, 1978).

9. Nikki Keddie, *Religion and Rebellion in Iran: The Tobacco Protest of 1891–1892* (London: Cass, 1966), 39–65.

10. Keddi, *Religion and Rebellion*, 1–10; Janet Afary, *The Iranian Constitutional Revolution, 1906–1911: Grassroots Democracy, Social Democracy and the Origins of Feminism* (New York: Columbia University Press, 1996); Nader Sohrabi, *Revolution and Constitutionalism in the Ottoman Empire and Iran* (New York: Cambridge University Press, 2011). For the divisions between secular nationalists and Islamic nationalists, see Vanessa Martin, *Iran between Islamic Nationalism and Secularism: The Constitutional Revolution of 1906* (London: I. B. Tauris, 2013), 36–37. See also Ali M. Ansari, ed., *Iran's Constitutional Revolution of 1906: Narratives of the Enlightenment* (London: Gingko Library, 2016).

11. Abbas Amanat, *Iran: A Modern History* (New Haven, CT: Yale University Press, 2017), 389–445; Homa Katouzian, "The Campaign against the Anglo-Iranian Agreement of 1919," *British Journal of Middle Eastern Studies* 25 (May 1998): 5–46; Michael P. Zirinsky, "Imperial Power and Dictatorship: Britain and the Rise of Reza Shah, 1921–1926," *International Journal of Middle Eastern Studies* 24 (1992): 639–63.

12. For the rise of Reza Shah, see Ali M. Ansari, *The Politics of Nationalism in Modern Iran* (New York: Cambridge University Press. 2121), 58–67; Stephanie Cronin, ed., *The Making of Modern Iran: State and Society under Riza Shah 1921–1941* (New York: Routledge Curzon, 2003); Touraj Atabaki and Eric J. Zurcher, eds., *Men of Order: Authoritarian Modernization under Ataturk and Reza Shah* (London: I. B. Tauris, 2004); Homa Katouzian, *Musaddiq and the Struggle for Power in Iran* (London: I. B. Tauris, 1990), 25.

13. Gregory Brew, "In Search of 'Equitability': Sir John Cadman, Rezā Shah and the Cancellation of the D'Arcy Concession, 1928–33," *Iranian Studies* 50 (2017): 115–48; Elm, *Oil, Power, and Principle*, 28–43.

14. Elm, *Oil, Power, and Principle*, 18.

15. J. H. Bamberg, *The History of the British Petroleum Company*, vol. 2: *The Anglo-Iranian Years, 1928–1954* (Cambridge: Cambridge University Press, 1994), 107–17; Blair, *Control of Oil*, 54-55.

16. Figures from Brew, "In Search of 'Equitability,'" 135; Elm, *Oil, Power, and Principle*, 18. According to some authors, the cancellation was the product of collusion between the shah and the oil company; see Mohammed Gholi Majd, *Great Britain and Rezā Shah: The Plunder of Iran, 1921–1941* (Gainesville: University of Florida Press, 2001), 253–59. Accounts of the decision (as well as documents from the company's archive) make it plain that the shah alone had made the decision to cancel the concession. See Sayyed Hasan Taqizadeh, *Zendegi-ye Tufani: Khaterat-e Sayyed Hasan Taqizadeh* [A Stormy Life: The Memoirs of Sayyed Hasan Taqizādeh], 2nd ed., edited by Iraj Afshar (Tehran: 'Elmi, 1993), 231–32; Mihdi Quli Khan Hidayat, *Khatirat va Khatarat* [Memoirs and Dangers] (Tehran: Shirkat-e Chap-e Rangin, 1950), 500–505.

17. Brew, "In Search of 'Equitability,'" 144–48.

18. Brew, "In Search of 'Equitability,'" 144–45; Elm, *Oil, Power, and Principle*, 38–39.

19. Yergin, *The Prize*, 263–85; Bamberg, *History of the British Petroleum Company*, vol. 2, 146–71.

20. Noel Maurer, "The Empire Struck Back: Sanctions and Compensation in the Mexican Oil Expropriation of 1938," *Journal of Economic History* 71 (September 2011): 560–615.

21. Taqizadeh, *Zendegi-ye Tufani*, 200–222; Ervand Abrahamian, *Iran between Two Revolutions* (Princeton, NJ: Princeton University Press, 1982), 149–65.

22. Shaul Bakhash, "Britain and the Abdication of Reza Shah," *Middle Eastern Studies* 52 (2016): 318–34; Elm, *Oil, Power, and Principle*, 41.

23. Figures from DeGolyer and MacNaughton, *Twentieth Century Petroleum Statistics: Historical Data* (Dallas, TX: DeGolyer & MacNaughton, n.d.); Bamberg, *History of the British Petroleum Company*, vol. 2, 216–19, 225–27, 230–35, 242; Elm, *Oil, Power, and Principle*, 38. Although Bamberg and Elm largely agree on production volumes, payments to Iran, and British tax payments, Bamberg gives larger figures for AIOC profits. Bamberg also gives slightly smaller figures for Iran's production in 1940 and 1945.

24. Stephen L. McFarland, "Anatomy of an Iranian Political Crowd: The Tehran Bread Riot of December 1942," *International Journal of Middle East Studies* 17 (February 1985): 51–65.

25. Harvard Interview, Sanjabi Interview, Tape 5, 12.

26. Analysis of Iran's social classes in the next two paragraphs comes from Abrahamian, *Iran between Two Revolutions*, 169–76; Fakhreddin Azimi, *Iran: The Crisis of Democracy: from the Exile of Reza Shah to the Fall of Moṣaddeq* (London: I. B. Tauris, 2009), 1–35.

27. Ervand Abrahamian, "Factionalism in Iran: Political Groups in the 14th Parliament (1944–46)," *Middle Eastern Studies* 14 (January 1978): 22–55.

28. Abrahamian, *Iran between Two Revolutions*, 281–90; Maziar Behrooz, "The 1953 Coup and the Legacy of the Tudeh," in *Mohammed Mosaddeq and the 1953 Coup in Iran*, edited by Mark J. Gasiorowski and Malcolm Byrne (Syracuse, NY: Syracuse University Press, 2004), 104–7.

29. T. H. Vail Motter, *The Persian Corridor and Aid to Russia* (Washington, DC: Office of the Chief of Military History, Department of the Army, 1952); Simon Davis, *Contested Space: Anglo-American Relations in the Persian Gulf, 1939–1947* (Boston: Martinus Nijhoff Publishers, 2009); Thomas M. Ricks, "U.S. Military Missions to Iran, 1943–1978: The Political Economy of Military Assistance," *Iranian Studies* 12 (Summer–Autumn 1979): 163–93; James A. Bill, *The Eagle and the Lion: The Tragedy of American-Iranian Relations* (New Haven, CT: Yale University Press, 1988), 15–27; Hamilton Lytle, *The Origins of the Iranian American Alliance, 1941–1953* (New York: Holmes and Meir, 1987), 41–46; Louise L'Estrange Fawcett, *Iran and the Cold War: The Azerbaijan Crisis of 1946* (Cambridge: Cambridge University Press, 1992), 110–22.

30. Yergin, *The Prize*, 373–76; David S. Painter, *Oil and the American Century: The Political Economy of U.S. Foreign Oil Policy, 1941–1954* (Baltimore: Johns Hopkins University Press, 1986), 100–101; Nathan J. Citino, "Internationalist Oilmen, the Middle East, and the Remaking of American Liberalism, 1945–1953," *Business History Review* 84 (Summer 2010): 227–28, 232–34.

31. FRUS 1943 4, doc. 398, Hull to Roosevelt, "American Policy in Iran," 16 August 1943; Painter, *Oil and the American Century*, 76–77.

32. Natalia Egorova, "Stalin's Oil Policy and the Iranian Crisis of 1945–1946," in *Cold War Energy: A Transnational History of Soviet Oil and Gas*, edited by Jeronim Perović (Cham, Switzerland: Palgrave Macmillan, 2017), 84–88; Painter, *Oil and the American Century*, 76–77.

33. Bruce R. Kuniholm, *The Origins of the Cold War in the Near East: Great Power Conflict and Diplomacy in Iran, Turkey and Greece* (Princeton, NJ: Princeton University Press, 1980), 192–97.

34. Katouzian, *Musaddiq and the Struggle for Power in Iran*, 56–58.

35. Jamil Hasanli, *At the Dawn of the Cold War: The Soviet-American Crisis over Iranian Azerbaijan, 1941–1946* (Lanham, MD: Rowman & Littlefield, 2006), 89–91; Egorova, "Stalin's Oil Policy and the Iranian Crisis of 1945–1946," 88; Fernand Scheid Raine, "The Iranian Crisis of 1946 and the Origins of the Cold War," in *The Origins of the Cold War: An International History*, 2nd ed., edited by Melvyn P. Leffler and David S. Painter (New York: Routledge, 2005), 93–111; Vladislov M. Zubok, "Stalin, Soviet Intelligence, and the Struggle for Iran, 1945–53," *Diplomatic History* 44 (January 2020): 25–26.

36. "Oil Concessions and the Problems in Iran," 11 December 1945, 891.6363 /12-1145.

37. Fawcett, *Iran and the Cold War*, 174–75.

38. Egorova, "Stalin's Oil Policy and the Iranian Crisis of 1945–1946," 84–88; Kuniholm, *The Origins of the Cold War in the Near East*, 188–91; Gary R. Hess, "The Iranian Crisis of 1945–46 and the Cold War," *Political Science Quarterly* 89 (March 1974): 117–46.

39. Bill, *The Eagle and the Lion*, 37–38; Fawcett, *Iran and the Cold War*, 108–40.

40. Zubok, "Stalin, Soviet Intelligence, and the Struggle for Iran," 27–28; Egorova, "Stalin's Oil Policy and the Iranian Crisis of 1945–1946," 95–96.

41. Habib Ladjevardi, *Labor Unions and Autocracy in Iran* (Syracuse, NY: Syracuse University Press, 1985): 121–36.

42. FRUS 1946 7, doc. 277, Tehran 384, 23 March 1946; Stephen L. McFarland, "A Peripheral View of the Origins of the Cold War: The Crises in Iran," *Diplomatic History* 4, no. 4 (October 1980): 345–51.

43. Habib Ladjevardi, "The Origins of US Support for an Autocratic Iran," *International Journal of Middle Eastern Studies* 15 (1983): 225–39.

44. Zubok, "Stalin, Soviet Intelligence, and the Struggle for Iran," 28; Scheid-Raine, "The Iranian Crisis of 1946," 93–111; Geoffrey Roberts, "Moscow's Cold War on the Periphery: Soviet Policy in Greece, Iran, and Turkey, 1943–8," *Journal of Contemporary History* 46 (January 2011): 68–70.

45. Katouzian, *Musaddiq and the Struggle for Power in Iran*, 44–48; Abrahamian, *Iran between Two Revolutions*, 242–50; Azimi, *Crisis of Democracy*, 183–217.

46. Abbas Milani, *The Shah* (New York: Palgrave Macmillan, 2011), 11–65; Gholam R. Afkhami, *The Life and Times of the Shah* (Berkeley: University of California Press, 2009), 61–85. For the turn in U.S. policy, see Richard A. Pfau, "Containment in Iran, 1946: The Shift to an Active Policy," *Diplomatic History* 1 (Fall 1977): 359–72.

47. Ervand Abrahamian, *Oil Crisis in Iran: From Nationalism to Coup d'Etat* (New York: Cambridge University Press, 2021), 88; Abrahamian, *Iran between Two Revolutions*, 249–50; Milani, *The Shah*, 130–33.

48. Quoted in Painter, *Oil and the American Century*, 113.

49. FRUS 1945 8, doc. 360; FRUS 1947 5, doc. 703; FRUS 1947 5, doc. 667, Tehran 866, 9 September 1947; Bill, *Eagle and the Lion*, 48–50; Pfau, "Containment in Iran," 361–62.

50. Bill, *Eagle and the Lion*, 38–39; Ladjevardi, "Origins of US Support for an Autocratic Iran," 225–39, Painter, *Oil and the American Century*, 113–14.

51. MemCon, 28 February 1946, 891.51/2-284; Dillon Glendinning and Clyde Dunn (US Embassy), General Classified Records US Embassy Tehran, 1945–1951, Box 23; FRUS 1949 6, doc. 304, State 477, 25 May 1949; James F. Goode, *The United States and Iran, 1946–51: The Diplomacy of Neglect* (New York: St. Martin's Press, 1989), 23–24.

52. Linda W. Qaimmaqami, "The Catalyst of Nationalization: Max Thornburg and the Failure of Private Sector Developmentalism in Iran, 1946–1951," *Diplomatic History* 19 (January 1995): 1–31.

53. Ricks, "U.S. Military Missions to Iran," 163–93.

54. Mark J. Gasiorowski, "The CIA's TPBEDAMN Operation and the 1953 Coup in Iran," *Journal of Cold War Studies* 15 (Fall 2013): 8; Mark J. Gasiorowski, "The US Stay-Behind Operation in Iran, 1948–1953," *Intelligence and National Security* 34 (2019): 174–75.

55. Douglas Little, *American Orientalism: The United States and the Middle East since 1945*, 3rd ed. (Chapel Hill: University of North Carolina Press, 2008), 123–24; Peter L. Hahn, *The United States, Great Britain, and Egypt, 1945–1956: Strategy and Diplomacy in the Early Cold War* (Chapel Hill: University of North Carolina Press, 1991), 49–56.

56. Wm. Roger Louis, *The British Empire in the Middle East: Arab Nationalism, the United States, and Postwar Imperialism* (New York: Clarendon Press, 1984), 632–35.

57. Cairo 2397, Enclosure No. 1, 3 April 1947, 891.6363/4-347.

58. FO 621, 14 June 1946, FO 371/52714. For oil's importance to Britain's postwar economy, see Stephen G. Galpern, *Money, Oil and Empire in the Middle East: Sterling and Postwar Imperialism, 1944–1971* (Cambridge: Cambridge University Press, 2009), 23–141.

59. Painter, *Oil and the American Century*; Yergin, *The Prize*, 391–544.

60. Painter, *Oil and the American Century*, 96–97.

61. David S. Painter, "The Marshall Plan and Oil," *Cold War History* 9 (May 2009): 159–75.

62. Painter, *Oil and the American Century*, 102–10; Yergin, *The Prize*, 392–404.

63. FRUS 1950 5, doc. 36, Paper Prepared in the Department of State, "Middle East Oil," September 1950; FRUS 1951 5, doc. 102, NIE-14, "The Importance of Iranian and Middle East Oil to Western Europe under Peacetime Conditions," 8 January 1951.

64. Elwell-Sutton, *Persian Oil*, 101–2; Fateh, *Panjah sal naft-e Iran*, 446–47.

65. International Labour Office, *Labour Conditions in the Oil Industry in Iran* (Geneva: ILO, 1950), 67, 76–79. For the company's welfare policies, see Bamberg, *History of the British Petroleum Company*, vol. 2, 347–82.

66. Personal Letter, 25 May 1951, John C. Wiley Papers, Series 1, Box 5, Franklin D. Roosevelt Library.

67. Richard Cottam, "Nationalism in Twentieth Century Iran," in *Musaddiq, Iranian Nationalism, and Oil*, edited by James A. Bill and Wm. Roger Louis (London: I. B. Tauris, 1988), 23–25.

68. Extract of *Shafaq-i Sorkh* from *Le Messager de Téhéran*, 2 March 1931; see Ansari, *Politics of Nationalism*, 124–39.

69. Ervand Abrahamian, *The Coup: 1953, the CIA and the Roots of Modern U.S.-Iranian Relations* (New York: New Press, 2013), 23–29; Katouzian, *Musaddiq and the Struggle for Power in Iran*, 63–66; Elwell-Sutton, *Persian Oil*, 86–96.

70. Katouzian, *Musaddiq and the Struggle for Power in Iran*, 67–68; Taqizadeh, *Zendegi-ye tufani*, 551–53.

71. Husayn Makki, *Naft va nutq-e Makki: Jarayan-e muzakirat-e naft dar Majlis-e Panzdahum dar barah-'e qarardad-e naft-e Iran va Ingilis* [Oil and the Speeches of Makki: The Course of Discussions in the Fifteenth Majlis Regarding the Anglo-Iranian Oil Concession] (Tehran: Intisharat-e Amir Kabir, 1978), 213–15.

72. Nikki R. Keddie, *Modern Iran: Roots and Results of Revolution* (New Haven, CT: Yale University Press, 2006), 110–22, 170–88; Sussan Siavoshi, "The Oil Nationalization Movement, 1949–1953," in *A Century of Revolution: Social Movements in Iran*, edited by John Foran, (Minneapolis: University of Minnesota Press, 1994), 106–34.

73. Galpern, *Money, Oil and Empire*, 88–89.

74. Bamberg, *History of the British Petroleum Company*, vol. 2, 385–98.

75. Le Rougetel to FO, 12 May 1949; Le Rougetel to Wright, 16 May 1949; Record of a Meeting, 19 May 1949, FO 371/75497; Bamberg, *History of the British Petroleum Company*, vol. 2, 393–99; Galpern, *Money, Oil, and Empire*, 89–93.

76. *Muzakirat-e Majlis* [Proceedings of Parliament], vol. 15, July 23–27, 1949; Makki, *Naft va nutq-e Makki*, 202–14, 220–406, 411–514.

77. Fateh, *Panjah sal naft-e Iran*, 392–403; Elm, *Oil, Power, and Principle*, 5–56.

78. Le Rougetel to FO, 28 July 1949, FO 371/75498; Le Rougetel to FO, 2 August 1949, FO 371/75499; Gass to Hobson, 18 August 1949, BP 80924.

79. State 157, 14 February 1950, 888.2553 AIOC/1-2650.

80. At the time of his birth, his name was Mirza Mohammed Khan Mosaddeq al-Saltaneh. The post-constitutional reforms mandated that Iranians adopt Western naming conventions, and Mosaddeq's name subsequently changed. See Katouzian, *Musaddiq and the Struggle for Power in Iran*, 1.

81. Fakhreddin Azimi, "The Reconciliation of Politics and Ethics, Nationalism, and Democracy: An Overview of the Political Career of Dr. Muhammed Musaddiq," in *Musaddiq, Iranian Nationalism, and Oil*, edited by James A. Bill and Wm. Roger Louis (London: I. B. Tauris, 1988), 47–68; Katouzian, *Musaddiq and the Struggle for Power*, 1–8; Abrahamian, *The Coup*, 33–34.

82. Mohammed Mosaddeq, *Musaddiq's Memoirs*, translated by Homa Katouzian and S. H. Amin (London: National Movement of Iran, 1988), 9; Katouzian, *Musaddiq and the Struggle for Power in Iran*, 33–61; Ansari, *Politics of Nationalism*, 130, 11; Ansari, *Modern Iran*, 131–34; Elm, *Oil, Power, and Principle*, 58–59; Christopher Dietrich, *Oil Revolution: Anticolonial Elites, Sovereign Rights and the Economic Culture of Decolonization* (Cambridge: Cambridge University Press, 2017), 30–35.

83. Taqizadeh, *Zendegi-ye tufani*, 366.

84. Ford to State, 10 March 1944, 891.00/3022.

85. Katouzian, *Musaddiq and the Struggle for Power in Iran*, 71–77; Abrahamian, *The Coup*, 53, 58; Fu'ad Ruhani, *Zindagi-e siyasi-e Musaddiq: Dar matn-e naḥzat-e milli-e Iran* [The Political Life of Musaddiq: In the National Front Movement of Iran] (London: Intisharat-e Nahzat-Muqavamat-e Milli-e Iran, 1987): 123–27; Fateh, *Panjah sal naft-e Iran*, 403–4; Sussan Siavoshi, *Liberal Nationalism in Iran: The Failure of a Movement* (Boulder, CO: Westview Press, 1990), 49–86.

86. Katouzian, *Musaddiq and the Struggle for Power in Iran*, 86–89; Abrahamian, *Iran between Two Revolutions*, 251–61; Abrahamian, *The Coup*, 48–54; Ali Shayegan, *Sayyed ʿAli Shayegan: Zendagi-nama-ye siasi.* [Sayyed Ali Shayegan: A Political Biography], vol. 1 (Tehran: Agaah, 2006), 329–39, 349–50; Harvard Interview with Mahdi Azar, No. 1, 1–16; for Kashani's role, see Shahrough Akhavi, "The Role of the Clergy in Iranian Politics, 1949–1954," in *Musaddiq, Iranian Nationalism, and Oil*, edited by James A. Bill and Wm. Roger Louis, see note 81, 94–96.

87. Katouzian, *Musaddiq and the Struggle for Power in Iran*, 90.

88. Harvard Interview with Sanjabi, Tape No. 8, 14–15.

89. Abrahamian, *Iran between Two Revolutions*, 260–61.

90. Shepherd to Wright, 14 April 1950, FO 371/82374.

91. Katouzian, *Musaddiq and the Struggle for Power in Iran*, 90.

92. Mark J. Gasiorowski, "US Perceptions of the Communist Threat in Iran during the Mossadegh Era," *Journal of Cold War Studies* 21 (Summer 2019): 193–94.

93. Tehran 416, 11 March 1950, General Classified Records US Embassy Tehran 1950–1952, Box 35.

94. FRUS 1950 5, doc. 232, "The Present Crisis in Iran," McGhee to Acheson, 19 April 1950; doc. 233, Memo for the Files, undated; doc. 234, McGhee to Acheson, 25 April 1950.

95. Melvyn P. Leffler, *A Preponderance of Power: National Security, the Truman Administration and the Cold War* (Stanford, CA: Stanford University Press, 1992), 312–60, Thomas J. McCormick, *America's Half-Century: United States Foreign Policy in the Cold War*, 2nd ed. (Baltimore: Johns Hopkins University Press, 1995), 88–98, 99.

96. FRUS 1950 5, doc. 233, Memo for the Files, undated.

97. David Collier contends that the United States used its leverage to convince the shah to appoint Razmara, though the evidence of direct pressure is mostly circumstantial. David R. Collier, *Democracy and the Nature of American Influence in Iran, 1941-1979* (Syracuse, NY: Syracuse University Press, 2017), 70-75.

98. Goode, *United States and Iran*, 68-69.

99. FRUS 1950 5, doc. 250, Tehran 968, 26 May 1950; doc. 253, Wiley to Acheson, 31 May 1950; doc. 254, Tehran 1168, 21 June 1950; doc. 255, State 763, 23 June 1950; Elm, *Oil, Power, and Principle*, 65-80.

100. Abrahamian, *Iran between Two Revolutions*, 263-64.

101. Abrahamian, *Iran between Two Revolutions*, 264-67.

102. Mary Ann Heiss, *Empire and Nationhood: The United States, Great Britain and Iranian Oil, 1950-1954* (New York: Columbia University Press, 1997), 26-27.

103. Note by Hankey, 28 July 1950, FO 371/82375; Henry F. Grady, *Memoirs of Henry F. Grady: From the Great War to the Cold War*, edited by John T. McKay (Columbia: University of Missouri Press, 2009).

104. Tehran 205, 25 July 1950, 888.2553/7-2450; Tehran 215, 26 July 1950, 888.2553/7-2550; Tehran 243, 28 July 1950, General Classified Records US Embassy Tehran 1950-1952, Box 38; Tehran 347, 9 August 1950; Tehran 395, 15 August 1950.

105. Minutes of a Meeting, 2 August 1950, FO 371/82375.

106. Galpern, *Money, Oil and Empire*, 98-101.

107. Memo by Furlonge: Persia, 11 August 1950, FO 371/82375.

108. FRUS 1950 5, doc. 261, London 399, 18 July 1950.

109. FRUS 1950 5, doc. 266, State 683, 7 August 1950.

110. FRUS 1950 5, doc. 267, London 839, 10 August 1950.

111. Painter, *Oil and the American Century*, 165-67.

112. FRUS 1950 5, doc. 38, Memorandum by Funkhouser, 14 September 1950.

113. FRUS 1950 5, doc. 277, MemCon, 21 September 1950.

114. FRUS 1950 5, doc. 281, Tehran 851, 12 October 1950.

115. Abrahamian, *Iran between Two Revolutions*, 265.

116. Gass to Furlonge, 26 Oct. 1950, FO 371/82376.

117. Heiss, *Empire and Nationhood*, 31-32.

118. Minute by E. W. Noonan, 15 November 1950, FO 371/82377.

119. FRUS 1950 5, doc. 285, Tehran 998, 31 October 1950.

120. Katouzian, *Musaddiq and the Struggle for Power in Iran*, 91.

121. Tehran 1199, 27 November 1950, 888.2253/11-2750.

122. Parker (US Treasury) to McGhee, 27 December 1950, 888.2553/12-2750.

123. Note from Furlonge, 9 December 1950; Nuttall to Furlonge, 15 December 1950, FO 371/82377; Qaimmaqami, "Catalyst for Nationalization," 23-24.

124. Yergin, *The Prize*, 427-31, Painter, *Oil and the American Century*, 167-71.

125. Tehran 465, 21 December 1950, 888.2553/12-2150.

126. British Embassy Tehran (BET) 662, 7 December 1950, FO 371/82377.

127. Elm, *Oil, Power, and Principle*, 73-74; Elwell-Sutton, *Persian Oil*, 204.

128. Furlonge to Flett, 11 January 1951, FO 371/91485.

129. Northcroft to Rice, No. 657, 5 March 1951, BP 126353; Tehran 1847, 17 February 1951, 888.2553 AIOC/2-1651; Tehran 1929, 1 March 1951, 888.2553 AIOC/2-2851.

130. Northcroft to Directors, Rice, No. 8396, 4 March 1951, BP 126353.

131. Heiss, *Empire and Nationhood*, 53.

132. FRUS 1952–1954 Retro, doc. 2, Editorial Note; doc. 3, Memo Prepared by the Office of National Estimates, CIA, 9 March 1951. U.S. Ambassador Henry F. Grady noted that the shah, the British, and the National Front had all opposed Razmara. Homa Katouzian, "Editor's Note," in Musaddeq, *Musaddiq's Memoirs*, 30–31; Katouzian, *Musaddiq and the Struggle for Power in Iran*, 83–84. For a study of available documentary evidence, see Mohammed Torkaman, *Asrar-e Qatl-e Razmara* [Secrets of Razmara's Assassination] (Tehran: Rasa, 1991).

Chapter 2

1. Tehran 2094, 16 March 1951, 888.2553/3-1651; FRUS 1952–1954 10, doc. 4, State 1531, 7 March 1951; doc. 9, State 1623, 17 March 1951; Shepherd, "Interview with Mr. Ala," 15 March 1951, FO 248/1514; Shepherd to Morrison, 19 March 1951, FO 371/91524; L. P. Elwell-Sutton, *Persian Oil: A Study in Power Politics* (London: Lawrence and Wishart, 1955), 208.

2. Mostafa Elm, *Oil, Power and Principle: Iran's Oil Nationalization and Its Aftermath* (Syracuse, NY: Syracuse University Press, 1992), 81–82; Mohammed Mosaddeq, *Musaddiq's Memoirs*, translated by Homa Katouzian and S. H. Amin (London: National Movement of Iran, 1988), 32; Fu'ad Ruhani, *Tarikh-e milli shudan-e ṣanʿat-e naft-e Iran* (Tehran: Kitabhaye Jibi), 116–22.

3. AIOC management argued that high wages after the 1946 strike and the burgeoning cost of house construction and amenities forced a reduction in staff; Elkington to Fraser, 16 January 1950; Gobey for Rice and Northcroft, 14 March 1950, BP 101108.

4. J.H. Bamberg, *The History of the British Petroleum Company*, vol. 2: *The Anglo-Iranian Years, 1928–1954* (Cambridge: Cambridge University Press, 1994), 419–20, Habib Ladjevardi, *Labor Unions and Autocracy in Iran* (Syracuse, NY: Syracuse University Press, 1985), 188–89; Ervand Abrahamian, *The Coup: 1953, the CIA and the Roots of Modern U.S.-Iranian Relations* (New York: New Press, 2013), 64–74.

5. Wm. Roger Louis, *The British Empire in the Middle East: Arab Nationalism, the United States, and Postwar Imperialism* (Oxford: Clarendon Press, 1984), 642–57; FRUS 1952–1954 10, doc. 27, Attlee to Truman, 5 June 1951.

6. Louis, *British Empire in the Middle East*, 689.

7. Steven G. Galpern, *Money, Oil and Empire in the Middle East: Sterling and Postwar Imperialism, 1944–1971* (Cambridge: Cambridge University Press, 2009), 105–8.

8. FO 1612, 31 March 1951, FO 371/91470.

9. FO 1981, 11 March 1951, FO 371/91534; Draft for UK Delegation, April 1951, FO 371/91470. On the British determination to retain control of Iran's oil, see Abrahamian, *The Coup*, 81–89.

10. FRUS 1952–1954 10, doc. 6, NSC 107, "The Position of the United States with Respect to Iran," 14 March 1951; FRUS 1951 5, doc. 102, NIE-14, "The Importance of Iranian and Middle East Oil to Western Europe under Peacetime Conditions,"

8 January 1951; Moscow 1709, 23 March 1951, 788.13/323-5; NIE-26, "Key Problems Affecting US Efforts to Strengthen the Near East," National Intelligence Estimate, 25 April 1951, President's Secretary's File (PSF): Intelligence, HSTL. Figures on oil production from DeGolyer and MacNaughton, *Twentieth Century Petroleum Statistics: Historical Data* (Dallas, TX: DeGolyer and MacNaughton, N.D.).

11. FRUS 1952–1954 10, doc. 6, NSC 107, "The Position of the United States with Respect to Iran," 14 March 1951.

12. FRUS 1952–1954 Retro, doc. 5, Paper Prepared in the Directorate of Plans, CIA, undated; doc. 7, Roosevelt to Dulles, 15 March 1951.

13. FRUS 1952–1954 Retro, doc. 8, Berry to Matthews, 15 March 1951.

14. FRUS 1952–1954 Retro, doc. 11, Dulles to Smith, 28 March 1951.

15. FRUS 1952–1954 10, doc. 7, NSC Draft Statement of Policy, 14 March 1951; doc. 8, Editorial Note; FRUS 1952–1954 Retro, doc. 8, note 4.

16. FRUS 1952–1954 Retro, doc. 14, Memo from [classified] to Roosevelt, 11 April 1951; doc. 15, Memo from [name not declassified] to [name not declassified], 12 April 1951; doc. 18, Wisner to Dulles, 23 April 1951. It is not clear if the money was ever delivered.

17. George C. McGhee, *Envoy to the Middle World: Adventures in Diplomacy* (New York: Harper & Row, 1983), 326–27; Memo of Discussion, 2 April 1951, 788.00/4-1051; London tlg. 5239, 5 April 1951, 888.2553/4-451; FO 371/91470; Morrison to Franks, 3 April 1951, FO 800/649l.

18. British Embassy, Washington (BEW) 1079, 10 April 1951; BEW 1080, 10 April 1951; BEW 1081, 10 April 1951; FO 1454, all in FO 371/91470; FRUS 1952–1954 10, doc. 12, MemCon, 17 April 1951; doc. 13, MemCon, 18 April 1951; doc. 14, State 1909, 20 April 1951; McGhee to Acheson, 17 April 1951, 788.00/4-1751; Bamberg, *History of the British Petroleum Company*, vol. 2, 417–18.

19. BEW 1080, 11 April 1951, FO 371/91470.

20. BET 240, 21 March 1951, FO 371/91454; Louis, *British Empire in the Middle East*, 666–78.

21. The British had an informant on the oil committee; A. Haddad, "Oil-Subcommittee Meeting," 23 April 1951, FO 371/91528; British Embassy, Tehran (BET) 398, 27 April 1951, FO 371/91528.

22. Fakhreddin Azimi, *Iran: The Crisis of Democracy: From the Exile of Reza Shah to the Fall of Musaddiq* (London: I.B. Tauris, 2009), 253–58; Mosaddeq, *Musaddiq's Memoirs*, 33–34, Abrahamian, *The Coup*, 74–75; Homa Katouzian, *Musaddiq and the Struggle for Power in Iran* (London: I. B. Tauris, 1990), 93.

23. Karim Sanjabi, *Omidha va Namidha: Khatirat-e Siyasi* (London: Nashr-e Kitab 1989), 174.

24. FRUS 1952–1954 10, doc. 18, Tehran 2692, 7 May 1951.

25. Shepherd to Furlonge, 6 May 1951, FO 371/91459; Louis, *British Empire in the Middle East*, 637–38.

26. Minute by Hiller, 3 May 1951, FO 248/1514.

27. Louis, *British Empire in the Middle East*, 651–53; Abrahamian, *The Coup*, 99–101.

28. Morrison to Attlee, 1 May 1951, FO 371/91531.

29. Ian Spiller, "A Sputter of Musketry? The British Military Response to the Anglo-Iranian Oil Dispute, 1951," *Contemporary British History* 17 (Spring 2003): 43–48; Steve Marsh, "Anglo-American Relations and the Labour Government's 'Scuttle' from Abadan: A Declaration of Dependence?" *International History Review* 35 (2013): 823–27; Confidential Annex to COS (51) 109th Mtg, 2 July 1951, DEFE 4/44.

30. For Truman's comments, see Arthur Krock, *Memoirs: Sixty Years on the Firing Line* (New York: Funk & Wagnalls, 1968), 261–62; Dean Acheson, *Present at the Creation: My Years at the State Department* (New York: Norton, 1969), 505–7.

31. George C. McGhee, *Envoy to the Middle World: Adventures in Diplomacy* (New York: Harper & Row, 1983), 327.

32. Nitze Interview, 31 October 1984, Paul H. Nitze Papers, Manuscript Division, LC, Box 11C; Paul H. Nitze, *From Hiroshima to Glasnost: At the Center of Decision: A Memoir* (New York: Grove Weidenfeld, 1989), 131; Nitze quote from Princeton Seminars, Acheson Papers, Box 81, HSTL.

33. McGhee to Acheson, 20 April 1951, 888.2553/4-2051; extract in FRUS 1952–1954 10, doc. 13, note 4.

34. London 5654, 28 April 1951, 888.2553/4-2851.

35. Tehran 2787, 13 May 1951, 888.2553/5-1351.

36. FRUS 1952–1954 Retro, doc. 25, Minutes of CIA Director Smith's Meeting, 9 May 1951.

37. FRUS 1952–1954 Retro, doc. 24, Telegram from Station in Iran to CIA, 6 May 1951.

38. FRUS 1952–1954 Retro, doc. 20, Memo Prepared in Office of National Estimates, CIA, 1 May 1951; doc. 23, Tehran Desp. 899, 4 May 1951.

39. FRUS 1952–1954 10, doc. 20, State 2067, 10 May 1951.

40. FRUS 1952–1954 Retro, doc. 9, SE-3, "The Current Crisis in Iran," 16 March 1951; FRUS 1952–1954 10, doc. 9, State 1623, 17 March 1951; CIA, "Iran's Position in the East-West Conflict," 5 April 1951, PSF: Intelligence, HSTL.

41. State-JCS Mtg., 2 May 1951, PPS Papers.

42. FO 1981, 11 May 1951, FO 371/91534.

43. FRUS 1952–1954 10, doc. 21, State 2088, 11 May 1951; BEW 488, 12 May 1951, FO 371/915341; BEW 1524, 16 May 1951, FO 371/91534; State 2139, 18 May 1951, 888.2553/5-1651; Robert Beisner, *Dean Acheson: A Life in the Cold War* (New York: Oxford University Press, 2006), 544–45.

44. FRUS 1952–1954 10, doc. 16, Editorial Note; FRUS 1952–1954 Retro, doc. 28, SE-6, "Current Development in Iran," 22 May 1951; "Position Paper for Discussion with British Ambassador," 15 May 1951, attached to McGhee to Acheson, 17 May 1951, 888.2553/5-1751; State 2120, 16 May 1951, 888.2553/5-1651; Memorandum for the President, 17 May 1951, National Security Council Meetings, Meeting Discussions 1951, HSTL

45. FRUS 1952–1954 10, doc. 22, London 5966, 16 May 1951; BEW 1524, 16 May 1951, FO 371/91534; State 2139, 18 May 1951, 888.2553/5-165.

46. FRUS 1951 5, doc. 124, MemCon, 14 May 1951.

47. *Department of State Bulletin*, 28 May 1951, 851 (hereafter DSB); Beisner, *Dean Acheson*, 544–45.

48. Varasteh to Fraser, 20 May 1951, BP 126464.

49. "Iran Briefs," 31 May 1951, RG 59, OIR 557.1; Bamberg, *History of the British Petroleum Company*, vol. 2, 422.

50. Bamberg, *History of the British Petroleum Company*, vol. 2, 422–30. For Iranian views, see Mostafa Fateh, *Panjah sal naft-e Iran* (Tehran: Entesharat-e Payam, 1979), 524–52; Ruhani, *Tarikh-e milli shudan-e ṣanʿat-e naft-e Iran*, 145–57.

51. Effect of the Withdrawal of British Staff on Producing and Refining Operations in Persia, 11 June 1951; Briefing Note for Gass, 11 June 1951; Abadan Refinery: Note on Complexity of Operations, 11 June 1951, BP 72363.

52. First Meeting, 14 June 1951, FO 371/91575; FO 549, 16 June 1951, FO 371/91548; Minutes of Second Meeting, 18 June 1951, FO 371/91575.

53. Notes on a Second Meeting Held at the Summer Office of the Prime Minister, 17 June 1951, BP 72363.

54. BET 674, 19 June 1951, FO 371/91548; see also Richards to Grady, 19 June 1951, 888.2553/6-1951; Heads of Agreement Prepared by AIOC, 25 June 1951, BP 2834.

55. Tehran 3186, 15 June 1951, 888.2553/6-1551; Tehran 3347, 19 June 1951, 888.2553/6-1951.

56. State 2430, 19 June 1951, 888.2553 AIOC/6-1951; Tehran 3372, 20 June 1951, 888.2553/6-2052; Tehran 3404, 22 June 1951, 888.2553/6-2251; Tehran 3399, 22 June 1951, 888.2553/6-2251.

57. Tehran 3373, 21 June 1951, 888.2553 AIOC/5-2151.

58. June Copy of Working Group Note, Annex I, "Action by AIOC," 19 June 1951; Note on AIOC's Customers, undated, BP 28431.

59. Elm, *Oil, Power, and Principle*, 145.

60. Economic Sanctions against Persia (second draft), 3 May 1951; Shepherd to Furlonge, 26 June 1951, FO 371/91497; Shepherd to Fry, 25 June 1951, FO 371/91498; "Persia," n.d., FO 371/91531; Ross to Shepherd (draft), 8 May 1951, FO 371/91534; FO 2347, 5 May 1951, FO 371/91531; "Persian Concession: 'Free' Tanker Tonnage," 4 June 1951, FO 371/91546.

61. Ramsbotham, Economic Sanctions against Persia, 23 June 1951, FO 371 /91498.

62. Shepherd to Fry, 25 June 1951, FO 371/91498.

63. Berthoud, "Persia," 15 June 1951; FO 73, 20 June 1951, FO 371/191548; Louis, *British Empire in the Middle East*, 660–61; Abrahamian, *The Coup*, 150–51; for British activities among the tribes, Tehran, 3095, 4 June 1591, 888.2553/6-351.

64. Wm. Roger Louis, "Britain and the Overthrow of the Mosaddeq Government," in *Mohammed Mosaddeq and the 1953 Coup in Iran*, edited by Mark J. Gasiorowski and Malcolm Byrne (Syracuse, NY: Syracuse University Press, 2004), 137–38.

65. Darbyshire Transcript, 3, National Security Archive.

66. Shepherd to Morrison, 2 July 1951, FO 248/1514.

67. Shepherd to Morrison, 4 July 1951, FO 248/1514.

68. London 6495, 12 June 1951, 888.2553/6-1251; McGhee to Matthews, 14 June 1951, 888.2553/6-145; State 2399, 15 June 1951, 888.2553/6-1251; "Persian Concession: 'Free' Tanker Tonnage," 4 June 1951, FO 371/91546; Logan and Fry,

"Persian Oil," 6 June 1951, FO 371/91546; London 6780, 23 June 1951, 888.2553/6-2351; Strang Minutes, 23 June 1951, FO 371/91556.

69. GTI, "Future Course of Action in Iran," 23 June 1951, RG 59, Lot 57 D 155, "1951—Oil."

70. MemCon, 6 July 1951, Acheson MemCons, HSTL.

71. Young to Grady, 20 June 1951, Tehran Post File (TPF) 350 Iran, RG 84; Richards to Grady, 23 June 1951, TPF 350 Iran.

72. Mark J. Gasiorowski, "The US Stay-Behind Operation in Iran, 1948–1953," *Intelligence and National Security* 34 (2019): 176.

73. FRUS 1952–1954 Retro, doc. 34, MemCon, 25 June 1951.

74. FRUS 1952–1954 Retro, doc. 36, Memo for the Record, 29 June 1951.

75. FRUS 1952–1954 Retro, doc. 41, Project Outline Prepared in the CIA, undated.

76. McGhee to Matthews, "Memorandum: United States Position in Iranian Oil Controversy," 14 June 1951, 888.2553/6-1451; State 2399, 15 June 1951, 888.2553/6-1251; McGhee to Acheson, 21 June 1951, 888.2553/6-2151.

77. Bamberg, *History of the British Petroleum Company*, vol. 2, 424–25.

78. For the documents taken from the AIOC information office, see *Asrar-e khanah-e Siddan* (Tehran: Mu'assasah-'e Intisharat-e Amir Kabir, 1979). For a firsthand account, see Harvard Interview, Mozaffar Baqa'i, Tape No. 12, 1–3. According to Baqa'i, most of the company's more sensitive documents were evacuated with the Jackson mission, carried out of the country "in fifty suitcases."

79. Tehran 3398, 22 June 1951, 888.2553 AIOC/6-2251.

80. Tehran 3381, 21 June 1951, 888.2553 AIOC/6-2151; Tehran 3398, 22 June 1951, 888.2553/6-2251; Tehran 3399, 22 June 1951, 888.2553/6-2251; Tehran 3436, 25 June 1951, 888.2553/6-2551.

81. Proclamation from Temporary Board of NIOC, 25 June 1951, BP 72363.

82. London 6495, 12 June 1951, 888.2553/6-1251; McGhee to Matthews, "Memorandum: United States Position in Iranian Oil Controversy," 14 June 1951, 888.2553/6-1451; State 2399, 15 June 1951, 888.2553/6-1251; "Persian Concession: 'Free' Tanker Tonnage," 4 June 1951, FO 371/91546; Logan and Fry, "Persian Oil," 6 June 1951, FO 371/91546; London 6780, 23 June 1951, 888.2553/6-2351; Strang Minutes, 23 June 1951, FO 371/91556.

83. FO 660, 28 June 1951, BP 72363.

84. FRUS 1952–1954 10, doc. 35, Tehran 6, 1 July 1951.

85. FRUS 1952–1954 Retro, doc. 35, NSC 107/2, 27 June 1951; FRUS 1952–1954 10, doc. 34, Prime Minister Mosaddeq to President Truman, 28 June 1951; doc. 37, President Truman to Prime Minister Mosaddeq, 8 July 1951; Acheson, *Present at the Creation*, 507–8; David S. Painter, *Oil and the American Century: The Political Economy of U.S. Foreign Oil Policy, 1941–1954* (Baltimore: Johns Hopkins University Press, 1986), 176.

86. State 72, 4 July 1952, 888.2553/7-451.

87. FRUS 1952–1954 10, doc. 37, Truman to Mosaddeq, 8 July 1951.

88. FRUS 1952–1954 10, doc. 38, MemCon, 11 July 1951.

89. Mary Ann Heiss, *Empire and Nationhood: The United States, Great Britain and Iranian Oil, 1950–1954* (New York: Columbia University Press, 1997), 82.

90. Minute of Meeting, 16 July 1951, Records of the Cabinet (CAB) 128-21-12; FRUS 1952–1954 10, doc. 36, MemCon, 7 July 1951; Tehran 94, 8 July 1951, 888.2553/7-851; State 44, 8 July 1951, Harriman Papers, Box 294, Library of Congress (LC); on Truman's offer, see Acheson, *Present at the Creation*, 507–8. For the ICJ action, see *I.C.J. Pleadings, Anglo-Iranian Oil Co. Case (United Kingdom v. Iran)*, 715–16.

91. Seddon to Rice, 17 July 1951, BP 72363.

92. Levy recounted his efforts in *The Present Situation in Iran: A Survey of Political and Economic Problems Confronting the Country* (Washington, DC: Middle East Institute, 1953). There are numerous documents on his efforts in Iran in his papers at the American Heritage Center at the University of Wyoming, but almost all are duplicates of documents in State Department Records. Walters has a colorful account in *Silent Missions* (Garden City, NY: Doubleday & Co., 1978), 241–59.

93. Tehran 260, 18 July 1951, Harriman Papers, Box 293, LC; Tehran Desp. 125, 28 July 1951, 788.00/7-2851; Tehran 484, 3 August 1951, TPF 361.2; Seddon to Northcroft, 16 July 1951, BP 72363; Mark J. Gasiorowski, "The CIA's TPBEDAMN Operation and the 1953 Coup in Iran," *Journal of Cold War Studies* 15 (Fall 2013): 13; Kermit Roosevelt, *Countercoup: The Struggle for the Control of Iran* (New York: McGraw-Hill, 1979), 98.

94. Memo(s) of Conversation, 16 July 1951, Harriman Papers, Box 292, LC.

95. FRUS 1952–1954 10, doc. 42, Tehran 240, 17 July 1951; doc. 43, Tehran 276, 19 July 1951; Harriman Diary, 22 July 1951, Harriman Papers, Box 292, LC.

96. FRUS 1952–1954 10, doc. 44, Tehran 285, 19 July 1951; doc. 47, Tehran 301, 20 July 1951; doc. 49, Tehran 321, 22 July 1951; Ali Rahnema, *Behind the 1953 Coup in Iran: Thugs, Turncoats, Soldiers, and Spooks* (Cambridge: Cambridge University Press, 2015), 13.

97. FIS, Interview with Sir Peter Ramsbotham, 1–3.

98. Technical Oil Discussions between Mr. Levy of the Harriman Mission and Iranian and British Officials, July–August 1951; "Conversation with Hassibi and Saleh," 16 July 1951, 888.2553/8-3151.

99. FRUS 1952–1954 10, doc. 46, Tehran 287, 20 July 1951; doc. 50, Tehran 322, 22 July 1951; doc. 52, Tehran 340, 24 July 1951; doc. 54, Tehran 380, 25 July 1951; Tehran 318, 21 July 1951, 888.2553/7-2151; Grady to Acheson, Note from Harriman, 22 July 1951, 888.2553/7-2251.

100. MemCon, 25 July 1951, Harriman Papers, Box 292, LC; Harriman Diary, n.d., Harriman Papers, Box 292, LC.

101. Tehran 341, 24 July 1951, Harriman Papers, Box 293, LC.

102. FRUS 1952–1954 10, doc. 53, Tehran 352, 24 July 1951.

103. "Technical Oil Discussions between Mr. Levy of the Harriman Mission and Iranian and British Officials, July–August 1951," 28 July 1951; MemCon, 29 July 1951, 888.2553/8-3151; Ramsbotham, Record of Meeting, 30 July 1951, FO 371/91575; Butler, "Mr. Levy's Dilution Plan," 31 July 1951, FO 371/91575.

104. "Lord Privy Seal's Mission to Persia," undated, BP 126364.

105. Flett Note, 31 July 1951, FO 371/91575; Ramsbotham, "Persian Oil," 1 August 1951, FO 371/91575.

106. Logan, Minute, 31 July 1951, FO 371/91575.

107. Ramsbotham, Record of Meeting, 31 July 1951 (misdated 21 July), FO 371/91575; Gass to Bowker, 31 July 1951, FO 371/91575; "Lord Privy Seal's Mission to Persia," n.d., T236/2828.

108. Heiss, *Empire and Nationhood*, 89–91.

109. London 669, 1 August 1951, Harriman Papers, Box 294, LC; MemCon, 2 August 1951, 788.00/8-251.

110. Ramsbotham, Record of Meeting, 5 August 1951, FO 371/91583; Stokes made the same points in a meeting with the Iranian delegation the following day; Record of Remarks, 6 August 1951, FO 371/91583.

111. *Documents on International Affairs (DIA)* 1951, 502–4; Berry to Acheson, 13 August 1951, 788.00/8-1351; FRUS 1952–1954 10, doc. 67; Louis, *British Empire in the Middle East*, 678–81; Heiss, *Empire and Nationhood*, 90.

112. Elwell-Sutton, *Persian Oil*, 251–53.

113. Tehran 601, 13 August 1951, PSF: Iran: Harriman, HSTL; BET 1105, 14 August 1951, FO 371/91577.

114. Tehran 1082, 12 August 1951, FO 371/91575.

115. Record of Meeting, 16 August 1951, FO 371/91580. See Fateh, *Panjah sal naft-e Iran*, 552–61, Ruhani, *Tarikh-e milli shudan-e ṣanʿat-e naft-e Iran*, 188–209.

116. Meeting, 15 August 1951; Meeting with the Shah, 16 August 1951; Furlonge, AIOC Personnel, 20 August 1951, FO 371/91580.

117. Reply of the Persian Delegation to the Proposals of the British Delegation, 18 August 1951, BP 126364.

118. *DIA*, 1951, 504–6; Berry to Acheson, 13 August 1951, 788.00/8-1351; Tehran 601, 13 August 1951, PSF: Iran: Harriman, HSTL; Painter, *Oil and the American Century*, 178.

119. FRUS 1952–1954 10, doc. 71, Tehran 675, 17 August 1951; doc. 72, Tehran 705, 19 August 1951; doc. 73, Tehran 709, 19 August 1951. The head of the Iranian delegation made an eloquent reply to Harriman; see *Iranian Documents*, 39–43; Berry to Acheson, 20 August 1951, PSF: Iran: Harriman, HSTL.

120. Tehran 709, Note from Harriman 19 August 1951, 888.2553/8-1951.

121. Tehran 704, 18 Aug. 1951, 888. 2553/8-1851; Stokes, "History of Events on 21st August 1951, FO 371/91583; Stokes, "Short Account of Talks on 22nd August 1951," T 235/2828.

122. MemCon, 22 August 1951, 888.2553/8-2251.

123. BET 1188, 22 August 1951, FO 371/91580.

124. MemCon, 22 August 1951, Harriman Papers, Box 292, LC; MemCon, 23 August 1951, Harriman Papers, Box 292, LC; MemCon, 24 August 1951, Harriman Papers, Box 292, LC; FRUS 1952–1954 10, doc. 74, Tehran 736, 22 August 151; doc. 75, Tehran 163, 22 August 1951; doc. 76, Tehran 761, 23 August 1951; Tehran 781, 23 August 1951, PSF: Iran: Harriman, HSTL. Harriman left Iran on 25 August.

125. FRUS 1952–1954 10, doc. 74, Tehran 736, 22 August 1951.

126. Note for Rothnie, 3 September 1951; Seddon to Rice, 27 August 1951, BP 126361.

127. Attlee to Truman, 23 August 1951, 888.2553/8-2351.

128. Zaehner, "Interview with Monsieur Perron," 27 August 1951, FO 248/1514.

129. Zaehner, "Perron Again," 29 August 1951, FO 248/1514.

130. BET 1248, 29 August 1951, FO 248/1514.

131. "The Position of the United States in Iran (drafted by McGhee and Ferguson)," n.d., appendix to WFM B-2/2b, 788.00/9-651; Ferguson, "Our Next Steps in Iran," attached to Ferguson to Dorsz, 16 August 1951, RG 59, Lot 55 D 155, "Iran—Oil."

132. Bonright to Raynor, 24 August 1951, 888.2553/8-2451.

133. FRUS 1952–1954 10, doc. 84, State 524, 7 September 1951.

134. Memo: Current Developments in Iranian Situation, 30 August 1951, 888.2553 /8-3051.

135. Shepherd Minute, 6 September 1951, FO 248/1514; BET 1298, 6 September 1951, FO 371/91463.

136. *DIA*, 1951, 506–18, 520–26, 531–40; see also Acheson's remarks in U.S. Congress, House, Committee on Foreign Affairs, *Selected Executive Session Hearings of the Committee, 1951–1956*, vol. 16: *The Middle East, Africa, and Inter-American Affairs*, 86–87, 107–8. The quote is from Brian Lapping, *End of Empire* (New York: St. Martin's Press, 1985), 209; Tehran 1017, 14 September 1951, 888.2553/9-1451; London 1490, 24 September 1951, Harriman Papers, Box 294, LC.

137. Shepherd to Strang, 11 September 1951, FO 371/91463.

138. BEW 3074, 22 September 1951, FO 371/91590.

139. FRUS 1952–1954 10, doc. 89, State 655, 26 September 1951.

140. Acheson, TelCon, 26 September 1951, 888.2553/9-2651; FRUS 1952–1954 10, doc. 90, note 3; Memorandum of two telephone conversations between Lovett and Acheson, 28 September 1951, *Declassified Documents Quarterly 1985*, doc. 1045.

141. Spiller, "Sputter of Musketry," 60–62; Marsh, "The Labour Government's 'Scuttle' from Abadan," 832–37.

142. FRUS 1952–1954 10, doc. 93, Tehran 1180, 27 September 1951; Tehran 1205, 28 September 1951, Harriman Papers, Box 294, LC.

143. Tehran 1204, 28 September 1951, Harriman Papers, Box 294, LC; FRUS 1952–1954 10, doc. 98, Tehran 1215, 30 September 1951; Tehran 1209, 29 September 1951, Harriman Papers, Box 294, LC.

144. Louis, *British Empire in the Middle East*, 671–76.

145. Text of Mosaddeq Speech, 27 September 1951, BP 126464A.

146. FRUS 1952–1954 10, doc. 95, Tehran 1208, 28 September 1951.

147. *Times*, 3 October 1951; Norman Kemp, *Abadan: A First-Hand Account of the Persian Oil Crisis* (London: Wingate, 1953), 239–50; Daniel Yergin, *The Prize: The Epic Quest for Oil, Money, and Power* (New York: Simon & Schuster, 1991), 463–64.

148. Sir Peter Ramsbotham, Interview with David S. Painter, Winchester, 17 July 1991; Yergin, *The Prize*, 464.

149. FRUS 1952–1954 Retro, doc. 47, Villard to Nitze, 26 September 1951.

150. Tehran 1296, 5 October 1951, 888.2553/10-551.

Chapter 3

1. FRUS 1952–1954 10, doc. 97, State 1754, 30 September 1951; Tehran 1230, 1 October 1951, 888.2553/10-151; McGhee and Hickerson to Webb, 1 October 1951, 888.2553/10-151; State 1840, 4 October 1951, Harriman Papers, Box 294, LC; Tehran 1236, 2 October 1951, and Tehran 1245, 2 October 1951, both in Harriman Papers, Box 294, LC; Tehran 1276, 4 October 1951, RG 84, Box 29; Tehran 1283, 4 October 1951, 888.2553/10-451; George C. McGhee, "Recollections of Dr. Muhammed Musaddiq," in *Musaddiq, Iranian Nationalism, and Oil,* edited by James A. Bill and Wm. Roger Louis (London: I. B. Tauris, 1988), 296–97.

2. CIA, "Analysis of Iranian Political Situation," 12 October 1951, PSF; FRUS 1952–1954 Retro, doc. 51, CIA Station in Iran to CIA, 12 October 1951; Tehran 1306, 6 October 1951, 888.2553/10-651.

3. Harvard Interview, Karim Sanjabi, Tape No. 10, 4–5.

4. Quotes in Mostafa Elm, *Oil, Power, and Principle: Iran's Oil Nationalization and Its Aftermath* (Syracuse, NY: Syracuse University Press, 1992), 175; Ervand Abrahamian, *The Coup: 1953, the CIA and the Roots of Modern U.S.-Iranian Relations* (New York: New Press, 2013), 124; Harvard Interview, Karim Sanjabi, Tape No. 10, 5; Fu'ad Ruhani, *Tarikh-e milli shudan-e ṣan'at-e naft-e Iran* (Tehran: Kitabhaye Jibi), 219–28; Mostafa Fateh, *Panjah sal naft-e Iran* (Tehran: Entesharat-e Payam, 1979), 567–74.

5. FRUS 1952–1954 10, doc. 114, Editorial Note; Mary Ann Heiss, *Empire and Nationhood: The United States, Great Britain and Iranian Oil, 1950–1954* (New York: Columbia University Press, 1997), 99.

6. Dean Acheson, *Present at the Creation: My Years at the State Department* (New York: W. W. Norton, 1969), 510; William A. Dorman and Mansour Farhang, *The U.S. Press and Iran: Foreign Policy and the Journalism of Deference* (Berkeley: University of California Press, 1987), 31–62.

7. Quoted in Christopher R. W. Dietrich, *Oil Revolution: Anti-Colonial Elites, Sovereign Rights, and the Economic Culture of Decolonialization* (New York: Cambridge University Press, 2017), 36.

8. Dietrich, *Oil Revolution,* 34–37; James F. Goode, *In the Shadow of Musaddiq* (New York: St. Martin's Press, 1997), 57.

9. Tehran 866, 27 April 1951, 888.2553/4-2751; Gregory Brew, "The Collapse Narrative: The United States, Mohammed Mossadegh, and the Coup Decision of 1953," *Texas National Security Review* 2 (November 2019): 38–59.

10. FRUS 1952–1954 Retro, doc. 4, Memo by Jackson, 12 March 1951.

11. Villard to Nitze, 9 October 1951, 888.2553/10-951.

12. MemCon, 10 October 1951, Acheson MemCons, HSTL.

13. FRUS 1952–1954 10, doc. 111, JCS to Lovett, 10 October 1951.

14. McGhee to Acheson, 16 October 1951, 888.2553/10-1651; DOS Briefing Memo for the President, 22 October 1951, PSF: Harriman, HSTL.

15. George C. McGhee, *Envoy to the Middle World: Adventures in Diplomacy* (New York: Harper & Row, 1983), 390–404; Vernon Walters, *Silent Missions* (Garden City, NY: Doubleday, 1978), 259–63; McGhee, "Recollections of Dr. Muhammed

Musaddiq," 296–304; Nathan J. Citino, "Internationalist Oilmen, the Middle East, and the Remaking of American Liberalism, 1945–1953," *Business History Review* 84 (Summer 2010): 245–48.

16. Abrahamian, *The Coup*, 126.

17. Quoted in Abrahamian, *The Coup*, 125; McGhee, "Recollections of Dr. Muhammed Musaddiq," 298; Elm, *Oil, Power, and Principle*, 183.

18. FRUS 1952–1954 10, doc. 113, MemCon, 11 October 1951; doc. 115, MemCon, 15 October 1951; doc. 117, MemCon, 23 October 1951; doc. 118, MemCon, 28 October 1951.

19. Memoranda of most, but not all, of the discussions are printed in FRUS 1952–1954 10, docs. 108, 109, 113, 115, 117, 118, and a summary doc. 119, State 2256, 30 October 1951. Memoranda of meetings on 8, 9 (A.M.), 11, 12, 17, and 25, all by Walters, can be found in Box 294, Harriman Paper, LC. See also McGhee, *Envoy to the Middle World*, 390–404; Walters, *Silent Missions*, 259–63.

20. Edith T. Penrose, *The Large International Firm in Developing Countries: The International Petroleum Industry* (London: George Allen & Unwin, Ltd., 1968), 25–52.

21. Acheson MemCon, 24 October 1951, Acheson Papers, HSTL; Acheson, *Present at the Creation*, 510–11.

22. "Courses of Action with Respect to the Iranian Problem," 30 October 1951, RG 59, PPS Papers, "Iran" (folder 2).

23. Funkhouser to Linder, 24 October 1951, 888.2553/10-2451; Minutes of Meeting, 2 November 1951, 888.2553/11-251; MemCon, 25 October 1951, 888.2553 /10-2551; MemCon, 5 November 1951, 888.2553/11-551; Basic Premises of US Good Offices Proposals, November 1951, RG 59, Box 5506, Nitze-Linder Working Group.

24. FRUS 1952–1954 10, doc. 119, State 2256, 30 October 1951, note 4.

25. Fergusson to Stokes, 3 October 1951, FO 371/91599; Wm. Roger Louis, *The British Empire in the Middle East, 1945–1951: Arab Nationalism, the United States and Postwar Imperialism* (Oxford: Clarendon Press, 1984), 682–85.

26. Louis, *British Empire in the Middle East*, 682.

27. "Persian Oil," n.d.; BET 1580, 23 October 1951; BET 1585, 24 October 1951; Logan, "Persian Oil Working Party," 18 October 1951, FO 371/91606; Flett (T) to Rowan (T), 19 October 1951, FO 371/91606; Rowan to Flett, 22 October 1951, FO 371/91606.

28. Furlonge, "Persian Oil," 30 October 1951; Berthoud to Furlonge, 29 October 1951; Makins Minute, 30 October 1951; "Persian Oil," n.d., FO 371/91608; Berthoud to Furlonge, 29 October 1951; Strang to Eden, 31 October 1951; "Persia," 29 October 1951, FO 371/91607.

29. Berthoud to Furlonge, 29 October 1951; Makins Minute, 30 October 1951; Strang to Eden, 31 October 1951, all in FO 371/91608. For the tanker survey, see Nuttall (M/FP) to Rothnie (FO), 8 October 1951, FO 371/91599.

30. FRUS 1952–1954 6, part 1, doc. 332, Acheson MemCon, 6 January 1952; Louis, *The British Empire in the Middle East*, 682–85.

31. Furlonge, "Persian Oil," 1 November 1951, FO 371/91607; Furlonge, "Persian Oil: Notes on Washington Telegram No. 3485," 1 November 1951, FO 371/91607; "Persian Oil," November 1951, FO 371/91608; "Persian Oil: Notes for Discussion with Mr. Harriman," n.d., FO 371/91609; FO 5436, 4 November 1951, FO 371/91608;

Ramsbotham, "Persian Oil," 8 November 1951, FO 371/91609; FO 1596, 6 November 1951, FO 371/91608; Makins, "Persian Oil," 7 November 1951, FO 371/91610; FO 1613, 7 November 1951, FO 371/91608.

32. Seddon, Note on Treasury Meeting, 6 November 1951, BP 100572.

33. FRUS 1952–1954 10, doc. 120, MemCon, 4 November 1951.

34. FRUS 1952–1954 10, doc. 124, Paris Actel 8, 7 November 1951; doc. 127, Paris 2743, 9 November 1951; British Embassy Paris (BEP) 487, 6 November 1951, FO 800/812; Persian (Official) Committee, 7 November 1951, CAB 134/1145; "Persian Oil," 6 November 1951, CAB 134/1145; Statement of Principles, 8 November 1951, CAB 134/1145; BEP 512, 8 November 1951, FO 371/91609; Paris 512, Heiss, *Empire and Nationhood*, 103–4.

35. FRUS 1952–1954 10, doc. 129, Paris 2808, 10 November 1951.

36. FRUS 1952–1954 10, doc. 130, Paris 2862, 14 November 1951; "Persia," 14 November 1951, FO 800/812.

37. McGhee, *Envoy to the Middle World*, 403.

38. Abrahamian, *The Coup*, 129; Lior Sternfeld, "Iran Days in Egypt: Mosaddeq's Visit to Cairo in 1951," *British Journal of Middle Eastern Studies* 43 (2016): 1–20.

39. Wm. Roger Louis, "Britain and the Overthrow of the Mosaddeq Government," in *Mohammad Mosaddeq and the 1953 Coup in Iran*, edited by James Bill and Wm. Roger Louis (Syracuse, NY: Syracuse University Press, 2004), 138, 140–41; Fakhreddin Azimi, "Unseating Mosaddeq: The Configuration and Role of Domestic Forces," in *Mohammad Mosaddeq and the 1953 Coup in Iran*, edited by James Bill and Wm. Roger Louis, see note 1, 29–51.

40. Louis, "Britain and the Overthrow of the Mosaddeq Government," 141–42.

41. Azimi, "Unseating Mosaddeq," 49; Fakhreddin Azimi, *Iran: The Crisis of Democracy: From the Exile of Reza Shah to the Fall of Musaddiq* (London: I.B. Tauris, 2009), 274–75.

42. FRUS 1952–1954 Retro, doc. 58, Memo Prepared in Office of National Estimates, CIA, undated; Mark J. Gasiorowski, "US Perceptions of the Communist Threat in Iran during the Mossadegh Era," *Journal of Cold War Studies* 21 (Summer 2019): 198–202.

43. Gholam R. Afkhami, *The Life and Times of the Shah* (Berkeley: University of California Press, 2009), 132–34; Abbas Milani, *The Shah* (New York: Palgrave Macmillan, 2011), 152–53.

44. Brew, "The Collapse Narrative," 45–47.

45. FRUS 1952–1954 10, doc. 116, Tehran 1478, 22 October 1951; Bayne MemCon 24 October 1951, 350 Iran, TPF.

46. FRUS 1952–1954 10, doc. 121, State 2704, 5 November 1951; doc. 122, note 3, doc. 123, Tehran 24, 7 November 1951; BET 1630, 7 November 1951, FO 248/1514; Webb, Meeting with the President, 5 November 1951. 888.2553/11-551.

47. Tehran 1730, 7 November 1951, 888.2553/11-751; FRUS 1952–1954 10, doc. 120, MemCon, 4 November 1951; Furlonge, "Persian Oil," 1 November 1951, FO 371/91607; Furlonge, "Persian Oil: Notes on Washington Telegram No. 3485," 1 November 1951, FO 371/91607; "Persian Oil," November 1951, FO 371/91608; "Persian Oil: Notes for Discussion with Mr. Harriman," n.d., FO 371/91609; FO 5436, 4

November 1951, FO 371/91608; Ramsbotham, "Persian Oil," 8 November 1951, FO 371/91609; FO 1596, 6 November 1951, FO 371/91608; Makins, "Persian Oil," 7 November 1951, FO 371/91610; FO 1613, 7 November 1951, FO 371/91608.

48. FRUS 1952–1954 10, doc. 138, Tehran 2329, 26 December 1951; Tehran, 10 December 1951, 788.00/12-1051; Tehran 2158, 12 December 1951, 350 Iran, TPF; Tehran 2165, 12 December 1951, 788.00/12-1251; Tehran 2216, 16 December 1951, 788.13 /12-1651.

49. Tehran 1792, 14 November 1951, 788.00/11-1451; Tehran 1796, 14 November 1951, Harriman Papers, Box 293, LC; "The Iranian Situation," 15 November 1951, PSF: Iran, HSTL; Tehran 1869, 20 November 1951, 888.2553/11-3051; FRUS 1952–1954 10, doc: 116, Tehran 1478, 22 October 1951; State-JCS Meeting, 21 November 1951, PPS, RG 59; Pyman Minute, 23 December 1951, FO 248/1531.

50. FRUS 1952–1954 Retro, doc. 56, Tehran 1984, 28 November 1951.

51. Middleton to Furlonge, 19 November 1951, FO 248/1514.

52. FRUS 1952–1954 Retro, doc. 54, Tehran 1829, 16 November 1951.

53. FRUS 1952–1954 10, doc. 126, MemCon, 9 November 1951.

54. Tehran 1603, 31 October 1951, RG 84 Box 35 501.

55. Tehran 2126, 10 December 1951, 888.2553/12-1051; Berry to Acheson, 14 December 1951, 888.2553/12-1451; Tehran 2201, 14 December 1951, 888.2553/12-1451; Tehran 2290, 21 December 1951, 888.2553/12-2151; TelCon, Perkins and Linder (Paris) and Nitze, McGhee, Rountree, and Bonright (Washington), 8 November 1951, Harriman Papers, Box 293, LC; State 1616, 9 November 1951, Harriman Papers, Box 29, LC; Washington Telac 21, 10 November 1951, Harriman Papers, Box 293, LC; Musaddiq to Truman, 9 November 1951, OF 134-13, Iranian Oil Controversy, HSTL.

56. State-JCS Meeting, 21 November 1951, PPS, RG 59; Funkhouser MemCon, 19 November 1951, plus attachment, 888.2553/11-1951.

57. FRUS 1952–1954 10, doc. 132, State Telac 40, 20 November 1951; doc. 133, State 2642, 23 November 1951; State 2913, 15 November 1951, Harriman Papers, Box 294, LC; Tehran 1832, 16 November 1951, Harriman Papers, Box 293, LC; Actels 16 and 17 November 1951, Harriman Papers, Box 293, LC; London 2432, 20 November 1951, Harriman Papers, Box 293, LC; State-JCS Meeting, 21 November 1951, PPS Papers; Murphy to Webb, 14 November 1951, PSF: Iran, HSTL; Unnumbered Tlg. White House to Acheson, 14 November 1951. 788.13/11-1451; on aid for the British, see David S. Painter, *Oil and the American Century: The Political Economy of U.S. Foreign Oil Policy, 1941–1954* (Baltimore: Johns Hopkins University Press, 1986), 261, note 30.

58. Tehran 2289, 21 December 1951, 888.2553/12-2151.

59. MemCon, 14 November 1951, RG 59, 888.2553/11-1751; Rome 2391, 28 November 1951, 888.2553/11-1251; Amy L. S. Staples, "Seeing Diplomacy through Bankers' Eyes: The World Bank, the Anglo-Iranian Oil Crisis, and the Aswan High Dam," *Diplomatic History* 26 (Summer 2002): 397–418; Fateh, *Panjah sal naft-e Iran*, 586–92.

60. Richard W. Cottam, Interview with David S. Painter, 20 July 1988, Pittsburgh, PA; Richard W. Cottam, *Iran and the United States: A Cold War Case Study* (Pittsburgh: University of Pittsburgh Press, 1988), 97. A distinguished scholar on Iranian

nationalism, Cottam was in Iran in 1951–52 conducting research. He joined the CIA in 1953, and later served at the U.S. embassy in Tehran, 1956–58.

61. Persia (Official) Committee Meeting, 26 November 1951 (with attached note by AIOC), CAB 134/1105; Record of Conversation between the Secretary of State and Mr. Garner, 27 November 1951, FO 800/812; Cabinet Persia Committee, "International Bank Proposals," 29 November 1951, Prime Minister's Office (PREM) 11/725; Foreign Office, "Persia," 1 December 1951, PREM 11/725.

62. Garner to McCloy, 15 March 1949, Iran—General—Correspondence 03, 1805821, World Bank Group Archive (WBGA); Michele Alacevich, "The World Bank and the Politics of Productivity: The Debate on Economic Growth, Poverty, and Living Standards in the 1950s," *Journal of Global History* 6 (2011): 53–74.

63. FRUS 1952–1954 10, doc. 134, State 1102, 28 November 1951.

64. Digest of a Meeting, Robert L. Garner, "The Role of the International Bank as a Mediator in the Iranian Crisis," 18 March 1952, Records of Meetings, vol. 17, Archives of the Council on Foreign Relations (CFR).

65. Record of a Meeting, 5 December 1951, Iran—General—Memoranda of Meetings—Correspondence, 1806448, WBGA.

66. Notes of a Meeting, 1 December 1951, Iran—General—Calculations—Correspondence, 1806456, WBGA.

67. Cabinet Persia Committee, "International Bank Proposals," 29 November 1951, PREM 11/725; Elm, *Oil, Power, and Principle*, 195–96.

68. FRUS 1952–1954 6, doc. 323, Paper Prepared in the Department of State, 21 December 1951; doc. 326, London 2898, 28 December 1951; doc. 327, London 2903, 29 December 1951; doc. 329, Memo by Acheson, 5 January 1952; doc. 330, Notes by Bradley, 5 January 1952; doc. 332, Memo by Acheson, 6 January 1952; doc. 333, Minutes of First Formal Meeting, 7 January 1952; State-JCS Mtg., 23 January 1951, PPS; Heiss, *Empire and Nationhood*, 115.

69. FRUS 1952–1954 10, doc. 142, Memo of Foreign Ministers Meeting, 9 January 1952. The document incorrectly cites the figure as £42 million, when in fact it was £49 million.

70. FRUS 1952–1954 10, doc. 139, Tehran 2462, 4 January 1952; doc. 140, Tehran 2480, 5 January 1952; Tehran 2448, 3 January 1952, 888.2553/1-352.

71. Minutes of Meeting, 17 January 1952, 888.2553/1-2352; MemCon, 25 January 1952, 888.2553/1-2252; Heiss, *Empire and Nationhood*, 114–17.

72. Adam Hochschild, "The Untold Story of the Texaco Oil Tycoon Who Loved Fascism," *The Nation*, 21 March 2016, https://www.thenation.com/article/archive/the-untold-story-of-the-texaco-oil-tycoon-who-loved-fascism/.

73. "Review of the International Bank's Negotiations Concerning the Iranian Oil Problem," 3 April 1952, Iran—General—Correspondence 1, 1805819, WBGA.

74. Prud'homme to Garner, 1 January 1952, RG 84, General Classified Records of the US Embassy in Tehran, 1950–1952, Box 40.

75. Tehran 2448, 3 January 1952, 888.2553/1-352.

76. Prud'homme for Garner, 2479, 6 January 1952, 888.2553/1-552; Edward S. Mason and Robert E. Asher, *The World Bank since Bretton Woods* (Washington, DC:

Brookings Institution, 1973), 604; Staples, "Seeing Diplomacy through Bankers' Eyes," 405; Elm, *Oil, Power, and Principle*, 196–98.

77. Prud'homme for Garner, 2462, 4 January 1952, RG 84, General Classified Records of the US Embassy in Tehran, 1950–1952, Box 40.

78. FRUS 1952–1954 10, doc. 144, Tehran 2598, 12 January 1952.

79. Burrows to Bowker, 26 January 1952, Ministry of Fuel and Power (POWE) 33/1929; Makins, Meeting with Fraser (AIOC), 5 February 1952, CAB 134/1147.

80. Prud'homme to Garner, 31 January 1952, Iran—General—Secret and Confidential Files—Negotiations—Volume 3, 1806452, WBGA.

81. State. 2609, 14 January 1952, 888.00 TA/1-1452.

82. FRUS 1952–1954 10, doc. 141, Berry to Acheson, 8 January 1952; Bradley to SecDef, 2 January 1952, DOD Records (RG 330), 092 Iran; Heiss, *Empire and Nationhood*, 113, 118.

83. FRUS 1952–1954 10, doc. 145, Tehran 2640, 15 January 1952.

84. Lovett to Acheson, 23 January 1952, RG 330, CD 092 Iran. According to a note on the source text, Acheson requested that the letter not be officially sent; State-JCS Mtg., 23 January 1952, PPS Papers.

85. FRUS 1952–1954 10, doc. 147, Attachment, Borel to Smith, 17 January 1952.

86. FRUS 1952–1954 10, doc. 148, London 3136, 18 January 1952.

87. GTI, "Position Paper," 15 January 1952, RG 59, Lot 57D 155, "Situation Reports & Briefing Memos, 1951 & 1952"; FRUS 1952–1954 10, doc. 151, State 1485, 22 January 1952.

88. Funkhouser, BOP Background Paper, 18 December 1951, RG 59, Box 5506, Nitze-Linder Papers.

89. Painter, *Oil and the American Century*, 179–81; Mary Ann Heiss, "The International Boycott of Iranian Oil and the Anti-Mosaddeq Coup of 1953," in *Mohammad Mosaddeq and the 1953 Coup in Iran*, edited by Mark J. Gasiorowski and Malcolm Byrne (Syracuse, NY: Syracuse University Press, 2004), 187–89.

90. Bank Memo, "Importance of Iran in World Oil Industry," 28 January 1952, Iran—General—Calculations—Correspondence, 1806456, WBGA.

91. Heiss, "International Boycott," 198.

92. U.S. Embassy to State, 22 October 22, 1951, General Classified Records US Embassy Tehran 1950–1952, Box 35.

93. FRUS 1952–1954 Retro, doc. 62, Kent to Smith, 30 January 1952.

94. FRUS 1952–1954 10, doc. 151, State 1485, 22 January 1952; doc. 152, State 1526, 26 January 1952.

95. Minutes of Meeting, 17 January 1952, 888.2553/1-2352.

96. FRUS 1952–1954 10, doc. 152, State 1526, 26 January 1952; doc. 156, State 1648, 9 February 1952; for the letter, see Tehran 2849, 888.2553/1-2952.

97. Notes from Meeting in Secretary's Office, 4 February 1952, RG 59, Box 5506, Nitze-Linder Working Group.

98. FRUS 1952–1954 10, doc. 157, Tehran 3031, 11 February 1952.

99. Butler, "Persia—International Bank Proposals," 2 February 1952, POWE 33/1929; Elm, *Oil, Power, and Principle*, 202–3.

100. "International Bank Mission to Tehran," 22 February 1952, CAB 134/1137; FRUS 1952–1954 10, doc. 159, Tehran 3137, 17 February 1952; Elm, *Oil, Power, and Principle*, 204–5.

101. Tehran 3206, 21 February 1952, 888.2553/2-2152.

102. Record of a Meeting, 21 February 1952, Iran—General—Memoranda of Meetings—Correspondence, 1806448, WBGA.

103. Tehran 3479, 12 March 1952, 888.2553/3-1252; Prud'homme to Garner, Draft note (never sent), March 1952, Iran—General—Secret and Confidential Files—Negotiations—Volume 3, 1806453, WBGA.

104. Garner to Richards, 20 March 1952, Iran—General—Secret and Confidential Files—Negotiations—Volume 3, 1806453, WBGA.

105. Digest of a Meeting, Robert L. Garner, "The Role of the International Bank as a Mediator in the Iranian Crisis," 18 March 1952, Records of Meetings, vol. 17, CFR.

106. Garner to Mossadegh, 4 April 1952, Iran—General—Secret and Confidential Files—Negotiations—Volume 3, 1806453, WBGA.

107. Staples, "Seeing Diplomacy through Bankers' Eyes," 406–7.

108. Linder to Acheson, Summary of British Talks, 16 February 1952, RG 59, Box 5506, Nitze-Linder Working Group Papers.

109. Acheson, *Present at the Creation*, 679.

Chapter 4

1. FRUS 1952–1954 Retro, doc. 67, CIA Memo, 28 March 1952; Harvard Interview, Karim Sanjabi, Tape No. 10, 9–10; Richard W. Cottam, *Nationalism in Iran: Updated through 1979* (Pittsburgh: University of Pittsburgh Press, 1979), 256–57, 274–76; Ervand Abrahamian, *The Coup: 1953, the CIA, and the Roots of Modern U.S.-Iranian Relations* (New York: New Press, 2013), 131–33; Ervand Abrahamian, *Oil Crisis in Iran: From Nationalism to Coup d'Etat* (New York: Cambridge University Press, 2021), 90–100; Habib Ladjevardi, "Constitutional Government and Reform under Musaddiq," in *Musaddiq, Iranian Nationalism, and Oil*, edited by James A. Bill and Wm. Roger Louis (London: I. B. Tauris, 1988), 71–74.

2. Tehran 3769, 4. April 1952, 888.2553/4-452; Tehran 3777, 4 April 1952, 350 Iran, TPF; Tehran 3916, 14 April 1952, 350 Iran, TPF; Tehran 3939, 15 April 1952, 350 Iran, TPF; Pyman Minute, 17 April 1952, FO 248/1531; Falle Minute, 20 April 20, 1952, FO 248/1531; Middleton Minute, 18 April 1952, FO 248/1531.

3. FRUS 1952–1954 Retro, doc. 67, CIA Memo, 28 March 1952.

4. Tehran 3865, 10 April 1952, 788.00/4-1052; see also Tehran Desp. 1077, "The Iranian Political Situation," 11 April 1952, 788.00/4-1152; FRUS 1952–1954 Retro, doc. 67, note 5.

5. FRUS 1952–1954 10, doc. 171, State 2312, 21 April 1952; doc.172, Tehran 4068, 23 April 1952; doc.173, State 2334, 23 April 1952; doc. 174, State 5535, 29 April 1952; Rountree to Byroade, 24 April 1952, RG 59, Lot 57 D 155, "Situation Rpts."

6. Gholam Reza Afkhami, *The Life and Times of the Shah* (Berkeley: University of California Press, 2009); Abbas Milani, *The Shah* (New York: Palgrave Macmillan, 2011), 137–40.

7. FRUS 1952–1954 Retro, doc. 67, CIA Memo, 28 March 195; doc. 68, Paris 5970, 28 March 1952; doc. 69, Tehran 3715, 31 March 1952.

8. Tehran 103, 22 July 1946, 891.00/7-2246.

9. Middleton Minutes, 16 and 18 April 1952, FO 248/1531; State 2441, 1 May 1952, 888.2553/5-152; FRUS 1952–1954 Retro, doc. 72, Tehran 4349, 9 May 1952; Tehran 4362, 10 May 1952, 500 General, TPF; BET 22, 14 May 1952, FO 371/98689.

10. MemCon, "The Iranian Situation," 15 May 1952, 888.2553/5-1552; "The Current Political Situation in Iran," 16 May 1952, Intelligence Report 5881, RG 59; Burrows to Ross, 17 May 1952, FO 371/98689; BEW 514, 18 May 1952, FO 371/98689; Logan Minute, 19 May 1952, FO 371/98689; Nitze to Acheson, 19 May 1952, RG 59, Lot 57 D 155, "Oil-1952"; Logan Minute, 21 May 1952, FO 371/98689.

11. FRUS 1952–1954 Retro, doc.73, MemCon, 16 May 1952; Abrahamian, *Oil Crisis in Iran*, 24–29.

12. FRUS 1952–1954 Retro, doc. 75, Tehran 4540, 24 May 1952.

13. FRUS 1952–1954 Retro, doc. 78, Tehran 4812, 12 June 1952; Middleton Minute, 11 June 1952, FO 248/1531.

14. FRUS 1952–1954 Retro, doc. 79, Tehran 4837, 13 June 1952. The British also opposed Saleh; Ross Minute, 7 June 1952, FO 371/98690.

15. BET 417, 13 June 1952, FO 371/98600; Fergusson, "Persian Oil," 11 June 1952, POWE 33/1934; Ross, "Persia: The Internal Situation and Prospects of Settlement over Oil," 14 June 1952, FO 371/98690; FO 395, 15 June 1952, FO 371/98690.

16. Churchill to Eden, 17 June 1952, FO 371/98600. Rather than strengthening the British position in Egypt, the "decisive volley at Ismailia" accelerated the decline of British influence and was an important factor in the seizure of power by nationalist army officers in July 1952. Michael Mason, "'The Decisive Volley': The Battle of Ismailia and the Decline of British Influence in Egypt, January-July 1952." *Journal of Imperial and Commonwealth History* 19 (1991): 45–64.

17. Falle Minute, 12 June 1952, FO 248/1531; Middleton Minute, 14 June 1952, FO 248/1531; Middleton to Ross, 16 June 1952, FO 248/1531; Middleton Minute, 9 June 1952, FO 248/1531.

18. Falle Minute, 12 June 1952, FO 248/1531; BET 417, 13 June 1952, FO 371/98600. Zaehner disagreed, arguing that Qavam could not be trusted; Zaehner, "Possible Prime Ministers," 15 June 1952, FO 248/1531; FRUS 1952–1954 Retro, doc. 79, Tehran 4837, 13 June 1952.

19. BET 426, 17 June 1952, FO 248/1531; London 5783, 18 June 1952, 888.2553 /6-1852; Falle, "Stray News," 18 June 1952, FO 248/1531.

20. Tehran 5048, 27 June 1952, 350 Iran, TPF.

21. FRUS 1952–1954 10, doc. 182, Minutes of Ministerial Talks, 24 June 1952; doc. 184, Minutes of Ministerial Talks, 28 June 1952; Ramsbotham, "The Form of a Settlement of the Dispute over the Persian Oil Industry," 19 June 1952, FO 371/98690; Makins Minute, 19 June 1952, FO 371/98690; Cabinet, Persia Committee, Meeting Minutes, 20 June 1952, CAB 134/1143; Makins, "Note on Persian Oil Dispute," 21 June 1952, FO 371/98690; Ross, "Brief for the Secretary of State's Meeting with Mr. Acheson," 23 June 1952, FO 371/98690; "Record of a Meeting Held at the Foreign Office," 24 June 1952, FO 800/813.

22. FRUS 1952–1954 10, doc. 179, Editorial Note; Sundhya Pahuja and Cait Storr, "Rethinking Iran and International Law: The *Anglo-Iranian Oil Company Case* Revisited," in *The International Legal Order: Current Needs and Possible Responses: Essays in Honor of Djamchid Montaz*, edited by James Crawford, Abdul G. Koroma, Said Mahmoudi, and Alain Pellet (Leiden: Brill Nijhoff, 2017), 60–63; Katayoun Shafiee, *Machineries of Oil: An Infrastructural History of BP in Iran* (Cambridge, MA: MIT Press, 2018), 166–75.

23. FRUS 1952–1954 Retro, doc. 79, Tehran 4837, 13 June 1952.

24. BET 211, 23 June 1952, FO 371/98625; *Ettelaat*, 18 June 1952.

25. FRUS 1952–1954 10, doc. 185, Tehran 98, 7 July 1952; Tehran 63, 5 July 1952, 350 Iran, TPF; BET 454, 5 July 1952, FO 371/98600; Tehran 457, 6 July 1952, FO 371/98600; Tehran 84, 7 July 1952, 788.2553/7-752; Tehran 108, 8 July 1952, 788.13/7-852; Tehran 117, 9 July 1952, 350 Iran, TPF; Tehran 471, 11 July 1952, FO 371/98600; Falle Minute, 15 July 1952, FO 248/1531; Tehran 201, 15 July 1952, 350 Iran, TPF.

26. Rothnie Minute, 7 July 1952, FO 371/98600; Ross Minute, 9 July 1952, FO 371/98600; Falle Minute, 12 July 1952, FO 248/1531; Falle Minute, 13 July 1952, FO 248/1531; BET 234, 14 July 1952, FO 371/98601; FRUS 1952–1954 10, doc. 186, London 153, 9 July 1952; for the portion of London 153 deleted from *Foreign Relations*, see 788.13/7-952; State 262, 11 July 1952, 788.13/7-952; Tehran 162, 13 July 1952, 788.13/7-1252; FRUS 1952–1954 Retro, doc. 98, Tehran 377, 24 July 1952; Tehran 201, 15 July 1952, 350 Iran, TPF.

27. Printed in *Ettelaat*, 17 July 1952, quoted in Ervand Abrahamian, *Iran between Two Revolutions* (Princeton, NJ: Princeton University Press, 1982), 271.

28. Harvard Interview, Mozaffar Baqa'i, Tape No. 15, 4; Mohammed Musaddeq, *Musaddiq's Memoirs*, translated by Homa Katouzian and S. H. Amin (London: National Movement of Iran, 1988), 52; FRUS 1952–1954 Retro, doc. 97, Position Paper, 22 July 1952.

29. FRUS 1952–1954 Retro, doc. 84, Tehran 239, 18 July 1952.

30. Abrahamian, *The Coup*, 138–39.

31. Husayn Makki, *Vaqayi'-e 30 Tir 1331* [Events of 30 Tir 1331] (Tehran: Bungah-e Tarjumah va Nashr-e Kitab, 1982), 64.

32. C. M. Woodhouse, *Something Ventured* (London: Granada, 1982), 115; Jackson (Woodhouse) handwritten comments on Zaehner Minute, 26 May 1952, FO 248/1531.

33. FRUS 1952–1954 Retro, doc. 85, Tehran 242, 18 July 1952; doc. 86, State 431, 18 July 1952; Byroade to Acheson, 19 July 1952, 888.2553/7-1952.

34. Bowker, "Persia," July 19, 1952, FO 371/98691.

35. Fergusson, "Persian Oil," 17 July 1952, FO 371/98690; Fergusson, "Note of Interview with Sir William Fraser," 18 July 1952, FO 371/98690; Makins, "Persian Oil," 18 July 1952, FO 371/98690; Cabinet, Persia (Official) Committee, Minutes, 18 July 1952, CAB 134/1146; London 352, 18 July 1952, 888.2553/7-1852; Makins, "Persian Oil," 19 July 1952, FO 371/98691; Bowker, "Persian Oil," 19 July 1952, FO 371/98691; London 359, 19 July 1952, 888.2553/7-1952; minute by Eden, 18 [?] July 1952, FO 371/98690.

36. Harvard Interview, Mozaffar Baqa'i, Tape No. 15, 7–13; "Kashani's Declaration," *Shahed*, July 19, 1952, *Kayhan*, 19 July 1952; "National Front Proclamation,"

Journal de Tehran, July 21, 1952, in FO 248/1531; Mary Ann Heiss, *Empire and Nation-hood: The United States, Great Britain and Iranian Oil, 1950–1954* (New York: Columbia University Press, 1997), 133; Abrahamian, *Iran between Two Revolutions*, 271.

37. FRUS 1952–1954 Retro, doc. 88, Tehran 263, 19 July 1952; doc. 89, Tehran 265, 19 July 1952; BET 531, 27 July 1952, FO 248/1531; BET 244, 28 July 1952, FO 248/1531.

38. FRUS 1952–1954 Retro, doc. 91, Tehran 276, 20 July 1952.

39. Abrahamian, *Iran between Two Revolutions*, 272; Abrahamian, *The Coup*, 140; *End of Empire*, Transcript of Interview with M. Azar, 2; Transcript of Interview with S. Bakhtiar, 14; Makkī, *Vaqayi'-I 30 Tir 1331*, 65; BET 531, 27 July 1952, BET. 244, 28 July 1952, FO 248/1531.

40. FRUS 1952–1954 Retro, doc. 92, Tehran 308, 21 July 1952; BET 494 and 496, 20 July 1952, FO 371/98601; BET 316, 21 July 1952, 350 Iran, TPF; BET 502 and 503, 21 July 1952, FO 371/98601; Ross, "Internal Persian Situation," 21 July 1952, FO 371/98601; FO 451 and 435, 21 July 1952, FO 371/98601; Fergusson, "The Iranian Situation," 22 July 1952, 788.00/7-2252; Bowker Minute, 22 July 1952, FO 371/98601.

41. International Court of Justice, Anglo-Iranian Oil Co. Case, Judgment of July 22, 1952, 112, 115; Pahuja and Storr, "Rethinking Iran and International Law," 63.

42. Mary Ann Heiss, "The International Boycott of Iranian Oil and the Anti-Mosaddeq Coup of 1953," in *Mohammad Mosaddeq and the 1953 Coup in Iran*, edited by Mark J. Gasiorowski and Malcolm Byrne (Syracuse, NY: Syracuse University Press, 2004), 194–95.

43. BET 244, 28 July 1952; BET 531, 27 July 1952, FO 248/1531; Abrahamian, *The Coup*, 141.

44. Richard W. Cottam, *Iran and the United States: A Cold War Case Study* (Pittsburgh: University of Pittsburgh Press, 1988), 100.

45. John Waller interview with David S. Painter, 29 June 1992, McLean, VA. Waller was CIA station chief in Iran from 1947 to 1949, and deputy station chief, 1951–52. In 1953, he returned to Washington to serve as chief of the Iran Branch, Directorate of Plans.

46. Maziar Behrooz, "Tudeh Factionalism and the 1953 Coup in Iran," *International Journal of Middle East Studies* 33 (August 2001): 370–71.

47. BET 518 and BET 519, 25 July 1952, FO 371/9869. Henri Rollin, the Belgian lawyer representing Iran before the International Court of Justice, had raised the possibility of an agreement on compensation on 22 July, but the British had shown no interest; Rothnie, "Offer to Discuss Compensation," 23 July 1952, and Ross Minute, 24 July 1952, FO 371/98692.

48. BET 523, 25 July 1952, FO 371/9869; Foreign Office 3012, 26 July 1952, FO 371/98691; BET 531, 27 July 1952, FO 371/98691.

49. FRUS 1952–1954 Retro, doc. 98, Tehran 377, 24 July 1952; doc. 99, State 585, 26 July 1952; Tehran 387, 25 July 1952, 888.2553/7-2552; Tehran 407, 27 July 1952, 888.2553/7-2752; Tehran 416, 27 July 1952, 888.2553/7-2752.

50. State 255, 29 July 1952, 788.00/7-2952; Burrows to Bowker, 30 July 1952, FO 371/98603.

51. Sam Falle, *My Lucky Life: In War, Revolution, Peace, and Diplomacy* (Sussex, UK: Book Guild, 1996), 68–86.

52. BET 533, July 28, 1952, FO 371/98691; Falle, "Recent Interviews," July 28, 1952, FO 248/1531; Ross Minute, July 28, 1952, FO 371/98691; Logan Minute, July 28, 1952, FO 371/98691; Middleton to Bowker, 28 July 1952, FO 371/98602; Ali Rahnema, *Behind the 1953 Coup in Iran: Thugs, Turncoats, Soldiers, and Spooks* (Cambridge: Cambridge University Press, 2014), 19–21.

53. Falle, "Recent Interviews," 28 July 1952, FO 248/1531; Ross Minute, 28 July 1952, FO 371/98691; Logan Minute, 28 July 1952; FO 371/98691; Tehran 423, 28 July 1952, 350 Iran, TPF; Ross Minute, 29 July 1952, FO 371/98603; War Office to Military Attaché, 29 July 1952, FO 371/98602; Cabinet Minute, 29 July 1952, CC 74 (52), CAB 128/24; Commonwealth Relations Office 310, 30 July 1952, FO 371/98602.

54. BEW 1448, July 29, 1952, FO 371/98691; FRUS 1953–1954 Retro, doc. 101, Byroade to Acheson, 29 July 1952; doc. 103, State 255, 29 July 1952.

55. FRUS 1952–1954 10, doc. 188; London 428, 23 July 1952, 888.2553/7-2352; FRUS 1952–1954 Retro, doc. 97, Position Paper, 22 July 1952; doc. 96, Memorandum for the Record, 21 July 1952; doc. 98, Tehran 377, 24 July 1952.

56. FRUS 1952–1954 10, doc. 190, Tehran 460, 30 July 1952; doc. 191, Tehran 480, 31 July 1952; FRUS 1952–1954 Retro, doc. 107, Tehran 481, 31 July 1952; for the embassy's estimate, see FRUS 1952–1954 Retro, doc. 112, Tehran 514, 3 August 1952.

57. FRUS 1952–1954 Retro, doc. 104, Minutes of Director of Central Intelligence Smith's Meeting, 30 July 1952.

58. FRUS 1952–1954 10, doc. 193, MemCon, 31 July 1952; doc. 194, State 276, 31 July 1952; doc. 195, Memo for the President, 6 August 1952; Tehran 435, 31 July 1952, 888.2553.7-2952; FRUS 1952–1954 Retro, doc. 106, MemCon, 31 July 1952; BEW 1469 and 1470, 31 July 1952, FO 371/98691.

59. BET 564, 7 August 1952, FO 371/98692.

60. Minute by Middleton, 22 July 1952, FO 248/1531.

61. Falle, "American Estimate," 2 August 1952; Falle, "The American Proposals," 4 August 1952, FO 248/1531; Middleton to FO, No. 547, 31 July 1952, FO 371/98691; Middleton to FO, No. 555, 2 August 1952, FO 371/98692; Middleton to Ross, 4 August 1952; Ross, "Persia," 6 August 1952; BET 559, 6 August 1952, all FO 371/98603. See also BET 561, 7 August 1952, FO 371/98602.

62. FO 939, 6 August 1952, FO 800/813.

63. FRUS 1952–1954 10, doc. 197, British Embassy to the Department of State, 9 August 1952; Tehran 588, 8 August 1952, 420 Iranian Army, TPF.

64. C.C. 76 (52), 7 August 1952, CAB 128/24; FO 416, 7 August 1952, FO 371/98692; FO 3231 and 3232, 9 August 1952, FO 371/98691.

65. "Compensation for AIOC Assets," 28 August 1951, BP 91031.

66. FRUS 1952–1954 10, doc 197, British Embassy to the Department of State, 9 August 1952.

67. BET 579, 11 August 1952, FO 371/98693.

68. FO 416, 7 August 1952, FO 371/98692.

69. BEW 1510, 12 August 1952, FO 371/98693.

70. FRUS 1952–1954 9, doc. 82, MemCon, 8 August 1952.

71. "Preliminary NEA Comments on Mr. Eden's Message to Secretary Acheson, August 8, 1952," 9 August 1952, 888.2553/8-9552; MemCon, 11 August 1952, and MemCon 12 August 1952, Acheson MemCons, HSTL; Tehran 626, 12 August 1952, 888.2553/8-1252; FRUS 1952–1954 10, doc. 199, State 1019, 13 August 1952.

72. BET 587, 14 August 1952, FO 371/98693; FRUS 1952–1954 10, doc. 201, Memo by Byroade to Bruce, 15 August 1952.

73. Bruce Memo, 14 August 1952, 788.00/8-1452; Bruce Memo, 14 August 1952, 888.2553/8-1652; State 412, 16 August 1952, 888.2553/8-1652.

74. FRUS 1952–1954 10, doc. 202, State 1159, 18 August 1952.

75. FO 3419, 20 August 1952, FO 371/98694; printed in FRUS 1952–1954 10, doc. 203, Bruce to Gifford, 22 August 1952.

76. FRUS 1952–1954 10, doc. 207, State 1310, 24 August 1952.

77. Minute from Bowker, 23 August 1952, FO 371/98694.

78. Minutes of a Meeting at the White House, 21 August 1952, Acheson Mem-Cons, HSTL.

79. FRUS 1952–1954 10, doc. 207, State 1310, 24 August 1952.

80. Tehran 3781, 4 April 1952, General Classified Records US Embassy Tehran 1950–1952, Box 36.

81. FO 3476, 22 August 1952, FO 371/98694.

82. "Persia," Note from Ross, 27 August 1952, FO 371/98696.

83. FO 331, 26 August 1952, FO 800/813; A. D. M. Ross, "Persia: Cities Service Company," 20 August 1952, POWE 33/1928; Tehran 848, 25 August 1952, 888.2553/8-2552; Churchill to Eden, 25 August 1952, FO 371/98695; Tehran 857, 26 August 1952, 888.2553/8-2652.

84. FRUS 1952–1954 10, doc. 211, Tehran 892, 27 August 1952; Middleton to Bowker, 1 September 1952, FO 371/98697.

85. FRUS 1952–1954 10, doc. 212, Truman to Churchill, 28 August 1952, doc. 213, State 511, 28 August 1952; FO 3605, 29 August 1952, FO 800/813.

86. BET 633, 28 August 1952, FO 371/98695; see also BET 640, 29 August 1952, FO 371/98695.

87. BEW 1651, 29 August 1952, FO 371/98695.

88. FO 616, 29 August 1952; FO 3607, 29 August 1952, FO 371/98695.

89. FO 3581, 28 August 1952; BET 632, 28 August 1952, FO 371/98695.

90. FRUS 1952–1954 10, doc. 214; Tehran 931, 30 August 1952, Tehran 938, 31 August 1952, 888.2553/8-3152; BET 643, 30 August 1952, FO 371/98695.

91. FO 3638, 1 September 1952, FO 371/98695.

92. Middleton to Bowker, 1 September 1952, FO 371/9869.

93. Karim Sanjabi, *Omidha va Namidha: Khaṭirat-e Siyasi* (London: Nashr-e Kitab, 1989), 174–75; Abrahamian, *The Coup*, 144–46; Gregory Brew, "The Collapse Narrative: The United States, Mohammad Mossadegh, and the Coup Decision of 1953," *Texas National Security Review* (August 2019): 47–48; Ladjevardi, "Constitutional Government and Reform under Musaddiq," 76–79.

94. Sanjabi, *Omidha va Namidha*, 179.

95. Abrahamian, *Iran between Two Revolutions*, 275–76.

96. BET 566, 7 August 1952, FO 248/1531.

97. FRUS 1952–1954 Retro, doc. 120, Telegram from Station in Iran to CIA, 5 September 1952. The idea may have come with British prompting: Middleton suggested that an approach be made to King Ibn Saud, encouraging the Saudi ruler to urge Kashani to act against Mosaddeq "[and] save his country for Islam. . . . Kashani is a poor instrument to use but we cannot afford to miss our chance." BET 548, 1 September 1952, FO 371/98695.

98. Ladjevardi, "Constitutional Government and Reform under Musaddiq," 78.

99. Rahnema, *Behind the Coup*, 22–23.

100. Mark J. Gasiorowski, "The 1953 Coup d'Etat in Iran," *International Journal of Middle East Studies* 19, no. 3 (August 1987): 266; FRUS 1952–1954 Retro, doc. 125, Monthly Report, September 1952.

101. Mark J. Gasiorowski, "The CIA's TPBEDAMN Operation and the 1953 Coup in Iran," *Journal of Cold War Studies* 15 (Fall 2013): 14.

102. Note from Falle, 3 September 1952, FO 248/1531.

103. Middleton to Bowker, 1 September 1952, FO 371/98697; Falle, "Observations," 11 September 1952, FO 248/1531; Falle, "Miscellaneous Information," 15 September 1952, FO 248/1531; Sarell MemCon, 12 September 1952, FO 371/98604; Logan, "Persia," 15 September 1952, FO 371/98604; Middleton to Ross, 15 September 1952, FO 371/98604; Middleton to Eden, 23 September 1952, FO 371/98604; Burrows, "Situation in Persia," 29 September 1952, FO 371/98604; Burrows Minute, 30 September 1952, FO 371/98604; Rothnie Minute, 30 September 1952, FO 371/98604; Middleton to Eden, 30 September 1952, FO 371/98604.

104. Tehran 1195, 18 September 1952, 888.2553/9-1852; FRUS 1952–1954 Retro, doc. 127, CIA Station, 2 October 1952.

105. BET 708, 16 September 1952; BET 714, 17 September 1952; BET 715, 17 September 1952, FO 371/98697; Tehran Despatch 210, 17 September 1952, 888.2553/9-1752; Tehran 1189, 17 September 1952, 888.2553/9-1752.

106. Tehran 1295, 27 September 1952, 888.2553/9-2752; Acheson to Truman, 30 September 30, 1952, White House Central Files, "Confidential State Department Correspondence," HSTL; "Iran and Egypt," 30 September 1952, Acheson MemCons, HSTL; BEW 1883, 3 October 1952, FO 371/98700; FRUS 1952–1954 10, doc. 218, State 805, 2 October 1952, 1952; doc. 216, Memo by the Secretary of State to the President, 26 September 1952; doc. 217, State 784, 29 September 1952.

107. BEW 1883, 3 October 1952, FO 371/98700; BET 771, 5 October 1952, FO 371/98700; FRUS 1952–1954 10, doc. 219, State 820, 3 October 1952; doc. 220, London 1986, 4 October 1952; see also State-JCS Meeting, 8 October 1952, RG 59, PPS Papers.

108. FRUS 1952–1954 10, doc. 221, Tehran 1374, 5 October 1952; doc. 222, Tehran 1428, 7 October 1952; BET 783, 7 October 1952, FO 371/98700; Tehran 1390, 6 October 1952, 888.2553/10-652; Tehran 1449, 8 October 1952, 888.2553/10-852.

109. FRUS 1952–1954 10, doc. 227, Henderson to Acheson, 16 October 1952; doc. 228, Tehran 1591, 18 October 1952; Tehran 1566, 16 October 1952, 888.2553/10-1652; Tehran 1591, 18 October 1952, 888.2553/10-1852; Tehran 1577, 16 October 1952, 350 Iran, TPF.

110. British Embassy, Tehran, "Persian Internal Affairs," 6 October 1952, FO 371/98604; British Embassy, Tehran, "Internal Affairs Report, 13 October 1952, FO 371/98604; British Embassy, Tehran, "Internal Affairs," 20 October 1952, FO 371/98604; BET 813, 20 October 1952, FO 371/98604; Middleton to Ross, 12 October 1952, FO 371/98605; Middleton to Ross, 13 October 1952, FO 371/98605; Middleton to Ross, 20 October 1952, FO 371/98605.

111. Gasiorowski, "The 1953 Coup d'Etat," 269.

112. Zahedi's Speech before the Senate, 23 Mehr 1331/15 October 1952, in Mostafa Fateh, *Panjah sal naft-e Iran* (Tehran: Entesharat-e Payam, 1979), 648.

113. Rahnema, *Behind the 1953 Coup*, 24–26; Abrahamian, *Iran between Two Revolutions*, 273; Fakhreddin Azimi, "Unseating Mosaddeq: The Configuration and Role of Domestic Forces," in *Mohammad Mosaddeq and the 1953 Coup in Iran*, edited by Mark J. Gasiorowski and Malcolm Byrne, 77–78.

114. FRUS 1952–1954 Retro, doc. 132, Special Estimate (SE-33): Prospects for Survival of Mosaddeq Regime in Iran, 14 October 1952.

115. Dean Acheson, *Present at the Creation: My Years in the State Department* (New York: W. W. Norton, 1969), 681–82.

Chapter 5

1. Princeton Seminars, 15 May 1954, Dean G. Acheson Papers, Box 81, HSTL.

2. FRUS 1952–1954 Retro, doc. 121, Byroade to Acheson, 10 September 1952; Byroade to Acheson, 16 September 1952, 888.2553/9-1652; Tehran 1285, 26 September 1952, 888.2553/9-2652; Tehran 1295, 27 September 1952, 888.2553/9-2752.

3. Linda W. Qaimmaqami, "The Catalyst of Nationalization: Max Thornburg and the Failure of Private Sector Developmentalism in Iran, 1946–1951," *Diplomatic History* 19 (January 1995): 1–31.

4. FRUS 1952–1954 Retro, doc. 116, MemCon, 20 August 1952.

5. FRUS 1952–1954 Retro, doc. 118, Memo Prepared by Max W. Thornburg, 22 August 1952.

6. Harvard Interview, Sanjabi, Tape No. 8, 9–10.

7. Scott A. Koch, *Zendebad, Shah! The Central Intelligence Agency and the Fall of Iranian Prime Minister Mohammed Mossadeq, August 1953*, June 1998, appendix E, 118–20, https://nsarchive.gwu.edu/document/16330-document-2-zendebad-shah; FRUS 1952–1954 Retro, doc. 119, Wisner to Roosevelt, undated.

8. FRUS 1952–1954 Retro, doc. 122, Leavitt to Roosevelt, 22 September 1952; doc. 83, Memo Prepared in the Office of National Estimates, CIA, 1 July 1952.

9. FRUS 1952–1954 Retro, doc. 123, Wilber Memo for the Record, 23 September 23, 1952; doc. 83, Memo Prepared in the Office of National Estimates, CIA, 1 July 1952.

10. FRUS 1952–1954 Retro, doc. 126, Memo from [name not declassified] to Roosevelt, 1 October 1952, note 3.

11. FRUS 1952–1954 Retro, doc. 133, Attachment, "The Communist Danger in Persia," undated.

12. FRUS 1952–1954 Retro, doc. 133, Byroade to Matthews, 15 October 1952.

13. Tehran 1220, 20 September 1952, 888.2553/9-2052. This document appears in the 1989 FRUS volume, with mention of the tribes and arms support excised. See FRUS 1952–1954 10, doc. 215.

14. FRUS 1952–1954 Retro, doc. 138, Memo, Study of CIA Capabilities in Iran, undated.

15. FRUS 1952–1954 Retro, doc. 117, Wisner to Smith, 20 August 1952; Bradley to Lovett, 5 September 1952, RG 330, 092 (Iran).

16. Metzger to Tate, "Some Legal Considerations Relating to the 'Blockade' by AIOC of Iranian Oil," 16 September 1952, and Richards to Henderson, 1 October 1952, RG 59, Office of Greek, Turkish, and Iranian Affairs, 1950–1958, Lot 60 533, Box 9; MemCon, 19 September 1952, 888.2553/9-1952; MemCon, 22 September 1952, 888.2553/9-2252.

17. FRUS 1952–1954 Retro, doc. 121, Byroade to Acheson, 10 September 1952; Byroade to Acheson, 16 September 1952, 888.2553/9/16-52; MemCon, 22 September 1952, 888.2553/9-2252; State 2091 to London, 23 September 1952, 888.2553/9-2352.

18. Tehran 968, 3 September 1952, 888.2553/9-352; Tehran 971, 3 September 1952, 888.2553/9-352; Tehran 1128, 14 September 1952, 888.2553/9-1452; Tehran 1216, 22 September 1952, 888.2552/9-2052; Persia Official Committee to Cabinet, 25 September 1952, CAB 134/1147; Middleton to Eden, 30 September 1952, FO 371/98604; for background on Jones trip, see Tehran 1068, 9 September 1952, 888.2553/9-952; Ross, "Persia: Cities Service Company," 20 August 1952, POWE 33/1928.

19. FRUS 1952–1954 Retro, doc. 121, Byroade to Acheson, 10 September 1952; Byroade to Acheson, 16 September 1952, 888.2553/9-1652.

20. Draft Background for Possible Use in Discussions of the Iranian Situation with the British, 19 September 1952, 888.2553/9-1952; MemCon, 22 September 1952, 888.2553/9-2252; State 2091 to London, 23 September 1952, 888.2553/9-2352; MemCon, "Iranian Oil Problem," 6 November 1952, 888.2553/11-652.

21. State-JCS Meeting, 8 October 1952, RG 59, PPS Papers; Nitze to Acheson, 8 October 1952, 888.2553/10-852.

22. FRUS 1952–1954 10, doc. 223, State 889, 10 October 1952; doc. 224, State 2592, 12 October 1952; doc. 225, State 2593, 12 October 1952; doc, 226, London 2160, 13 October 1952; doc. 229, London 2288, 20 October 1952; doc. 230, London 2296, 20 October 1952; London 2297, 20 October 1952, 888.2553/10-2052; BEW 1910 to Foreign Office, 9 October 1952, FO 371/98700.

23. Federal Trade Commission, *The International Petroleum Cartel: Staff Report Submitted to the Subcommittee on Monopoly of the Select Committee on Small Business, United States Senate* (Washington DC: U.S. Government Printing Office, 1952).

24. MemCon, 8 October 1952, 888.2553/10-852; Franks to Eden, 9 October 1952, 888.2553/8-952; David S. Painter, *Oil and the American Century: The Political Economy of U.S. Foreign Oil Policy, 1941–1954* (Baltimore: Johns Hopkins University Press, 1986), 186–87.

25. Lovett to Acheson, 24 October 1952, 888.2553/10-2452; FRUS 1952–1954 10, doc, 234, note 2.

26. FRUS 1952–1954 10, doc 234; Memo of Telephone Conversation, 6 November 1952, Acheson MemCons, HSTL; OIR "The British Position in the Middle East," Intelligence Report No. 5980, 2 October 1952, DDRS 1978: 415A.

27. FRUS 1952–1954 10, doc. 236, Acheson to Truman, 7 November 1952.

28. FRUS 1952–1954 Retro, doc. 146, MemCon, 18 November 1952.

29. FRUS 1952–1954 Retro, doc. 145, Bradley to Lovett, 18 November 1952; Francis J. Gavin, "Politics, Power, and U.S. Policy in Iran, 1950–1953," *Journal of Cold War Studies* 1 (Winter 1999): 76–80.

30. FRUS 1952–1954 Retro, doc. 147, NSC 136/1, The Present Situation in Iran, 20 November 1952.

31. FRUS 1952–1954 10, doc. 241, State 3510, 22 November 1952; see also New York to FO 855, FO 800/813.

32. FRUS 1952–1954 10, doc. 241, State 3510, 22 November 1952; doc. 242, State 3556, 25 November 1952; Princeton Seminars, 15 May 1954, Acheson Papers, HSTL.

33. Eastern Department, "Notes for the Bukit Serve Conference," 21 November 1952, FO 371/98703; Conversation between the Secretary of State and General Eisenhower, 20 November 1952, FO 800/813; Bowker Minute, 3 December 1952, FO 371/98703; FO 5044, 3 December 1952, FO 371/98703; BEW 2033, 6 December 1952, FO 371/98703; Persia (Official) Committee, "Persian Oil: Resumed Discussions with Mr. P. Nitze of the State Department," 9 December 1952, CAB 134/1147.

34. Bowker Minute, 29 November 1952, FO 371/98703, with marginal note, "I agree. AE"; Dixon Minute, 30 November 1952, FO 371/98703.

35. FRUS 1952–1954 10, doc. 252, State 1497, 19 December 1952.

36. FRUS 1952–1954 Retro, doc. 134, MemCon 23 October 1952; C. M. Woodhouse, *Something Ventured* (London: Granada, 1982), 117.

37. FRUS 1952–1954 Retro, doc. 148, Byroade to Matthews, "Proposal to Organize a Coup d'Etat in Iran," 26 November 1952; doc. 149, MemCon, 3 December 1952; Woodhouse, *Something Ventured*, 118–19; Donald Wilber, *Overthrow of Premier Mosaddeq of Iran, November 1952–August 1953*, 1–2, https://nsarchive2.gwu.edu /NSAEBB/NSAEBB28/l; Mark J. Gasiorowski, "The 1953 Coup d'Etat in Iran," *International Journal of Middle East Studies* 19 (August 1987), 270.

38. Princeton Seminars, May 15, 1954, Dean G. Acheson Papers, Box 81, HSTL.

39. MemCon, 21 November 1952, 888.2553/11-2152; "Iranian Oil Problem," 29 November 1952, 888.2552/11-2952; Memo of Meeting, 4 December 1952, 888.2553/12-452; Minutes of Meeting, 9 December 1952, 888.2553/12-952. For a shorter record, see FRUS 1952–1954 10, doc. 245, State 3763, 4 December 1952.

40. Beckett to Butler, 2 December 1952, FO 371/98668.

41. MemCon, 21 November 1952, RG 59, Office of Greek, Turkish, and Iranian Affairs, 1950–1958, Lot 60 533, Box 9.

42. FRUS 1952–1954 10, doc. 249, Paris 3475, 14 December 1952; Linder to Chapman, 17 December 1952, 888.2553/12-1752.

43. *Department of State Bulletin*, 15 December 1952, 946.

44. FRUS 1952–1954 10, doc. 247, MemCon, 10 December 1952; Mostafa Elm, *Oil, Power and Principle: Iran's Nationalization and Its Aftermath* (Syracuse, NY: Syracuse University Press, 1992), 261.

45. FRUS 1952–1954 10, doc. 253, Paris 3582, 19 December 1952.

46. FRUS 1952–1954 10, doc. 251, State 4101, 18 December 1952; doc. 254, Nitze to Acheson, 22 December 1952.

47. Paris 3475, 14 December 1952, 888.2553/12-145: Briefing Notes for Eden Meeting, 14 December 1952, 888.2553/12-1452.

48. FRUS 1952–1954 Retro, doc. 150, Memo Prepared in ONE, CIA, 11 December 1952.

49. Briefing Memo: Iran, 17 December 1952, 888.2553/12-1752.

50. FRUS 1952–1954 10, doc. 244, State 1338, 3 December 1952.

51. Tehran. 2425, 26 December 1952, 888.2553/12-2652; FRUS 1952–1954 10, doc. 255, Tehran 2430, 27 December 1952; "Oil Dispute—The Next Steps, 8 January 1953," P.O. (M) 2nd Mtg., 8 January 1953, CAB 134/1144.

52. State 1568, 29 December 1952, 888.2553/12-2652.

53. FRUS 1952–1954 10, doc. 256, State 4273, 29 December 1952.

54. FRUS 1952–1954 10, doc. 263, Tehran 2506, 2 January 1953.

55. FRUS 1952–1954 10, doc. 261, London 3611, 1 January 1953.

56. Minute by Ross, 3 January 1953, CAB 129/58.

57. London 3662, 6 January 1953, 888.2553/1-553; FRUS 1952–1954 10, doc. 266, London 3696, 6 January 1953; doc. 267, London 3694, 6 January 1953; doc. 268, State 4505, 7 January 1953; doc. 269, London 3737, 8 January 1953; Mary Ann Heiss, *Empire and Nationhood: The United States, Great Britain, and Iranian Oil, 1950–1954* (New York: Columbia University Press, 1997), 161.

58. FO 69, 8 January 1953, FO 371/ FO 371/104607.

59. *Etellaat*, 20 Dey 1331/10 January 1953; *Tehran Musavvar*, 19 Dey 1331/9 January 1953.

60. Tehran 2539, 5 January 1953, 888.2553/1-553; Tehran 2569, 6 January 1953, 888.2553/1-653.

61. Tehran 2608, 8 January 1953, 888.2553/1-853.

62. Tehran 2647, 11 January 1953, 888.2553/1-1153; Elm, *Oil, Power, and Principle*, 264.

63. FRUS 1952–1954 10, doc. 270, London 3738, 8 January 1953.

64. London 3645, 4 January 1953, 888.2553/1-453; Current Status of Iranian Oil Problem, 8 January 1953, 888.2553/1-853.

65. FRUS 1952–1954 10, doc. 270, London 3738, 8 January 1953; doc. 275, London 3790, 11 January 1953; "Current Status of Iranian Oil Problem," 8 January 1953, 888.2553/1-853; Note from Fitzmaurice, 13 January 1953, FO 371/104609.

66. FRUS 1952–1954 10, doc. 275, London 3790, 11 January 1953.

67. Tehran 2652, 12 January 1953, 888.2553/1-1253; Tehran. 2654, 12 January 1953, 888.2553/1-1253.

68. FRUS 1952–1954 10, doc. 276, State 4607, 12 January 1953.

69. Ross, "Property, Rights and Interests," 13 January 1953, FO 371/104609.

70. FRUS 1952–1954 10, doc. 279, London 3840, 14 January 1953; FO 137, 15 January 1953, FO 371/104607.

71. Heiss, *Empire and Nationhood*, 160–63, Elm, *Oil, Power, and Principle*, 262-66; J. H. Bamberg, *The History of the British Petroleum Company*, vol. 2: *The Anglo-Iranian Years, 1928–1954* (Cambridge: Cambridge University Press, 1994), 481–82, 485–86.

72. Eden to Churchill, 14 January 1953, FO 371/104608.

73. FRUS 1952–1954 10, doc. 282, London 3844, 14 January 1953.

74. FRUS 1952–1954 1, part 2, doc. 159, NSC 138/1, 6 January 1953; Nathan J. Citino, "Internationalist Oilmen, the Middle East, and the Remaking of American Liberalism, 1945–1953," *Business History Review* 84 (Summer 2010): 248–49.

75. FRUS 1952–1954 1, part 2, doc. 161, NSC Meeting, 9 January 1953; FRUS 1952–1954 9, part 1, doc. 282, Bohlen to Acheson, 9 January 1953; Heiss, *Empire and Nationhood*, 157.

76. Memo for Attorney General, 14 January 1953, 888.2553/1-1454.

77. Homa Katouzian, *Khalil Maleki: The Human Face of Iranian Socialism* (London: One World Academic, 2018), 153–54.

78. FRUS 1952–1954 Retro, doc. 151, Mattison to Richards, 18 December 1952; Homa Katouzian, *Musaddiq and the Struggle for Power in Iran* (London: I. B. Tauris, 1990), 167.

79. Tehran 2420, 26 December 1952, 888.2553/12-2652; Note for Shuckburgh, 9 January 1953, FO 371/104608.

80. Tehran 2435, 28 December 1952, 888.2553/12-2852.

81. Katouzian, *Musaddiq and the Struggle for Power in Iran*, 171.

82. Abbas Milani, *The Shah* (New York: Palgrave Macmillan, 2011), 154.

83. Harvard Interview, Sanjabi, Tape No. 11, 3–4.

84. Fortnightly Reviews from UK Embassy, Karachi, 12 February 1953, FO 371/104562.

85. Ervand Abrahamian, *The Coup: 1953, the CIA and the Roots of Modern U.S.-Iranian Relations* (New York: New Press, 2013), 165–66; Richards to Byroade, 22 January 1953, 888.2553/1-2253.

86. Katouzian, *Khalil Maleki*, 152.

87. Tehran 2768, 18 January 1953, 888.2553/1-1853.

88. FRUS 1952–1954 10, doc. 284, Tehran 2754, 17 January 1953.

89. FRUS 1952–1954 10, doc. 285, Tehran 2761, 17 January 1953; doc. 286, Tehran 2762, 17 January 1953.

90. Tehran 2741, 16 January 1953, 888.2553/1-1653; Tehran 2727, 16 January 1953, 888.2553/1-1653.

91. FRUS 1952–1954 10, doc. 287, Tehran 2763, 17 January 1953.

92. FRUS 1952–1954 10, doc. 289, London 3935, 18 January 1953; doc. 290, London 3936, 18 January 1953; Cabinet, Persia (Official) Committee, "Dr. Musaddiq's Reply to the 'Package' Proposals," 19 January 1953, P.O.(O)(53)37, CAB 134/1149.

93. FRUS 1952–1954 10, doc. 291, Tehran 2802, 19 January 1953.

94. Tehran 2804, 10 January 1953, 888.2553/1-1953.

95. Tehran 2803, 19 January 1953, 888.2553/1-1953.

96. Brook to Ramsbotham, 24 January 1953, FO 371/104611.

97. FO 302, 23 January 1953, FO 371/104610.

98. FRUS 1952–1954 10, doc. 292, State 4941, 26 January 1953; State Department Memo, 28 January 1953, FO 371/104611.

99. BEW 172, 27 January 1953; BEW 184, 28 January 1953, FO 371/104610.

100. Tehran 2865, 24 January 1953, 888.2553/1-2453; Note to Dulles, 5 March 1953, 888.2553/3-553.

101. State 1900, 29 January 1953, 888.2553/1-2453; State 1850, 25 January 1953, 888.2553/1-2553.

102. FRUS 1952–1954 10, doc. 293, Tehran 2934, 28 January 1953. AIOC estimated such an award at £1-2 billion, or £150 million for six to thirteen years.

103. Tehran 2948, 30 January 1953, 888.2553/1-3053.

104. Tehran 3016, 4 February 1953, 888.2553/2-353.

105. Tehran 3035, 4 February 1953, 888.2553/2-453.

106. BEW 217, 1 February 1953, FO 371/104611.

107. L. P. Elwell-Sutton, *Persian Oil: A Study in Power Politics* (London: Lawrence and Wishart, 1955), 296–98; "The Rose Mary's Test Run," *Economist* 163 (21 June 1952): 800; "International Law for the Rose Mary," *Economist* 166 (7 January 1953): 134; "Mossadegh's Dangerous Deal," *Economist* 166 (24 January 1953): 191–92; FO 31, 17 January 1953, FO 371/104617; Copy of Tehran 2820, 21 January 1953, FO 371/104617; Note from Rothnie, 24 January 1953, FO 371/104617.

108. FRUS 1952–1954 10, doc. 296, State 5294, 10 February 1953.

109. BEW 288, 10 February 1953, FO 371/104612.

110. FRUS 1952–1954 10, doc. 297, Tehran 3184, 14 February 1953.

111. Allen Dulles to John Foster Dulles, 18 February 1953, 888.2553/2-1853.

112. BEW 288, 10 February 1953, FO 371/104612.

113. FO 716, 18 February 1953, FO 371/104612.

114. State 2140, 18 February 1953, 888.2553/2-1853.

115. FRUS 1952–1954 10, doc. 298, State 2139, 18 February 1953; Heiss, *Empire and Nationhood*, 171.

116. FRUS 1952–1954 10, doc. 299, State 2145, 19 February 1953.

117. State 2146, 19 February 1953, 888.2553/2-1953.

118. FRUS 1952–1954 10, doc. 300, Tehran 3304, 20 February 1953.

119. Dixon Memo, 19 February 1953; BEW 359, 20 February 1953, FO 371/104613.

120. Abrahamian, *The Coup*, 166.

121. Abrahamian, *The Coup*, 166–68.

122. Katouzian, *Musaddiq and the Struggle for Power in Iran*, 171.

123. Milani, *The Shah*, 155–62.

124. FRUS 1952–1954 Retro, doc. 153, Briefing Note, 18 February 1953; Ali Rahnema, *Behind the 1953 Coup in Iran: Thugs, Turncoats, Soldiers, and Spooks* (Cambridge: Cambridge University Press, 2014), 34.

125. FRUS 1952–1954 10, doc. 297, Tehran 3184, 14 February 1953.

126. Milani, *The Shah*, 161.

127. *Ettelaat*, 18 February 1953; Minute from Rothnie, 18 February 1953; Tehran 3264, 19 February 1953, FO 371/104562.

128. FRUS 1952–1954 Retro, doc. 155, Tehran 3306, 20 February 1953.

129. FRUS 1952–1954 Retro, doc. 156, Tehran 3342, 23 February 1953; Rahnema, *Behind the 1953 Coup in Iran*, 31.

130. Harvard Interview, Sanjabi, Tape No. 11, 8–9.

131. *Bahktar-e Emruz*, 22 February 1953; FRUS 1952–1954 10, doc. 301, Tehran 3334, 22 February 1953.

132. FRUS 1952–1954 10, doc. 302, Tehran 3355, 23 February 1953; doc. 303, Tehran 3356, 23 February 1953.

133. FRUS 1952–1954 10, doc. 301, Tehran 3334, 22 February 1953.

134. Tehran 3345, 24 February 1953, FO 371/104562; FRUS 1952–1954 10, doc. 304, Tehran 3358, 24 February 1953; FRUS 1952–1954 Retro, doc. 159, Briefing Notes, undated; Rahnema, *Behind the 1953 Coup in Iran*, 35; Mohammad Musaddiq, *Musaddiq's Memoirs*, translated by Homa Katouzian and S. H. Amin (London: National Movement of Iran, 1988), 343.

135. FRUS 1952–1954 Retro, doc. 157, CIA Memo, 24 February 1953.

136. FRUS 1952–1954 Retro, doc. 161, Tehran 3393, 25 February 1953; also printed in FRUS 1952–1954 10, doc. 305; Soraya Esfandiary-Bakhtiari, *Palace of Solitude*, reprinted in Ardeshir Zahedi, *The Memoirs of Ardeshir Zahedi*, vol. 1: *From Childhood to the End of My Father's Premiership*, translated by Farhang Jahanpour (Bethesda, MD: Ibex Publishers, 2012), 134–35.

137. FRUS 1952–1954 Retro, doc. 162, Tehran 3397, 26 February 1953. News of Henderson's intervention was relayed to the British; Ross Minute, 28 February 1953, FO 371/104562.

138. FRUS 1952–1954 Retro, doc. 165, Tehran 3431, 27 February 1953. This telegram appeared in FRUS 1952–1954 10, doc. 306.

139. Milani, *The Shah*, 164.

140. Gholam R. Afkhami, *The Life and Times of the Shah* (Berkeley: University of California Press, 2009), 149.

141. Mohamed Reza Pahlavi, *Mission for My Country* (London: Hutchinson, 1961), 97.

142. FRUS 1952–1954 Retro, doc. 165, Tehran 3431, 27 February 1952.

143. State 4844, 27 February 1953, 788.11/2-2753.

144. FRUS 1952–1954 Retro, doc. 166, Tehran 3449, 28 February 1953.

145. Harvard Interview, Khosrovani, Tape No. 1, 6–7.

146. Rahnema, *Behind the 1953 Coup in Iran*, 35, 36–38; Harvard Interview, Sanjabi, Tape No. 11, 9–10.

147. Milani, *The Shah*, 166.

148. Zahedi, *The Memoirs of Ardeshir Zahedi*, vol. 1, 124.

149. Harvard Interview, Sanjabi, Tape No. 11, 10.

150. FRUS 1952–1954 Retro, doc. 166, Tehran 3449, 28 February 1953.

151. FRUS 1952–1954 10, doc. 309, Tehran 3454, 28 February 1953; Milani, *The Shah*, 166.

152. Eden (from RMS *Queen Elizabeth*) to FO, No. 17, 1 March 1953, FO 371/104562.

153. FRUS 1952–1954 Retro, doc. 169, Allen Dulles to Eisenhower, 1 March 1953. In a 1992 interview, CIA operative John Waller argued that once Mosaddeq had lost

access to Kashani's "street organization," he would inevitably become dependent on the Tudeh; Waller interview with David S. Painter, 29 June 1992, McLean, VA; C.I.B., "Comment on Tudeh position in current Iranian Situation, 3 March 1953, *Declassified Documents Quarterly* 1981, doc. 275D.

154. FRUS 1952–1954 Retro, doc. 167, State 2254, 28 February 1953.

Chapter 6

1. FRUS 1952–1954 Retro, doc. 168, Monthly Report Prepared in the Directorate of Plans; doc. 169, Memo from Dulles to Eisenhower, 1 March 1953. According to a 2015 MA thesis, Major Margaret Taafe-McMenamy, "Operation Ajax: Study of Analyst-Policy Maker Tensions and the Challenges of Estimative Intelligence" (Fort Leavenworth, KS: School of Advance Military Studies, United States Army Command and General Staff College, 2015), 49–50, there is no indication in the source text that the CIA's Office of National Estimates prepared the report, suggesting that Dulles may have drafted the report himself.

2. "The Iranian Situation," 3 March 1953, RG 59, Records Relating to State Department Participation in the Operations Coordinating Board and the National Security Council, 1947–1963, Lot 63 D 351, Box 68.

3. FRUS 1952–1954 10, doc. 311, State 2266, 2 March 1953.

4. FRUS 1952–1954 Retro, doc. 171, NSC Meeting, 4 March 1953.

5. FRUS 1952–1954 Retro, doc. 171, NSC Meeting, 4 March 1953.

6. FRUS 1952–1954 10, doc. 311, note 2.

7. Tehran 3548, 5 March 1953, 888.2553/3-553.

8. FRUS 1952–1954 10, doc. 313, Tehran 3576, 6 March 1953.

9. FRUS 1952–1954 Retro, doc. 173, Tehran 3597, 8 March 1953.

10. FO 1068, 7 March 1953, FO 371/104614.

11. FRUS 1952–1954 6, part 1, doc. 381, Minutes of Meeting, 6 March 1953; FRUS 1952–1954 10, doc. 314, State 5959, 7 March 1953.

12. FRUS 1952–1954 6, part 1, doc. 383, Communique on the US-UK Political Talks, 7 March 1953.

13. Anthony Eden, *Full Circle: The Memoirs of the Rt. Hon. Sir Anthony Eden* (London: Cassell, 1960), 213.

14. British Embassy Washington (BEW), Washington 526, 9 March 1953, FO 371/104614; FRUS 1952–1954 Retro, doc. 181, Memo Prepared in the Office of Intelligence and Research, 31 March 1953, note 2.

15. BEW 526, 9 March 1953, FO 371/104614.

16. FRUS 1951–1953 10, doc. 316, Tehran 3627, 10 March 1953; RG 59 888.2553 /3-553; Tehran 3548, 5 March 1953.

17. FRUS 1952–1954 10, doc. 316, Tehran 3627, 10 March 1953.

18. FRUS 1952–1954 10, doc. 317, Tehran 3644, 11 March 1953.

19. FRUS 1952–1954 Retro, doc. 174, Byroade to Dulles, 10 March 1953; Tehran 2865, 24 January 1953, 888.2553/1-2453; Stutesman Memo, 5 March 1953, 888.2553/3 -553; Byroade to Dulles, 6 March 1953, 788.00/3-653. See also Tehran 3548, 5 May 1953, 888.2553/3-553, where Henderson again defended the sanctity of contracts.

20. FRUS 1952–1954 Retro, doc. 177, Memorandum Prepared in the Office of National Estimates, CIA, 11 March 1953.

21. FRUS 1952–1954 Retro, doc. 176, NSC Meeting, 11 March 1953. Beginning in March 1953 court cases against companies importing Iranian oil began to go against AIOC, and more and more companies successfully imported Iranian oil, albeit in relatively small volumes. See L. P. Elwell-Sutton, *Persian Oil: A Study in Power Politics* (London: Lawrence and Wisehart, 1955), 298–300.

22. FRUS 1952–1954 10, doc. 319, State 2387, 13 March 1953.

23. On 14 March, Mosaddeq told Henderson that he was "disappointed" Jones would not be coming to Iran; Tehran 3689, 14 March 1953, 888.2553/3-1453. Secretary Dulles finally told Jones on 9 June that it would be against U.S. interests for him to provide technicians to Iran at the present time; State 3170, 9 June 1953, 523.1 AIOC, RG 84, Tehran Post File (TPF).

24. FRUS 1952–1954 Retro, doc. 179, Memo for the Record, 18 March 1953.

25. Mary Ann Heiss, *Empire and Nationhood: The United States, Great Britain and Iranian Oil, 1950–1954* (New York: Columbia University Press, 1997), 175.

26. FRUS 1952–1954 Retro, doc. 180, Progress Report to the National Security Council, 20 March 1953.

27. Tehran Despatch 873, 24 April 1953, 788.00/4-2453.

28. FRUS 1952–1954 Retro, doc. 178, Information Report, 16 March 1953, note 2.

29. FRUS 1952–1954 10, doc. 322, Tehran 3853, 31 March 1953.

30. FRUS 1952–1954 Retro, doc. 181, Memo Prepared in the Office of Intelligence and Research, 31 March 1953.

31. FRUS 1952–1954, Retro, doc. 154, Allen Dulles to Smith, 19 February 1953, with attachment, Thornburg to Allen Dulles, 10 February 1953.

32. Donald Wilber, *Adventures in the Middle East: Excursions and Incursions* (Princeton, NJ: Darwin, 1986), 189.

33. Wm. Roger Louis, "Britain and the Overthrow of the Mosaddeq Government," in *Mohammad Mosaddeq and the 1953 Coup in Iran*, edited by Mark J. Gasiorowski and Malcolm Byrne (Syracuse, NY: Syracuse University Press, 2004), 168.

34. FRUS 1952–1954 Retro, doc. 183, Morgan to Dulles, 3 April 1953.

35. FRUS 1952–1954 Retro, doc. 184, Roosevelt to Dulles, 4 April 1953; Donald Wilber, *Overthrow of Premier Mosaddeq of Iran, November 1952-August 1953, CIA Clandestine Service History*, 2–3, https://nsarchive2.gwu.edu/NSAEBB/NSAEBB28/l.

36. FRUS 1952–1954 Retro, doc. 192, Waller to Roosevelt, 16 April 1953.

37. FRUS 1952–1954 Retro, doc. 170, Memo Prepared in the Directorate of Plans, CIA, 3 March 1953.

38. Wilber mentions this report in *Overthrow of Mossadeq*, 3; it appears in FRUS 1952–1954 Retro, doc. 192, Waller to Roosevelt, 16 April 1953.

39. Kermit Roosevelt, *Countercoup: The Struggle for the Control of Iran* (New York: McGraw-Hill, 1979), 79, 98. Roosevelt refers to these two actors as "the Boscoe Brothers," but context makes it clear that he is referring to Jalali and Keyvani.

40. Mark J. Gasiorowski, "The CIA's TPBEDAMN Operation and the 1953 Coup in Iran," *Journal of Cold War Studies* 15 (Fall 2013): 10–11.

41. FRUS 1952–1954 Retro, doc. 5, Paper Prepared in the Directorate of Plans, CIA, undated; doc. 123, Wilber Record by Wilber, 23 September 1952; Scott A. Koch, *Zendebad Shah! The Central Intelligence Agency and the Fall of Iranian Prime Minister Mohammed Mossadeq, August 1953*, 44, https://nsarchive.gwu.edu /document/16330-document-2-zendebad-shah.

42. FRUS 1952–1954 Retro. doc. 169, Dulles to Eisenhower, 1 March 1953; doc. 170, Memo Prepared in the Directorate of Plans and Operations, 3 March 1953; Mark J. Gasiorowski, "The US Stay-Behind Operation in Iran, 1948–1953," *Intelligence and National Security* 34 (2019): 180; Ervand Abrahamian, *The Coup: 1953, the CIA and the Roots of Modern U.S.-Iranian Relations* (New York: New Press, 2013), 157–58.

43. Abrahamian, *The Coup*, 150–57; Louis, "Britain and the Overthrow of the Mosaddeq Government," 138–41.

44. FRUS 1952–1954 Retro, doc. 193, Information Report Prepared in the CIA, 17 April 1953.

45. FRUS 1952–1954 Retro, doc. 188, Information Report Prepared in the CIA, 8 April 1953.

46. Quoted in Louis, "Britain and the Overthrow of the Mosaddeq Government," 169.

47. FRUS 1952–1954 Retro, doc. 192, Waller to Roosevelt, 16 April 1953; Wilber, *Overthrow of Mosaddeq*, 3–4.

48. FRUS 1952–1954 10, doc. 322, Tehran 3853, 31 March 1953.

49. FRUS 1952–1954 Retro, doc. 192, Waller to Roosevelt, 16 April 1953.

50. FRUS 1952–1954 10, doc. 322, Tehran 3853, 31 March 1953.

51. Abrahamian, *The Coup*, 165–68.

52. Fakhreddin Azimi, "Unseating Mosaddeq: The Configuration and Role of Domestic Forces," in *Mohammad Mosaddeq and the 1953 Coup in Iran*, edited by Mark J. Gasiorowski and Malcolm Byrne, 82; Ervand Abrahamian, *Oil Crisis in Iran: From Nationalism to Coup d'Etat* (New York: Cambridge University Press, 2021), 108.

53. FRUS 1952–1954 10, doc. 322, Tehran 3853, 31 March 1953.

54. FRUS 1952–1954 Retro, doc. 189, CIA Station in Iran, TEHE 945, 12 April 1953; doc. 191, Information Report Prepared in the CIA, 16 April 1953.

55. FRUS 1952–1954 10, doc. 324, Tehran 4027, 15 April 1953.

56. FRUS 1952–1954 10, doc. 324, Tehran 4027, 15 April 1953.

57. FRUS 1952–1954 Retro, doc. 192, Waller to Roosevelt, 16 April 1953.

58. U.S. Embassy No. 65, 19 April 1953, 888.00TA/4-1953; FRUS 1952–1954 Retro, doc. 195, Information Report Prepared in the CIA, 24 April 1953.

59. FRUS 1952–1954 Retro, doc. 185, Information Report Prepared in the CIA, 6 April 1953.

60. FRUS 1952–1954 Retro, doc. 207, Warne to Henderson, 20 May 1953.

61. Karim Sanjabi, *Omidha va Namidha: Khaṭirat-e Siyasi* (London: Nashr-e Kitab, 1989), 198–99; Abrahamian, *The Coup*, 174.

62. FRUS 1952–1954 Retro, doc. 196, Information Report Prepared in the CIA, 27 April 1953; *Bakhtar-e Emruz*, 27 April 1953; Darbyshire Transcript, National Security Archive, 11–12.

63. Azimi, "Unseating Mosaddeq," 83.

64. FRUS 1952–1954 Retro, doc. 203, Tehran 4356, 8 May 1953; Azimi, "Unseating Mosaddeq," 83.

65. FRUS 1952–1954 Retro, doc. 197, Information Report Prepared in the CIA, 28 April 1953.

66. FRUS 1952–1954 Retro, doc. 203, Tehran 4356, 8 May 1953; doc. 200, Tehran 4311, 4 May 1953.

67. Tehran 4350, 7 May 1953, 788.00/5-753; Tehran 4463, 19 May 1953, 78800.5-1953.

68. Wilber, *Overthrow of Mosaddeq*, 6, 10; Louis, "Britain and the Overthrow of the Mosaddeq Government," 163.

69. Wilber, *Overthrow of Mosaddeq*, appendix B, 2.

70. FRUS 1952–1954 Retro, doc. 208, Tehran Desp. 982, 20 May 1953, with attachment.

71. Gasiorowski, "The CIA's TPBEDAMN Operation," 15.

72. Koch, *Zendebad, Shah!* 22; Kermit Roosevelt, *Arabs, Oil, and History: The Story of the Middle East* (London: Gollanz, 1949).

73. Hugh Wilford, "'Essentially a Work of Fiction': Kermit 'Kim' Roosevelt, Imperial Romance, and the Iran Coup of 1953," *Diplomatic History* 40 (November 2016): 922–47.

74. Mostafa Elm, *Oil, Power and Principle: Iran's Nationalization and Its Aftermath* (Syracuse, NY: Syracuse University Press, 1992), 286–87; FRUS 1952–1954 Retro, doc. 176, NSC Meeting, 11 March 1953; FRUS 1952–1954 4, part 1, doc. 407, Eisenhower to Churchill, 8 May 1953.

75. Tehran 4348, 7 May 1953, 888.2553/5-753.

76. MemCon, 20 May 1953, 888.2553/5-2053; Levy to Jones, 25 May 1953, 888.2553/5-2553; Elm, *Oil, Power, and Principle*, 289–90. The award for British assets in Mexico had been $85 million, paid over fifteen years. British interests in Mexico in 1938 had produced roughly one-eighth as much oil as Iran produced in 1950, so Levy estimated a lump sum compensation award for AIOC of around $800 million. Although the British complained about the settlement, detailed analysis by economic historian Noel Mauer points out that both the British settlement and the earlier settlement for the U.S. companies gave the companies significantly more than their properties were worth. See Noel Maurer, "The Empire Struck Back: Sanctions and Compensation in the Mexican Oil Expropriation of 1938," *Journal of Economic History* 71 (Sept. 2011): 560–615.

77. FRUS 1952–1954 Retro, doc. 206, Mattison to Henderson, 19 May 1953.

78. FRUS 1952–1954 Retro, doc. 215, MemCon, 2 June 1953.

79. H. W. Brands, "The Cairo-Tehran Connection in Anglo-American Rivalry in the Middle East, 1951–1953," *International History Review* 11 (August 1989): 434–56; Francis J. Gavin, "Politics, Power, and U.S. Policy in Iran, 1950–1953," *Journal of Cold War Studies* 1 (Winter 1999): 58–60.

80. FRUS 1952–1954 Retro, doc. 218, Jernegan to Matthews, 15 June 1953; Elm, *Oil, Power, and Principle*, 291.

81. FRUS 1952–1954 Retro, doc. 204, Tehran Desp. 953, 15 May 1953, with attached MemCon dated 14 May 1953; doc. 205, Tehran Desp. 975, 19 May 1953, with attached MemCon, undated.

82. FRUS 1952–1954 10, doc. 326, Tehran 4472, 20 May 1953; doc. 327, State 4524, 25 May 1952; doc. 327, note 1.

83. FRUS 1952–1954 10, doc. 330, Memo by Byroade for Dulles, 5 June 1953. Henderson delivered the letter to Eisenhower on 5 June.

84. FRUS 1952–1954 Retro, doc. 212, MemCon, 30 May 1953. A heavily redacted summary was published in FRUS 1952–1954 10, doc. 329, Tehran 4573, 30 May 1953.

85. FRUS 1952–1954 Retro, doc. 210, Memo for the Record, Message from British Prime Minister Churchill, 21 May 1953.

86. FRUS 1952–1954 Retro, doc. 212, MemCon, 30 May 1953.

87. FRUS 1952–1954 Retro, doc. 212, MemCon, 30 May 1953.

88. Tehran 7579, 31 May 1953, RG 84, London Embassy Files, 350 Iran.

89. The title appears in the 2017 *Foreign Relations* volume, but the document is redacted in its entirety; FRUS 1952–1954 Retro, doc. 214, Summary of Operational Plan, 1 June 1953. There is a copy in appendix A of Wilber, *Overthrow of Mosaddeq*, entitled "Summary of Preliminary Plans Prepared by SIS and CIA Representatives in Cyprus, June 1, 1953."

90. Wilber, *Overthrow of Mosaddeq*, appendix A.

91. FRUS 1952–1954 Retro, doc. 216, MemCon, 6 June 1953. While the document is redacted, it is possible to perceive its content in the discussion. This briefing is also mentioned in *Battle for Iran*, CIA History, National Security Archive, 38–39, https://nsarchive2.gwu.edu/NSAEBB/NSAEBB476/.

92. FRUS 1952–1954 Retro, doc. 218, Jernegan to Matthews, 15 June 1953.

93. Tehran 4350, 7 May 1953, 788.00/5-753; Tehran 4463, 19 May 1953, 788.00 /5-1953; Makins to Bowker, 26 June 1953, FO 371/104616, which is summarized in FRUS 1952–1954 Retro, doc. 226, Editorial Note.

94. *Department of State Bulletin*, 20 July 1953, 74–76; Dulles to Eisenhower, 26 June 1953, John Foster Dulles Papers, Chronological Series, 1 June 1953 (2), Dwight D. Eisenhower Library (DDEL); FRUS 1952–1954 Retro, doc. 230, State 3295, 30 June 1953; David S. Painter, *Oil and the American Century: The Political Economy of U.S. Foreign Oil Policy, 1941–1954* (Baltimore: Johns Hopkins University Press, 1986), 191.

95. Wilber, *Overthrow of Mosaddeq*, 12. A "Beirut Draft" of the coup plan was produced on 13 June, but a copy has not been made available and may no longer exist.

96. Wilber, *Overthrow of Mosaddeq*, appendix B, 3, 11–12, 21–24, 26.

97. FRUS 1952–1954 Retro, doc. 232, Editorial Note; Roosevelt, *Countercoup*, 1–19; Roosevelt may have been referring to the meeting on June 6 where he and other CIA officials briefed Ambassador Henderson about the operation; doc. 216, MemCon, 6 June 1953.

98. Koch, *Zendebad Shah!* 39; Wilber, *Overthrow of Mosaddeq*, 18; *Battle for Iran*, 31, 41.

99. FRUS 1952–1954 10, doc. 331, Tehran 4658, 16 June 1953; FRUS 1952–1954 Retro, doc. 219, Tehran 4684, 19 June 1953; Mark J. Gasiorowski, "The 1953 Coup

d'Etat against Mosaddeq," in *Mohammad Mosaddeq and the 1953 Coup in Iran*, edited by Mark J. Gasiorowski and Malcolm Byrne (Syracuse, NY: Syracuse University Press, 2004), 244.

100. Abrahamian, *Oil Crisis in Iran*, 114.

101. FRUS 1952–1954 10, doc. 332, Tehran 79, 13 July 1953; doc. 333, Tehran 91, 14 July 1953.

102. Azimi, "Unseating Mosaddeq," 83.

103. Abrahamian, *Oil Crisis in Iran*, 79–80, 115.

104. FRUS 1952–1954 Retro, doc. 246, Tehran 142, 22 July 1953; *New York Times*, July 22, 1953. Although historians have long relied on his reports, Love had just arrived in Iran and had very limited knowledge of the situation, leaving him dependent on his driver to explain what he witnessed; Kennett Love remarks at an October 2003 conference at Georgetown University; David S. Painter, notes from the conference.

105. FRUS 1952–1954 Retro, doc. 244, Tehran 116, 17 July 1953; doc. 246, Tehran 142, 22 July 1953.

106. Wilber, *Overthrow of Mosaddeq*, 20; *End of Empire*, Transcript of Interview with R. Cottam, Roll 60, 1; Gasiorowski, "The CIA's TPBEDAMN Operation," 17.

107. Wilber, *Overthrow of Mosaddeq*, 19, appendix D, 2.

108. Wilber, *Overthrow of Mosaddeq*, appendix D, 10–11, 13.

109. FRUS 1952–1954 Retro, doc. 245, Acting Chief of Near East and Africa Division to Mitchell, 22 July 1953.

110. Wilber, *Overthrow of Mosaddeq*, appendix D, 13.

111. *Battle for Iran*, 41; Wilber, *Overthrow of Mosaddeq*, appendix D, 8.

112. FRUS 1952–1954 Retro, doc. 237, Tehran 74, 13 July 1953.

113. FRUS 1952–1954 Retro, doc. 238, Roosevelt to Mitchell, 14 July 1953; doc. 249, Memo from Acting Chief of the Near East and Africa Division to Mitchell, undated.

114. FRUS 1952–1954 10, doc. 335, Telephone Conversation, 24 July 1953.

115. FRUS 1952–1954 Retro, doc. 223, Memo Prepared in the Bureau of Near Easter, South Asian, and African Affairs, undated.

116. FRUS 1952–1954 Retro, doc. 250, Makins to Smith, 23 July 1953; *Battle for Iran*, 39–40.

117. Wilber, *Overthrow of Mosaddeq*, 23; *End of Empire*, Transcript of Interview with S. Meade, Roll 54, 3–6. In an interview for *End of Empire*, Darbyshire claims he bribed Ashraf with a "wad of notes"; Darbyshire Transcript, National Security Archive, 9-10.

118. Wilber, *Overthrow of Mosaddeq*, 23, 25.

119. Wilber, *Overthrow of Mosaddeq*, 28.

120. Wilber, *Overthrow of Mosaddeq*, 25; FRUS 1952–1954 Retro, doc. 227, MemCon, 26 June 1953; doc. 229, Dulles to Schwarzkopf, 30 June 1953.

121. Wilber, *Overthrow of Mosaddeq*, 29–30.

122. FRUS 1952–1954 Retro, doc. 254, Paper Prepared in the CIA, 29 July 1953.

123. Briefing Notes for National Security Council, 5 August 1953, CREST Online Archive.

124. Some accounts claim that the new Soviet ambassador to Iran, Anatoly Lavrentiev, who arrived in early August, had been ambassador to Czechoslovakia in 1948 and presided over the communist takeover there. Lavrentiev had been in Yugoslavia not Czechoslovakia in 1948, however, so his arrival in Iran seems less ominous; Artemy Kalinovsky, "The Soviet Union and Mosaddeq: A Research Note," *Iranian Studies* 47 (2014): 415, note 60.

125. FRUS 1952–1954 Retro, doc. 252, Waller to Dulles, 27 July 1953; Wilber, *Overthrow of Mosaddeq*, 29.

126. Wilber, *Overthrow of Mosaddeq*, 34.

127. FRUS 1952–1954 10, doc. 335, Memo of Telephone Conversation, 24 July 1953; doc. 337, Memo of Telephone Conversation, 25 July 1953; "Iran—Reds Take Over," *Newsweek*, 10 August 1953, 36–38.

128. *New York Times*, 15 August 1953.

129. Tehran 300, 12 August 1953, Attachment, "Control of the Armed Forces of Iran," 10 August 1953, 788.00/8-1253.

130. Abrahamian, *The Coup*, 180.

131. Wilber, *Overthrow of Mosaddeq*, 32–36, appendix D. 14–15.

132. Ali Rahnema, *Behind the 1953 Coup in Iran: Thugs, Turncoats, Soldiers, and Spooks* (Cambridge: Cambridge University Press, 2014), 78.

133. Siavush Randjbar-Daemi, "'Down with the Monarchy': Iran's Republican Moment of August 1953," *Iranian Studies* (December 2016): 6.

134. FRUS 1952–1954 Retro, doc. 260, CIA Station Iran TEHE 686, 14 August 1953.

135. Gasiorowski, "Coup d'Etat against Mosaddeq," 248–49.

136. FRUS 1952–1954 Retro, doc. 270, CIA Station Iran TEHE 710, 17 August 1953.

137. Abrahamian, *The Coup*, 184–85, Rahnema, *Behind the 1953 Coup*, 102.

138. FRUS 1952–1954 Retro, doc. 270, CIA Station Iran TEHE 710, 17 August 1953, contains a timeline of these events; Wilber, *Overthrow of Mosaddeq*, 39–43.

139. Wilber, *Overthrow of Mosaddeq*, 39.

140. Wilber, *Overthrow of Mosaddeq*, 45.

141. FRUS 1952–1954 Retro, doc. 262, Tehran 337, 16 August 1953.

142. Gasiorowski, "Coup d'Etat against Mosaddeq," 249.

143. Wilber, *Overthrow of Mosaddeq*, 49. Fatemi wrote three editorials that appeared in *Bakhtar-e Emruz* on 16, 17, and 18 August.

144. FRUS 1952–1954 Retro, doc. 267, Tehran 345, 16 August 1953; Wilber, *Overthrow of Mosaddeq*, 46.

145. Rahnema, *Behind the 1953 Coup*, 105.

146. FRUS 1952–1954 Retro, doc. 263, CIA Station Iran TEHE 704, 16 August 1953.

147. Wilber, *Overthrow of Mosaddeq*, 39.

148. FRUS 1952–1954 Retro, doc. 307, Record of Meeting, 28 August 1953.

149. Wilber, *Overthrow of Mosaddeq*, 45; FRUS 1952–1954 10, doc. 342, Tehran 331, 16 August 1953.

150. FRUS 1952–1954 Retro, doc. 307, Record of Meeting, 28 August 1953.

151. FRUS 1952–1954 Retro, doc. 271, Bagdad 92, 17 August 1953.

152. Randjbar-Daemi, "'Down with the Monarchy,'" 6–7.

153. *Mardom-e Iran*, 26 Mordad 1332 (17 August 1953).

154. Abrahamian, *The Coup*, 186–87.

155. Randjbar-Daemi, "'Down with the Monarchy,'" 13.

156. Harvard Interview, Sanjabi, Tape No. 11, 15–17.

157. FRUS 1952–1954 Retro, doc. 264, CIA Station Iran TEHE 707, 16 August 1953; doc. 269, CIA Station Iran TEHE 705, 16 August 1953.

158. FRUS 1952–1954 Retro, doc. 266, Tehran 342, 16 August 1953; FRUS 1952–1954 10, doc. 342, Tehran 331, 16 August 1953.

159. FRUS 1952–1954 Retro, doc. 272, Telegram from CIA to [text not declassified], 17 August 1953, note 3.

160. FRUS 1952–1954 Retro, doc. 273, CIA Station Iran TEHE 717, 17 August 1953.

161. FRUS 1952–1954 Retro, doc. 274, Memo Prepared in the Directorate of Plans, 17 August 1953.

162. FRUS 1952–1954 Retro, doc. 275, Memo from the Office of National Estimates, 17 August 1953.

163. FRUS 1952–1954 Retro, doc. 278, CIA to CIA Station Iran, 18 August 1953, note 3.

164. FRUS 1952–1954 10, doc. 346, Smith to the President, 18 August 1953.

165. FRUS 1952–1954 Retro, doc. 278, CIA to CIA Station Iran, 18 August 1953.

166. FRUS 1952–1954 Retro, doc. 307, Record of Meeting, 28 August 1953.

167. Rahnema, *Behind the 1953 Coup*, 147; Maziar Behrooz, "Tudeh Factionalism and the 1953 Coup in Iran," *International Journal of Middle East Studies* 33 (August 2001): 366.

168. Mark J. Gasiorowski, "The 1953 Coup d'Etat in Iran," *International Journal of Middle East Studies* 19 (August 1987): 274.

169. Sanjabi, *Omidha va Naomidiha*, 142.

170. Wilber, *Overthrow of Mosaddeq*, 56–57; Roosevelt, *Countercoup*, 180. The British account of the coup suggests the decision to attempt a second coup was made on 17 August; FRUS 1952–1954 10, doc. 362, British Memorandum, "Political Review of the Recent Crisis," 2 September 1953.

171. Gasiorowski, "The 1953 Coup d'Etat in Iran," 274.

172. Wilber, *Overthrow of Mosaddeq*, 57.

173. Rahnema, *Behind the 1953 Coup*, 126.

174. Rahnema, *Behind the 1953 Coup*, 138–39. Ja'far Behbehani, son of Ayatollah Behbehani, became a Majlis deputy. Shahid Tayyeb Haj Reza'i was given an import license for bananas; Harvard Interview, Reza Muqaddam, Tape No. 1, 15–17.

175. Ardeshir Zahedi's meetings with Love are mentioned in both FRUS volumes. For Love's own account, see Kennett Love, "The American Role in the Pahlavi Restoration on August 19, 1953" (unpublished paper, 1960), 31–32, available in the Allen W. Dulles Papers, Seeley-Mudd Manuscript Library, Princeton University. Woodhouse credits Roosevelt with distributing the *firmans*; C. M. Woodhouse,

Something Ventured (London: Granada, 1982), 128. Roosevelt credits the "Boscoe Brothers," with context implying it is Keyvani and Jalali; Roosevelt, *Counter-coup*, 179.

176. FRUS 1952–1954 Retro, doc. 307, Record of Meeting, 28 August 1953.

177. Wilber, *Overthrow of Mosaddeq*, 65–66. Harvard Interview, Mehdi Hairi-Yazdi, No. 2, 3–4; Mark J. Gasiorowski, "The Causes of Iran's 1953 Coup: A Critique of Darioush Bayandor's *Iran and the CIA*," *Iranian Studies* 45 (September 2012): 669–78.

178. FRUS 1952–1954 Retro, doc. 280, Tehran 384, 18 August 1953.

179. Abrahamian, *The Coup*, 190–91.

180. FRUS 1952–1954 Retro, doc. 283, Tehran 419, 20 August 1953.

181. FRUS 1952–1954 Retro, doc. 307, Record of Meeting, 28 August 1953.

182. See Gasiorowski, "The CIA's TPBEDAMN Operation," 19–20.

183. Rahnema, *Behind the 1953 Coup*, 156–61, 167–68, 179–80; Richard Cottam, *Nationalism in Iran Updated Through 1978* (Pittsburgh: University of Pittsburgh Press, 1979), 37–38.

184. Wilber, *Overthrow of Mosaddeq*, 65; FRUS 1952–1954 Retro, doc. 306, Chief of Station in Iran to Roosevelt, 28 August 28, 1953.

185. Harvard Interview, Mohammed Daftari, Tape 2, 13.

186. FRUS 1952–1954 Retro, doc. 306, Chief of Station in Iran to Roosevelt, 28 August 1953.

187. Rahnema, *Behind the 1953 Coup*, 188

188. Rahnema, *Behind the 1953 Coup*, 198–203.

189. Wilber, *Overthrow of Mosaddeq*, 69.

190. Wilber, *Overthrow of Mosaddeq*, 71.

191. Rahnema, *Behind the 1953 Coup*, 124; Wilber, *Overthrow of Mosaddeq*, 69–73; Roosevelt, *Countercoup*, 188–92.

192. FRUS 1952–1954 Retro, doc. 307, Record of Meeting, 28 August 1953.

193. Wilber, *Overthrow of Mosaddeq*, 73; FRUS 1952–1954 Retro, doc. 307, Record of Meeting in the CIA, 28 August 1953.

194. FRUS 1952–1954 Retro, doc. 286, CIA Station Iran TEHE 742, 19 August 1953.

195. FRUS 1952–1954 Retro, doc. 288, Tehran 400, 19 August 1953.

196. Abrahamian, *The Coup*, 196.

197. FRUS 1952–1954 10, doc. 362, British Memorandum, "Political Review of the Recent Crisis," 2 September 1953.

198. Wilber, *Overthrow of Mosaddeq*, 73–74; FRUS 1952–1954 Retro, doc. 283, Tehran 419, 20 August 1953.

199. FRUS 1952–1954 Retro, doc. 291, Waller Memo, 20 August 1953.

200. Gasiorowski, "The 1953 Coup d'Etat in Iran," 274; Abrahamian, *The Coup*, 197–98.

201. Ardeshir Zahedi, *The Memoirs of Ardeshir Zahedi*, vol. 1: *From Childhood to the End of My Father's Premiership*, translated by Farhang Jahanpour (Bethesda, MD: Ibex Publishers, 2012), 179–83.

202. Darioush Bayandor, *Iran and the CIA: The Fall of Mossadeq Revisited* (Basingstoke, UK: Palgrave Macmillan, 2010), 96–97, 131.

203. Ray Takeyh, *The Last Shah: America, Iran, and the Fall of the Pahlavi Dynasty* (New Haven, CT: Yale University Press, 2021), 115.

204. FRUS 1952–1954 10, doc. 348, Tehran 419, 20 August 1953.

205. Cottam, *Nationalism in Iran*, 229.

206. Gasiorowski, "The CIA's TPBEDAMN Operation," 18–19.

207. Abrahamian, *The Coup*, 157–58.

208. Gasiorowski, "The 1953 Coup d'Etat in Iran," 273.

209. FRUS 1952–1954 Retro, doc. 306, Chief of Station in Iran to Roosevelt, 28 August 1953.

210. FRUS 1952–1954 Retro, doc. 282, Memo for the Record, 19 August 1953.

211. Mark J. Gasiorowski, *U.S. Foreign Policy and the Shah: Building a Client State in Iran* (Ithaca, NY: Cornell University Press, 1991), 93–95, 101–3.

212. Behrooz, "Tudeh Factionalism," 369.

213. Sanjabi, *Omidha va Naomidiha*, 148.

214. David S. Painter, notes from the conference.

Chapter 7

1. FRUS 1952–1954 10, doc. 353, Tehran 466, 23 August 1953; FRUS 1952–1954 Retro, doc. 315, Memo from Bryant to Warne, 9 September 1953; Abbas Milani, *The Shah* (New York: Palgrave Macmillan, 2011), 190.

2. Byroade to Bowie, 21 August 1953, RG 59, Lot 57D 155, "Situation Rts." There is a redacted version in FRUS 1952–1954 10, doc. 352.

3. London 3268, 23 August 1953, PREM 11/726; Foreign Office Brief for the Cabinet, "Persia," FO 371/104577; FRUS 1952–1954 10, doc. 355, MemCon, 25 August 1953; BEW 1902, 3 September 1953, PREM 11/726.

4. FRUS 1952–1954 Retro, doc. 294, Memo by Wisner, 20 August 1953; doc. 303, Tehran 489, 26 August 1953; FRUS 1952–1954 10, doc. 357, Tehran 497, 27 August 1953.

5. FRUS 1952–1954 Retro, doc. 256, Stutesman Memo, undated; doc. 299, Nash to Cutler (draft), undated; doc. 301, Zahedi to Eisenhower, 26 August 1953; doc. 302, Eisenhower to Zahedi, 26 August 1953.

6. FRUS 1952–1954 Retro, doc. 308, CIA Monthly Report, August 1953; doc. 295, Cabell to Eisenhower, undated; doc. 296, CIA Station Tehran to CIA, 21 August 1953; doc. 297, Wisner to Mitchell, 21 August 1953; doc. 319, Briefing Notes for Dulles, undated; see also the British intelligence report on the internal situation in Iran for September and October, FO 371/104571.

7. FRUS 1952–1954 Retro, doc. 322, Roosevelt Memo, 21 September 1953; doc. 326, CIA Monthly Report, September 1953.

8. FRUS 1952–1954 Retro, doc. 309, Memo from [name not declassified] to Dulles, 2 September 1953.

9. FRUS 1952–1954 Retro, doc. 329, Roosevelt Memo, 9 October 1953; Homa Katouzian, *Musaddiq and the Struggle for Power in Iran* (London: I. B. Tauris, 1990), 208–9; David R. Collier, *Democracy and the Nature of American Influence in Iran, 1941–1979* (Syracuse, NY: Syracuse University Press, 2017), 151–55.

10. FRUS 1952–1954 Retro, doc. 314, CIA Information Cable, 8 September 1953.

11. FRUS 1952–1954 Retro, doc. 315, Bryant to Warne, 9 September 1953.

12. FRUS 1952–1954 Retro, doc. 316, Tehran Desp. 154, 11 September 1953; doc. 321, Tehran Desp. 172, 18 September 1953.

13. FRUS 1952–1954 Retro, doc. 324, Memo by Chief of Station in Iran to Henderson, 25 September 1953; doc. 326, CIA Monthly Report, September 1953.

14. FRUS 1952–1954 Retro, doc. 303, Tehran 489, 16 August 1953.

15. FRUS 1952–1954 Retro, doc. 322, Memo by Roosevelt, 21 September 1953.

16. FRUS 1952–1954 Retro, doc. 325, Tehran Desp. 187, 26 September 1953.

17. FRUS 1952–1954 Retro, doc. 343, CIA Monthly Report, October 1953.

18. FRUS 1952–1954 10, doc. 368, Tehran 703, 18 September 1953; doc. 374, Tehran 866, 9 October 1953.

19. Byroade to Bowie, 21 August 1953, RG 59, Lot 57D 155, "Situation Rts."

20. FRUS 1952–1954 Retro, doc. 312, McClure to Ridgway, 6 September 1953; doc. 317, CIA Information Report, 14 September 1953; doc. 319, Briefing Notes for Dulles, undated; FRUS 1952–1954 10, doc. 368, Tehran 703, 18 September 1953; doc. 370, Tehran 783, 29 September 1953.

21. FRUS 1952–1954 Retro, doc. 325, Tehran Desp. 187, 26 September 1953.

22. FRUS 1952–1954 Retro, doc. 320, Editorial Note. See also FRUS 1952–1954 10, doc. 367, NSC Meeting, 17 September 1953.

23. FRUS 1952–1954 Retro, doc. 304. NSC Meeting, 27 August 1953; doc. 299, Nash to Cutler (draft), undated.

24. FO Memo, "Persian Oil Problem," 31 August 1953, CAB 134/1149; FO 3531, 10 September 1953, PREM 11/726; BEW 1961, 11 September 1954, PREM 11/726; "Persian Oil," 11 September 1953, RG 59, Lot 57 D 155, "British Memoranda"; FO 3709, 25 September 1953, PREM 11/726; FRUS 1952–1954 10, doc. 369, note 3, Tehran 749, 25 September 1953.

25. FRUS 1952–1954 10, doc. 367, NSC Meeting, 17 September 1953.

26. FRUS 1952–1954 10, doc. 369, State 853, 23 September 1953.

27. MemCon, "Discussion Regarding the Iranian Oil Problem," 25 September 1953, 888.2553/9-2553; FRUS 1952–1954 10, doc. 369, State 853, 23 September 1953; Mary Ann Heiss, *Empire and Nationhood: The United States, Great Britain, and Iranian Oil, 1950–1954* (New York: Columbia University Press, 1997), 191.

28. FRUS 1952–1954 10, doc. 371, State 897, 29 September 1953; Heiss, *Empire and Nationhood*, 193.

29. FRUS 1952–1954 10, doc. 372, State 956, 8 October 1953; doc. 375, State 1964, 13 October 1953; doc. 376, Editorial Note on Foreign Ministers Conference, 2nd Tripartite Meeting, 17 October 1953; J. H. Bamberg, *The History of the British Petroleum Company*, vol. 2: *The Anglo-Iranian Years, 1928–1954* (Cambridge: Cambridge University Press, 1994), 490–91.

30. Tehran 940, 22 October 1953, 888.2553/10-2253; there are also copies in RG 59, Lot 55 D 155, "Middle Eastern Oil"; Tehran 956, 23 October 1953, 888.2553/10-2253; Tehran 970, 888.2553/10-2453; Persia (Official) Committee, Note by the Joint Secretariat, "The Persian Oil Problem," 23 October 1953, CAB 134/1149; Persia

(Official) Committee, Note by the Joint Secretariat, "Visit of Mr. Hoover to Teh-ran," 28 October 1953, CAB 134/1149; Eakens to Hoover, 22 September 1953, RG 59, Lot 57 D 155, "Iran—Oil"; MemCon, "Iranian Oil Problem," 6 November 1952, 888.2553 /11-652.

31. FRUS 1952–1954 10, doc. 377, Tehran 996, 29 October 1953; Fry, "Persia," FO 371/104585; Tehran 998, 29 October 1953, 888.2553/10-2953. Zahedi and Hoover also discussed the possibility of the World Bank acting as a middleman between the companies and the Iranian government. Although this idea initially received considerable attention, it was eventually dropped due to the objections of the oil companies.

32. FRUS 1952–1954 10, doc. 378, Tehran 1022, 2 November 1953.

33. Persia (Official) Committee, "Persia: Record of Meeting with Mr. Hoover held at the Foreign Office," 6 November 1953, CAB 134/1149; Committee, "Mr. Hoover's Visit to London: Note by Joint Secretaries," 7 November 1953, CAB 134/1149; Persia (Official) Committee, "Mr. Hoover's Visit to London: Note by the Joint Secretariat," 12 November 1953, CAB 134; London 1968 to State, 6 November 1953, 888.2553/11-653; FRUS 1952–1954 10, doc. 379, London 1945, 5 November 1953; doc. 370, Tehran 783, 29 September 1953; doc. 380, London 1965, 5 November 1953; doc. 382, London 2002, 7 November 1953; doc. 384, Tehran 1088, 12 November 1953. For summaries of the talks, see London 381, 10 November 1953, PREM 11/726; London 331, FO 371/10485; "Persian Oil," undated, CAB 134/1149.

34. Persia (Official) Committee, "Persia: Record of Meeting with Mr. Hoover Held at the Foreign Office," 6 November 1953, CAB 134/1149; Persia (Official) Com-mittee, "Mr. Hoover's Visit to London: Note by Joint Secretaries," 7 November 1953, CAB 134/1149; Persia (Official) Committee, "Mr. Hoover's Visit to London: Note by the Joint Secretariat," 12 November 1953, CAB 134/1149; Memo to Fry, 9 Janu-ary 1954, FO 371/110046.

35. "Persian Oil," 24 November 1953, CAB 134/1149.

36. Message Q, "Memorandum," 30 November 1953, CAB 134/1149; FRUS 1952–1954 Retro, doc. 347, NIE-102, 16 November 1953; Tehran 108, 11 November 1953, 888.2553/11-1153; FRUS 1952–1954 10, doc. 379, London 1945, 5 Novem-ber 1953; doc. 380, London 1965, 5 November 1953; doc. 381, London 1969, 6 No-vember 1953; doc. 382, London 2002, 7 November 1953; doc. 386, London 2099, 14 November 1953; doc. 388, Tehran 1140, 19 November 1953; doc. 390, London 2158, 19 November 1953; doc. 391, London 2228, 24 November 1953; doc. 393, Teh-ran 1227, 3 December 1953; Heiss, *Empire and Nationhood*, 194; Bamberg, *History of the British Petroleum Company*, vol. 2, 492–93; Selwyn Lloyd memo, 15 Novem-ber 1953, FO 371/104586.

37. FRUS 1952–1954 Retro, doc. 330, CIA Information Report, 14 October 1953; doc. 341, Tehran Desp. 245, 30 October 1953; Katouzian, *Musaddiq and the Struggle for Power in Iran*, 209.

38. FRUS 1952–1954 Retro, doc. 339, Memo from the Near East and Africa Divi-sion, CIA, 29 October 1953.

39. FRUS 1952–1954 Retro, doc. 336, CIA Information Report, 20 October 1953.

40. FRUS 1952–1954 Retro, doc. 347, NIE-102, 16 November 1953; doc. 348, Tehran 1141, 19 November 1953.

41. FRUS 1952–1954 Retro, doc. 338, Wisner to Dulles, 27 October 1953.

42. FRUS 1952–1954 Retro, doc. 349, Roosevelt to Dulles, 20 November 1953; FRUS 1952–1954 10, doc. 385, Tehran 1102, 14 November 1953.

43. Katouzian, *Musaddiq and the Struggle for Power in Iran*, 194–207.

44. Jalil Bozorgmehr, *Musaddiq dar mahkameh-ye nezami* [Musaddiq in Military Court], vol. 2 (Tehran: Nehzat-e Moqavemat-e Melli, 1985), 52–53.

45. Milani, *The Shah*, 194.

46. FRUS 1952–1954 Retro, doc. 353, MemCon, 22 December 1953.

47. FRUS 1952–1954 10, doc. 405, Tehran 1481, 7 January 1954; doc. 407, Tehran 1491, 8 January 1954.

48. FRUS 1952–1954 10, doc. 409, Tehran 1581, 18 January 1954.

49. FRUS 1952–1954 Retro, doc. 346, Tehran CIA Desp. 1472, 13 November 1953; doc. 354, Monthly Report, "Iran: Dec 1953," undated.

50. FRUS 1952–1954 Retro, doc. 356, CIA Information Report, 6 January 1954.

51. FRUS 1952–1954 Retro, doc. 358, Tehran Desp. 410, 11 January 1954.

52. 178th Meeting of the National Security Council, 30 December 1953, Eisenhower Papers, NSC Series, DDEL; FRUS 1952–1954 Retro, doc. 355, NSC 5402: United States Policy toward Iran, 2 January 1954. NSC 5402 superseded NSC 136/1. There is a redacted version in FRUS 1952–1954 10, doc. 403.

53. Heiss, *Empire and Nationhood*, 196–99; Bamberg, *History of the British Petroleum Company*, vol. 2, 493–94; Dixon MemCon, 8 December 1953, PREM 11/726; FRUS 1952–1954 10, doc. 392, London 2340, 30 November 1953; doc. 394, London 2444, 5 December 1953; MemCon, 5 January 1954, FO 371/11046.

54. George W. Stocking, *Middle East Oil: A study in Political and Economic Controversy* (Nashville, TN: Vanderbilt University Press, 1970), 157–58; Wanda Jablonski, "Masterstroke in Iran." *Collier's* (21 January 1955), 34. For an earlier assessment of company views, see MemCon, 6 November 1952, 888.2443/11-652.

55. MemCon, "Iranian Oil," 12 November 1953, 888.2553/11-1253.

56. FRUS 1952–1954 10, doc. 395, Phleger Memo, 8 December 1953.

57. Heiss, *Empire and Nationhood*, 198; Bamberg, *History of the British Petroleum Company*, vol. 2, 494–95; FRUS 1952–1954 10, doc. 397, London 2678, 18 December 1953; Belgrave, "Persian Oil," 22 December 1953, FO 371/110046.

58. FRUS 1952–1954 10, doc. 398, Editorial Note; doc. 399, Byroade to the Secretary of State, 23 December 1953.

59. FRUS 1952–1954 10, doc. 401, NSC Meeting, 30 December 1953; doc. 402, Cutler to Dulles, 4 January 1954.

60. FRUS 1952–1954 Retro, doc. 355, NSC 5402: United States Policy toward Iran, 2 January 1954.

61. Tehran 25, 29 December 1953, PREM 11.726; Wright to Allen, 31 December 1953, FO 371/110046; Tehran 15, 6 January 1954, PREM 11/726; Heiss, *Empire and Nationhood*, 198–200; Bamberg, *History of the British Petroleum Company*, 495, 496.

62. Tehran 18, 7 January 1954, PREM 11/726; "Persian Oil: Memorandum by the Secretary of State for Foreign Affairs," 5 January 1953, PREM/726; Cabinet Conclusion C.C. (54) 1 (5), 7 January 1954; CAB 128, 5 January 1954; Dixon Minute, "Persian Oil," 5 January 1954, FO 371/110046; London 4, 8 January 1954, PREM/11/726; Belgrave, "Persian Oil," 22 December 1953, FO371/110046.

63. FO 292, 18 January 1953, FO 371/11046; Bamberg, *History of the British Petroleum Company*, vol. 2, 497–98.

64. *Consortium Documents*, 60–61; FRUS 1952–1954 Retro, doc. 357, Henderson to Armstrong, 7 January 1954.

65. FRUS 1952–1954 10, doc. 413, Hoover to the Secretary of State, 21 January 1954.

66. FRUS 1952–1954 10, doc. 411, Brownell to the NSC, 20 January 1954; doc. 414, NSC Meeting, 21 January 1954.

67. FRUS 1952–1954 10, doc. 415, London 3171, 26 January 1954; doc. 416, London 3230, 28 January 1954; doc. 418, London 3314, 3 February 1954; Belgrave, "Statement Made by Mr. Hoover to the Middle East Oil Committee," 29 January 1954, CAB 134/1144.

68. Middle East Oil (Official) Committee, "Formation of a Consortium for Persian Oil," 2 February 1954, PREM 11/726; Cabinet, Persia Committee, "Minutes of a Meeting," 2 February 1953, PREM 11/726.

69. Cabinet, Persia Committee, "Minutes of a Meeting," 2 February 1953, PREM 11/726; Berlin Seco 75, 3 February 1953; FRUS 1952–1954 10, doc. 420, note 2, summarizes a telegram from Secretary Dulles about his meeting with Eden; Fry Minute, 4 February 1954, FO 371/110047.

70. FRUS 1952–1954 10, doc. 423, Tedul 50, 15 February 1954; doc. 424, Merchant to the Secretary of State, 16 February 1954; doc. 425, State 1745, 18 February 1954; British Embassy Berlin 223, 18 February 1953, PREM/11/72.

71. FRUS 1952–1954 10, doc. 426, State 1749, 19 February 1954; doc. 428, State 4334, 23 February 1954; doc. 429, State 4365, 23 February 1954; BEW 300, 19 February 1954, FO 371/110047.

72. State 4507 to London, 3 March 1954, 888.2553/3-354; FO 814, 2 March 1954, FO 371/11047; Hopwood to Fraser, 2 March 1954, FO 371/110048; BEW 385, 4 March 1954, PREM 11/726; FRUS 1952–1954 10, doc. 432, State 4533, 4 March 1954; doc. 433, State 4547, 5 March 1954.

73. London 3948, 13 March 1954, 888.2553/3-1354; London 3949, 13 March 1954, 888.2553/3-1348; London 3973, 15 March 1954, 888.2553/3-1553; London 3986, 16 March 1954, 888.2553/3-1654; FRUS 1952–1954 10, doc. 436, State 4773, 17 March 1954; doc. 437, London 3992, 17 March 1954; Bamberg, *History of the British Petroleum Company*, vol. 2, 501; Mostafa Elm, *Oil, Power, and Principle: Iran's Oil Nationalization and Its Aftermath* (Syracuse, NY: Syracuse University Press, 1992), 316–17.

74. Tehran 1948, 16 March 1954, 888.2553/3-1654; London 3986, 16 March 1954, 888.2553/3-1654.

75. Dulles TelCon with Secretary Wilson, 17 March 1954, JFD TelCons, DDEL; BEW 447, 17 March 1954; BEW 448, 17 March 1954; BEW 449, 17 March 1954, PREM 11/726; Dulles TelCon with Secretary Wilson, 17 March 1954, JFD TelCons, DDEL;

189th Meeting of the National Security Council, Eisenhower Papers, NSC Series, DDEL.

76. 189th Meeting of the National Security Council, 18 March 1954, Eisenhower Paper, NSC Series, DDEL; FRUS 1952–1954 Retro, doc. 364, Waller to Jackson, 19 March 1954; Heiss, *Empire and Nationhood*, 206.

77. Heiss, *Empire and Nationhood*, 206–7; FRUS 1952–1954 10, doc. 440, London 4024, 18 March 1954; doc. 441, Tehran 1977, 20 March 1954; doc. 442, London 4062, 22 March 1954; FO 1073, 20 March 1954, PREM 11/726; FO 1076, 20 March 1954, PREM 11/726.

78. FO 1076, 20 March 1954, PREM 11/726; MemCon, 22 March 1954, 888.2553 /3-2254.

79. London 4057, 21 March 1954, 888.2553/3-2154; FRUS 1951–1954 10, doc. 442, London 4062, 22 March 1954; doc. 443, State 4885, 22 March 1954; doc. 444, London 4104, 23 March 1954; Elm, *Oil, Power, and Principle*, 317–18; Bamberg, *History of the British Petroleum Company*, vol. 2, 501–2; Dulles TelCon with Secretary Humphrey, 22 March 1954, JFD TelCons, DDEL; MemCon, "Iranian Oil—Compensation Problem," 24 March 1954, 888.2553/3-2453; Dulles TelCon with Secretary Humphrey, 24 March 1954, JFD TelCons, DDEL.

80. BEW 474, 22 March 1954, PREM 11/726; FRUS 1951–1954 10, doc. 444, London 4104, 23 March 1954; doc. 445, London 4118, 24 March 1954; doc. 446, London 4150, 25 March 1954; doc. 447, London 4178, 26 March 1954; State 4969, 26 March 1954, 888.2553/3-2654; MemCon, "Further British Observations on Iran Negotiations," 25 March 1954, 888.2553/3-2554; Bamberg, *History of the British Petroleum Company*, vol. 2, 501–2; Elm, *Oil, Power, and Principle*, 317–18.

81. "Memorandum of Understanding on the Basis for the Settlement with Anglo-Iranian," 9 April 1954, PREM 11/726; Bamberg, *History of the British Petroleum Company*, vol. 2, 504. In April 1955, each of the five U.S. companies gave up one-eighth of its shares so that a 5 percent share could be made available to a new organization, the Iricon Agency, which was jointly owned by nine smaller U.S. companies; David S. Painter, *Oil and the American Century: The Political Economy of U.S. Foreign Oil Policy, 1941–1954* (Baltimore: Johns Hopkins University Press, 1986), 196, which, due to a transcription error, gives a figure of £188 million instead of £182 million.

82. Daniel Yergin, *The Prize: The Epic Quest for Oil, Money, and Power* (New York: Simon & Schuster, 1991), 478.

83. FRUS 1952–1954 10, doc. 449, London 4311, 1 April 1954; doc. 457, Editorial Note.

84. Tehran 2134, 15 April 1954, 888.2553/4-1554; Tehran 2206, 26 April 1954, 888.2553/4-2654.

85. Tehran 2248, 8 May 1954; FRUS 1952–1954 10, doc. 459, Tehran 2288, 8 May 1954; doc. 465, NSC Meeting, 27 May 1954; Tehran 2147, 16 April 1954, 888.2553/4-1654; Tehran 2210, 26 April 1954, 888.2553/4-2654; MemCon, 28 May 1954, 888.2553/5-2854; London 5401, 28 May 1954, 888.2553/5-2854; Steven G. Galpern, *Money, Oil, and Empire in the Middle East: Sterling and Postwar Imperialism, 1944–1971* (New York: Cambridge University Press, 2009), 134.

86. Tehran 2206, 26 April 1954, 888.2553/4-2654; Tehran 2210, 26 April 1954, 888.2553/4-2654; FRUS 1952–1954 10, doc. 458, Tehran 2287, 8 May 1954.

87. Tehran 2265, 4 May 1954, 888.2553/5-454; Stevens to Caccia, 4 May 1954, FO 371/110062; FRUS 1952–1954 10, doc. 467, Tehran 2432, 29 May 1954; MemCon, 3 June 1954, 888.2553/6-254.

88. FRUS 1952–1954 10, doc. 459, Tehran 2288, 8 May 1954.

89. MemCon, 28 May 1954, 888.2553/5-2854; London 5401, 28 May 1953, 888.2553/5-2554; State 6577, 4 June 1954, 888.2553/6-454.

90. FO 65, 8 April 1954, PREM 11/726; BET 20, 5 May 1964, PREM 11/726.

91. Tehran 2147, 16 April 1954, 888.2553/4-1654; London 4912, 5 May 1954, 888.2553/5-554; Galpern, *Money, Oil, and Empire*, 130–41.

92. FRUS 1952–1954 10, doc. 460, Jernegan to Murphy, 15 May 1954; doc. 462, Tehran 2356, 18 May 1954; Tehran 2323, 18 May 1954, 888.2553/5-1854.

93. Byroade to Murphy, "Iranian Oil," 20 May 1954, 888.2553/5-2054; MemCon, "Iranian Oil Negotiations," 21 May 1954, 888.2553/5-2154; FRUS 1952–1954 10, doc. 464, State 6287, 24 May 1954.

94. Tehran 2210, 26 April 1954, 888.2553/4-2654. There are numerous references to possible oil deals in the 888.2553 file.

95. M. A. Adelman, *The World Petroleum Market* (Baltimore: Johns Hopkins University Press, 1972), 148–50; Douglas R. Bohi and Milton Russell, *Limiting Oil Imports: An Economic History and Analysis* (Baltimore: Johns Hopkins University Press, 1978), 22–23; Albert L. Danielsen, *The Evolution of OPEC* (San Diego: Harcourt Brace Jovanovich, 1982), 134; Jerrold L. Walden, "The International Petroleum Cartel in Iran—Private Power and the Public Interest," *Journal of Public Law* 11 (Spring 1962): 100–102.

96. Heiss, *Empire and Nationhood*, 212; Tehran 2444, 1 June 1954, 888.2553/6-154; Tokyo 3238, 26 June 1954, 888.2553/6-2654.

97. MemCon, "Iranian Oil Negotiations, 1 June 1954, Lot 57 D 155, "Extra Oil Papers," RG 59; FRUS 1952–1954 10, doc 478, State 6903, 17 June 1954; doc. 481, Tehran 10, 1 July 1954; doc. 484, State 44, 8 July 1954; State 93, 14 July 1954, 888.2553/7-1454.

98. FRUS 1952–1954 10, doc. 480, Tehran 2611, 30 June 1954; Tehran Desp. 12, 12 July 1954.

99. *Consortium Documents*, 95–116; see summary by Howard Page, Tehran 239, 31 July 1954, 888.2553/7-3154. The State Department also circulated a summary of the agreement prepared by Standard Oil of New Jersey, State Circular 71, 4 August 1954, 888.2553/8-454.

100. Stocking, *Middle East Oil*, 157–61; Elm, *Oil, Power, and Principle*, 329; Jablonski, "Masterstroke in Iran," 34.

101. FRUS 1952–1954 Retro, doc. 375, NIE 34-54, 7 December 1954; on the formula, see John M. Blair, *The Control of Oil* (New York: Pantheon, 1977), 103–8; Theodore H. Moran, "Managing an Oligopoly of Would-Be Sovereigns: The Dynamics of Joint Control and Self-Control in the International Oil Industry Past, Present, and Future," *International Organization* 41 (Autumn 1987): 590–92.

102. FRUS 1952–1954 10, doc. 491, Tehran 311, 5 August 1954; Galpern, *Money, Oil, and Empire*, 138.

103. "Persia: Memorandum by the Secretary of State for Foreign Affairs," 28 July 1954, PREM 11/726; Cabinet Conclusions: Minutes, 28 July 1954, PREM 11/726; FRUS 1952–1954 10, doc. 486, London 549, 30 July 1954; doc. 487, Tehran 241, 31 July 1954; doc. 489, Tehran 307, 5 August 1954; doc. 490, Tehran 309, 5 August 1954; Heiss, *Empire and Nationhood*, 214–15.

104. FRUS 1952–1954 10, doc. 492, Tehran 385, 15 August 1954; doc. 495, Jernegan to Bowie, 18 September 1954.

105. FRUS 1952–1954 10, doc. 466, Tehran 2418, 28 May 1954; doc. 468, State 2337, 29 May 1954; doc. 471. State 2343, 31 May 1954; doc. 475, Tehran 2513, 11 June 1954; FRUS 1952–1954 Retro, doc. 367, CIA Information Report, 14 June 1954; doc. 370, CIA Information Report, 17 June 1954; doc. 371, Quarterly Report, 8 July 1954.

106. FRUS 1952–1954 Retro, doc. 368, Project Outline Proposed in CIA, 15 June 1954; doc. 375; NIE 34-54, "Probable Developments in Iran through 1955," 7 December 1954; Ervand Abrahamian, *The Coup: 1953, the CIA and the Roots of Modern U.S.-Iranian Relations* (New York: New Press, 2013), 214–15.

107. FRUS 1952–1954 Retro, doc. 374, Quarterly Report, 12 October 1954.

108. FRUS 1952–1954 10, doc. 493, State 532, 15 September 1954; doc. 494, State 549, 17 September 1954.

109. Burton I. Kaufman, *The Oil Cartel Case: A Documentary Study of, Antitrust Activity in the Cold War Era* (Westport, CT: Greenwood Press, 1978), 59–60; Painter, *Oil and the American Century*, 197.

110. FRUS 1952–1954 10, doc. 465, NSC Meeting, 27 May 1954; MemCon, "Iranian Oil Negotiations, 1 June 1954, Lot 57 D 155, "Extra Oil Papers," RG 59.

111. FRUS 1952–1954 10, doc. 497, MemCon, 12 October 1954; doc. 498, State 729, 13 October 1954; doc. 503, Dulles to Wilson, 8 November 1954.

112. FRUS 1952–1954 10, doc. 497, MemCon, 12 October 1954; Bennet H. Wall, *Growth in a Changing Environment: A History of Standard Oil Company (New Jersey) 1950-1972 and Exxon Corporation 1972-1975* (New York: McGraw-Hill, 1988), 494–95.

113. FRUS 1952–1954 10, doc. 501, Editorial Note; doc. 502, State 843, 28 October 1954; Elm, *Oil, Power, and Principle*, 327–28.

114. FRUS 1952–1954, Retro, doc. 375, NIE 34-54, "Probable Developments in Iran through 1955," 7 December 1954. NIE 34-54 drew in part on an intelligence note, "Political Prospects in Iran," 30 July 1954, FRUS 1952–1954 10, doc. 487.

115. FRUS 1952–1954 Retro, doc. 154, Thornburg to Dulles, 10 February 1953, attached to Dulles to Smith, 19 February 1953.

History and Contested Memories

1. William A. Dorman and Mansour Farhang, *The U.S. Press and Iran: Foreign Policy and the Journalism of Deference* (Berkeley: University of California Press, 1987), 31–62; John Foran, "Discursive Subversions: *Time* Magazine, the CIA Over-

throw of Musaddiq, and the Installation of the Shah," in *Cold War Constructions: The Political Culture of United States Imperialism, 1945–1966*, edited by Christian G. Appy (Amherst: University of Massachusetts Press, 2000), 157–82.

2. John F. Harter, "Mr. Foreign Service on Mossadegh and Wristonization: An Interview with Loy W. Henderson," *Foreign Service Journal* 57 (November 1980): 16–18.

3. Second Oral History Interview with Loy W. Henderson by Richard D. McKinzie, Washington, DC, 5 July 1973, HSTL.

4. Henderson to Bruce Riedel, 30 October 1975, Henderson Papers, Manuscript Division, LC, Box 9, "Iran—Misc."

5. Henderson to Ron Cockrell, 25 January 1978, Henderson Papers, Manuscript Division, LC, Box 10, "Iran—Misc."

6. Kermit Roosevelt, *Countercoup: The Struggle for the Control of Iran* (New York: McGraw-Hill Book Company, 1979).

7. Donald Wilber, *Overthrow of Premier Mosaddeq of Iran, November 1952–August 1953, CIA Clandestine Service History*, 1–2, https://nsarchive2.gwu.edu/NSAEBB /NSAEBB28/; Scott A. Koch, *Zendebad Shah! The Central Intelligence Agency and the Fall of Iranian Prime Minister Mohammed Mossadeq, August 1953*, June 1998, 2–3, https://nsarchive.gwu.edu/document/16330-document-2-zendebad-shah; *The Battle for Iran*, CIA History, 1, https://nsarchive2.gwu.edu/NSAEBB/NSAEBB476/.

8. Secretary of State Madeleine K. Albright, "Remarks before the American-Iranian Council," March 17, 2000, *U.S. Department of State Archive*, https://1997 -2001.state.gov/statements/2000/000317.html. The CIA unofficially admitted its involvement in the coup when it declassified several sections of its internal history, "The Battle for Iran," in 2013; Malcolm Byrne, "CIA Admits It Was behind Iran's Coup," *Foreign Policy*, 12 August 2013, http://foreignpolicy.com/2013/08/19/cia -admits-it-was-behind-irans-coup/.

9. FRUS 1952–1954 Retro, doc. 328, Editorial Note.

10. John Prados, *Safe for Democracy: The Secret Wars of the CIA* (Chicago: Ivan R. Dee, 2006), Tim Weiner, *Legacy of Ashes: The History of the CIA* (New York: Double-day, 2007); Piero Gleijeses, *Shattered Hope: The Guatemalan Revolution and the United States, 1944–1954* (Princeton, NJ: Princeton University Press, 1992).

11. FRUS 1952–1954 Retro.

12. FRUS 1952–1954 Retro, doc. 353, Memo of Conversation, 22 December 1953; Abbas Milani, *The Shah* (London: Palgrave Macmillan, 2011), 193–94.

13. Homa Katouzian, *Musaddiq and the Struggle for Power in Iran* (London: I. B. Tauris, 1990), 215.

14. FRUS 1969–1976 36, doc. 202, Editorial Note.

15. Christopher R. W. Dietrich, *Oil Revolution: Anti-Colonial Elites, Sovereign Rights, and the Economic Culture of Decolonization* (New York: Cambridge University Press, 2017), 40–41; Giuliano Garavini, *The Rise and Fall of OPEC in the Twentieth Century* (New York: Oxford University Press, 2019), 86–87.

16. Ervand Abrahamian, *The Coup: 1953, the CIA and the Roots of Modern U.S.-Iranian Relations* (New York: New Press, 2013); 206-7; Jalal Al-e Ahmed, *Gharbza-degi* [Westoxification] (Costa Mesa, CA: Mazda Publishers, 1982).

17. "The Disputes between Iran and the U.S. Stem from the 1953 Coup in Iran," *Khamenei.ir*, November 3, 2019, http://english.khamenei.ir/news/7135/The-disputes-between-Iran-and-the-U-S-stem-from-the-1953-coup; Karim Sadjapour, *Reading Khamenei: The World View of Iran's Most Powerful Leader* (Washington, DC: Carnegie Endowment for Peace, 2009), 15–16.

18. Melvyn P. Leffler, *Safeguarding Democratic Capitalism: U.S. Foreign Policy and National Security, 1920–2015* (Princeton, NJ: Princeton University Press, 2017), 24–25, 317–35.

19. David S. Painter, *Oil and the American Century: The Political Economy of U.S. Foreign Oil Policy, 1941–1954* (Baltimore: Johns Hopkins University Press, 1986); Daniel Yergin, *The Prize: The Epic Quest for Oil, Money and Power* (New York: Simon & Schuster, 1991), 391–449.

20. FRUS 1952–1954 1, part 2, doc.159, NSC 138/1, "National Security Problems Regarding Free World Petroleum Demands and Supplies," 6 January 1953. NSC 138/1 is also printed in FRUS 1952–1954 9, part 1, doc. 279.

21. Steve Marsh, "HMG, AIOC and the Anglo-Iranian Oil Crisis: In Defence of AIOC," *Diplomacy and Statecraft* 12 (December 2001): 143–74; Steven G. Galpern, *Money, Oil, and Empire in the Middle East: Sterling and Postwar Imperialism, 1944–1971* (Cambridge: Cambridge University Press, 2009).

22. Charles Bright and Michael Geyer, "For a United History of the World in the Twentieth Century," *Radical History Review* 39 (Fall 1987): 82–84; David S. Painter, "Oil and the American Century," *Journal of American History* 99 (June 2012): 24–39.

23. FRUS 1952–1954 5, doc. 102, NIE-14, "The Importance of Middle East Oil to Western Europe under Peacetime Conditions," 8 January 1951; FRUS 1952–1954 Retro, doc. 375, NSC-5402, "United States Policy toward Iran," 2 January 1954; Gregory Brew, *Petroleum and Progress: Oil, Development, and the American Encounter with Iran, 1941–1965* (Cambridge: Cambridge University Press, 2022).

24. Walter J. Levy, "The Progressive Threat to the U.S. Position in Foreign Oil," 25 July 1952, Oscar L. Chapman Papers, Box 102, Petroleum Cartel File, Harry S. Truman Library.

25. This is a key argument in Ervand Abrahamian's work on the crisis.

26. Wilber, *Overthrow of Mosaddeq*, appendix B, 2.

27. *End of Empire*, Transcript of Interview with Cottam, Roll 60, 2.

28. *End of Empire*, Transcript of Interview with Byroade, 7.

29. FRUS 1952–1954 Retro, doc. 259, Draft National Intelligence Estimate, 12 August 1953; Gregory Brew, "The Collapse Narrative: The United States, Mohammad Mossadegh, and the Coup Decision of 1953," *Texas National Security Review* 2 (August 2019): 58–59.

30. Vladislav M. Zubok, "Stalin, Soviet Intelligence, and the Struggle for Iran, 1945–53," *Diplomatic History* 44 (January 2020): 22–25.

31. Koch, *Zendebad Shah!* appendix E, 118–20; Margaret Taafe-McMenamy, "Operation Ajax: A Case Study of Analyst—Policy Maker Tensions and the Challenges of Estimative Intelligence" (Fort Leavenworth, KS: School of Advanced Military Studies, U.S. Army Command and General Staff College, 2015).

32. Mark J. Gasiorowski, "The 1953 Coup d'Etat in Iran," *International Journal of Middle East Studies* 19 (August 1987): 270.

33. Donald N. Wilber, *Adventures in the Middle East: Excursions and Incursions* (Princeton, NJ: Darwin, 1986), 189.

34. Gregory Brew, "Misreading the 1953 Coup," *Lobelog,* 20 May 2019, https://lobelog.com/misreading-the-1953-coup/.

35. Mostafa Elm, *Oil, Power, and Principle: Iran's Oil Nationalization and Its Aftermath* (Syracuse, NY: Syracuse University Press, 1992), 306–7.

36. Mary Ann Heiss, "Real Men Don't Wear Pajamas: Anglo-American Cultural Perceptions of Mohammed Mossadegh and the Iranian Oil Nationalization Dispute," in *Empire and Revolution: The United States and the Third World Since 1945*, edited by Peter Hahn and Mary Ann Heiss (Columbus: Ohio State University Press, 2001), 178–91; Abrahamian, *The Coup*, 98–108.

37. Charles Bergquist, *Labor and the Course of American Democracy: U.S. History in Latin American Perspective* (London: Verso, 1995), 197–209.

38. Michael H. Hunt and Steven I. Levine, *Arc of Empire: America's Wars in Asia from the Philippines to Vietnam* (Chapel Hill: University of North Carolina Press, 2012), 272.

Bibliography

Archival Sources—United States

Dwight D. Eisenhower Presidential Library, Abilene, Kansas
  John Foster Dulles Papers
  Dwight D. Eisenhower Papers (Ann Whitman File)
Firestone Library, Princeton University
  John Foster Dulles Telephone Transcripts
Franklin Delano Roosevelt Library, Hyde Park, New York
  John C. Wiley Papers
Harry S. Truman Library, Independence, Missouri
  Dean Acheson Papers
  Oscar L. Chapman Papers
  Henry F. Grady Papers
  President's Secretary's File
  White House Central Files
Library of Congress, Manuscript Division, Washington, DC
  Averell Harriman Papers
  Loy W. Henderson Papers
  Paul H. Nitze Papers
Seeley G. Mudd Manuscript Library, Princeton University, Princeton, New Jersey
  Allen W. Dulles Papers
  John Foster Dulles Papers
  Arthur Krock Papers
United States National Archives and Records Administration, College Park, Maryland
  Record Group 59: General Records of the Department of State
  Record Group 84: Records of the Foreign Service Posts of the Department of State
  Record Group 330: Records of the Office of the Secretary of Defense

Archival Sources—Great Britain

Bodleian Library, University of Oxford
  End of Empire, Transcripts of Interviews
BP Archive, University of Warwick
The National Archives of the United Kingdom, Kew Gardens, UK
  CAB 128, 129 Records of the Cabinet Office

DEFE 4 Records of the Chiefs of Staff Committee

FO 248 Foreign Office: Embassy and Consulates, Iran (Formerly Persia):
General Correspondence

FO 371 Foreign Office: Political Departments: General Correspondence,
1906–1966

POWE 33 Ministry of Fuel and Power: Petroleum Division

PREM 11 Prime Minister's Office Records, 1951-1964

T Treasury Office

Published Primary Sources

Folliot, Denise, ed. *Documents on International Affairs, 1951–1954*. London: Royal
Institute of International Affairs, 1954–57.

Foreign Relations of the United States 1943, vol. 4: *Near East and Africa.*
Washington, DC: U.S. Government Printing Office, 1964.

Foreign Relations of the United States 1945, vol. 8: *The Near East and Africa.*
Washington, DC: U.S. Government Printing Office, 1969.

Foreign Relations of the United States 1946, vol. 7: *Near East and Africa.*
Washington, DC: U.S. Government Printing Office, 1969.

Foreign Relations of the United States 1947, vol. 5: *The Near East and Africa.*
Washington, DC: U.S. Government Printing Office, 1971.

Foreign Relations of the United States 1949, vol. 6: *The Near East, South Asia and
Africa.* Washington, DC: U.S. Government Printing Office, 1977.

Foreign Relations of the United States, 1950, vol. 5: *The Near East, South Asia and
Africa.* Washington, DC: U.S. Government Printing Office, 1978.

Foreign Relations of the United States, 1951, vol. 5: *The Near East, South Asia and
Africa.* Washington, DC: U.S. Government Printing Office, 1982.

Foreign Relations of the United States, 1952–1954, vol. 5, part 1: *Western European
Security.* Washington, DC: U.S. Government Printing Office, 1983.

Foreign Relations of the United States, 1952–1954, vol. 1, part 2: *General: Economic
and Political Matters.* Washington, DC: U.S. Government Printing Office, 1983.

Foreign Relations of the United States, 1952–1954, vol. 9, part 1: *The Near and
Middle East.* Washington, DC: U.S. Government Printing Office, 1986.

Foreign Relations of the United States, 1952–1954, vol. 6, part 1: *Western Europe and
Canada.* Washington, DC: U.S. Government Printing Office, 1986.

Foreign Relations of the United States, 1952–1954, vol. 10: *Iran, 1951–1954.*
Washington, DC: U.S. Government Printing Office, 1989.

Foreign Relations of the United States, 1952–1954, Iran, 1951–1954, 2nd ed.
Washington, DC: U.S. Government Printing Office, 2018.

Iranian Embassy. *Some Documents on the Nationalization of the Oil Industry in
Iran.* Washington, DC: Iranian Embassy, 1951.

U.S. Congress, Senate Committee on Foreign Relations, Subcommittee on
Multinational Corporations. *The International Petroleum Cartel, the Iranian
Consortium and U.S. National Security.* Washington DC: U.S. Government
Printing Office, 1975.

U.S. Senate, Select Committee on Small Business. *The International Petroleum Cartel.* Staff Report to the Federal Trade Commission. Washington, DC: U.S. Government Printing Office, 1952.

Miscellaneous Archival Collections

American Heritage Center, University of Wyoming
  Walter J. Levy Papers
Foundation for Iranian Studies
  Development Series. *Siyasat va siyasatguzari-ye eqtesadi dar iran, 1340–1350.* https://fis-iran.org/fa/resources/development-series/financialpolicy/.
  Development Series. *Tahavvul-e san`at-e naft-e Iran: Negahi az darun.* Interview with Parviz Mina. https://fis-iran.org/fa/resources/development-series/oil/.
  FIS Interview, Peter Ramsbotham
Harvard Iran Oral History Project (HIOHP): Interviews
  Mahdi Azar
  Mozaffar Baqa'i
  Mohammed Daftari
  Mehdi Hairi-Yazdi
  Parviz Khosrovani
  Gholam Reza Muqaddam
  Karim Sanjabi
National Security Archive
The Battle for Iran. CIA History. https://nsarchive2.gwu.edu/NSAEBB /NSAEBB476/.
Iran Collection, Document Archive. https://nsarchive.gwu.edu/events/iran -mosaddeq-overthrow-1953?page=1.
Koch, Scott A. *Zendebad, Shah! The Central Intelligence Agency and the Fall of Iranian Prime Minister Mohammed Mossadeq, August 1953.* June 1998. Reviewed for Declassification in November 2017. https://nsarchive.gwu .edu/document/16330-document-2-zendebad-shah.
Wilber, Donald. *Overthrow of Premier Mosaddeq of Iran, November 1952–August 1953. CIA Clandestine Service History.* https://nsarchive2.gwu.edu/NSAEBB /NSAEBB28/l.
World Bank Group Archives
  Records of the Middle East and North Africa Regional Vice Presidency, Iran Oil Nationalization Inventory List http://pubdocs.worldbank.org/en /458211475595816522/Archives-mediation-exhibit-Iran-oil-folder-list-2.pdf.

Periodicals

Bakhtar-e Emruz	*New York Times*
Economist	*Newsweek*
Ettelaat	*Shahed*
Le Messager de Téhéran	*Shojat*
Mardom-e Iran	*Tehran Musavvar*

Interviews by the Authors

Richard W. Cottam
George C. McGhee
George Middleton
Peter Ramsbotham
John Waller

Other Interviews

Harter, John F. "Mr. Foreign Service on Mossadegh and Wristonization: An Interview with Loy W. Henderson." *Foreign Service Journal* 57 (November 1980): 16–18.

Second Oral History Interview with Loy W. Henderson by Richard D. McKinzie. Washington, DC, 5 July 1973, Harry S. Truman Library.

Persian Secondary Sources

Asrar-e khanah-e Siddan. Tehran: Mu'assasah-'e Intisharat-e Amir Kabir, 1979.

Bozorgmehr, Jalil. *Musaddiq dar mahkameh-ye nezami*, vol. 2. Tehran: Nehzat-e Moqavemat-e Melli, 1985.

Fateh, Mostafa. *Panjah sal naft-e Iran*. Tehran: Entesharat-e Payam, 1979.

Hidayat, Mihdi Quli Khan. *Khatirat va Khatarat*. Tehran: Shirkat-e Chap-e Rangin, 1950.

Makki, Hossein. *Naft va nutq-e Makki: Jarayan-e muzakirat-e naft dar Majlis-e Panzdahum dar barah-e qarardad-e naft-e Iran va Ingilis*. Tehran: Intisharat-e Amir Kabir, 1978.

Makki, Husayn. *Vaqayi'-e 30 Tir 1331*. Tehran: Bungah-i Tarjumah va Nashr-i Kitab, 1982.

Ruhani, Fu'ad. *Tarikh-e milli shudan-e san'at-e naft-e Iran*. Tehran: Kitabhaye Jibi, 1973.

———. *Zindagi-ye siyasi-ye Musaddiq: Dar matn-e nahzat-e milli-ye Iran*. London: Intisharat-e Nahzat-e Muqavamat-e Milli-ye Iran, 1987.

Sanjabi, Karim. *Omidha va Namidha: Khatirat-e Siyasi*. London: Nashr-e Kitab, 1989.

Shayegan, 'Ali. *Sayyed 'Ali Shayegan: Zendagi-nama-ye siasi*, vol. I. Tehran: Agaah, 2006.

Taqizadeh, Sayyed Hasan. *Zendegi-ye Tufani: khaterat-e Sayyed Hasan Taqizadeh*, 2nd ed. Edited by Iraj Afshar. Tehran: 'Elmi, 1993.

Tavanayan-Fard, Hasan. *Duktur Mosaddeq va iqtisad*. Tehran: Sazman-e Intishrat-e 'Alavi, 1983.

Torkaman, Mohammed. *Asrar-e Qatl-e Razmara*. Tehran: Rasa, 1991.

Memoirs and Diaries

Acheson, Dean. *Present at the Creation: My Years at the State Department*. New York: Norton, 1969.

Eden, Anthony. *Full Circle: The Memoirs of Sir Anthony Eden*. London: Cassell, 1960.

Falle, Sam. *My Lucky Life: In War, Revolution, Peace, and Diplomacy.* Sussex, UK: The Book Guild, 1996.

Grady, Henry F. *Memoirs of Henry F. Grady: From the Great War to the Cold War.* Edited by John T. McKay. Columbia: University of Missouri Press, 2009.

Kennan, George F. *The Kennan Diaries.* Edited by Frank Costigliola. New York: W. Norton & Company, 2014.

Krock, Arthur. *Memoirs: Sixty Years on the Firing Line.* New York: Funk & Wagnalls, 1968.

McGhee, George C. *Envoy to the Middle World: Adventures in Diplomacy.* New York: Harper & Row, 1983.

Melbourne, Roy M. "America and Iran in Perspective: 1953 and 1980." *Foreign Service Journal* 57 (1980): 10–17.

Mosaddeq, Mohammed. *Musaddiq's Memoirs.* Translated by Homa Katouzian and S. H. Amin. London: National Movement of Iran, 1988.

Nitze, Paul H. *From Hiroshima to Glasnost: At the Center of Decision: A Memoir.* New York: Grove Weidenfeld, 1989.

Pahlavi, Mohammed Reza. *Mission for My Country.* London: Hutchinson, 1961.

Roosevelt, Kermit. *Countercoup: The Struggle for the Control of Iran.* New York: McGraw-Hill, 1979.

Truman, Harry S. *Memoirs*, vol. 1: *Year of Decisions.* Garden City, NY: Doubleday & Co., 1955.

———. *Memoirs*, vol. 2: *Years of Trial and Hope.* Garden City, NY: Doubleday & Company, 1956.

Walters, Vernon. *Silent Missions.* Garden City, NY: Doubleday & Co., 1978.

Wilber, Donald N. *Adventures in the Middle East: Excursions and Incursions.* Princeton, NJ: Darwin, 1986.

Woodhouse, C. M. *Something Ventured.* London: Granada, 1982.

Zahedi, Ardeshir. *The Memoirs of Ardeshir Zahedi*, vol. 1: *From Childhood to the End of My Father's Premiership.* Translated by Farhang Jahanpour. Bethesda, MD: Ibex Publishers, 2012.

Secondary Sources

Abrahamian, Ervand. *The Coup: 1953, the CIA and the Roots of Modern U.S.-Iranian Relations.* New York: New Press, 2013.

———. "Factionalism in Iran: Political Groups in the 14th Parliament (1944–46)." *Middle Eastern Studies* 14 (January 1978): 22–55.

———. *Iran between Two Revolutions.* Princeton, NJ: Princeton University Press, 1982.

———. *Oil Crisis in Iran: From Nationalism to Coup d'Etat.* New York: Cambridge University Press, 2021.

Adelman, M. A. *The World Petroleum Market.* Baltimore: Johns Hopkins University Press, 1972.

Afary, Janet. *The Iranian Constitutional Revolution, 1906–1911: Grassroots Democracy, Social Democracy and the Origins of Feminism.* New York: Columbia University Press, 1996.

Afkhami, Gholam R. *The Life and Times of the Shah.* Berkeley: University of California Press, 2009.

Ahmed, Jalal Al-e. *Gharbzadegi* [Westoxification]. Costa Mesa, CA: Mazda Publishers, 1982.

Alacevich, Michele. "The World Bank and the Politics of Productivity: The Debate on Economic Growth, Poverty, and Living Standards in the 1950s." *Journal of Global History* 6 (March 2011): 53–74.

Amanat, Abbas. *Iran: A Modern History.* New Haven, CT: Yale University Press, 2017.

Ansari, Ali M., ed. *Iran's Constitutional Revolution of 1906: Narratives of the Enlightenment.* London: Gingko Library, 2016.

———. *The Politics of Nationalism in Modern Iran.* New York: Cambridge University Press, 2012.

Aram, Bethany. "Exporting Rhetoric, Importing Oil: United States Relations with Venezuela, 1945–1948." *World Affairs* 154 (Winter 1992): 94–106.

Atabaki, Touraj, and Erik Zürcher, eds. *Men of Order: Authoritarian Modernization under Ataturk and Rezā Shah.* London: I. B. Tauris, 2004.

Azimi, Fakhreddin. *Iran: The Crisis of Democracy: from the Exile of Reza Shah to the Fall of Moşaddeq.* London: I. B. Tauris, 2009.

———. "The Overthrow of the Government of Mosaddeq Reconsidered." *Iranian Studies* 45 (2012): 693–712.

Bakhash, Shaul. "Britain and the Abdication of Reza Shah." *Middle Eastern Studies* 52 (2016): 318–34.

———. *Iran: Monarchy, Bureaucracy and Reform under the Qajars, 1858–1896.* London: Ithaca Press, 1978.

Bamberg, J. H. *The History of the British Petroleum Company,* vol. 2: *The Anglo-Iranian Years, 1928–1954.* Cambridge: Cambridge University Press, 1994.

———. *The History of the British Petroleum Company,* vol. 3: *British Petroleum and Global Oil, 1950–1975.* Cambridge: Cambridge University Press, 2000.

Bayandor, Darioush. *Iran and the CIA: The Fall of Mossadeq Revisited.* Basingstoke, UK: Palgrave Macmillan, 2010.

Behrooz, Maziar. "Tudeh Factionalism and the 1953 Coup in Iran." *International Journal of Middle East Studies* 33 (August 2001): 363–82.

Beisner, Robert L. *Dean Acheson: A Life in the Cold War.* New York: Oxford University Press, 2006.

Bessner, Daniel, and Fredrik Logevall. "Recentering the United States in the History of American Foreign Relations." *Texas National Security Review* 3 (Spring 2020): 38–55.

Bergquist, Charles. *Labor and the Course of American Democracy: U.S. History in Latin American Perspective.* London: Verso, 1995.

Bill, James A. *The Eagle and the Lion: The Tragedy of American-Iranian Relations.* New Haven, CT: Yale University Press, 1988.

Bill, James A., and Wm. Roger Louis, eds. *Musaddiq, Iranian Nationalism and Oil.* London: I. B. Tauris, 1988.

Blair, John. *The Control of Oil.* New York: Pantheon Books, 1976.

Bohi, Douglas R., and Milton Russell. *Limiting Oil Imports: An Economic History and Analysis*. Baltimore: Johns Hopkins University Press, 1978.

Brands, H. W. "The Cairo-Tehran Connection in Anglo-American Rivalry in the Middle East, 1951–1953." *International History Review* 11 (August 1989): 434–56.

Brew, Gregory. "The Collapse Narrative: The United States, Mohammed Mossadegh, and the Coup Decision of 1953." *Texas National Security Review* 2 (November 2019): 38–59.

———. "The 1953 Coup d'État in Iran: New FRUS, New Questions." Wilson Center, *Sources and Methods*, 30 October 2017. https://www.wilsoncenter.org/blog -post/the-1953-coup-detat-iran-new-frus-new-questions.

———. *Petroleum and Progress in Iran: Oil, Development, and the Cold War*. New York: Cambridge University Press, 2022.

———. "A Review of *Foreign Relations of the United States, Retrospective: Iran, 1951–1954*." *Passport: The Society for Historians of American Foreign Relations Review* 48 (2018): 53–55.

———. "In Search of 'Equitability': Sir John Cadman, Rezā Shah and the Cancellation of the D'Arcy Concession, 1928–33." *Iranian Studies* 50 (2017): 115–48.

Bright, Charles, and Michael Geyer. "For a United History of the World in the Twentieth Century." *Radical History Review* 39 (Fall 1987): 69–91.

Bull, Hedley. "The Revolt against the West." In *The Expansion of International Society*, edited by Adam Watson and Hedley Bull, 217–28. New York: Oxford University Press, 1985.

Byrne, Malcolm. "When History Meets Politics: The Challenging Case of the 1953 Coup in Iran." In *United States Relations with China and Iran*, edited by Osamah F. Khalil, 121–40. London: Bloomsbury Academic, 2019.

Citino, Nathan J. *From Arab Nationalism to OPEC: Eisenhower, King Saud, and the Making of U.S.-Saudi Relations*, 2nd ed. Bloomington: Indiana University Press, 2010.

———. "Internationalist Oilmen, the Middle East, and the Remaking of American Liberalism, 1945–1953." *Business History Review* 84 (Summer 2010): 227–51.

Clawson, Patrick, and Cyrus Sassanpour. "Adjustment to a Foreign Exchange Shock: Iran, 1951–1953." *International Journal of Middle East Studies* 19 (February 1987): 1–22.

Collier, David R. *Democracy and the Nature of American Influence in Iran, 1941–1979*. Syracuse, NY: Syracuse University Press, 2017.

Cottam, Richard W. *Nationalism in Iran Updated Through 1978*. Pittsburgh, PA: University of Pittsburgh Press, 1979.

Cronin, Stephanie, ed. *The Making of Modern Iran: State and Society Under Riza Shah, 1921–1941*. New York: Routledge, 2003.

Cumings, Bruce. *The Origins of the Korean War*, vol. 2: *The Roaring of the Cataract, 1947–1950*. Princeton, NJ: Princeton University Press, 1990.

Danielsen, Albert L. *The Evolution of OPEC*. San Diego: Harcourt Brace Jovanovich, 1982.

Darmstadter, Joel, and Hans H. Landsberg. "The Economic Background." In *The Oil Crisis*, edited by Raymond Vernon, 15–37. New York: W. W. Norton & Company, 1976.

Davis, Simon. *Contested Space: Anglo-American Relations in the Persian Gulf, 1939–1947*. Boston: Martinus Nijhoff, 2009.

DeGolyer and MacNaughton. *Twentieth Century Petroleum Statistics: Historical Data*. Dallas, TX: DeGolyer and MacNaughton, n.d.

Dietrich, Christopher. *Oil Revolution: Anti-Colonial Elites, Sovereign Rights, and the Economic Culture of Decolonization*. New York: Cambridge University Press, 2017.

Dorman, William A., and Mansour Farhang. *The U.S. Press and Iran: Foreign Policy and the Journalism of Deference*. Berkeley: University of California Press, 1987.

Ediger, Volkan S., and John V. Bowlus. "A Farewell to King Coal: Geopolitics, Energy Security, and the Transition to Oil, 1898–1917." *Historical Journal* 62 (June 2019): 427–49.

Egorova, Natalia. "Stalin's Oil Policy and the Iranian Crisis of 1945–1946." In *Cold War Energy: A Transnational History of Soviet Oil and Gas*, edited by Jeronim Perović, 79–104. Cham, Switzerland: Palgrave Macmillan, 2017.

Elm, Mostafa. *Oil, Power, and Principle: Iran's Oil Nationalization and Its Aftermath*. Syracuse, NY: Syracuse University Press, 1992.

Elwell-Sutton, L. P. *Persian Oil: A Study in Power Politics*. London: Lawrence and Wishart, 1955.

Fawcett, Louise L'Estrange. *Iran and the Cold War: The Azerbaijan Crisis of 1946*. Cambridge: Cambridge University Press, 1992.

———. "Revisiting the Iranian Crisis of 1946: How Much More Do We Know?" *Iranian Studies* 47 (2014): 379–99.

Ferrier, R. W. *The History of the British Petroleum Company*, vol. I: *The Developing Years, 1901–1932*. Cambridge: Cambridge University Press, 1982.

Foran, John. "Discursive Subversions: *Time* Magazine, the CIA Overthrow of Musaddiq, and the Installation of the Shah." In *Cold War Constructions: The Political Culture of United States Imperialism, 1945–1966*, edited by Christian G. Appy, 157–82. Amherst: University of Massachusetts Press, 2000.

Galpern, Stephen S. *Money, Oil and Empire in the Middle East: Sterling and Postwar Imperialism, 1944–1971*. Cambridge: Cambridge University Press, 2013.

Garavini, Giuliano. *The Rise and Fall of OPEC in the Twentieth Century*. New York: Oxford University Press, 2019.

Gasiorowski, Mark J. "The Causes of Iran's 1953 Coup: A Critique of Darioush Bayandor's *Iran and the CIA*." *Iranian Studies* 45 (September 2012): 669–78.

———. "The CIA's TPBEDAMN Operation and the 1953 Coup in Iran." *Journal of Cold War Studies* 15 (Fall 2013): 4–24.

———. "The 1953 Coup d'Etat in Iran." *International Journal of Middle East Studies* 19 (August 1987): 261–86.

———. "U.S. Perceptions of the Communist Threat in Iran during the Mossadegh Era." *Journal of Cold War Studies* 21 (Summer 2019): 185–221.

———. "The US Stay-Behind Operation in Iran, 1948–1953." *Intelligence and National Security* 34 (2019): 170–88.

Gasiorowski, Mark J., and Malcolm Byrne, eds. *Mohammed Moṣaddeq and the 1953 Coup in Iran.* Syracuse, NY: Syracuse University Press, 2004.

Gavin, Francis J. "Politics, Power, and U.S. Policy in Iran, 1950–1953." *Journal of Cold War Studies* 1 (Winter 1999): 56–89.

Gleijeses, Piero. *Shattered Hope: The Guatemalan Revolution and the United States.* Princeton, NJ: Princeton University Press, 1991.

Goode, James F. *The United States and Iran: In the Shadow of Musaddiq.* New York: St. Martin's Press, 1997.

Hahn, Peter L. *The United States, Great Britain, and Egypt, 1945–1956: Strategy and Diplomacy in the Early Cold War.* Chapel Hill: The University of North Carolina Press, 1991.

Harmer, Tanya. *Allende's Chile and the Inter-American Cold War.* Chapel Hill: The University of North Carolina Press, 2011.

Hasanli, Jamil. *At the Dawn of the Cold War: The Soviet-American Crisis over Iranian Azerbaijan, 1941–1946.* Lanham, MD: Rowman & Littlefield, 2006.

Heiss, Mary Ann. *Empire and Nationhood: The United States, Great Britain and Iranian Oil, 1950–1954.* New York: Columbia University Press, 1997.

———. "Real Men Don't Wear Pajamas: Anglo-American Cultural Perceptions of Mohammed Mossadegh and the Iranian Oil Nationalization Dispute." In *Empire and Revolution: The United States and the Third World Since 1945*, edited by Peter Hahn and Mary Ann Heiss, 178–91. Columbus: Ohio State University Press, 2001.

Hess, Gary R. "The Iranian Crisis of 1945–46 and the Cold War." *Political Science Quarterly* 89 (March 1974): 117–46.

Hochschild, Adam. "The Untold Story of the Texaco Oil Tycoon Who Loved Fascism." *The Nation*, 21 March 2016. https://www.thenation.com/article/archive/the-untold-story-of-the-texaco-oil-tycoon-who-loved-fascism/.

Hunt, Michael H. "Internationalizing U.S. Diplomatic History: A Practical Agenda." *Diplomatic History* 15 (January 1991): 1–11.

Hunt, Michael H., and Steven I. Levine. *Arc of Empire: America's Wars in Asia from the Philippines to Vietnam.* Chapel Hill: The University of North Carolina Press, 2012.

Hurst, Steven. *The United States and Iraq since 1979: Hegemony, Oil, and War.* Edinburgh: Edinburgh University Press, 2009.

Jablonski, Wanda. "Masterstroke in Iran." *Collier's* (21 January 1955): 32, 34, 36.

Jack, Marian. "The Purchase of the British Government's Shares in the British Petroleum Company, 1912–1914." *Past & Present* 39 (1968): 139–68.

Jacobs, Matthew. *Imagining the Middle East: The Building of an American Foreign Policy, 1918–1967.* Chapel Hill: The University of North Carolina Press, 2011.

Kalinovsky, Artemy. "The Soviet Union and Mosaddeq: A Research Note." *Iranian Studies* 47 (2014): 401–18.

Katouzian, Homa. "The Campaign against the Anglo-Iranian Agreement of 1919." *British Journal of Middle Eastern Studies* 25 (May1998): 5–46.

———. *Khalil Maleki: The Human Face of Iranian Socialism*. London: One World Academic, 2018.

———. *Musaddiq and the Struggle for Power in Iran*. London: I. B. Tauris, 1990.

———. *The Political Economy of Modern Iran: Despotism and Pseudo-Modernism, 1926–1979*. New York: New York University Press, 1981.

Kazemzadeh, Firuz. *Russia and Britain in Persia, 1864–1914: A Study in Imperialism*. New Haven, CT: Yale University Press, 1968.

Keddie, Nikki. *Roots of Revolution: An Interpretive History of Modern Iran*. New Haven, CT: Yale University Press, 1981.

———. *Modern Iran: Roots and Results of Revolution*. New Haven, CT: Yale University Press, 2006.

———. *Religion and Rebellion in Iran: The Tobacco Protest of 1891–1892*. London: Cass, 1966.

Kemp, Norman. *Abadan: A First-Hand Account of the Persian Oil Crisis*. London: Wingate, 1953.

Kent, Marian Kent. *Oil and Empire: British Policy and Mesopotamian Oil, 1900–1920*. London: Macmillan, 1976.

Khalil, Osamah F. *America's Dream Palace: Middle East Expertise and the Rise of the National Security State*. Cambridge, MA: Harvard University Press, 2016.

———, ed. *United States Relations with China and Iran*. London: Bloomsbury Academic, 2019.

Kuniholm, Bruce R. "Foreign Relations, Public Relations, Accountability, and Understanding," *Perspectives on History* 28, no. 5 (May–June 1990).

———. *The Origins of the Cold War in the Near East: Great Power Conflict and Diplomacy in Iran, Turkey and Greece*. Princeton, NJ: Princeton University Press, 1980.

Ladjevardi, Habib. *Labor Unions and Autocracy in Iran*. Syracuse, NY: Syracuse University Press, 1985.

———. "The Origins of U.S. Support for an Autocratic Iran." *International Journal of Middle East Studies* 15 (May 1983): 225–39.

Lapping, Brian. *End of Empire*. New York: St. Martin's, 1985.

Leffler, Melvyn. *A Preponderance of Power: National Security, the Truman Administration, and the Cold War*. Stanford, CA: Stanford University Press, 1992.

———. *Safeguarding Democratic Capitalism: U.S. Foreign Policy and National Security, 1920–2015*. Princeton, NJ: Princeton University Press, 2017.

Leffler, Melvyn P., and David S. Painter, eds. *The Origins of the Cold War: An International History*, 2nd ed. New York: Routledge, 2005.

Leffler, Melvyn P., and Odd Arne Westad, eds. *The Cambridge History of the Cold War*, vol. 1: *Origins*. New York: Cambridge University Press, 2010.

Little, Douglas. *American Orientalism: The United States and the Middle East Since 1945*, 3rd ed. Chapel Hill: The University of North Carolina Press, 2008.

———. "Mission Impossible: The CIA and the Cult of Covert Action in the Middle East." *Diplomatic History* 28 (November 2004): 663–701.

Louis, Wm. Roger. *The British Empire in the Middle East, 1945–1951: Arab Nationalism, the United States and Postwar Imperialism*. Oxford: Clarendon Press, 1984.

Lüthi, Lorenz M. *Cold Wars: Asia, the Middle East, Europe.* Cambridge: Cambridge University Press, 2020.

Lytle, Mark H. *The Origins of the Iranian-American Alliance, 1941–1953.* New York: Holmes and Meier, 1987.

MacFarlane, S. Neil. *Superpower Rivalry and Third World Radicalism: The Idea of National Liberation.* Baltimore: Johns Hopkins University Press, 1985.

McAlister, Melani. *Epic Encounters: Culture, Media, and U.S. Interests in the Middle East,* 2nd ed. Berkeley: University of California Press, 2005.

McAllister, William B., Joshua Botts, Peter Cozzens, and Aaron W. Marrs. *Toward "Thorough, Accurate, and Reliable": A History of the Foreign Relations of the United States Series.* Washington, DC: United States Department of State, 2015.

McCormick, Thomas J. *America's Half-Century: United States Foreign Policy in the Cold War,* 2nd ed. Baltimore: Johns Hopkins University Press, 1995.

McFarland, Stephen L. "Anatomy of an Iranian Political Crowd: The Tehran Bread Riot of December 1942." *International Journal of Middle East Studies* 17 (February 1985): 51–65.

———. "A Peripheral View of the Origins of the Cold War: The Crises in Iran, 1941–1947." *Diplomatic History* 4, no. 4 (October 1980): 333–51.

McFarland, Victor. *Oil Powers: A History of the U.S.-Saudi Alliance.* New York: Columbia University Press, 2020.

McMahon, Robert J., ed. *The Cold War in the Third World.* New York: Oxford University Press, 2013.

———. "Eisenhower and Third World Nationalism: A Critique of the Revisionists." *Political Science Quarterly* 101 (Fall 1986): 453–73.

Marsh, Steve. "Anglo-American Crude Diplomacy: Multinational Oil and the Iranian Crisis, 1951–53." *Contemporary British History* 21 (March 2007): 25–53.

———. "Anglo-American Relations and the Labour Government's 'Scuttle' from Abadan: A 'Declaration of Dependence.'" *International History Review* 35 (2013): 817–43.

———. "Continuity and Change: Reinterpreting the Policies of the Truman and Eisenhower Administrations toward Iran, 1950–1954." *Journal of Cold War Studies* 7 (Summer 2005): 79–123.

———. "HMG, AIOC and the Anglo-Iranian Crisis: In Defence of Anglo-Iranian." *Diplomacy and Statecraft* 12 (December 2002): 143–74.

Martin, Vanessa. *Iran between Islamic Nationalism and Secularism: The Constitutional Revolution of 1906.* London: I. B. Tauris, 2013.

———. *The Qajar Pact: Bargaining, Protest, and the State in Nineteenth-Century Persia.* London: I. B. Tauris, 2005.

Mason, Edward S., and Robert E. Asher. *The World Bank since Bretton Woods.* Washington, DC: Brookings Institution, 1973.

Mason, Michael. "'The Decisive Volley': The Battle of Ismailia and the Decline of British Influence in Egypt, January-July 1952." *Journal of Imperial and Commonwealth History* 19 (1991): 45–64.

Maurer, Noel. "The Empire Struck Back: Sanctions and Compensation in the Mexican Oil Expropriation of 1938." *Journal of Economic History* 71 (September 2011): 560–615.

Middle East Institute. *The Present Situation in Iran: A Survey of Political and Economic Problems Facing the Country.* Washington, DC: Middle East Institute, 1953.

Milani, Abbas. *The Shah.* New York: Palgrave Macmillan, 2011.

Motter, T. H. Vail. *The Persian Corridor and Aid to Russia.* Washington, DC: Office of the Chief of Military History, Department of the Army, 1952.

Pahuja, Sundhya, and Cait Storr. "Rethinking Iran and International Law: The *Anglo-Iranian Oil Company Case* Revisited." In *The International Legal Order: Current Needs and Possible Responses: Essays in Honor of Djamchid Montaz,* edited by James Crawford, Abdul G. Koroma, Said Mahmoudi, and Alain Pellet, 53–74. Leiden: Brill Nijhoff, 2017.

Painter, David S. *The Cold War: An International History.* New York: Routledge, 1999.

——. "Explaining U.S. Relations with the Third World." *Diplomatic History* 19 (Summer 1995): 525–48.

——. "The Marshall Plan and Oil." *Cold War History* 9 (May 2009): 159–75.

——. "Oil and the American Century." *Journal of American History* 99 (June 2012): 24–39.

——. *Oil and the American Century: The Political Economy of U.S. Foreign Oil Policy, 1941–1954.* Baltimore: Johns Hopkins University Press, 1986.

——. "Overthrowing Mosaddeq." *Diplomatic History* 42 (June 2019): 492–95.

Penrose, Edith T. *The Large International Firm in Developing Countries: The International Petroleum Industry.* London: George Allen & Unwin, Ltd., 1968.

Pfau, Richard. "Containment in Iran, 1946: The Shift to an Active Policy." *Diplomatic History* 1 (Fall 1977): 359–72.

Podobnik, Bruce. *Global Energy Shifts: Fostering Sustainability in a Turbulent Age.* Philadelphia: Temple University Press, 2006.

Prados, John. *Safe for Democracy: The Secret Wars of the CIA.* Chicago: Ivan R. Dee, 2006.

Qaimmaqami, Linda W. "The Catalyst of Nationalization: Max Thornburg and the Failure of Private Sector Developmentalism in Iran, 1946–1951." *Diplomatic History* 19 (January 1995): 1–31.

Rabe, Stephen G. *The Road to OPEC: United States Relations with Venezuela, 1919–1976.* Austin: University of Texas Press, 1982.

Rahnema, Ali. *Behind the 1953 Coup in Iran: Thugs, Turncoats, Soldiers, Spooks.* New York: Cambridge University Press, 2015.

Randjbar-Daemi, Siavush. "'Down with the Monarchy': Iran's Republican Moment of August 1953." *Iranian Studies* (2016): 1–21.

Ricks, Thomas M. "U.S. Military Missions to Iran, 1943–1978: The Political Economy of Military Assistance." *Iranian Studies* 12 (Summer–Autumn 1979): 163–93.

Roberts, Geoffrey. *Molotov: Stalin's Cold Warrior.* Washington, DC: Potomac Books, 2013.

——. "Moscow's Cold War on the Periphery: Soviet Policy in Greece, Iran, and Turkey, 1943–8." *Journal of Contemporary History* 46 (January 2011): 58–81.

Roosevelt, Kermit. *Arabs, Oil, and History: The Story of the Middle East.* London: Gollanz, 1949.

Rubino, Anna. *Queen of the Oil Club: The Intrepid Wanda Jablonski and the Power of Information.* Boston: Beacon Press, 2008.

Sadjapour, Karim. *Reading Khamenei: The World View of Iran's Most Powerful Leader.* Washington, DC: Carnegie Endowment for Peace, 2009.

Sampson, Anthony. *The Seven Sisters: The Great Oil Companies and the World They Shaped.* New York: Viking, 1975.

Schmitz, David F. *Thank God They Are on Our Side: The United States and Right-Wing Dictatorships, 1921–1965.* Chapel Hill: The University of North Carolina Press, 1999.

Shafiee, Katayoun. *Machineries of Oil: An Infrastructural History of BP in Iran.* Cambridge, MA: MIT Press, 2018.

Siavoshi, Sussan. *Liberal Nationalism in Iran: The Failure of a Movement.* Boulder, CO: Westview Press, 1990.

——. "The Oil Nationalization Movement, 1949–1954." In *A Century of Revolution: Social Movements in Iran,* edited by John Foran, 106–34. Minneapolis: University of Minnesota Press, 1994.

Simpson, Bradley R. *Economists with Guns: Authoritarian Development and U.S.-Indonesian Relations, 1960–1968.* Stanford, CA: Stanford University Press, 2008.

——. "Explaining Political Economy." In *America in the World,* 3rd ed., edited by Frank Costigliola and Michael J. Hogan, 58–73. New York: Cambridge University Press, 2016.

Sohrabi, Nader. *Revolution and Constitutionalism in the Ottoman Empire and Iran.* New York: Cambridge University Press, 2011.

Staples, Amy L. S. "Seeing Diplomacy through Bankers' Eyes: The World Bank, the Anglo-Iranian Oil Crisis, and the Aswan High Dam." *Diplomatic History* 26 (Summer 2002): 397–418.

Sternfeld, Lior. "Iran Days in Egypt: Mosaddeq's Visit to Cairo in 1951." *British Journal of Middle Eastern Studies* 43 (2016): 1–20.

Stocking, George W. *Middle East Oil: A Study in Political and Economic Controversy.* Nashville, TN: Vanderbilt University Press, 1970.

Taafe-McMenamy, Margaret. "Operation Ajax: A Case Study of Analyst-Policy Maker Tensions and the Challenges of Estimative Intelligence." Fort Leavenworth, KS: School of Advanced Military Studies, United States Army Command and General Staff College, 2015.

Tabatabai, Ariane M. *No Conquest, No Defeat: Iran's National Security Strategy.* Oxford: Oxford University Press, 2020.

Takeyh, Ray. *The Last Shah: America, Iran, and the Fall of the Pahlavi Dynasty.* New Haven, CT: Yale University Press, 2021.

Toprani, Anand. *Oil and the Great Powers: Britain and Germany, 1914–1945.* New York: Oxford University Press, 2019.

Vitalis, Robert. *America's Kingdom: Mythmaking on the Saudi Oil Frontier.* New York: Verso, 2009.

Walden, Jerrold L. "The International Petroleum Cartel and Iran—Private Power and the Public Interest." *Journal of Public Law* 11 (Spring 1962): 64–121.

Wall, Bennet H. *Growth in a Changing Environment: A History of Standard Oil Company (New Jersey) 1950–1972 and Exxon Corporation 1972–1975.* New York: McGraw-Hill, 1988.

Weiner, Tim. *Legacy of Ashes: The History of the CIA.* New York: Doubleday, 2008.

Weis, W. Michael. *Cold Warriors and Coups d'Etat: Brazilian-American Relations, 1946–1964.* Albuquerque: University of New Mexico Press, 1993.

Westad, Odd Arne. *The Cold War: A World History.* New York: Basic Books, 2017.

———. *The Global Cold War: Third World Interventions and the Making of Our Times.* New York: Cambridge University Press, 2005.

Wilford, Hugh. "'Essentially a Work of Fiction': Kermit 'Kim' Roosevelt, Imperial Romance, and the Iran Coup of 1953." *Diplomatic History* 40 (November 2016): 922–47.

Wolfe-Hunnicutt, Brandon. *The Paranoid Style in American Diplomacy: Oil and Arab Nationalism in Iraq.* Stanford, CA: Stanford University Press, 2021.

Yergin, Daniel. *The Prize: The Epic Quest for Oil, Money and Power.* New York: Simon & Schuster, 1991.

Zirinsky, Michael P. "Imperial Power and Dictatorship: Britain and the Rise of Reza Shah, 1921–1926." *International Journal of Middle East Studies* 24 (November 1992): 639–63.

Zubok, Vladislav M. *A Failed Empire: The Soviet Union in the Cold War from Stalin to Gorbachev.* Chapel Hill: The University of North Carolina Press, 2007.

———. "Soviet Intelligence and the Cold War: The 'Small' Committee of Information, 1952–53." *Diplomatic History* 19 (July 1995): 453–72.

———. "Stalin, Soviet Intelligence, and the Struggle for Iran, 1945–53." *Diplomatic History* 44 (January 2020): 22–46.

Zunes, John Stephen. "Decisions on Intervention: United States Response to Third World Nationalist Governments." Ph.D. dissertation, Cornell University, 1990.

Index

Carroll, George: coup organizing, 162, 168

Central Intelligence Agency (CIA): assets in Iran, 152–53; Baqa'i, Mozaffar, contacts with, 113, 115; British, coordination with, 156, 172–73; control of "the street," 102, 143, 253n153; coup feasibility, 105, 120, 149, 210; coup planning, 152, 156, 159–63; coup role, 164–65, 167–71, 172–73; internal histories, 3–4, 119, 152, 160, 204; Iran, prospects for stability, 200; Kashani, Ayatollah Abolqassem, 146; and Majlis elections, 90–91, 184; Mosaddeq, 44, 91, 116, 140, 146, 147; propaganda, 40, 162, 164; Qashqa'i, relations with, 50, 105, 120, 153, 177; on Razmara assassination, 36; records, 3–4, 160, 205; shah, 119, 146–47, 184; Soviet ability to move Iranian oil, 68, 85, 137; TPAJAX, 160; TPBEDAMN, 50, 170; Tudeh, 77, 154–55, 164; Zahedi, Fazlollah, 155

Churchill, Winston S.: Abadan and "splutter of musketry," 74, 95; APOC share purchase, 11–12; coup, 158, 160; Jones, Alton, 108–9; Royal Navy, conversion from coal to oil, 11; Truman-Churchill proposal, 109–12, 114; United States, relations with, 7, 83, 109, 156; "volley at Ismailia," 95, 241n16

Cilley, 152

coal, 11. *See also* Coal Nationalization Act of 1945

Coal Nationalization Act of 1945 (Great Britain): basis for compensation, 129; British reservations, 130–31, 135; compensation precedent, 57

Cold War: Anglo-American relations, 7, 22; control of oil, 207–08; Global South, 1, 4–7; Iranian crisis, 203; Third World nationalism, 9

colonialism: context, 5: Mosaddeq trial, 184; Mosaddeq at United Nations, 67

Committee of Eight (Majlis): public support, 161; opposition to, 154, 161; report, 150

Compagnie française des pétroles (CFP): consortium discussion, 186; consortium share, 189–90, 192; Iraq Petroleum Company, 14

compensation: Acheson proposal, 83; AIOC compensation demands, 186, 190–93, 252n102; British policy, 75, 81, 96, 107, 109, 115, 117, 124, 128–29, 130–32, 163, 179, 191–92, 195–96, 198, 208; Coal Nationalization Act, 57, 129, 130–31, 135; consortium, 182, 183, 189, 190; February proposal, 138; Henderson, Loy W., views, 149, 157; Iranian position, 47, 182; Jackson proposal, 47; Levy proposal, 157; loss of enterprise, 109, 115, 131–133, 135, 136, 138, 179, 208; major oil companies' views, 127, 190–91; McGhee proposal, 70–71; Mexican precedent, 14–15; Mosaddeq's views, 57, 71, 102–4, 107, 108, 111, 114, 129, 133, 135–36, 208; Nitze plan, 121, 126; package proposal, 126–29, 134–35; settlement, 199–200; Stokes proposal, 57; U.S. views, 105, 106; 149, 157, 160, 192; World Bank proposal, 87–88

consortium, 2, 209; and antitrust, 132, 186, 188, 200; British view, 56, 180, 182–83, 185, 188, 193–94; final agreement, 198–99, 201; Foreign Office proposal, 74; Hoover proposal, 179–80, 182–83; inter-company agreement; 192–93, 268n81; Iranian proposal, 181–82; June 1952 agreement, 96; Levy proposal, 56; major oil companies' views, 185–86; membership shares, 182, 186, 188–90; National Security Council decisions, 132, 188; negotiations with Iran, 193–95; Nitze proposal, 121; package proposal, 135 constitution (Iran): 1906 constitution and monarchical power, 8, 12, 97, 102; 1949 amendment, 19–20; Committee of Eight, 150, 161

Constitutional Revolution (Iran), 12

control of oil, 10, 37, 203, 205, 211–12; Azerbaijan crisis, 18; British position, 11, 39, 41, 103, 205, 207, 208, 226n; consortium, 175, 193–96, 198–99, 202; Hoover plan, 179–80; Jackson proposal, 54–55; McGhee plan, 70–72, 75; Mosaddeq's view, 75, 133, 208–9; oil cartel, 122, 200; package proposal, 125–26; postwar petroleum order, 21–22; Seven Sisters, 5; Stokes proposal, 57–58; U.S. position, 5–6, 8, 22, 39, 40, 64, 123, 187, 207–9

Cottam, Richard W.: background, 237–38n60; fears of communism, 209; July Uprising, 102

countercoup narrative: Kermit Roosevelt, 167

covert action: Eisenhower, Dwight D., views on, 205

cultural bias, 8–9, 39, 49, 211; Gardner, Robert L., 82; Kennan, George F., 8–9; Mattison, Gordon, 166; Shepherd, Francis, 42; Stokes, Richard, 57; Stutesman, John, 9, 128

Cutler, Robert: Iranian threat to world oil markets, 150

Czechoslovakia: popular front strategy; 77; Soviet ambassador, 260n124

Darbyshire, Norman: MI6, 49–50; Afshartus murder, 155; coup planning, 156, 159–60; Pahlavi, Ashraf, 163; 259n117

D'Arcy, William Knox: background, 10

D'Arcy Concession: terms, 10–11, 14

decolonization, 29, 67: context, 207

Defense Production Act: major oil companies, 126; Nitze Plan, 122–23; Petroleum Administration for Defense, 86

DeGolyer, Everett Lee: Middle East oil potential, 16

Devotees of the Shah: opposition to Mosaddeq, 113

Dooher, Gerald; Qashqa'i: 50

Drake, Eric: AIOC General Manager, 52

Duce, James Terry: NSC report, 132

Dulles, Allen W.: background, 118–19; coup, support for, 44, 125; Iran, situation in, 146–47, 185, 254n1; propaganda campaign; 40; shah, concern about, 163; Thornburg, Max, ties to, 50, 118–19, 202, 210

Dulles, John Foster: AIOC demands, 192; British, relations with, 124, 137–38, 143, 149–50, 189–90; communism in Iran, 164; ending negotiations with Mosaddeq, 150, 157; independent oil companies, concerns about, 137; Jones, Alton, 137, 148, 255n23; Mosaddeq and the shah, 146–47; "northern tier" strategy, 167; "second chance," 179, 180; support for shah, 178; TPAJAX, approval of, 160

Eden, Anthony: AIOC return to Iran, 185, 188; AIOC share in consortium, 189; British policy, 75; compensation to AIOC, 191–92; coup, prospects for, 106–7; Fraser in "cloud cuckoo land," 99; Hoover visit to Iran, 180; Jones, Alton, 148; Kashani, Ayatollah Abolqassem, 149; Mosaddeq's proposals, 103; Nitze plan, 124; package proposal, 132, 136, 148; pushing Mosaddeq out, 96; Truman-Churchill joint proposal, 112, 114; U.S. aid to Iran, 91, 127–28; World Bank proposals, 81, 82

Egypt: Anglo-American relations, 7, 83, 150; Ismailia incident, 95, 241n16; military coup, 106; Mosaddeq visit, 76; northern tier concept, 157

Eisenhower, Dwight D.: aid to Iran, 147; British, relations with, 7–8, 147, 191;

cartel case, 188, 200; coup authorization, 160; covert action, 205; Mosaddeq, letter to, 160; Soviet threat, 156, 164; U.S. oil concessions, concern about, 150; Zahedi, Fazlollah, letter to, 176. *See also* Eisenhower administration

Eisenhower administration: coup decision, 2, 145; coup planning, 151, 158; economic aid to Iran, 175; package proposal, 138; sanctity of contracts, 156. *See also* Eisenhower, Dwight D.

Eisenhower Library, 3

Emami, Hasan: Majlis speaker, 97; Qavam, Ahmed, appointment as Prime Minister, 98; shah, comment on Qavam, Ahmed, 96

Emami, Jamal: Mosaddeq., appointment as Prime Minister, 41; Mossadeq prospects, 42

Entezam, Abdullah: AIOC return to Iran, 187; Iran, position on oil settlement, 181

Export-Import Bank loan to Iran: British opposition, 33, 127–28; freeze, 60; Grady, promise to Razmara, 32; Mosaddeq request, 79; revival, 127–28

Falle, Sam; coup as solution, 104; coup planning, 104, 111, 114–15, 125; "self-sacrificing line," 106–07; Zahedi, 153

Fateh, Mostafa, AIOC and Iran, 11

Fatemi, Hossein: arrest and execution, 1; Mosaddeq, health, 139; National Front, 29, 114; nationalization of AIOC, 30; October 1952 coup attempt, 114; republic, call for, 166–68

February crisis (1953), 138–46

February proposals, 149, 179, 180. *See also* final offer

Fedayeen-e Islam: Razmara assassination, 36

Federal Trade Commission: oil cartel report, 122

Fergusson, Donald: British policy options, 73

fifty-fifty profit sharing: AIOC offer, 36; British proposal, 179; British tax code, 25; consortium agreement, 199; Iranian goal, 25; Iranian proposal, 182; Jackson proposal, 47; McGhee, George C., advice to British, 40–44; McGhee plan, 71, 74; Nitze plan, 121, 127; major companies' position, 196; and posted price, 82; Saudi Arabia, 35; Stokes proposal, 58; World Bank proposal, 81, 88

Foreign Relations of the United States (FRUS): 1989 volume on Iran, 3; Retrospective volume on Iran, 3–4, 205

Foundation for Iranian Studies (FIS), 4

Franks, Oliver: British policy, 52–53, 108, 111–12; Mosaddeq, replacing, 107; use of force, 44–45

Fraser, William J., 43; AIOC return to Iran, 188, 189; compensation demands, 190–92; consortium shares, 186, 189; July Uprising, 99; letter to major oil companies, 186; Supplemental agreement, 25–26, 32; tenacity, 193

Funkhouser, Richard: major oil companies, 33

Furlonge, Geoffrey: Razmara, 32–33; nationalization movement, 41

Galpern, Steven G.: control of oil and British power, 207

Garner, Robert L.: cultural bias, 82; Rieber, Torkild, 84; World Bank mediation, 81–82, 87–89

Gass, Neville: nationalization impact, 74; posted price, 82; Supplemental Agreement, 26

Global South, 214n1; and Cold War, 1, 4–5; corporate control of resources, 180, 203, 205–7, 212; U.S. policy, 9. *See also* Third World

Goiran, Roger: doubts about coup, 210; Mosaddeq and National Front, 44

Golsha'ian, Abbasqoli: Supplemental Agreement, 25–26

Grady, Henry F.: British, criticism of, 33–34; Jackson proposal, 47–48; nationalization, Iranian support for, 51–52; nationalization, opposition to, 44; Razmara and Supplemental Agreement, 32; Truman letter, 7

Great Britain, 7, 207; Abadan, 39; AIOC return to Iran, 180, 182–83, 188; "Communist Danger to Persia," 119; compensation, 75, 81, 96, 107, 109, 115, 117, 128–29, 130–32, 135, 179, 191–93, 195–96, 198–200, 208; consortium, 56, 74, 96, 180, 182–83, 185, 188–190, 194–95; control of oil, 11, 39, 41, 103, 205, 207, 208, 226n9; coup, 90, 104–7, 111, 114–15, 119, 124–25, 145, 162, 168, 172–73, 210–11; covert assets, 153; economic concerns, 39; end of empire, 7, 63; Humphrey proposal, 156; independent oil companies, concern about, 124, 197; International Court of Justice, 52, 81, 97, 101; Iran, restoration of relations, 183; Jones, Alton (Cities Service), 108–9, 111, 148; Kashani, Ayatollah Abolqassem, 148; Majlis, influence in, 29, 153; Mosaddeq, policy toward, 42, 48, 56, 60–61, 73–74, 90, 96, 103–7, 109, 115, 119, 124–25, 148, 208; nationalization, opposition to, 7, 37–39, 58, 73–74, 89, 197, 212; oil boycott, 2, 48–49, 61, 65, 78, 86, 120, 137, 208–9, 255n21; Operation Boot, 125; and package proposal, 124, 137, 148; Pahlavi, RezaShah/Reza Khan, 13, 15; political pressure, 49, 52–53, 55, 118, 139; Qavam, Ahmed, 76, 79, 92, 95–96; records, 3, 174, 203; Royal Navy and Iranian oil, 11; Russia, competition with, 11–12; sanctity of contracts, 65;

"self-sacrificing line," 106–7, 115; settlement requirements, 75, 96, 99, 103, 107, 115, 117, 179; shah (Mohammed Reza Pahlavi), 15, 96; sterling, 7, 21, 32, 39, 56, 193, 196–98, 199; strategy, 83, 95, 107, 109, 111, 115, 124, 138, 208–9; tax law and fifty-fifty, 25; Truman-Churchill proposals, 109–12, 114; Tudeh threat, assessment of, 78, 93, 106, 125, 199; United Nations, 65–67; United States, relations with, 7, 83, 107, 109, 111–12, 115, 124, 136–38; use of force, 37, 42–43, 45, 57, 58, 61–62; World Bank, 81–83; World War I, 13; World War II, 15; Zahedi, Fazlollah, 94, 104, 106, 111, 153; Zia, Sayyed, 41, 62, 66, 76, 78, 92

Gulf Oil Company, 13; compensation to AIOC, 191; consortium discussion, 186; Kuwait Oil Company, 14, 48; nationalization, opposition to, 68

Haerizadeh, Abdolhossin, 29; Mosaddeq, break with, 134, 138, 139; ties to Zahedi, Fazlollah, 139

Harriman, Averell; background, 53; control of oil, 53, 58–59, 126; Harriman mission, 52–56, 58–60; Mosaddeq, critique of, 59; Mosaddeq, replacing, 55, 59

Harvard Iran Oral History Project (HIOHP), 4

Hassibi, Kazem: nationalization, benefits, 47; Harriman mission, 55; British UN complaint, 66; arrest, 177

Henderson, Loy W.: Amini, Abolqassem, views on, 155, 159–60; British policy, critique of, 64, 78, 88; British position in Iran, 78; AIOC return to Iran, 69; 178, 184; Coal Nationalization Act, 129, 135–36; compensation, 114, 129, 135–36, 157, 159; coup, doubts about, 105, 157, 159, 210; coup, narrative, 204; coup, role in, 169–70, 173; coup, support for, 151; democracy in Iran, 178, 204; February crisis, 140–43, 147; Iranian nationalism, views about, 78, 128; July Uprising, 99–101; Majlis elections (1954), 178, 184; military assistance, support for, 183–84, 201; monarchy, views on, 141; Mosaddeq, replacing, 62, 79, 94–95, 158–59; Mosaddeq, views about, 66, 78, 83, 91, 94–95, 103, 139; oil settlement, views on, 136, 139, 160; Qavam, Ahmed, support for, 79, 92, 94; reporting, shift in, 136, 149; Saleh, Allahyar, opposition to, 94, 95; sanctity of contracts, 148, 254n19; shah, views about, 78, 93 ("Persian Hamlet"), 96, 105, 128, 148, 159; Zahedi, Fazlollah, 128, 153

41, 227n21; Prime Minister, power to choose, 151; Qavam, Ahmed, elected Prime Minister, 98; Rashidian influence in, 76; referendum on dissolution, 161, 163, 164; Reza Khan named shah, 13; Senate dissolved, 115; Seventeenth Majlis elections, 90–91; Soviet oil concession rejected, 19; Supplemental agreement, 26, 35; Zahedi, Fazlollah, support in, 153–54

major oil companies: antitrust, 121–22, 123, 126, 132, 188, 200; consortium, 185–86, 196–97; control of oil, 5, 48, 72, 123, 181, 191, 202, 205, 209; control of oil tankers, 48, 137; Hoover plan, 179, 182; nationalization, 46, 68, 207; Nitze plan, 121, 126–28; Petroleum Administration for Defense, 86; postwar petroleum order, 5, 21–22, 175, 209; sanctity of contracts, 68, 127; U.S. support for, 45–46, 123, 132, 180, 207

Makins, Roger: Anglo-American relations, 136–37, 190–91, 192; AIOC, 74, 190–91; coup, 168; Qavam, Ahmed, 99

Makki, Hossein: 1933 oil agreement, 23–24; AIOC, takeover of facilities, 51; February crisis, 140; Mosaddeq, break with, 113, 134, 139, 160; National Front, 29; Qashqa'i negotiations, 177; Qavam, Ahmed, 92; Supplemental Agreement, 26; Zahedi, Fazlollah, ties to, 139

Maleki, Khalil: Third Force, 134; arrest and imprisonment, 177. *See also* Third Force

Mansur, 'Ali: Majlis oil committee, 30

Marsh, Steve: control of oil and British power, 207

Mattei, Enrico: "Seven Sisters," 5

Mattison, Gordon: cultural bias, 166; Mossadeq, "leftist dictatorship," 161; shah, 162; coup, 166

Mauritius: British expulsion, 63

McClure, Brigadier General Robert A.: U.S, military mission, 152; military aid to Iran, 201

McGhee, George C.: AIOC, 43; fifty-fifty profit sharing, 40, 69; Iran, concerns about, 31; Iran, situation in, 40; 43; McGhee plan, 70, 72, 74; Mosaddeq, discussions with, 69–75, 79; nationalization, 40, 43–44; shah, 31, 40; Supplemental Agreement, 34; U.S. policy, 45–46, 60

McGranery, James: cartel case, 122, 132

Meade, Colonel Stephen: meeting with Pahlavi, Ashraf, 163

Melbourne, Roy: Mosaddeq trial, 178

Mexican oil nationalization, 14–15; settlement, 157, 257n76

Middle East: Anglo-American cooperation, 7, 21, 83, 89; northern tier, 157; strategic importance, 9, 11

Middle East/Persian Gulf oil: European and Japanese reconstruction, 5–6, 22, 39, 208; major oil concessions, 13–14; postwar petroleum order, 21–22; strategic and economic importance, 5–6, 22, 39, 207; surplus of oil, 180–81; U.S. interests, 16–17, 33

Middleton, George: Anglo-American unity, 111–12; coup promotion, August 1952, 104–8; coup prospects, 104, 111; elections for Seventeenth Majlis, 79; Iranian nationalism, 78; July Uprising, 99, 101; Qavam, Ahmed, 95–96; shah, doubts about, 96; Zahedi, Fazlollah, contacts with, 104, 114–15

military attachés (United States): influence, 153; loyalty of Iranian military, 164–65

military missions to Iran (United States): during World War II, 16; influence of, 78; 152–53, 211

Ministry of Fuel and Power (Great Britain), AIOC, support for, 99; compensation, 124

MI6: Iran, operatives in, 49–50, 76, 153, 156, 172–73

Molotov, Vyacheslav: Azerbaijan crisis, 18

Morrison, Herbert: AIOC, cessation of operations, 52; AIOC, negotiations with Iran, 46; use of force, 42–43, 45, 61

Mosaddeq, Mohammad, 1–2; AIOC, expulsion of staff, 61–62; advisers, 47, 67, 133; 'Ala, Hossein, 155; Amini, Abolqassem, 155; army, 97–98, 102, 113, 164; background, 28–29, 223n80; British Coal Nationalization Act, 57, 129; British subversion efforts, 76, 81, 85, 114, 139; Committee of Eight, 150; compensation, 57, 71, 102–4, 107, 111, 114, 129, 133, 135–36, 149, 208; constitution, 1, 8, 13; control of oil, 75, 133, 208–9; coup, 165, 167, 169–71, 173; emergency powers, 112, 134; February crisis, 139–40, 142–43; financial policies, 68, 91, 112–13, 125, 133; Great Britain, breaks relations, 115; Harriman, 53–55; International Court of Justice, 53, 97, 101, 108, 114; Jackson proposal, 54–55; Jones, Alton, 108, 120; July Uprising, 97–98; Majlis elections (1952), 90–91; Majlis oil committee, 30, 34, 35, 38, 41; McGhee, George C., discussions with, 69–75; monarchy, 8, 13, 28, 167; National Front, 8, 29; nationalization, 10, 26, 35, 37–38, 41, 48, 51; negative equilibrium, 17, 29, 133; October 1952 coup attempt, response to, 114–15; oil pricing, 72–73, 81; opposition to, 75–76, 113, 153–54; package proposal, 129, 135, 138, 149, 150; Prime Minister, 37, 41–42, 102; referendum on dissolving Majlis, 161, 164, 169; reform agenda, 112–13, 134; Reza Khan, opposition to, 13; shah (Mohammed Reza Pahlavi), opinion of, 149; Soviet oil concession,

opposition to, 17; Soviet Union, 133; Stokes mission, 57–58, 59; Supplemental Agreement, 30, 34, 35; trial, 184; Truman-Churchill proposals, 111, 112, 114; Tudeh, 133, 155, 170, 173, 210; United Nations, 66, 67; U.S. economic aid, requests for, 79–80, 85, 87, 149, 157–58, 160; U.S. military assistance, 80, 85, 91–92; unpaid royalties, 106, 111, 114; World Bank mediation, 81, 84–85, 87–88, 102

Nassiri, Ne'matallah, 162; first coup attempt, 165, 169

National Archives (Great Britain), 3

National Archives and Records Administration (United States), 3

National Front, 8; coup, 166, 170–71, 173; divisions in, 113, 134, 138–39; February crisis, 143; founding, 29; July crisis, 99–101; Kashani, Ayatollah Abolqassem, 30, 38, 66, 91, 113, 134, 139, 143; membership, 29; National Resistance Movement, 183; oil issue, 30, 36, 37, 38, 41; Qashqa'i, 105; referendum on dissolving the Majlis, 161; reform agenda, 42; Senate, dissolution, 115; Seventeenth Majlis elections, 90–91; suppression, 177; Tudeh, 7, 77, 90–91, 101, 102, 149, 161

National Iranian Oil Company (NIOC): creation, 47; Iranian proposal, 58–59; McGhee proposal, 70; package proposal, 129; Iranian proposal, 181–82; oil settlement agreement, 198

National Security Archive, 4

National Security Council (United States): antitrust, 132, 188, 200; Britain, relations with, 191; recommendations/decisions: aid to Iran, 39, 149–50; settlement of oil dispute, 40, 52, 123, 147, 187; special political measures, 120, 152

negative equilibrium: Mosaddeq, 17, 29, 133

Nerren, 152

Newsweek: CIA propaganda, 164

New York Times: CIA internal history, 3; coup, role in, 167, 169; Mosaddeq, 164

9 *Esfand*: turning point, 143

Nine-Point Nationalization Law: compensation, 104; Jackson mission, 47; Majlis passage, 41; shah, 194

Nitze, Paul: aid to Iran, 80, 83; final attempt, 120–24, 137; major oil companies, discussions with, 126–27; Mosaddeq, discussions with, 70; NSC-68, 31; shah, view of, 43–44; World Bank, 87

Nixon, Richard M.: British policy, 186; nationalization, 205; shah, view of, 186

Northcroft, Ernest: Razmara and Supplemental Agreement, 35–36

Office of Greek, Turkish, and Iranian Affairs (State Department): Mosaddeq, 50; Pyman, Launcelot, meeting with, 94

Office of the Historian (State Department), 3

Office of Intelligence and Research (State Department): Kashani, Ayatollah Abolqassem report on, 151

Office of Strategic Services (OSS): Iran, stay-behind mission, 21

oil: British imperial policy, 11; economic and military importance, 1, 213n5; and Cold War, 6, 22, 207; Iranian nationalism, 8; postwar petroleum order, 5, 21–22

oil boycott, 2; components, 61; feasibility, 48–49; impact, 68, 76–80, 86–87, 92–93, 120; legacy, 205; objective, 65, 78, 208; weakening, 120, 137, 149, 209, 255n21

oil cartel: Justice Department case, 121–22; operation, 200; Seven Sisters, 5

oil imports: and U.S. economy, 186, 191, 197, 198

oil-less economy: economic strategy, 112–13, 133

oil markets: Iranian oil, reintegrating, 157, 179–81, 186–188, 202; Iranian threat to oil markets, 49, 83, 137, 145, 149–50, 197, 209; U.S. oil companies and AIOC's markets, 123

oil price(s): Admiralty, 21; consortium agreement, 199; and fifty-fifty profit sharing, 71–72, 81, 121, 199; Iranian threat to price structure, 121, 150, 185, 197; Mosaddeq-McGhee discussions, 70–73, 75, 79; Nitze plan, 121, 126, 145; Policy Planning Staff recommendation, 72–73; posted price, 82; vertical integration, 72; World Bank proposals, 81, 84, 87–88

oil tankers; control by major oil companies, 48; "free" tankers, availability of, 74; 84–85, 120, 137, 149–50

Operation Boot: British coup plan, 125

package proposal, 125–26, 128–29, 137; British concerns, 130–32, 135; major oil companies' objections, 126–27, 132; negotiations with Mosaddeq, 128, 134–36, 138, 150–51; resubmittal, 137–38. *See also* February proposals

Pahlavi, Ashraf, coup, role in, 163; MI6 bribe, 259n117

Pahlavi, Mohammad Reza, 2,15; background, 19; British, distrust of, 62, 77, 154, 158, 163; consortium, 195–95, 200; coup, 145, 154, 158, 162–66, 172, 205, 211; February crisis, 140–43; Jackson mission, 48; July Uprising, 97–102; Majlis elections, 178, 184; military, control of, 97–98, 102, 163; Mosaddeq, appointment as Prime Minister, 41; Mosaddeq, relations with, 55, 59, 60, 62, 65, 77, 79, 95; Mosaddeq, trial, 177–78, 184, 205; nationalization, 41, 42, 62, 65, 194; 1949 assassination attempt, 19; 1949 constitution, amendment to, 19–20; 1949 elections, 29; Qavam,

Standard Oil Company of California (SOCAL), 13; Aramco share, 33; compensation to AIOC, 191; consortium discussion, 186; nationalization, view of, 68; 118; Saudi Arabia concession, 14

State Department (U.S. Department of State): antitrust suit, 121, 132, 186; military assistance to Iran, 184, 201; world oil industry, 69

state-owned/state supported oil companies: British boycott, 108, 209; Iranian oil, interest in, 185; oil price structure, 121

sterling: British boycott, 48, 61; consortium, 196–98, 199; Iranian oil and British balance of payments, 6, 7, 21, 32, 39, 56

Stevens, Roger: compensation negotiations, 193

Stokes, Richard: cultural bias, 57; mission to Iran, 56–60; proposal, 57–58, 88, 126

Stutesman, John: cultural bias, 9; Mosaddeq, analysis of, 9; political assessment, 128

Suez Canal: strategic asset, 9, 39, 157; Shinwell, Emmanuel, warning, 43

SUMKA: CIA asset, 154; coup, 170

Supplemental Agreement, 24–26, 30–36

Tahmasabi, Khalil: assassination of Razmara, 36

Takeyh, Ray: coup, local agency, 172

Texas Company (Texaco), 13; compensation to AIOC, 191; consortium discussion, 186; concession in Saudi Arabia, 14; share in Aramco, 33; nationalization, view of, 68

Texas Railroad Commission: oil imports, 197

Third Force: coup, 171; Mosaddeq, support for, 138. See also Maleki, Khalil

Third World: nationalism, 9, 80; resource sovereignty, 67. See also Global South

Thornburg, Max Weston: background, 118; coup, ideas about, 50, 118, 119, 151, 202; Dulles, Allen, 50, 118, 119, 202, 210; and Razmara, 'Ali, 32, 35

Toilers Party. See Baqa'i, Mozaffar

TPAJAX: CIA coup plan, 160

TPBEDAMN: CIA anti-communist program, 50; October 1952 coup attempt, 115

Treasury (Great Britain): compensation, 124; Iranian oil and balance of payments, 32, 56; July Uprising, 99; sterling controls, 197–98, 199

Truman, Harry S.: aid to Iran, 79–80, 87; Attlee, Clement, letters, 60, 61; British use of force, 45; cartel case, 121, 132; Defense Production Act, 122–23; 132; ICJ interim judgment, 53; Iran as diversion, 6; Krock, Arthur, interview, 43; letter to Grady, Henry F.; Jones, Alton, 108–9; Mosaddeq, meeting with, 69; Truman-Churchill proposals, 109–112, 114; Truman Doctrine, 20–21; U.S. support for settlement, 52. See also Truman administration

Truman administration, military assistance, 22; Petroleum Administration for Defense, 86; package proposal, 117, 128. See also Truman, Harry S.

Truman Library, 3

Tudeh, 6–7; coup, 165–71, 173, 211; Eighteenth Majlis elections, 90; February crisis, 140, 143, 146; Harriman riot, 53–54; Iranian army, network in, 200; July Uprising, 98, 100–2; Mosaddeq and National Front, 65, 133, 134, 138, 154–55, 209–10, 253–54n153; and oil workers, 18–19, 38, 77; Qavam, Ahmed, 18–19; referendum dissolving Majlis, 164;

shah and monarchy, 143, 166, 168; Soviets, 7, 16, 19; strength and capabilities, 6–7, 77, 161, 164, 209–10; suppression of, 177, 183, 185

28 *Mordad*, 145, 172, 174, 175

vertical integration: control of oil; 200; oil pricing; 72

Villard, Henry: British as obstacle to settlement, 64; Soviets and Iranian oil, 68

Waller, John: background, 21, 243n45; on "street organizations," 253n153

Walters, Vernon: Harriman mission, 53

War Ministry (Iran): control of, 97–98, 102

Warne, William E.: Point Four, 114; Mossadeq letter, 154; Minister of Economy meeting, 155

Webb, Robert: on Gardner, Robert L., 82

Wilber, Donald: CIA history, 4; coup central idea, 151–52; coup, failure of first attempt, 166; coup, plan for second attempt, 168; coup timing, 162; on Darbyshire, Norman, 156; June operational plan, 159; "London Draft," 160; on Schwarzkopf, H. Norman, 163; shah, doubts about; 119, 154; on Zahedi, 153

Wiley, John C.: Anglo-Iranian Oil Company, criticism of, 23; Iranian economic and political problems, 31

Wilson, Charles E.: sanctity of contracts, 150; anger at British policy, 190

Wisner, Frank: British intelligence, coordination with, 153; CIA records; 4; coup, support for, 125

Woodhouse, Christopher Montague: communist threat, 125; coup planning, 160; July Uprising, 99; MI6 operations in Iran, 49

World Bank (International Bank for Reconstruction and Development) mediation effort, 65; British support, 82–83; Gardner, Robert L., views, 83; Gardner, Robert L. visit to Iran,

87–88; obstacles, 81, 88–89; origins, 81; Prud'homme-Rieber mission, 84–85; U.S. view, 87

Wright, Denis: AIOC return to Iran, 187–88

Yergin, Daniel: AIOC and oil settlement, 193

Young, T. Cuyler, view of Mosaddeq, 50

Zaehner, Robin: background, 49; British network in Iran, 49–50, 60, 76, 104, 106; Qavam, Ahmed, 241n18

Zahedi, Ardeshir: coup, foreign involvement, 172; coup role, 167, 169; February crisis, 139, 142; Pollard, Eric, contacts with, 139, 153

Zahedi, Major General Fazlollah, 2; April 1953 coup plans, 154–55; background of, 153; Baqa'i, Mozaffar, contact with, 113, 114; British views of, 94, 153; British support, 104, 107, 111, 114–15, 156; coup plans, 159–60, 162–65; coup, role in, 164–69, 171–72; dismissal, 54; February crisis, 139–40; Haerizadeh, Abdolhossin, contact with, 139; and independent oil companies, 182, 185, 187–88; Kashani, Ayatollah Abolqassem, contact with, 114, 139, 155; Makki, Hossein, contact with, 139; October 1952 coup attempt, 114–15; and oil settlement, 179, 180, 182–83, 187–88; Qashqa'i, 177, 183; shah, 151, 158, 178, 183, 200; U.S. assessments, 128, 153, 186; U.S. assistance, request for, 145, 156; U.S. economic assistance, 173, 175–77; World Bank, 265n31

Zia, Sayyed: British support, 41, 62, 76, 78, 92; shah, 60, 66